OXFORD STUDIES IN MODERN EUROPEAN HISTORY

General Editors
SIMON DIXON, MARK MAZOWER,
and
JAMES RETALLACK

'A View of the Marmara's Sorrowful Shore,' from *Tasvir-i Efkar*, 5 June 1921.

Sorrowful Shores

Violence, Ethnicity, and the End of the Ottoman Empire, 1912–1923

RYAN GINGERAS

OXFORD
UNIVERSITY PRESS

Great Clarendon Street, Oxford OX2 6DP

Oxford University Press is a department of the University of Oxford.
It furthers the University's objective of excellence in research, scholarship,
and education by publishing worldwide in

Oxford New York

Auckland Cape Town Dar es Salaam Hong Kong Karachi
Kuala Lumpur Madrid Melbourne Mexico City Nairobi
New Delhi Shanghai Taipei Toronto

With offices in

Argentina Austria Brazil Chile Czech Republic France Greece
Guatemala Hungary Italy Japan Poland Portugal Singapore
South Korea Switzerland Thailand Turkey Ukraine Vietnam

Oxford is a registered trade mark of Oxford University Press
in the UK and in certain other countries

Published in the United States
by Oxford University Press Inc., New York

© Ryan Gingeras 2009

The moral rights of the authors have been asserted
Database right Oxford University Press (maker)

First published 2009
First published in paperback 2011

All rights reserved. No part of this publication may be reproduced,
stored in a retrieval system, or transmitted, in any form or by any means,
without the prior permission in writing of Oxford University Press,
or as expressly permitted by law, or under terms agreed with the appropriate
reprographics rights organization. Enquiries concerning reproduction
outside the scope of the above should be sent to the Rights Department,
Oxford University Press, at the address above

You must not circulate this book in any other binding or cover
and you must impose the same condition on any acquirer

British Library Cataloguing in Publication Data
Data available

Library of Congress Cataloging in Publication Data
Gingeras, Ryan.
Sorrowful shores: violence, ethnicity, and the end of the Ottoman
Empire, 1912–1923 / Ryan Gingeras.
p. cm. — (Oxford studies in modern european history)
Includes bibliographical references and index.
ISBN 978-0-19-956152-0
1. Turkey—History—Mehmed V, 1909-1918. 2. Turkey—History—Revolution,
1918-1923. 3. Ethnic conflict—Turkey—History—20th century.
4. Turkey—Ethnic relations—History—20th century. I. Title.
DR584.G56 2009 956'.02—dc22 2008049481

Typeset by Laserwords Private Limited, Chennai, India
Digitally printed and bound in Great Britain by
CPI Antony Rowe, Chippenham and Eastbourne.

ISBN 978-0-19-956152-0 (Hbk.)
ISBN 978-0-19-969834-9 (Pbk.)

This book is dedicated to two people:
my wife, Mariana Chavez Vazquez,
and my grandfather, Charles Fitzpatrick

Preface

If the truth be told, this work was born out of an act of cowardice. My ambitions leading up to my comprehensive exams tended towards some kind of radical, challenging project. There was little question in my mind that I wanted to write my dissertation on some corner of Anatolia during the First World War and/or the early Turkish Republic. Going for the jugular, I turned towards eastern Anatolia. A couple of ideas came to me: perhaps a study of how the small town of Naxçıvan became a part of Azerbaijan; better yet, the reconstruction of Kars following the establishment of the Turkish Republic.

Either, I thought, would serve wonderfully. I was told otherwise. Friends and colleagues with years of experience in Ottoman studies warned me that I was essentially contemplating professional suicide. First there was the question of sources. Where would I get them? Do such documents even exist? More importantly, would Turkish archivists even allow me to see the records (a question followed by anecdotal horror stories about scholars denied access to state archives in Turkey)? Then there were the political consequences to consider. A dissertation dealing with Kurds, Armenians, or other taboo subjects in Turkey was bound to bring troubles down around me. No matter what I did, I was told, someone would be very unhappy with my work. Someone, be it a member of the Turkish government, members of the Armenian diaspora, or other Ottoman scholars, would eat me alive for having challenged, upheld, or ignored some aspect of eastern Anatolia's recent history. In short, the advice I had was: don't do it. Drop it. Don't kill your career before it begins.

The dissertation that I wrote ultimately was founded upon this advice. My time in the archives instead led me to focus on western Anatolia and drew my attention to the roles of Albanian and North Caucasian immigrants during the Turkish War of Independence. The research for this project generally went swimmingly. None of the nightmare scenarios I was forewarned of came to fruition. No lifetime bans. No hate mail. Nothing.

Still, I cannot say for sure that my friends and colleagues, people whom I believe genuinely had my best interests at heart, were wrong. Yes, archivists, scholars, and staff I met in Istanbul and Ankara were indeed helpful, courteous, and, at times, a real pleasure to be around. The sheer mention of my interest in Muslim immigrants in Anatolia was greeted with sincere enthusiasm and support by the archivists who helped make my research possible. More often than not, though, I rarely broached the topic of Armenians and Greeks with archival staff. Since it was not the central focus of my work, the parallel fate of non-Muslims in western Anatolia during the war years was a subject I kept under my hat. Earlier admonitions continued to play in my head.

This roundabout preface is meant as both an apology and an explanation for the continuities and discontinuities between my dissertation and this book. The question of what happened to Anatolian Greeks and Armenians (as well as other criminalized groups) between the years 1912 and 1923 lingers on like some proverbial 500-pound gorilla in the room. Recent events such as the murder of Hrant Dink confirm this. Yet I do not believe that the wartime persecution of Ottoman Christians should be approached in isolation. More to the point, it is quite clear to me that there is a more universal story to be told of the level and significance of human suffering in Anatolia during this period of time. As will become clearer through the coming pages, similar patterns of reasoning and behaviour on the part of the Ottoman government, as well as the occupational forces of Greece and others, led to the mass removal, extermination, and suppression of Christians and Muslims alike. The degree to which various communities were victimized by competing statist forces certainly differed tremendously (if I was forced to compare, clearly Armenians and Greeks collectively shared a more unenviable position by 1923 than Muslim immigrants). Whether one can compare levels of hardship, however, is not the point. Rather, this book takes up the question of precisely how and why large groups of people living around the southern coast of the Marmara Sea were subjected to a series of deliberate campaigns to do them harm.

In order better to highlight the unanimity of suffering found among various communities living around the southern shores of the Sea of Marmara, I have put greater emphasis on Armenian and Greek affairs. Although by no means absolutely comprehensive, I believe these steps help better to bridge the historical gap between Christian natives and immigrant Muslims than my previous attempt.

Although the text that follows is not in execution a comparative work, it must be said that the history of Anatolia during this period of time is not unique in a global sense. The mass disenfranchisement and liquidation of home populations is a phenomenon that can be found the world over. State terror of this sort is a modern phenomenon, and is part and parcel of the logic of modern state building. In situating this study within a finite region and approaching a fairly finite collection of peoples, I take up several critical, but admittedly dense, historical concepts: state modernization, organized violence, identity formation, immigration, and network politics. By placing both geographic and social restrictions upon my research, it was my hope to make a discussion of these various historical threads more wieldy, and the narrative more seamless.

Looking back, I do not regret following the advice of my trusted peers. Ultimately I feel that it has led me back to addressing my original goals. I do hope, however, that others (with thicker skin than myself) take on the histories of Kars and Naxçıvan, and other vital stories yet to be told.

Acknowledgements

During the course of my doctoral research and the follow-up research for this monograph, I found myself travelling, at times regularly, between Toronto, San Diego, New York, London, Istanbul, Ankara, Skopje, and Mexico City. Yet, before I extend my gratitude to those I met along the way, I must first thank my family and close friends. Above all, I want to thank my wife, Mariana Chavez Vazquez, who has given so much of herself and has had to endure too many long absences in exchange. Te quiero mucho, Marianita. Gracias por todo. Without my parents, Tom and Dedee Gingeras, I doubt that many of my dreams would have become realities. My incredible sister Alison and my loving grandparents Dot and Charlie Fitzpatrick each played vital roles in inspiring and supporting me. My family's love and encouragement have made me who I am today. I want to thank Metin Bezikoğlu, Shane Cotter, Kevin Franks, Steve Maddox, Mike Mastroeni, William Silverman, and Mark Tkach for their genuine friendship, encouragement, and criticisms over the years. You have each been a wonderful friend to me.

I have been a beneficiary of outstanding teachers and colleagues both at the University of California, San Diego, and at the University of Toronto. I will for-ever be indebted to Virginia Aksan and Hasan Kayalı. Over the years I have come to see both as wonderful friends, trusted advisers, and consistent models for how to conduct myself as a scholar and a human being. I would especially like to thank Robert Edelman. Doctor Bob, who has been my rabbi and my friend for many years, has long counselled me on how to become the historian I am today. I would like to thank my colleagues at Long Island University for their support and guidance as my career takes its next step.

A great deal of the research that went into the creation of this book was made possible by the support of the American Research Institute in Turkey and the International Research and Exchange Board. Specifically, I would like to thank Michelle Duplissis, Tony Greenwood, Pelin Gurol, Gülden Günleri, Nancy Leinwand, and Tova Pertman for all of their assistance during my times (and ordeals) away from home. I have nothing but thanks and kind words for the staff of the Ottoman and Republican archives in Istanbul and Ankara. I would specifically like to thank Yıldırım Ağanoğlu, Noray Bozbora, Thomas Goltz, Ayhan Kaya, Nurcan Özgür-Baklacıoğlu, Stanford Shaw, Nicole van der Os, and members of the Türk-Arnavut Kardeşliği Derneği for their help in my research in Turkey. I cannot forget the kindness and generosity shown to me by the staff and students of Sabancı University. I would like to thank Halil Berktay, Hakan Erdem, Rossitsa Gradeva, Peter Holt, Kerimcan Kavaklı, Cemil Koçak, Metin Kunt, Şerif Mardin, Akşin Somel, and Mary Wynn for making my stay there so rewarding. I would like to thank Ramiz Abdyli for his generosity and help in Skopje (falaminderit shumë). Antonis Hadjikyriacou and Gaby and Brendon Smith cannot be thanked enough for putting me up and taking me out for drinks during my various stays in London. Special thanks go to Aren Sarikyan and the Zoryan Institute of Canada, who generously allowed me access to their collection.

I would lastly like to thank those colleagues of mine who have read my material, offered advice on research and writing, or simply shared a beer with me after a long day: Isa Blumi, Gavin Brockett, John Colarusso, Howard Eissenstat, Tolga Ezmer, Ben Fortna, Fatma Müge Göçek, Jens Hanssen, Peter Holquist, Reşat Kasaba, Tijana Krstic, Donald Quataert, Michael Reynolds, Safa Saracoğlu, Erik Jan Zürcher, and many others. Last, but far from least, I want sincerely to thank Mark Mazower and Christopher Wheeler for all of their help in making this book possible.

Contents

List of Abbreviations	xiii
Map of the South Marmara	xiv

Introduction	1
A Note on Geography and Sources	8

1. Before They Became Turks: Immigration, Political Economy, and Identity in the Pre-war South Marmara — 12

- New Elites, New Identities: Revolution, Class, and Identity during the Young Turk Period — 13
- Resident Aliens: Reassessing Native Armenians and Greeks in the Ottoman Empire during the Nineteenth Century — 19
- The Mountaineers: North Caucasian Migrants and the Ottoman State in the Nineteenth Century — 23
- Bandits or Bureaucrats: Albanian Migrants and the Ottoman State in the Nineteenth Century — 30

2. The Politics of the Condemned: The South Marmara during the First World War — 37

- Boycotts and Refugees: The CUP's First Steps — 38
- 'Tehcir' for All: Reassessing the Wartime Deportations — 41
- The Condemned Come Home: The Return of Non-Muslims and its Immediate Aftermath — 52

3. In the Company of Killers: Crime, Recruitment, and the Birth of the National Movement in the South Marmara — 55

- Killer Patriots: Circassians and the Origins of the Ottoman Clandestine Service — 56
- Under the Reign of Gunmen: Paramilitarism and Instability in Wartime South Marmara — 65
- Turning Back the Clock: Origins of the Turkish National Movement — 68
- After Izmir: Contriving a Military/Bureaucratic Response — 71
- Çetecilik: Arming the Movement — 77

Contents

The Politics of Revenge: The Rise and Fall of the Loyalist Opposition in the South Marmara ... 81

The Loyalist Confederacy: The Sultanate and the Opposition to the *Kuva-yı Milliye* ... 83
Blood Feuds: The Prelude to Rebellion ... 86
'Protector of the Government and Slave to the Shariah': Reconsidering the Rise of Ahmet Anzavur ... 94
A Village Saint's Last Act: The İzmit Uprising and the Death of Ahmet Anzavur ... 104

5. Separatism, Violence, and Collaboration in Bandit Country: The South Marmara during the Greek Occupation ... 107

The Onset of Occupation: Greece, Britain, and Non-Muslims ... 108
'Those who stay will be destroyed by our hands': The National Movement under Occupation ... 113
From Rebels to Collaborators: Circassian Paramilitarism and the Greek Occupation ... 118
Resistance by Another Means: The Move towards Circassian Separatism in the South Marmara ... 123

6. Settling Accounts: Circassians, Albanians, and the Founding of the Turkish Republic ... 136

Killing Anzavur's Ghost: Republican Politics and the End of Circassian Resistance in the South Marmara ... 138
The Unwelcome Prodigal Sons: Albanians and the Contradictions of Turkish State Building ... 148

Conclusion ... 166

Appendix 1: Cast of Characters ... 171

Appendix 2: Glossary of Terms ... 182

Notes ... 185
Bibliography ... 239
Index ... 253

List of Abbreviations

ABCFM   American Board of Commissioners of Foreign Missions
BCA   Başbakanlık Cumhuriyet Arşivi
BOA   Başbakanlık Osmanlı Arşivi
CUP   Committee of Union and Progress
PRO   Public Records Office
VMRO   Vutreshna Makedonska Revoliutsıona Organizatsija

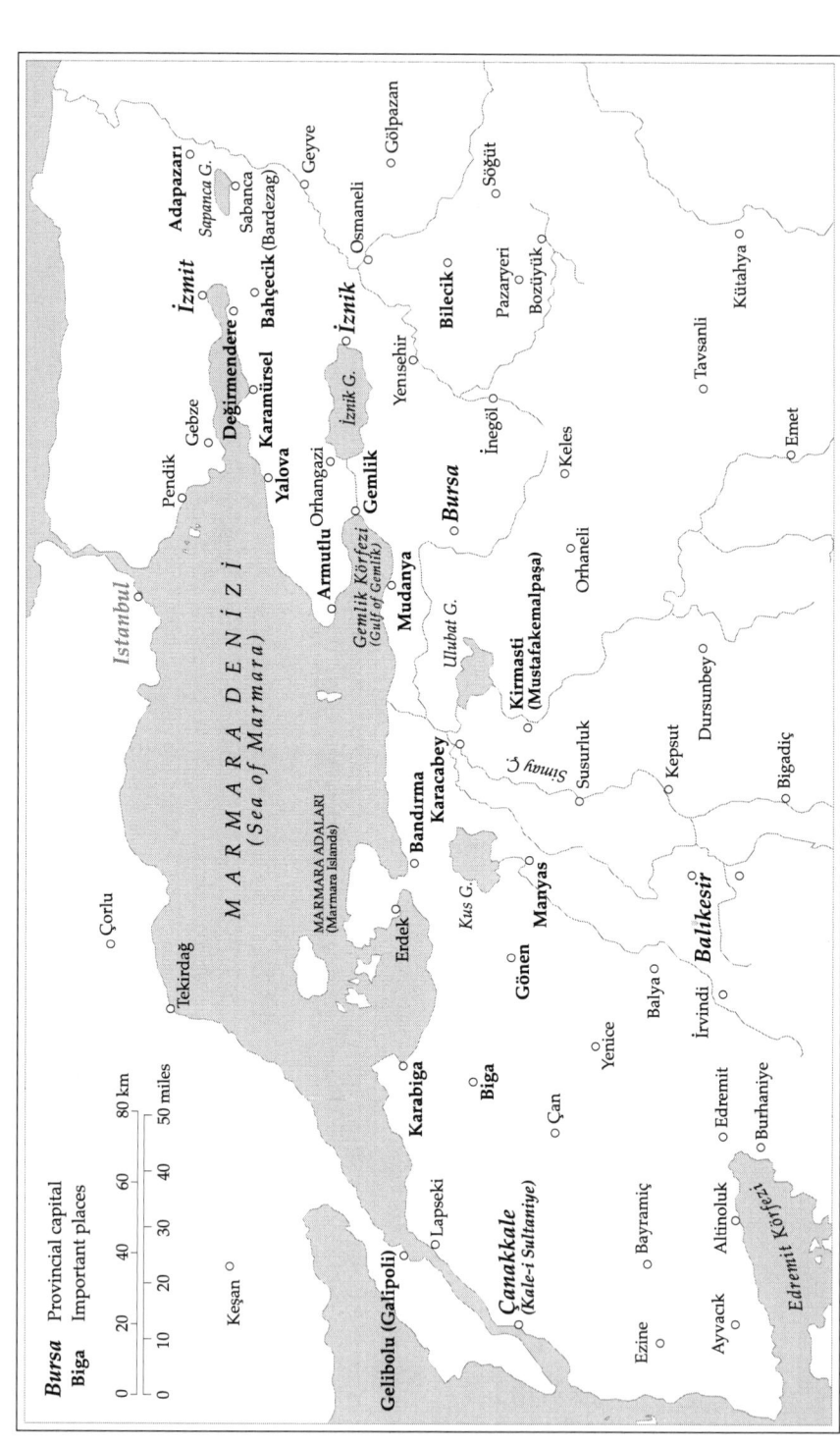

Introduction

For the last five years two small photos have hung behind my work desk. I bought them on my second trip to Istanbul in an antique shop off İstiklal Caddesi, a shop which subsequently went out of business. The pictures are delicately glued on to two separate exit visas from Turkey during the early 1920s. The man and woman in the photos, in both appearance and background, come from very different worlds. Muharrem stares blankly at the camera lens, dressed in a dark fez, coat, and shirt. The faded blacks and greys, contrasted with the deep lines on his face, make him look old, weather-worn, and tired. The application asks him for his religion (*din*), ethnicity or nationality (*millet*), destination, and the purpose of his trip. He declares that he is a Muslim Albanian destined for Debre, located in the western mountains of southern Serbia (now the Republic of Macedonia). There, he explains, he will attend to a piece of property still in his possession. At the age of 57, one would assume he had once lived on this land and had at some point left it behind.

The woman, by comparison, appears young, fair, and healthy. The image sharply portrays the 24-year-old Navart Odabaşiyan posing comfortably in a studio or parlour. Her fine dress and posture betray confidence and affluence. She is from Istanbul and is bound for Paris in order to visit family. She professes that she is Armenian, which she denotes as both her ethnicity and her religion. Without knowing the context of her life or her ultimate intensions, nothing in her exit application appears out of the ordinary. Yet, through my research and writing, I do wonder if Navart ever returned home to Istanbul.

This book is an effort to give the lives of these two individuals, as unknowable as they are, a context. Despite their apparent differences in class, religion, and ethnicity, both Muharrem and Navart share a common history of tragedy and metamorphosis. At the heart of this shared history is the story of Anatolia between the outbreak of the Balkan Wars in 1912 and the establishment of the Republic of Turkey in 1923. Although one could argue that they, as citizens of the once mighty Ottoman Empire, share a much a deeper historical past than these eleven years, this period possesses greater immediate and more profound significance than any other that had preceded the twentieth century. In the lifetimes of both of these individuals, they would see the passing of the Ottoman Empire, a state that had been in existence since the fourteenth century, and the establishment of a new nation-state upon its ashes. The years that accompanied this radical transition from empire to nation-state were defined by war, oppression, and upheaval. When the fighting ended in 1923, the physical and social contours of their lives had changed irrevocably.

Yet the contemporary retelling of this shared history often excludes the roles played by ordinary people. More importantly, historians of this period have deliberately approached the experiences of Muslims and Christians as separate and exclusive. This book offers an alternative perspective on the polities represented by Navart and Muharrem during this period between the imperial and the post-imperial. It draws similarities and contrasts between four distinct groups that were respectively Muslim and Christian, as well as native and immigrant in nature. In order to understand the proper context of these communities and individuals in the years between the Balkan Wars and the establishment of the Turkish Republic, close attention is paid to the evolution of a specific region within northwestern Anatolia. By taking up the roles of these four discrete groups, this book demonstrates the ways in which a series of provincial communities were both the objects and the engines of radical social and political change.

The focus of this book is the southern coastal corridor of the Marmara Sea, an area stretching roughly from the small garrison town of Çanakkale to the industrialized centres of İzmit and Adapazarı. During the interregnum between the Ottoman Empire and the Republic of Turkey, the South Marmara, as I refer to this region, constituted four strategically significant sub-provinces (*sancak*s) located to the south of the imperial capital of Istanbul. The middle section of the South Marmara littoral comprised two massive *sancak*s, Karesi (modern-day Balıkesir) and Hüdavendigar (Bursa).[1] On either side of these two districts were the independently run *sancak*s of Kale-i Sultaniye (Çanakkale), on the mouth of Dardanelles, and İzmit (Kocaeli), encompassing a vital railway junction east of the capital. These four districts did not belong to what one would consider the political 'periphery' of the Ottoman Empire; all four provinces were in fact within a day's journey of the very epicentre of the empire.

As the primary setting for this narrative, the South Marmara was the home to two of the largest immigrant groups of Anatolia: Muslim Albanians and North Caucasians. Although comparatively recently settlers from respectively distant corners of the Ottoman world, both of these groups are deeply tied to the empire's historical evolution. Through the history of the Ottoman Empire, migrant Albanians and North Caucasians (otherwise known more colloquially as Circassians) can be found at the most extreme ends of the social and political spectrum. From the first centuries of Ottoman expansion, Circassians and Albanians were counted among the highest-ranking officials and officers as well as the most insidious bandits and rebels. This internal dichotomy within the Albanian and North Caucasian diasporas takes centre stage in this look at the South Marmara during the war years.

The South Marmara at the turn of the century was also the home of the two largest native Christian populations of Anatolia: Armenians and native Greeks (or Rum in Turkish). Like Circassians and Albanians, Rum and Armenians were also seminal actors in the construction of the Ottoman state. Known for their contributions to the fields of commerce and industry, these two groups often straddled the nexus betwen Ottoman society and the wider Western world. In the midst of war and political chaos in the years between the Balkan Wars and the establishment of the Republic of Turkey, all four of these polities came under extreme state scrutiny. By the end of the war years, violence would decimate each of these communities in the South Marmara.

The years under discussion in this book encompass the most central period in Anatolia's modern development. It is a time that is celebrated within many venues of Turkish public life and represents both the origins and the destiny of the state. Be it in the confines of the classroom, the parliament, or street demonstrations, the retelling of the story often begins against the backdrop of the closing years of the Ottoman Empire, the political and cultural antecedent of the Republic of Turkey. There were glimmers of hope in the Ottoman Empire at the turn of century, an era when modern reform and 'national awakening' began to take hold among the 'Turks' of Anatolia. During the First World War, the story continues, young men from across Anatolia served bravely and valiantly in spite of invasion, rebellion, and economic hardship. Yet the sacrifices of the nation's soldiers and civilians could not forestall the empire's defeat at the hands of the Allied powers. In the dark months following Istanbul's surrender in 1918, foreign troops occupied large swaths of the country. Separatism and partition seemed inevitable. It is at this same moment when true patriots under the command of Mustafa Kemal (Atatürk) took up arms in the name of the Turkish nation, casting out the foreign invaders and unseating the long corrupt and backward Ottoman sultan. Mustafa Kemal's final ascendancy after the declaration of a Turkish Republic in 1923 sealed Anatolia's deliverance. Through the subsequent decades, a radical series of reforms transformed Anatolia forever, making it the heartland of a secular (yet Muslim), democratic, modern nation-state worthy of Western recognition.

Like many epic nationalist narratives, there is something reminiscent of the classic 'passion play' structure within this official interpretation. After years of decay and impending doom, when all seemed lost, a saviour appeared. This saviour, in leading his people out of lethargy, assumed a righteous mantle and attracted to his side equally righteous men. Nationalism, and not Islam, was the creed that he promoted as the ideological foundation for his struggle against the occupiers. In declaring victory over both the occupying Allied powers and the treacherous sultan, Atatürk's announcement of republican rule represents a moment of resurrection and, indeed, redemption of the 'Turkish people'. This official narrative not only signifies the triumph of Turkish Anatolia over both foreign and domestic challengers, but signals the emergence of a progressive and revitalizing ethos negating the centuries of backwardness and decline in Anatolia. This narrative structure, which is embodied in Atatürk's own account, the *Nutuk*, is reproduced in literally scores of books and articles covering the war years.[2]

This understanding of the war years is not without its detractors, however. Parallel to this nationalist discourse over the roots of the Turkish Republic are numerous studies documenting the victims of Anatolia's transformation from imperial core to nation-state. For many, Mustafa Kemal's National Movement (*Milli Mücadele*) was built upon the death and banishment of hundreds of thousands of Armenians and Greeks from Anatolia, ending centuries of history within a few short years. The suppression of Kurdish nationalism soon followed the establishment of the Turkish Republic, an act ultimately culminating in a violent protracted struggle over the fate of eastern Anatolia. Critics have also pointed to the silencing of independent Islamic expression in the face of Ankara's stringent secularist laws and statist interpretations of Islamic identity. In the present day, critical debate over the legacies of the war years has increasingly spilled into the political arena. One needs only look at the recent controversies that have swirled around author Orhan Pamuk, the rise of the Justice and Development Party, or the trials of Layla Zana to witness the violence and urgency with which this period is approached.

The most vivid example of scholarly disagreement over the historical significance of this decade is the bitter debate over the fate of Armenians during the First World War. Recent works produced by Taner Akçam and Stanford Shaw typify the essence of this debate. Akçam, in his most recent work, *A Shameful Act*, places heavy emphasis on Turkish nationalism in motivating the Ottoman government to undertake a series of genocidal policies towards its non-Muslim population. As an agenda many years in the making (and seemingly rooted in ancient Islamic tradition), the violence unleashed by Istanbul, which comprised mass deportations, executions, and economic disenfranchisement, barrelled over innumerable helpless and innocent Christian communities.[3] Shaw, however, paints a very different picture. Armenian nationalists, Greek irredentists, and Western imperialists, he argues, had plotted the partition of the Ottoman Empire throughout the nineteenth century. Indigenous Armenians and Greeks in Anatolia, swayed by nationalist passions and foreign support, executed hideous crimes against Muslim civilians during the First World War.[4] Had it not been for the heroics of Mustafa Kemal and those who took up the national struggle, the lives and freedoms of millions of Turks would have been condemned. A similar series of debates between these historians and others can also be found in regards to atrocities committed by Greek and Turkish forces in western Anatolia during the Turkish War of Independence (as well as, to a limited degree, the actions of the Balkan states during the Balkan Wars).

This study of Muslim immigrants and native Christians in the South Marmara enters into this debate and takes it in a different direction. The role of the state (be it the Ottoman, Greek, British, or American governments) is an essential factor in fanning the violence seen in this portion of northwestern Anatolia between 1912 and 1923. But to look at the role of the state in this region as somehow exclusive or independent of the complexities of local society would be a gross mistake. Furthermore, particularly in the case of the Ottoman government, nationalism was only one of the motivating factors that drove the violence forward.

In the South Marmara we see an overlapping series of alliances between local, national, and international actors both collaborating with and resisting statist intervention. At the heart of this conflict that bound and divided Albanians, Rum, Armenians, and Circassians was the will of the late Ottoman state to centralize and consolidate its hold over Anatolia. Through to the end of the First World War, the ruling Committee of Union and Progress (CUP), a party made up of individuals drawn from the emerging Muslim elite of the empire, proved to be limitedly capable of co-opting or subduing the population of the South Marmara into accepting the totality of their plans of state consolidation. It is only with the resurgence of the CUP, reconstituted under the leadership of Mustafa Kemal after 1919, that the fierce, often militant resistance to state centralization was finally broken. Although native Greeks and Armenians are often seen as the core of this resistance, Muslim immigrants like Albanians and Circassians played definitive roles in defying, as well as cooperating with, the CUP and the National Movement. This book presents a departure from the traditional line of inquiry into this period by tracing the provincial origins and violent results of the alliances formed by both collaborationist and resistance elements that struggled over the South Marmara during the war years.

The issue of identity is indelibly tied to the violent nature of this period. Scholars have often pointed to discourses of nationalism as the primary engine in mobilizing and defining the factions that would decide the fate of Anatolia between 1912 and 1923. Yet in looking beyond the elite rhetoric of the conflicting indigenous forces in the South Marmara, one is struck by the relative absence of nationalism at the popular level. The narrative provided to us through memoirs, police reports, consular dispatches, and military orders instead reveals the pre-eminence of religion, ethnicity, and class as defining components of identity in the South Marmara. Although religion forms the primary axis of perception and allegiance in this region, observers from all sides extensively used the more refined, although still blurry, prism of ethnicity as a tool to understand and describe the motivations, goals, and patterns of the social and political behaviour of actors in the South Marmara. But in delving still deeper into this time of upheaval, ethnic monikers and identities do not take on monolithic cultural forms. Rather, individual and collective ethnic qualities are often deeply invested with class and regionalist undertones, giving the appearance that ethnic character, specifically among Muslims, could be ameliorated depending on one's social origins. The politics of identity in the South Marmara is crucial not only in determining how state and local actors perceived one another, but also in elucidating the principles and contradictions of the statist and anti-statist agendas ingrained within the violence of this period.

Paramilitarism is an important subtext within these themes of violence and identity. The propagation and employment of militia groups is a dominating trait found in the South Marmara during this period of upheaval. Paramilitarism was a political, economic, and social institution that enabled both statist and resistance factions to mobilize popular support. The significance of this universal reliance upon paramilitary forces, however, exceeds its military implications. As a socio-political phenomenon indigenous to the South Marmara, the region's 'culture of paramilitarism' (to borrow Ussama Makdisi's turn on the phrase) underscores critical rifts within the fabric of this segment of Ottoman state and society. The attention paid to paramilitary activity in this book serves to emphasize that the violence of this period, be it in the South Marmara or elsewhere, was fundamentally a provincial affair.

A number of notable comparative studies on provincial violence during the early twentieth century provide the inspirational foundation for this book. In the Ottoman context, research conducted by Ussama Makdisi, Isa Blumi, and Hans-Lukas Kieser convincingly demonstrates how competing national and international forces collided to produce mass violent actions in Lebanon, the southern Balkans, and eastern Anatolia during the nineteenth and twentieth centuries.[5] The force and conviction of the Ottoman centralizing agenda, together with the subversive interests of the Western powers, undermined the provincial integrity of these three respective regions. Local factions in these areas, comprising both elite and subaltern elements, interpreted and manipulated these forces in order to promote their own provincial prerogatives. Mass violence in Lebanon, the south Balkans, and eastern Anatolia ensued, with the creation of new systems of patronage (often along ethnic or sectarian lines) and the renegotiation of older political and economic orders.

Provincial violence on a grand scale was not unique to the late Ottoman Empire. The combined influences of the modernizing state, imperialism, global capitalism, and migration had violent consequences for states across the globe at the turn of the twentieth century. Gyanendra Pandey, Ranajit Guha, Stanley Tambiah, and Anton Blok have each demonstrated how provincial actors struggled over the limits of state centralization and the politics of identity.[6] Pandey reminds us that the perceived 'communal' nature of violence and mass mobilization is a product of state intervention (since it is the state that gives significance to the geographical and social characteristics of given territory). Even the notion of 'minorities' or 'majorities' within a specific political or geographical space is subject to the categories and constructs of the state. When violence in the provinces did erupt, 'primordial hatreds' were not to blame. Rather, it has been well documented that the reconfiguration of political, economic, and social networks that pre-date state reform and globalization produce violent returns.

Blok and Guha each show that provincial paramilitaries, or even violent mobs, are indispensable interlocutors between state and provincial society. Rather than being 'antiquarian' or 'fanatical', the words and actions of locally based armed factions provide essential insights into the concerns, desires, and tensions within communities they claim to represent.

In considering both the methodological and historiographical goals of this book, I have been particularly influenced by revisionist studies of the Mexican Revolution. As a comparative foil to the events seen in the Ottoman Empire between 1912 and 1923, revolutionary Mexico shared many qualities that defined Anatolia at the turn of the twentieth century: a strong imperial tradition, an emerging industrial base, antagonistic relations between centre and periphery, pervasive foreign influence in both the state and the economy, and complex localist social structures. The combined works of Alan Knight, Gilbert Joseph, Paul Vanderwood, John Hart, Ana Maria Alonso, and others demonstrate that, as in the war years in Anatolia, the Mexican Revolution represented an elitist struggle over the continuation of the centralizing and modernizing practices of the pre-war era rather than an absolute rupture with the past.[7] More importantly, the popular socio-political shifts that did occur during Mexico's nineteen-year internal conflict (such as in Sonora or the Yucatan) were the result of regional socio-economic tensions, and therefore can only be understood through a more refined localist lens.

The broader historical narrative of modern Middle Eastern history has traditionally embraced the Turkish nationalist reading of the war years almost to the letter. Successive generations of Turkish and non-Turkish academics and civic leaders have solidified the success of the Mustafa Kemal's National Movement as the touchstone of the republic's development. Its current significance exceeds the overthrow of the Ottoman sultans and the establishment of republican rule. Decades of scholarship and nation building have transformed the Nationalist victory of 1923 into a representation of the unity and singular purpose of the Turkish nation. Within the retelling of the war years, little room tends to be left for the genocidal policies of the Committee of Union and Progress or the convoluted tensions that defined the Turkish War of Independence. The picture we receive from the South Marmara muddles this figment of the collective imagination. The events that transpired in the South Marmara between 1912 and 1923 possessed the characteristics of both a civil war and a revolution, as rival elites sought to impose their own vision of the post-war Ottoman state. The war years proved only to entrench the region's governing factions and marked the end of organized, armed opposition to the institutionalized CUP/Nationalist elite and the agenda of reform that it represented. The carnage that accompanied the struggle over the region is the most lasting legacy of the war, one that allowed the newly founded republican government in Ankara a cleaner (yet by no means immaculate) slate upon which it could thoroughly remake Anatolia society.

A NOTE ON GEOGRAPHY AND SOURCES

No map one can find in a library will point to a region specifically called the South Marmara. It is a region I have delineated strictly for the purpose of my research. Early on in my research, I came to draw lines around this portion of northwestern Anatolia on the basis of what I perceive to be a logical pattern of perceptions on the part of historical and contemporary sources. Without naming it as such, the South Marmara formed a fairly coherent geographical space in the minds of policy-makers and other actors during the final years of the Ottoman Empire. The southern Marmara coast enveloped the interior eastern lines of communication and transport in and out of the capital. By either land or sea, migrants, troops, and commerce could be easily transported to and from the Anatolian hinterland and then transferred to one of two major railway heads in the region, one at Bandırma and the other at İzmit. Each of the provincial capitals, as well as a series of small market towns, were linked by a web of well-travelled roads. Provincial communities, like the Armenians of Bahçecik and the North Caucasians of Gönen, moved, worked, and intermarried across the region without giving much thought to provincial borders. Events and government decisions described in official documents and personal accounts seemed to bind the four provinces of the South Marmara together, making each a fundamental setting for the story I wished to tell.

The four counties comprising the South Marmara, İzmit, Hüdavendigar, Karesi, and Kale-i Sultaniye, cannot be characterized or essentialized in a word or phrase. The diversity of the region begins with its geography. Past the southern shores of the Marmara Sea, the land immediately gives way to flat marshy plains and gentle hills. A belt of highlands stretches east of Adapazarı and through the southern rim of Karesi south of Balıkesir. Lakes teeming with fish dot the landscape between Bursa and Balıkesir. Summers are humid and warm, yet seasonal rain leaves the land fairly lush and fertile. No singular mode of economy dominates. The South Marmara has historically produced bountiful crops of tobacco, opium, fruits, vegetables, and silk. As a crossroads encompassing the land and sea routes leading in and out of old Istanbul, local and transnational trade in and through the region has long been vibrant. By the turn of the twentieth century, the South Marmara boasted four major cities (Bursa, Balıkesir, İzmit, and Adapazarı), as well as several smaller towns, with growing manufacturing sectors financed by domestic and foreign capital.

Since the time of Osman Gazi, whose son Orhan established the first capital of the fledgling Ottoman Empire in Bursa in 1326, the South Marmara has been home to a rich mosaic of peoples. Various spellings and names of different cities and towns are testament to the multiple waves of peoples who came to call the southern shores of the Marmara Sea home.[8] The incredible diversity of this region extends beyond the Albanian, Rum, Armenian, and North Caucasian communities described in this book. Naturally, the countryside stretching from Çanakkale in the west to Adapazarı in the east, then and now, hosts a large Muslim Turkish-speaking population. Yet, contrary to the expectations of many, the native Turkish-speakers of the South Marmara have never formed a homogeneous whole. Notable differences in dialect and religion found among several distinct local groups (such as the Zeybeks and Yörüks of modern-day Balıkesir, the Çetmi of Çanakkale, and the Manav of Bursa, Kocaeli, and Sakarya) reflect the internal complexities of the original Turkic nomads who migrated into the region both before and after the establishment of the Ottoman Empire. Unfortunately, historians of the late Ottoman Empire and the modern Republic of Turkey have paid little heed to the ways in which administrators and locals differentiated between rural Turkish-speakers. Rather than essentialize the entire native Muslim population, I use the term 'Turk' only in very specific circumstances.

Since antiquity, the South Marmara has welcomed an ongoing stream of migrants. Beginning in the late eighteenth century, most of the settlers who arrived in the region were refugees. In addition to the Albanian and North Caucasian communities I discuss in this book, large numbers of Pomaks (Bulgarian-speaking Muslims) and Bosnians had come to reside in the South Marmara by the outbreak of the First World War. Smaller communities of Arabs, Tatars, and Kurds also added to the stew of Muslim migrants living in the area. Pockets of Christian settlers and expatriates also found their way into different towns and villages. In addition to European and American missionaries, diplomats and merchants, various generations of Russian and Ukrainian refugees arrived and established new lives along the interior of the Marmara's southern shores during the nineteenth century.

The sources I have employed for this book also influenced the emphasis and content of the pivotal turns described in the forthcoming pages. Documents from the Ottoman archives and contemporary memoirs consistently highlight the trials and affairs of Muslims in the South Marmara. Due to either self-censorship or deliberate purging, Ottoman accounts often ignore, condense, or denigrate the roles of Christians. Sources from the Public Records Office in London and the American Board of Commissioners of Foreign Missionaries unfortunately shed only a partial light on the evolution of the Armenians and Greeks during this period. Quite often too, these documents tell more about the Western perspectives on the South Marmara than offer revelations on the local communities themselves. I have also consulted newspapers and recorded interviews in order to round out patches of my work. I believe that what I have assembled in this book constitutes a concise overview of the region and key elements of local socio-political life during the war years. Still, a more definitive work, if it is at all possible, will have to wait.

Table I.1 Sancak statistical data, 1914

	Muslims	Rum	Armenians	Jews	Armenian Catholics	Protestants	Roma	Total
İzmit	226,859	40,048	55,403	428	449	1,937		325,153
Karesi	359,804	97,497	8,544	362	109	51	74	472,970
Hüdavendigar	474,114	74,927	58,921	4,126	1,278	992	1,869	667,790
Kale-i Sultaniye	149,903	8,531	2,474	3,642		67	369	165,815
Total	1,210,680	221,003	125,342	8,558	1,836	3,047	2,312	1,631,728

Source: Kemal Karpat, *Ottoman Population, 1830–1914: Demographic and Social Characteristics* (Madison: University of Wisconsin Press, 1985), 188–9.

Table I.2 Kaza statistical data, 1914

	Muslims	Rum	Armenians	Jews	Armenian Catholics	Protestants	Roma
Adapazarı	76,864	7,957	16,461	113	1	655	
Yalova	7,954	10,274	3,304				
İznik	13,785	1,632	126				
Gemlik	16,373	8,568	3,348				
Orhangazi	11,884		22,726		36	121	
Karacabey	25,763	9,921	987	44		49	530
İzmit	40,403	5,226	23,873	307	448	1,078	
Bilecik	59,508	9,877	7,774		479	183	
Söğüt	55,223	1,982	7,770		52	136	
İnegöl	56,238	34	7,101	106		225	
Geyve	32,508	7,108	8,363	4		225	
Yenişehir	26,408	1,683	1,660				
Lapseki	17,561	1,164	43	52			
Çanakkale	13,596	4,358	1,269	2,961		59	
Mudanya	7,677	17,389	100	53		20	
Kirmasti	56,599	1,381	1,016	184			
Bursa	111,301	24,048	6,433	3,687	691	278	1,339
Karamürsel	14,850	6,047	2,635				
Balıkesir	156,092	2,655	2,963	1	3		30
Gönen	34,979	2,251	53				
Bandırma	41,146	11,507	4,032	4	106	51	
Ezine	15,801	486	700	256			
Bayramiç	20,614	290	48	269		8	
Biga	65,242	2,243	409	103			

Source: Karpat, *Ottoman Population*, 176–7, 184–5, 186–7.

1

Before They Became Turks: Immigration, Political Economy, and Identity in the Pre-war South Marmara

Selahettin Bey appeared to have waited more than half of his life to tell his story. As a veteran of the Turkish War of Independence, the captain's distinguished service in Mustafa Kemal's National Forces remained a tale worth telling towards the end of the twentieth century. He was born in Edirne, a town in eastern Thrace that had once been the seat of the Ottoman Empire. His father, a state official, moved the family several times during Selahettin's youth. Between stops in Edirne, Tekirdağ, and Istanbul, he received an education fitting a young man with imperial ambitions.[1] His excellence as a student, as well as the years his father served the empire, finally brought him to the Ottoman Military Academy (*Harbiye Mektebi*) in Istanbul. The city, his friends, and the education he received both inside and outside the classroom would change his life. At a café in Istanbul, a classmate and old friend of Selahettin's asked him the following set of questions:

> 'What are you?'
> 'A student at the military school.'
> 'What else?'
> 'I don't know.'
> 'Think about it.'
> 'I am an Ottoman.'
> 'What else?'
> 'I am a Muslim.'
> 'No, before everything else, you are a Turk!'[2]

In citing this recollection, Selahettin emphasizes that his commitment to state service changed while at the academy. He began to read the work of Namık Kemal, the famed Ottoman nationalist writer of a generation before, and developed a strong interest and attachment to 'Turkishness' (*Türkçülük*).

Before discovering his Turkishness, Selahettin's personal account is largely silent on his life as an 'Ottoman Muslim'. He does, however, offer the reader an interesting hint. One of his first recollections as a boy occurred shortly before his circumcision. Offhandedly, he recalls one of his relatives presenting him with an Albanian costume as a gift to mark the occasion.³ The inclusion of this brief anecdote raises several questions about its significance. Is the reader to interpret this as a fragment of Selahettin's family history? Is he Albanian, or were members of his family of Albanian origin? Is the costume, an article representing tradition, to be juxtaposed with the success or progress of his future? Of greatest importance, how did Selahettin reconcile the provincial traditions symbolized by this gift with his cultivated devotion to 'Turkishness' later on in life?

The revelations and questions embedded within Selahettin's story resonate in the lives of many of the most prominent and defining figures of the Ottoman Empire during the early twentieth century.⁴ Selahettin's rise to prominence and the evolution of his life and career are intimately tied to the state. He and many others like him were at the same time the chief architects and beneficiaries of a reforming state fighting for its political survival. Their experiences of war, education, and social class further bound Selahettin's political generation together as the emerging elite of the empire. We see in the emergence of the Committee of Union and Progress, the party which ruled the Ottoman Empire during its very last years, the embodiment of this generation. In this chapter and others to follow, the interwoven relationship between the state and the collective identity of this new elite is crucial in order to understand the origins and direction of the policies that many critical bureaucrats and officers would undertake during the war years.

At the same time, the murkiness of Selahettin's past reflects less discussed aspects of the forces that would transform and defend the status quo in Anatolian society between 1912 and 1923. The Albanian costume that Selahettin received as a child points to cultures and groups in provincial society exclusive (and at times opposed) to the norms imposed by the state. The costume symbolizes those who neither dressed the part of an ambitious young officer nor subscribed to state nationalism, but who instead worked to maintain local tradition and autonomy. As we will see over the forthcoming pages, some individuals were able to reconcile their provincial roots with their attachment to the imperial state (often with a great deal of unease and confusion). Many others, however, struggled in their encounters with the modern Ottoman state. The bulk of this chapter presents an overview of the four principal social groups of this study within the context of their interactions with the Ottoman state. In this historical foundation, we begin to see the social origins of the provincial forces at the centre of the violence in the South Marmara during the war years.

NEW ELITES, NEW IDENTITIES: REVOLUTION, CLASS, AND IDENTITY DURING THE YOUNG TURK PERIOD

There is arguably no singular Ottoman or Anatolian equivalent to Bastille Day or the storming of the Winter Palace, definitive moments marking the beginning of French and Russian revolutionary history. Ottoman historians have given approximate significance to 23 July 1908, the day when then Sultan Abdülhamid II conceded defeat to the Young Turk revolt in Macedonia and restored the 1876 constitution. But to begin a discussion of the Ottoman revolutionary period with this date would be misleading. The Young Turk Revolution of 1908 was a moment that was decades in the making and was only one turn in a series of revolutionary steps towards top-down reform.[5] During the century of state transformation leading up to the ascendancy of the Committee of Union and Progress, one question dominated the motivations and actions of several generations of bureaucrats, statesmen, and intellectuals alike: How can this state be saved?[6] The CUP was only one voice that ventured an answer to this question. Yet, as we will see, it is this generation of political leaders and societal managers that would have the final word.

The constriction and consolidation of Ottoman rule over its lands during the eighteenth century, followed by increased Western influence and intervention during the early nineteenth century, provided the pretext for the first centralizing reforms instituted by Sultan Mahmud II. Sultan Abdülmecid's ascendancy in 1839 changed the tone of Mahmud's reforms with the commencement of the 'Reordering' period (the *Tanzimat*) between 1839 and 1876. This period featured the beginning of a centralized system of education, the creation of new criminal and commercial courts, and an ever-deepening commitment to the establishment of an effective and robust military. By 1876, the apparatus of the state took on the veneer of a more regularized, Western-style bureaucracy. The Ottoman constitution of 1876 was the invention of this new bureaucracy, which increasingly saw itself as the sole arbiter of modernism and reform in the empire. Abdülhamid II's abrogation of the constitution in 1878 sidelined this group of intellectuals and officials; yet the sultan continued down the path they first laid out. Through an expansion of the state education system, infrastructure, communications, conscription, and regional bureaucracy, Abdülhamid II furthered the goals of the *Tanzimat* in creating a more centralized and consolidated state. Yet, under the Hamidian regime the sultan and his personal offices cast themselves as the central managers of reform.[7]

Opposition to the Hamidian order began almost immediately after he took power. Largely based abroad, this opposition fervently rejected the 'despotism' of Abdülhamid and demanded the restoration of the constitution. The Committee of Union and Progress (or the 'Young Turks', as they were labelled by the French press) garnered a considerable following among younger members of the Ottoman bureaucracy and military still based in the empire. Yet this younger segment of the elite differed from its counterparts in exile in Europe. As Erik Jan Zürcher points out, the CUP's disciples in the empire were overwhelmingly the children of mid-level officials and officers of the imperial administration and army. Educated in the finest schools of the empire (such as the Military Academy and Civil Service School), many of these young dissidents spoke at least one

European language. In school they surreptitiously read the works of dissident Ottoman writers (such as Namık Kemal), who advocated total devotion to the Ottoman *vatan* or fatherland. They were for the most part Muslims, although during the initial stages some Christians and Jews were found among them.[8]

Many of these young dissidents in the empire were raised in the provinces of Ottoman Macedonia. The significance of their provincial origins is key for Zürcher, since Macedonia was among the most industrialized, urban, and cosmopolitan portions of the Ottoman Empire. In keeping with their education in Istanbul or their upbringing in the new urban centres of Selanik (Salonika/Thessaloniki) or Manastır (Bitola), this generation was profoundly influenced by the materialist and classist tendencies of elite culture found in Europe and elsewhere at the turn of the century.[9] Western dress, for example, was assigned extreme importance, since it was a marker for urbanity and status.[10]

Macedonia held another important significance for this group of dissidents. Since the 1890s, the region had become the epicentre of a massive, multidimensional insurgency against the Ottoman state. Many of these dissident officers and officials actively took part in the war against the Christian separatists in Macedonia, which from the beginning was hampered by European interference and Istanbul's ineptitude and impotence. The conflict resonates throughout the memoirs of the founders of the Committee of Union and Progress as the key factor that led to their revolt in the summer of 1908.[11]

The Revolution of 1908, which heralded the restoration of the constitution of 1876 and parliamentary rule, again shifted power away from the sultan and allowed the Ottoman bureaucracy and military greater authority in pressing forward a more stringent regime of centralization. In addition to attempting to extend Istanbul's control over the provinces (which included draconian measures against the press, trade unions, tribes, and 'vagrants'), the imperial bureaucracy renewed its commitment to education as a means to 'enlighten' and mould the population.[12] Meanwhile, the Committee of Union and Progress continued to grow after Abdülhamid was dethroned in 1909. At times, it appeared to many observers that the CUP provincial offices *were* the bureaucracy, since many local officials and bureaucrats (as well as merchants, intellectuals, landowners, and professionals) were active members.[13] Unionists also dominated the parliament and continued to exercise inordinate control over the army, regardless of the constitution and the chain of command.[14] Yet the CUP's first years in politics were far from tranquil. Major rebellions and crises in Albania, Kosova, Macedonia, Libya, and Yemen shook internal support for the party and gave further evidence of the weakening sovereignty and cohesion of the Ottoman Empire.[15]

Internal discord intensified with the progressive adaptation of Turkish as the language of provincial administration and education. Although Ottoman Turkish was codified as the language of the state in the 1876 constitution, the Ottoman government, under strong CUP pressure, took an especially hard line on its use after 1908.¹⁶ This led to accusations by Arab, Albanian, and other provincial officials and notables that the Unionist-led government was attempting to 'Turkify' the population and deny cultural expression in the empire. On the face of things, there was some merit to this accusation. The promotion of Ottoman Turkish did come at the expense of local languages in areas such as the Arab and Albanian lands, two regions that experienced a 'renaissance' in terms of local linguistic reform.¹⁷

Critics also argued that the CUP was in league with the 'Turkist' intellectual movement beginning to take root in the Balkans and Anatolia. The Turkist movement first manifested itself outside of the empire in the nineteenth century through the work of European and Russian Muslim intellectuals. With the turn of the century, a small clique of writers (such as Ziya Gökalp, Ahmet Ağaoğlu, and Yusuf Akçura) argued for the recognition of the Turkish people of Anatolia as the core demographic element of the empire and the cultural and political source of Ottoman imperial tradition. They advocated, in one form or another, greater ties between the Ottoman state and its Turkish brethren residing in Central Asia, the Caucasus, and the Crimea.¹⁸ The CUP's association with Turkist doctrine became cemented with the founding of the Turkish Hearth (*Türk Ocağı*) in 1911, an intellectual organization dedicated to the awakening of 'national feelings (*milliyet duygusu*)' in Anatolia.¹⁹ Chapters of the *Türk Ocağı* were established throughout Anatolia and the Balkans, and became an unofficial meeting place for CUP officials and members.

Scholars over the past decades have countered that the conflict over Turkish language policy reflected a larger debate on centre–periphery relations. The struggle between imperial centralization and provincial autonomy had a long history in the Ottoman Empire, with power shifting back and forth throughout the eighteenth and nineteenth centuries. The promotion of a state language was only one aspect of this conflict.²⁰ The diversity of language, in the words of Namık Kemal, was a 'barrier' to state centralization and national unity. In this light, the promotion of Turkish, the traditional language of the Ottoman state, was justified in achieving greater state cohesion.²¹ Şükrü Hanioğlu has added that the association between the Young Turks and the Turkists was an alliance of convenience. The Young Turks pushed the Turkist agenda when it suited them, employing it as an 'instrument' to 'save the state'.²² Both Hanioğlu and Kayalı maintain that the Young Turks, who were drawn from numerous ethno-linguistic groups, viewed themselves first and foremost as loyal Ottomans and often used the terms 'Ottoman' (*Osmanlı*) and 'Turk' (*Türk*) interchangeably.²³

The significance of the CUP's language policies and its association with the Turkist movement should not be confined to our understanding of state policy; rather, we should view these two facets of CUP rule as windows into how the Young Turks understood themselves in relationship to both state and society. From its roots in the dissident exile communities of Europe during the nineteenth century, the Committee of Union and Progress saw itself as representative of the political, intellectual, *and* cultural elite of the empire. They fancied themselves as members of a 'vanguard party' (to borrow a Leninist idiom) dedicated to bringing order to the state and enlightening the masses. This in part comes out of the ways in which the Young Turks read and perceived themselves in the context of the French revolutionary tradition. The French Revolution represented the ascendancy of the French intellectual elite as the pre-eminent political class of the nation. For the Young Turks, the revolution also symbolized the empowerment of the population at large. The revolutionaries hoped to illuminate the masses as to their plight and offer them a path and a medium through which they too could participate in the state's reformation.[24]

In other ways too, the formation of the CUP and the crafting of its policies speak to how this collective of individuals viewed themselves as members of a socio-economic class. The individuals comprising the CUP saw themselves as the elite of their generation, the sons and daughters of an emerging Muslim bourgeoisie. This sense of privilege was reinforced by their education and their deep ties to the urban centres of the empire, the two primary nodes of state modernization and centralization.[25] In joining the CUP, the Young Turks believed that their purpose, their charge to keep, was to teach and lead their fellow citizens, particularly Muslims. Language, education, and identity politics were tools in this effort to co-opt the masses.

Still, this world-view placed *fraternité* over *egalité*. The CUP's objective was not to raise the population to a level on a par with itself as a socio-economic or political group. Their elitism, based on their class backgrounds and close identification with the Ottoman state, was a right and a quality that separated them from the rest of society. State policy was to be used instead as a tool to instil a core set of values and qualities that levelled regional and ethno-linguistic differences and brought the population into the collective fold. By learning and adopting Turkish (particularly their brand of Ottoman Turkish) as the primary means of official communication, the CUP attempted to compel other Muslims to accept a shared set of values and priorities advocated by the state. Demanding loyalty was not enough. Citizens had to be mulded or re-engineered in order for state and society to function in coherent harmony with one another.[26]

The CUP's agenda of social and political re-engineering through compulsory education and language laws followed bifurcated lines of reasoning and approach. Non-Muslims, as we will see shortly, were initially not the focus of such rigorous state attention. For Muslims, however, 'ethnic' attachments were often subject to scrutiny and apprehension. One's ethno-linguistic background was immaterial to the CUP (whose members were drawn from a number of ethno-linguistic groups) so long as one accepted and adopted a select set of social and political norms pre-packaged in Istanbul.[27] But if one did not accept the norms put forward by the state (speaking proper Turkish, dressing in a 'modern', quasi-Western style, pursuing education, being loyal to the Ottoman state and the CUP), one's ethnicity did assume importance. Where this 'ethnic' opponent to state reforms could be found was in 'the provinces'. The provinces, which could mean either territories at a distance from the capital or an area lying just outside the city limits, constituted an environment that created and preserved social, cultural, and political differences. In other words, the conflict between the CUP's values, based on a 'non-ethnic', urban elitism, and the 'ethnics' who resisted the CUP's political and social agenda was in many ways an extension of the centre–periphery struggle. The difference between urban/imperial norms and provincial/peripheral heterodoxy contained an inherently classist component. Those who rejected state authority were not only labelled rebels (who were often coded as bandits or *eşkiya*), but were also considered 'vagrants' (*serseri*), a favourite term for low-class, uncouth individuals.[28]

Even if one looks at the CUP in association with Turkism, a doctrine that lavished affection upon the ethnic Turkish elements of Anatolia, it is clear that not all 'Turks' were viewed equally.[29] The writings of Ziya Gökalp, for example, are vague as to the ethnographical variations of Turkishness, referring to Turkish-speakers in Anatolia simply as the descendants of the Oğuz peoples who migrated from Central Asia.[30] What is not taken into account is the diversity among the indigenous Turkish-speakers of Anatolia. In the South Marmara, for example, large communities of indigenous Turcoman dotted the region, such as the Zeybeks, Manav, and Çetmi.[31] While 'Turks' in the absolute sense of the word, there were significant sectarian, dialectical, and cultural differences among these groups. Local Ottoman officials recognized these differences and often disparaged them (associating them with banditry and other antisocial or anti-state behaviour). These 'Turks' too would be forced to abandon their provincial character and accept the CUP's notion of uniformity.

Istanbul's confrontation with society was further complicated by the sheer multiplicity of groups living in the provinces. In areas such as the South Marmara, internal and transnational migration and trade created fluid socio-political networks. Along with older, more established groups, these provincial networks were able to preserve their local autonomy despite a century-long effort towards centralizing reform.

The 'ethnics' that so concerned the CUP were themselves not monolithic organisms. Integral fault lines, along sectarian, economic, and social lines, stymied many of the state's attempts to co-opt these groups into accepting the reformation of the empire. By looking at the construction of the various Albanian, Armenian, Rum, and Circassian communities in the South Marmara, we achieve greater insight into the fundamental issues that defined the violent contours of state–periphery negotiation during the war years.

RESIDENT ALIENS: REASSESSING NATIVE ARMENIANS AND GREEKS IN THE OTTOMAN EMPIRE DURING THE NINETEENTH CENTURY

Istanbul's efforts towards creating a loyal citizenry within its imperial domain was crystallized in the Gülhane Rescript of 1839, which first outlined a regime of political and legal equality between Christians and Muslims. Although intended as a means to change the way in which imperial institutions were supposed to function and to create a new precedent as to the meaning of being Ottoman, this new regime met with mixed results throughout the *Tanzimat* and Abdülhamid's reign.[32] The declaration of Muslim–Christian equality created confusion and discontent as the *millet* system (whereby non-Muslim communities were allowed a certain degree of autonomy within the Ottoman state) was gradually replaced by a more uniform code of law and civic responsibility. This fundamental change in Ottoman society, together with greater Western intervention and the growth of nationalism, proved a combustible mixture throughout the Ottoman lands. Between 1839 and 1908, sectarian violence tore through communities in Macedonia, eastern Anatolia, Syria, and Lebanon, leaving thousands dead and displaced.[33] Fatma Müge Göçek suggests that the rifts caused by the government's commitment to the creation of a more uniform notion of Ottoman citizenship went deeper than these outbreaks of civil strife. The reforms of the nineteenth century, she argues, created a bifurcated society of patronage, service, and economy. Ottoman Muslim society in the nineteenth century, through access to government education and recruitment, became anchored in the bureaucracy and military.[34] Abdülhamid's pan-Islamist posturing at home and abroad furthered this collective identity among Muslims.[35] Meanwhile, Ottoman Christians were simultaneously drawn closer to the West through a parallel system of patronage established through business contacts and foreign representatives.[36] This fundamental cleavage, she concludes, greatly contributed to the violence seen in the Ottoman lands during the early twentieth century.[37]

In the years leading up to the outbreak of war in 1912, evidence from the South Marmara suggests that Armenians and Greeks experienced the diverging effects of imperial reform and polarization in full. Internal and transnational forces profoundly changed their collective relationships with the Ottoman state. Yet these two Christian communities did not encounter or negotiate these changes as a harmonious whole. Issues of class, location, and contact with the West (as well as inherent linguistic and sectarian differences) among Rum and Armenians conditioned their collective interactions with the Ottoman state. Still, on the surface at least, there were few immediate signs that pointed to the catastrophe that would befall these two communities during the war years.

By the outbreak of the Balkan Wars, non-Muslims in the provinces of İzmit, Hüdavendigar, Karesi, and Kale-i Sultaniye comprised slightly more than 20 per cent of the population.[38] However, the population breakdown along *vilayet* and *kaza* lines shows dramatic disparities in the distribution of Muslims and Christians throughout the South Marmara. Armenians, though found throughout the region, were largely concentrated along the eastern rim of the Marmara Sea. The *kaza* of Adapazarı contained the highest percentage of Armenians, totalling more than 34 per cent of the population in 1912. In each *vilayet* the number of Greek Christians spanned from 5 per cent (Kale-i Sultaniye) to 21 per cent (Karesi). Distribution by district varied even more dramatically, with the Greek population of some districts and towns constituting as little as 1 or 2 per cent (Bayramiç and Balıkesir) to as high as 70 per cent (Mudanya). While Ottoman censuses in the South Marmara identify large numbers of individuals as members of the Catholic, Armenian, and Greek Christian *millet*s, the classification 'Protestant' leaves out any association with an 'Armenian' or 'Rum' ethnicity, allowing for the possibility that there were still slightly denser pockets of ethnic Armenians and Rum in the South Marmara.[39]

Western observers, particularly missionaries, readily identified the South Marmara and its Christian population with antiquity. In their reports back to the United States, American missionaries introduced İzmit (or Nicomedia in Greek) as the ancient capital of the province of Bythinia, a region steeped in biblical lore.[40] This geographic and historical association between the ancient South Marmara and native Christians, however, was naturally quite tenuous. Many individuals who belonged to the Orthodox, Catholic, or Gregorian faiths were descendants of fairly recent settlers to the region. The vast majority of the Armenians of İzmit and Adapazarı were descendants of settlers from Iran and eastern Anatolia who came to the region as traders and farmers during the seventeenth and eighteenth centuries.[41] Even many Greeks, such as in the environs of Bandırma, were recent immigrants from islands in the Aegean or from the Anatolian interior.[42]

This transience seen among Armenians and Greeks in the South Marmara developed new dimensions around the turn of the twentieth century. Family and business relations tied many Christians to Istanbul, Izmir, and entrepôts beyond the Ottoman Empire.[43] Economic and professional opportunities in the burgeoning cities of Bursa, İzmit, and Balıkesir brought Armenians and Greeks from as far away as Erzerum or Trabzon.[44] The migration of peasants from neighbouring villages further increased the urban Christian population of the South Marmara in the decades preceding the Balkan Wars.[45] Yet many of those who achieved success in the more economically vibrant coastal towns did not remain estranged from their co-religionists in the interior. One wealthy

Armenian merchant in Balıkesir, for example, organized a local relief effort on behalf of the Armenian victims of violence in Adana in 1909.[46] Still other Greeks and Armenians would cut all ties with the South Marmara and the Ottoman Empire and seek employment, education, or adventure abroad.[47]

By the turn of the twentieth century, movement to the cities and divisions of labour served to increase class stratification among Armenians and Greeks. The onset of mechanized production and the inflow of foreign capital transformed cities such as Bursa, Gemlik, Bilecik, and Adapazarı into vital centres of production and trade. At the heart of this economic shift was the manufacturing of silk, an industry associated with Greek and Armenian entrepreneurs.[48] As silk output increased and trade between the hinterland and the coast quickened, Christian owners, managers, and merchants increasingly became an elite class with transnational roots. Economic prosperity also provided the foundation for a sizeable professional class of Christian doctors, teachers, lawyers, and intellectuals. Perhaps even more profound was the establishment of a new urban working class, made up of factory workers and spinners, comprising large numbers of Armenians and Rum (as well as Muslims).[49] In the countryside, rural Christians serviced the new economic needs of the towns and contributed to other important sectors of the economy. In addition to providing the raw silk to urban factories, Christian peasants outside of Balıkesir, Bursa, and İzmit also engaged in the production of timber, tobacco, tiles, and foodstuffs.[50] In the coastal districts of Erdek, Bandırma, and Çanakkale, Greek fishermen and ferrymen continued to ply their trade on the Marmara Sea.[51]

The widening and expansion of class and provincial divisions had varying effects upon the ways in which Greeks and Armenians related to the society around them. Urban Christians largely remained tied to neighbourhoods long identified with the Armenian or Rum *millet*s.[52] Yet growing class divisions served to complicate this sectarian divide as working-class or elite Christians tended to mix together in poorer or wealthier quarters of town. As with Muslims, status and location also changed the tastes, ideals, and patterns of education for Christians in the South Marmara. The donning of 'modern' or 'traditional' clothing served to emphasize urban/rural rifts.[53] By the turn of the century, socialism and labour activism began to seep into the fabric of Christian urban life.[54] The greatest question that remains is the degree to which class and location affected the spread of nationalism (be it Armenian, Greek, or even Ottoman nationalism).[55] Although there are woefully few studies on the spread of nationalism among Christians in the South Marmara, comparative studies, as well as contemporary observations, suggest that Greek nationalism attracted greater adherents in both urban and rural communities.[56]

Perhaps the greatest levelling force within Christian society in the South Marmara was the influence wielded by Western actors. Mirroring the rise of foreign capital, the numbers and influence of agents representing European and American interests increased in magnitude through the turn of the century.

Among the most significant foreign elements to enter the South Marmara in the years before the Balkan Wars was the American Board of Commissioners for Foreign Missionaries (ABCFM), a Protestant evangelical organization based in New York and Boston. According to their own estimates in 1908, American missionaries established 140 churches and operated literally scores of primary, secondary, and Sunday schools in the South Mamara. Between 1850 and 1908, they reportedly educated thousands of students and attracted tens of thousands of adherents and attendees to their church services.[57] The reports they have left us, despite their omissions, biases, and obvious inaccuracies, provide invaluable insights into the nature of Western imperialism in the South Marmara and the effect it had upon communal Greek and Armenian life.

From the onset of their activities in the South Mamara in the early nineteenth century, correspondents from the ABCFM betray a highly calculated, almost militarized, line of thinking in discussing the proselytization of local Christians. General reports and documents speak of densities of Muslim and Christian populations, distances between towns, 'strategic' locations for schools and missions, and even the 'military' significance of specific cities.[58] American missionaries were careful to inform not only their superiors back in the United States, but also American embassy staff in Istanbul of their whereabouts and activities. Several decades of work in towns and villages in the South Marmara (as well as elsewhere) conditioned American missionaries as to where and how converts and clients could be made.

Reports written after 1900 repeatedly emphasize that Armenians were by far and away the most eager recipients of the Word. Although initially opposed to their activities, ordained and lay members of the Armenian Gregorian church at times supported, or even cooperated with, the activities of American missionaries. Greeks, on the other hand, were found to be generally indifferent, if not opposed, to their overtures. With the exception of a small community in the port town of Bandırma, Greeks sent far fewer students to missionary-run schools and remained 'fanatically' attached to the Orthodox Church and its schools.[59] Relating to Muslims in the region, who were collectively seen as the most 'backwards' and 'fanatical' of the three, proved to be an even more hopeless task. Although some wealthy Muslims were willing to send their children to missionary schools or seek help at missionary hospitals, conversion was painfully rare.[60]

Reflecting their success among native Armenians, American missionary efforts were largely confined to the geographic corridor between Bursa and Adapazarı. A handful of ordained and lay American and Armenian preachers both serviced the large congregations of the major towns and provided intermittent assistance to 'out station' rural communities. As testament to the Lord's work, as well as showcases for Western 'civilization' and modernity, most of the ABCFM's resources were invested in a handful of tuition-based secondary schools. Students who entered either the Bythinian High School in Bahçecik (Bardezag in Armenian), the Armenian Girls' High School in Adapazarı, or the Girls'

Boarding School in the Kayabaşı section of Bursa came from town, outlying villages, and from districts further east and west.61 They were offered a regime of religious and practical classes in Ottoman Turkish, Greek, and Armenian. A handful of exceptional graduates from these schools would return as teachers, seek education abroad, or be enrolled in Robert College, the crown jewel of the American missionary schools. Connection to missionary schools, orphanages, or churches also provided professional opportunities to those trained as craftsmen and for a few a means to emigrate to the United States.62

Scattered pieces of evidence suggest, however, that many of those who participated in these missionary institutions were not completely passive or compliant. In the years between 1908 and 1912, church officials grew exasperated with the infighting among parishioners in Bilecek over the leadership of the community.63 Even into the war years, Armenian churchgoers repeatedly clashed with their American counterparts over the future of their schools and parishes. The Board resisted calls for local autonomy and decried what one American commentator would later call the 'Bolshevik' tendency of some local Armenian leaders towards self-rule.64

Correspondence from American missionaries offers very few details as to the effect they had upon Muslim–Christian relations in the South Marmara. What the records of the ABCFM do suggest is the degree to which Armenians and Greeks functioned outside the institutions and outlets offered by the Ottoman state. Even though the 'revolutionary spirit' brought about by the restoration of the constitution in 1908 may have swayed some non-Muslims in the region to engage the state more directly, the evidence available to us suggests that Armenians and Greeks in the South Mamrara did so from their exclusive positions in society.65 The path to civic leadership, be it locally or in the parliament, remained overwhelmingly grounded in the economy and not in state service.66 Orthodox, Gregorian, and missionary schools remained predominantly outlets for upward mobility. Still, there appear to have been few signs pointing to a crisis over the horizon. In turning to Albanian and Circassian immigrants on the threshold of the war, we see some similarities. Although the pressures and nuances affecting these Muslim communities differed from those on their Christian counterparts, the Ottoman state faced similar limitations in its effort to integrate and interact with Circassian and Albanian elements in the South Marmara.

THE MOUNTAINEERS: NORTH CAUCASIAN MIGRANTS AND THE OTTOMAN STATE IN THE NINETEENTH CENTURY

Long before they came to reside in the South Marmara by the tens of thousands, men and women from the North Caucasus were critical supporting actors in the making of the modern Middle East. Prized for their beauty, female Circassian slaves were the wives and mothers of the rich and powerful of the Ottoman Empire and its historical antecedents. North Caucasian men, renowned for their military prowess, were mustered into countless armies and served as the loyal lieutenants of monarchs and potentates throughout the eastern Mediterranean.

Yet, until the mid-nineteenth century, the vast majority of peoples residing in the North Caucasus remained detached from the rise and fall of the states and empires of the Middle East. On the imperial peripheries of the Ottoman, Russian, and Persian lands, the peoples of the North Caucasus formed an intricate series of communities and confederations. A plethora of languages and dialects are spoken north of the Caucasus Mountains. Unique clan alliances, social ranks, and patterns of trade abound within the region. Islam, the religion of most North Caucasians migrants to the Ottoman Empire, arrived comparatively late to the region (with many remaining Christian or retaining earlier religious practices). It is still not fully understood how these native cultural traits were translated when the exile communities in the Ottoman Empire were formed after the nineteenth century.

War came to the North Caucasus in the late eighteenth century with the collapse and incorporation of the Crimean Tatar Khanate into the Russian state in 1783. During the first half of the nineteenth century, Chechen and Dagestani communities in the central and eastern mountain regions violently resisted repeated Russian assaults. The surrender of the last and most famous resistance fighter, Sheikh Shamil of Chechnya, marked a dramatic turn in Russian policy towards the peoples of the North Caucasus. When Russian forces subdued the Adige, Ubıh, and Abkhaz lands on the Black Sea coast between 1862 and 1863, hundreds of thousands of indigenous Muslims fled to the Ottoman Empire. The causes for this mass exodus were most probably multiple, including the threat of forced conversion and Russian atrocities, forced dispersal, the organized colonization of the region by Cossack settlers, and the influence of Ottoman propaganda.[67] The flow of refugees out of the North Caucasus reached its height in 1864 with almost the complete depopulation of the northeastern shore of the Black Sea (an act that was repeated further south with the outbreak of the Russo–Ottoman War of 1877–1878). By the early twentieth century, hundreds of thousands of North Caucasians of various ethnic, linguistic, and social backgrounds came to reside in the Ottoman lands. Although the final number is difficult to ascertain, scholars have estimated that as many as 2.5 million North Caucasians entered the Ottoman lands between 1859 and 1914.[68]

Despite the experience of past refugee crises during the eighteenth century, the Ottoman government was still unprepared for the massive numbers of North Caucasians arriving by sea and by land in such a short space of time.[69] The trickle of immigrants from the North Caucasus coming into Istanbul in 1858 and 1859 gave way to a flood of refugees in 1864, overwhelming the ports of Samsun, Trabzon, Istanbul, Varna, Sinop, and Burgas. New arrivals were shepherded into makeshift tent cities, where thousands contracted typhus, smallpox, and cholera.[70] Disease and starvation claimed up to 500,000 lives within these first years as provincial governments struggled to coordinate an effective response to the crisis.[71] Generations later, North Caucasians would continue to remember and rue the incompetence and disorganization of the Ottoman government that resulted in the deaths of hundreds of thousands of their kin.

A discrete, regulated policy of settlement slowly evolved through the successive waves of refugees arriving in the Ottoman lands. While some immigrants were allowed to take up residence around their first ports of entry, immigration officials gradually broke up the refugee camps and scattered the immigrants far and wide. Over the next several decades, Istanbul would instruct local administrators to construct new villages and ready provincial town quarters for the arrival of these largely poor refugees. Nearly every portion of Anatolia was required to house a certain portion of North Caucasians (see Table 1.1). Thousands of families would be settled through the southern Balkans and greater Syria.[72] Despite the immense effort devoted to this imperial project, not all North Caucasians chose or were allowed to stay in their appointed places of settlement. After the Russo–Ottoman War of 1877–8 and the Balkan Wars of 1912–13, tens of thousands of Caucasian and Crimean refugees were displaced again from the

Table 1.1 North Caucasians settling in Anatolia

1857–66		1879	
Name of region	Number of settlers	Name of region	Number of settlers
Kars	5,000	Ankara	60,000
Bitlis	2,500	Konya	12,000
Muş	2,500	Bolu	23,000
Erzurum	3,000	Antakya	1,500
Mardin	1,000	Afyon	5,000
Gümüşhane	1,000	Eskişehir	14,000
Antep	17,000	Sakarya (Adapazarı)	35,000
Sivas	49,000	Kütahya	3,000
Samsun	60,000	Bilecik	1,000
Amasya	6,000	Kocaeli (İzmit)	15,000
Tokat	33,000	Burdur	10,000
Hatay (Antakya)	1,500	Istanbul	1,000,000
Adana	13,000	Denizli	1,500
Kayseri	35,000	Balıkesir	35,000
Sinop	10,000	Manisa	2,000
Çorum	16,000	Aydın	9,000
Yozgat	7,000	Çanakkale	10,000
Mersin	1,000	İzmir	10,000
Kırşehir	2,000	Kastamonu	5,000

Source: Avagyan, *Osmanlı İmparatorluğu ve Kemalist Türkiye 'nin Devlet- İktidar Sisteminde Çerkesler*, 71.

Balkans and portions of eastern Anatolia.[73] An unknown number of refugees returned to the Caucasus on their own initiative.[74] A great many more moved in order to be closer to their extended family, to escape enslavement, or to find a warmer climate or better land.[75]

A specific set of agendas drove the concerted placement of North Caucasian refugees in the Ottoman Empire. The regions that were most densely settled by these immigrants largely constituted areas of high strategic value for the Ottoman state. This included the South Marmara, a basin that enveloped the capital and its lines of communication with the Anatolian interior.[76] Coupled with their services as loyal military auxiliaries, the presence of these Muslim refugees helped to dilute the number of native Christians. The result of this settlement policy was disastrous and bloody. During the Russo–Ottoman War of 1877–8 and the suppression of Ottoman Armenians in the 1890s, native Christians and the Great Powers accused both Crimean Tatars and North Caucasians of being particularly culpable in numerous massacres that had taken place.[77]

The integration of North Caucasians into Ottoman society went beyond these matters of settlement and internal politics. The introduction of hundreds of thousands of new subjects into the empire also compelled the imperial administration and civil society to welcome and accommodate a completely foreign body of men and women organized according to their own system of class, rank, and occupation. The historic ties between the sultan's palace and the North Caucasus helped facilitate the infusion of the new immigrant elite. Unlike menial slavery elsewhere in the Middle East or the Americas, the relationship between royal or elite households and Caucasian slaves was premissed upon loyalty and service to the state, thus becoming a tool for maintaining and perpetuating the integrity of the Ottoman ruling class. With the gradual replacement of slave administrators by professionally trained bureaucrats in the nineteenth century, the descendants of Ottoman-born Caucasian slaves began to establish their own households, in certain cases transforming themselves into interlocutors between Istanbul and newly arriving North Caucasians.[78]

Whether by design or by accident, the institution of slavery in the nineteenth century provided another medium by which the North Caucasian diaspora further integrated itself into Ottoman life. The Ottoman government sought to curry favour with North Caucasian slaves with offers of manumission in exchange for military service. During the reign of Sultan Abdülhamid II, the Ottoman Council of Ministers proposed a plan to draft North Caucasian agricultural slaves into the army with the consent of their masters. If the master accepted the offer, the slave would then be set free while the former owner would be compensated with the slave's previously tendered land.[79] In being drawn into the functioning of the state, North Caucasian officers and men were both made to feel privileged and unique. They were organized into special units of the gendarmerie and army and allowed to wear native dress (most notably the large fur hat, the *kalpak*, and a long overcoat with bandolier). Most importantly, it appears to have been the case that many units comprised members of the same extended family and were placed under the command of a regional or 'tribal' notable. It has traditionally been argued that Sultan Abdülhamid II was a crucial figure in bringing the 'war-like' North Caucasians into the highest ranks of the state. Contemporary observers often noted the number of North Caucasians promoted to the rank of general (*paşa*) and field marshal (*müşir*) and then appointed to sensitive positions within the Ottoman administration.[80]

By the end of the nineteenth century, high-ranking North Caucasian officers and bureaucrats began to band together independently to advocate policy towards the Caucasus and its refugee population in the Ottoman Empire. At the centre of this elite group of North Caucasians was Field Marshal *Deli* Fuad (Fuad the Mad), the son of an Ubıh family from Egypt.[81] Abdülhamid's best attempts to stem the influence of Fuad and other powerful Caucasians in the administration (which included Fuad's arrest and expulsion to Syria in 1902) ultimately did not silence this emerging elite of North Caucasian cadres. In 1908, just after the Young Turk Revolution, the Society for Circassian Unity and Mutual Aid (*Çerkes İttihat ve Teavün Cemiyeti*) was formed in Istanbul. Officially speaking, Deli Fuat and other founders of the organization limited their activism to advancing the political and cultural concerns of North Caucasians in the Ottoman lands. Along with subsequent groups based in Istanbul, such as the North Caucasian Political Committee (*Şimali Kafkas Cemiyet-i Siyasiyesi*) and the Circassian Womens' Mutual Aid Committee (*Çerkes Kadınları Teavün Cemiyeti*), the men and women who gathered around *Deli* Fuat campaigned to open Adige language schools (for men as well as women), published newspapers in both Turkish and Adige, and called for the creation of an independent North Caucasian state.[82] In practice, however, these organizations served as the political nexus for the most powerful North Caucasians, particularly Adige, in the empire. The Society for Circassian Unity and Mutual Aid and other such North Caucasian immigrant groups formed an exclusive network of officers, bureaucrats, and intellectuals, each sharing a general set of political and cultural agendas and values. As bodies gathering together the most elite strata of Ottoman North Caucasian society, these organizations became closely tied to the state's administrative apparatus, and in certain respects became quasi-arms of the state itself.

The semi-official nature of these elite North Caucasian organizations, like other organizations comprising migrant Albanian, Kurd, Laz, or Azeri intellectuals or officials, was complicated by the relationship some still held with their former homeland. Immediately following the First World War, the British High Commission in Istanbul reported on recent contacts it had with *Deli* Fuat regarding British assistance for a mass return of North Caucasians to Russia.[83] Although the British rejected Fuat's overtures, this brief exchange shows a continued willingness of at least a portion of the Istanbul Circassian elite to abandon the Ottoman lands and return to the Caucasus. Yet, by the outbreak of the First World War in 1914, some fifty years after the peak of the Circassian exodus, the Ottoman Empire was the only home that most young North Caucasians, regardless of their background, would have known.

The emergence of this elite Circassian element within the Ottoman state and society constituted only a fraction of the North Caucasian immigrant experience in Anatolia. Most refugees lived in a dire state of poverty and dislocation decades after arriving in the Ottoman Empire. While the state gave them land and tried to assist them in starting a new life (mostly by providing agricultural tools and supplies), the transition to a life in exile was difficult and often violent.[84] The arrival of Circassian immigrants was a disruptive force in a many different localities. State and economic resources (particularly foodstuffs) usually designated for native consumption were often diverted to recently established refugee communities. The redistribution of land was an especially sensitive matter, since borders and rights came into dispute. Above all, Circassian settlers gradually became synonymous with banditry, theft, and violence. Reports from local Ottoman officials consistently mention the prevalence of paramilitary activity among rural Circassians. Whole villages would be implicated in the creation, support, and recruitment of gangs that would rob wealthy merchants on the main roads, steal land, or carry out murder for hire.

The Circassian diaspora of the South Marmara was associated with each of the phenomena listed above. It is difficult to say how large the North Caucasian community in the region was by 1914. One survey made under the Greek occupation in 1922 estimated that a total of 108,000 North Caucasians lived in the *sancak* of Hüdavendigar alone.[85] Even if this estimate is inflated, it is still possible that the number of North Caucasians in the four provinces of İzmit, Hüdavendigar, Karesi, and Kale-i Sultaniye could have numbered in the tens of thousands. Villages outside the towns of Bursa, Bandırma, Gönen, İzmit, Balıkesir, Manyas, Karacabey, Kirmasti, Biga, and Susurluk were settled with Adige and Ubih refugees.[86] Large numbers of Abkhazians, Laz, Dagestanis, and Muslim Georgians came to reside in the counties of Adapazarı, Sabanca, Yalova, İzmit, and Bilecik.[87] Documents cited by Nedim İpek suggest that North Caucasians often had a violent impact upon the regions they settled. After a new wave of refugees arrived at the conclusion of the Russo–Ottoman War of 1877–8, cases of mass land and property theft were reported in Karacabey, Kirmasti, Manyas, İzmit, and Biga.[88] One British officer estimated in 1878 that 40,000 Circassians and Abhkazians in Adapazarı had created a general state of disorder in the county.[89]

The violence and social dislocation that followed the establishment of the largely poor North Caucasians communities did not subside with the turn of the twentieth century. Tensions between the native population and immigrant Circassians continued well into the war period and defined the local politics of such counties as Biga, İzmit, Gönen/Manyas, Karacabey, and Kirmasti. While many refugees continued to live on the economic and social margins of the region, the North Caucasian diaspora did integrate itself into the administrative and economic life of the South Marmara at various levels. Certain notable families grew to prominence in their adopted districts (such as the Maan, Koç, and Bağ families from Abkhazia in İzmit/Adapazarı) and were appointed to positions in the local administration. A select number of this local elite even obtained a higher status in the Istanbul, often through relatives living and working in the capital. Many more North Caucasians contributed to essential sectors in the local economy, particularly in raising and selling horses. Many of the figures discussed in later chapters found work as foot soldiers in the private armies of wealthy notables or as independent bandits. As we will see later, paramilitary life not only served as a means of survival but also offered an alternative path to state service.

Despite the internal divisions that distinguish the numerous groups that were exiled from the North Caucasus, there were two forces that had a homogenizing effect upon refugees in the South Marmara and elsewhere. Regardless of socioeconomic class (be it indigenous to North Caucasian culture or due to place in Ottoman society), the common experience of displacement, exodus, and resettlement was integral to the North Caucasian identity in the Ottoman Empire. The collective memory of *sürgün* (exile or deportation in Turkish) united the diaspora and was often used as the rallying cry for campaigns led by the Circassian political elite. Equally homogenizing was the collective designation of the term Circassian (*Çerkes*) for all refugees from the North Caucasus. Although usage of the term *Çerkes* (or the plural *Çerakise* in Ottoman, *Çerkesler* in modern Turkish) had a long history within the Ottoman lands, the diversity among North Caucasian refugees did little to break down this collective label. On the contrary, groups such as the Circassian Unity and Mutual Aid Society and North Caucasus Committee perpetuated its usage. Although it is not entirely clear whether this was because of the overwhelming Circassian (i.e., Adige and Ubıh) membership of such organizations, it is clear that other manifestations of North Caucasian identity (such as Chechen, Dagestani, or even Abkhazian) were marginalized in terms of self-representation.

The North Caucasian diaspora of Anatolia (including the communities of the South Marmara) was naturally no monolithic group. More than issues related to language or ethnic designation, class was the primary fault line that divided Ottoman Circassians. The North Caucasian urban elite were counted first among equals in the capital and other towns in the Ottoman Empire. They attended school alongside non-Circassians (not simply native Turkish-speakers) and shared the same feelings of loyalty (or disloyalty) to the Ottoman state as other members of the elite. At the opposite end of the spectrum were low-class North Caucasians. Whether they lived in town or in the countryside, the 'less reputable' Circassians constituted a well of recruitment for gangs, the military, or gendarmerie (and later on, the Ottoman clandestine service). It is this segment of the socio-economic spectrum that supplied the most negative popular perceptions associated with the North Caucasian diaspora.[90]

The class divide among Circassians also included an important nuance. More than the amount of money made or the occupation held, education was a central element in the class divide in Ottoman society. Education created the social networks that helped advance an individual's professional prospects and gave access to influential circles of power in both the capital and the provinces. It also elicited and changed one's cultural tastes, be it in terms of dress, behaviour, or system of beliefs. The constraints or advantages of class confronted not only North Caucasians, but all segments of Ottoman society. In Albanians we see similar internal social divisions. However, the experience of diaspora in the Ottoman Empire would have a radically different effect upon many of those who came from the Albanian lands.

BANDITS OR BUREAUCRATS: ALBANIAN MIGRANTS AND THE OTTOMAN STATE IN THE NINETEENTH CENTURY

The modern history of the Albanian people is intimately tied to the Ottoman Empire and its legacies. Although the roots of the Albanian language and culture pre-date the Ottoman invasion of the southern Balkans (arguably going back to the Illyrians in the classical period), the Ottoman conquest of the southern Balkans fundamentally shaped the evolution of the Albanian lands. Through the following centuries, a majority of Albanian-speakers came to accept Islam.[91] In turn, Albanians came to populate the ranks of the imperial administration in great numbers and at various levels of power.[92]

Like the North Caucasians, Albanians are defined by numerous internal differences. The Albanian language itself is composed of two main regional dialects, Gheg and Tosk. Although Islam historically is the dominant religion among Albanians, sizeable Catholic and Orthodox communities exist in northern and southern Albania respectively.[93] No singular social structure dominates Albanian life. In addition to the rural/urban divide (a topic to be discussed in greater detail shortly), many families in northern Albania and Kosova organized themselves into clan-like confederations (*fis*).[94]

These internal differences found among Albanians have traditionally been sidelined with the crafting of a 'national' Albanian history. The Albanian 'national movement' (*Rilindje Kombetarë*) officially began with the gathering of 300 Albanians in Prizren in 1878, who collectively declared their desire to create an autonomous Albanian state.[95] At the turn of the twentieth century, the cause of Albanian nationalism was further advanced by a broad alliance of Albanian politicians, intellectuals, and exiles. Many nationalist scholars point to the declaration of the Republic of Albania in 1912 as only a partial victory for the Albanian nationalist cause, citing the fact that most Albanians were placed under the Serb or Greek governments.[96] Scholars have only recently begun to question the crafting (and implications) of this national thesis.[97]

In principle, the nationalist narrative of Albanian history deliberately avoids an important subset of the population: those who simply opted out of Albanian nationalism altogether. This segment of the 'imaginary' Albanian nation was particularly represented by the large numbers of individuals who migrated outside the Albanian-speaking regions of the southern Balkans and settled elsewhere. It must be said that a select number of Albanians living in Anatolia and outside the Ottoman Empire were counted among the leading figures in the development of Albanian nationalism.[98] Yet both before and after the nineteenth century, a great many more Albanian-speakers would abandon the Balkans and create new, more detached identities in the diaspora. For many migrants living in the South Marmara and elsewhere in Anatolia, 'Albanianness' was a social designation, meaning that one still had not abandoned one's Balkan roots. Other individuals who were raised in the Albanian lands and then later settled in Anatolia would accept elite Ottoman norms. This latter group of migrants, mostly found among the urban, Albanian-speaking elite, would shed any identification with 'Albanianness' and come to call themselves 'Turks', that is, Turkish-speaking Ottoman citizens. To understand the origins of this variation in identity found among Muslim Albanian migrants, one must look more closely at the meaning of 'Albanianness' within the socio-economic structure of Ottoman life in the south Balkans.

The southern Balkans was historically one of the most densely populated regions of the Ottoman Empire, and became one of the most urbanized and politically integrated portions of the state during the nineteenth century.[99] In the heart of this region were the three *vilayet*s constituting Ottoman Macedonia, Kosova/Üsküp, Manastir, and Selanik. By 1900, the linguistically diverse provinces of Macedonia contained several prosperous cities and towns located within a short distance of the imperial capital of Istanbul, including Salonika, Üsküp (Skopje), Manastır, Priziren, Drama, Siroz (Serres), and Ohri (Ohrid).[100] As the Ottoman state became increasingly centralized at the turn of the century, towns and cities such as these became the harbingers of Ottoman modernity. The Muslim elites of these towns were by and large educated in schools established by the state or by foreign agencies and adapted themselves to the tastes and manners of the capital. Although the political allegiance of these Muslim urban dwellers (*şehirli*) to the Ottoman state may have diverged, Burcu Akan Ellis asserts that Ottoman Turkish remained their *lingua franca*.[101] In looking at the history of urban Muslim emigration from Macedonia in the twentieth century, she asserts that *şehirli* identity was an amalgamation of shared linguistic (Turkish) and socio-economic (elite, i.e., merchant, administrator, professional) traits. To be *şehirli* did not necessarily mean to be 'Turkish' in an ethno-linguistic sense, despite the fact that non-Muslims and villagers often referred to such people as 'Turks'.[102] The elite notion of being an urban dweller only sublimated one's relationship to Albanian-, Macedonian-, Bulgarian-, or even Romani-speakers. The allure of living in town required one to integrate and adopt Turkish as one's language of day-to-day expression and assume the dress and demeanour of the imperial upwardly mobile.[103]

Life beyond the city limits of these urban Ottoman centres differed dramatically. If to live in a city carried with it the cachet of being educated and affluent, the characteristics of a villager (*köylü*) were ignorance, coarseness, and provincialism. In this environment where state education and influence were less present, local languages, as opposed to the state language, Turkish, were more dominant. In the case of Kosova and to a large degree Macedonia, the dominant language among rural Muslim communities was Albanian. This did not mean, as in the case of urban Muslim society, that all Muslims living in the countryside were of some pure Albanian stock. Rather, in this multilingual environment, Albanian served as a *lingua franca* for Muslims who may have also spoken Turkish, Romani, Greek, or a Slavic language. Dress, customs, and other day-to-day social practices were also affected by the pervasiveness of Albanian-speakers.[104] Yet it is possible that both urban and rural families may have even been divided as to what language or customs predominated within the household.[105] In this sort of environment, be it in the town or in the village, there is no definite set of criteria to judge if an individual or family can be counted as Albanian or not. Situations such as these dilute the notion that there is a pure Albanian (or, for that matter, an individual of pure Anatolian Turkish descent). By adopting the language, dress, and norms of the local surroundings, one could 'become' an Albanian or an 'Ottoman Turk'. These ill-defined and permeable borders of Muslim identity in Macedonia and Kosova (and arguably in other parts of the Ottoman Empire) made the process of labelling, cataloguing, and even locating Albanians as an ethno-linguistic group difficult for the Ottoman state and other outside observers.[106]

The history of migration among Albanians is a long, storied one. Suraiya Faroqhi documents waves of Albanians coming from the Balkans to northwestern Anatolia, beginning in the sixteenth century. Many of these individuals found work in Anatolia as field labourers and watchmen for local landowners.[107] Evliya Çelebi speaks specifically of an Albanian presence in the South Marmara in the seventeenth century, citing the stationing of Albanian irregulars (*sekban*) in Bursa and the existence of a village named Arnavudköy (Albanian village) in the province of Mihaliç (Karacabey).[108] In the nineteenth century, labour migration greatly intensified, with many Albanians, as well as other inhabitants of the

Balkans, settling (either seasonally or permanently) in Anatolia, Romania, Egypt, Greece, Western Europe, and the United States.

As largely poor, unskilled, and transient labourers, Albanians in the diaspora were not taken to kindly. Eyal Ginio, in his study of Salonika during the eighteenth century, demonstrates that Muslim Albanian migrants were a source of great social tension and political concern. Most of the young Albanian men who came to the port found work as shepherds, craftsmen, dockworkers, or porters.[109] Many also supported themselves as criminals and bandits (some Albanian gangs had even taken over the mountain passes outside Salonika and demanded payment from passing travellers).[110] Still other Albanians arriving in the city were unable to find any work at all and congregated together in the city. Local authorities, as well as the central government in Istanbul, were suspicious of such a mass of unemployed Albanians, and feared the potential of social upheaval should these derelict men become restless. For this reason several sultans issued decrees forbidding Albanians to migrate and work in the capital.[111] In certain cases, these congregations of Albanians were forcibly broken up and deported back to their place of origin.[112] Centuries later, Ottoman officials in the South Marmara would also not shy away from using the threat of deportation in order to break up threatening groups of Albanian migrants.

Ottoman and foreign observers would associate low-class Albanians with crime and banditry above all other vices and ills. Fredrick Anscombe locates this association between Albanians and banditry in the crises of the eighteenth century, when the Ottoman Empire was locked in a desperate struggle with Russia and the Habsburgs. According to Anscombe, political and economic instability during this period of war and internal conflict in the Albanian lands induced thousands of Albanians to sack towns, farms, and government offices through the region in order to supplement their already meagre standard of living.[113] Certainly by the late nineteenth century, the Albanians became synonymous with violence, criminality, and wild behaviour. In the Western press, the Ottoman use of Albanian irregular militias (*başibozuk*s) to suppress revolts in the Balkans was understood as a lethal ingredient leading to massacres and indiscriminate destruction.[114] Ottoman writers were no less cynical and disparaging towards Albanians, even in the diaspora. In the traditional *Karagöz* shadow plays, the main characters, Karagöz and Hacivat, encounter 'the Albanian (*Arnavud*)' as a stock character on several adventures in Anatolia (including in Bursa and Yalova). 'The Albanian' speaks Turkish with a noted accent and is always dressed in his native costume.[115] He is quick to anger, always armed, and casually mentions murder without hesitation.[116]

To be considered Albanian (*Arnavud*) in the diaspora had inescapable classist overtones. It meant at the very least that one was not educated and not socialized into the norms of high Ottoman society. In its most extreme form, being Albanian meant being innately inclined towards crime and violence. In the absence of surnames, bandits and other lowly Albanian figures often carried the epithet *Arnavud* as a personal moniker (e.g., *Arnavud* Kazım, *Arnavud* Rahman). This is in contrast to the use of one's birthplace or point of origin to describe or introduce oneself, such as Mustafa from Salonika (*Selanikli* Mustafa) or İbrahim from Gostivar (*Gostivarlı* İbrahim), which tended to be used more by members of the elite.[117] The notion of Albanians as almost a criminal class in Ottoman society was not unique to them. Indeed, Ottoman and Western observers often viewed low-class Circassians, as well as Laz, Kurds, and Bosnians, as inherently inclined to congregate, steal, kill, and create havoc.[118]

Members of the Albanian elite living in the diaspora largely escaped this sort of association. Proponents of Albanian nationalism in the nineteenth and twentieth centuries tended to fear and degrade low-class Albanians who left their ancestral lands. For this segment of the intellectual, bureaucratic, and military elite who endeavoured to create and promote an autonomous Albanian identity and polity, the idea of permanently migrating to Anatolia carried with it dangerous consequences for the future of the Albanian lands. As one nationalist writer eloquently stated:

When Miss Turkey is driven out and expelled from these countries [the Balkans], as she has been driven out of other areas too, then the Albanians will also be dragged towards Anatolia by a chain which has taken the name of Islam with being afraid of God and without shame before the Prophet Peygamber [Mohammed], and they will change the name 'Albanian' into 'Muhacir' [immigrant]!ized[119]

In another article submitted sometime later, the same intellectual argued: 'For those who don't want to read and write Albanian and who like the language of the *halldup* [negative epithet for the Turks], they had better go quickly to Sivas and Ankara in order to buy land, because later on it will be more expensive.'[120] Despite having studied and lived in Istanbul or in other portions of Anatolia, most of those Albanians who devoted themselves to the budding Albanian nationalist cause during the late nineteenth and early twentieth centuries would ultimately abandon the Ottoman lands for good and throw in their lot with the newly founded state of Albania in 1912.

Another portion of the Albanian-speaking elite living abroad would come to think of itself in yet another way. This group appeared to be generally *şehirli* in origin and born in Macedonia or Kosova (or in certain cases in Anatolia). This group, often like Albanian nationalists, were educated in the empire's finest schools, landed well-paying, respectable jobs, or served within the middle and upper ranks of the bureaucracy and military. But unlike the Albanian nationalists, this segment of the diaspora freely and readily integrated itself into Turkish-speaking Ottoman culture and society. A certain number even participated in the growing Ottomanist and Young Turk movements of the late nineteenth and early twentieth century. Judging by the memoirs they left behind, this group of individuals was largely silent or demure in speaking about their Albanian backgrounds. With hindsight, they were simply Ottomans or Turks.

As well as in the recollections of Selahettin Bey, one sees this phenomenon in the recollections of Tahsin (Uzer), who served as governor of numerous provinces in Anatolia and was among the founding members of Mustafa Kemal's National Movement. He tells us that he was born in a village outside the town of Prizren in Kosova. Although his mother was born into a military family in Salonika, Tahsin was a descendant of a long line of village notables (*eşraf*) native to the Prizren region. During his childhood his father engaged in trade throughout the South Marmara and lived for a time in Karacabey, Bandırma, and Kirmasti.[121] After his father's death, Tahsin moved several times and attended military school in Manastır and Istanbul. Beyond these recollections of his family and his childhood, he makes no mention of his ethnic background. Yet, considering his deep roots in Kosova, it is reasonable to believe that he was at least partly grounded in Albanian culture and society.

The trend similar to that in the Selahettin memoir echoes larger questions about the meaning of being Albanian in the diaspora at the turn of the century. The notion of identifying oneself as Albanian transcended the fact that one spoke Albanian, had Albanian parents, or was raised among Albanians. To be Albanian meant that you were not satisfied with identifying yourself strictly with the Ottoman Empire, an association that had separatist connotations. For the elite, it meant rejecting a state education that taught unity among Muslims and among Ottoman citizens as a whole. For individuals such as Tahsin (Uzer) and Selahettin, two ambitious men rising through the ranks of the Ottoman state, these political and social realities left little room for more than one allegiance.

The outbreak of the Balkan Wars in 1912 changed the parameters of the Albanian diaspora in Anatolia profoundly. The war was brief but vicious. International observers implicated the armies of Serbia, Bulgaria, Greece, and Montenegro in scores of atrocities on innocent Muslim civilians.[122] Hundreds of thousands of Muslims fled their homes and sought all means of transportation available to ferry them to safety in Anatolia. The sheer size and speed with which these refugees poured into Istanbul and into ports throughout Anatolia overwhelmed local authorities charged with registering and comforting the victims. Many entered the remaining portions of the Ottoman Empire without being documented by immigration officials or the police. An official estimate of the number of refugees from the Balkans entering the Ottoman lands was finally formulated eight years after the end of hostilities. The estimate put the total number of refugees at 509,922 individuals, a number that included former citizens not only from the Balkans but also from Crete, Cyprus, and other islands.[123]

The refugee crisis sparked by the Balkan Wars heightened government sensitivity to the issue of Albanian migration. Considering the demographics of Kosova and Macedonia, it is clear that officials in Istanbul had little doubt that Albanians comprised a large portion of the unregistered immigrants now in Anatolia. Over the next decade, officials responsible for locating and settling

Balkan migrants paid special attention to Albanians, whose long history of creating havoc, particularly in the form of banditry, made them a suspect group, particularly in the South Marmara. By 1914, officials repeatedly expressed concern about large concentrations of Albanian refugees in areas such as Karacabey, Kirmasti, Edremit, Karamürsel, Değirmendere, and Bursa. As we will see, the outbreak of the First World War presented an opportunity for the Young Turk government to address these concerns.

2

The Politics of the Condemned: The South Marmara during the First World War

Arshag Dikranian could recall only a few political events before 1915. He was only ten years old at the time, an Armenian boy living in the Greek quarter of Adapazarı. During an interview conducted in the winter of 1986, Arshag, then living in Los Angeles, could still recount in great detail other memories from his childhood. He remembered his house fully, down to the floor plan. His father was a leading merchant of silk and dry goods in town. He went to an Armenian school and learned to read and write in Armenian from a teacher trained in Europe. His father hoped that Arshag would eventually become a farmer, and even laid plans to send him to America for his education.[1]

His earliest memories of his Turkish neighbours were for the most part warm. He learned Turkish in the street while playing marbles, hopscotch, and football with other children. He did not remember the presence of Armenian *fedayee* (or militias) as a boy and only as an adult found out that his father had been a member of the Hnchaktsutiun, one of the largest Armenian nationalist parties in the Ottoman Empire. His only sour memory related to the summer of 1910. At the age of 5 he recalled the passing of a parade marking the fifteen hundredth anniversary of the first translation of the Bible into Armenian.[2] Hundreds of people attended. Although approved by Istanbul, local police attempted to halt the parade and threatened to fire on the crowd. A fight broke out, and in the ensuing scuffle he remembered one policeman was killed. Other than that, Arshag claimed, life in his hometown progressed without incident until things seemed to change overnight.[3]

We now know that things did not change overnight. Arshag's exile from Adapazarı in the summer of 1915 was an act that the state had contemplated months, perhaps years, in advance. Within the space of three years, three pivotal events would dramatically change the lives of Arshag and others in the South Marmara. The first occurred in October 1912 when armies from Montenegro, Serbia, Bulgaria, and Greece swept across the Ottoman Macedonian borders. In the midst of the humanitarian disaster brought on by the First Balkan War, a second dramatic turn took place when officers loyal to the Committee of Union and Progress launched a coup against the sitting Ottoman cabinet and seized power for themselves. After the Bab-ı Ali coup of January 1913, the Young

Turks ruled virtually by decree, and became even less restrained in pursuing their policies of centralization. Istanbul's entry into the First World War upon the side of the Central Powers in October 1914 stands as the final turning point that would lead to disaster for many individuals like Arshag.

This chapter presents an intimate perspective on the origins and aftermath of Ottoman policies during the Great War in the South Marmara. Traditionally the debates over why and how the Young Turk government came to deport or murder its own citizens during the First World War have been confined to the actions and opinions of those in the capital. Through the prism of the South Marmara, our understanding of the role of the Ottoman state in prosecuting its wartime policies shifts dramatically. Native Armenians like Arshag Dikranian comprised only a portion of the victims of this period. Official documents and personal accounts cast a much broader light upon a multiplicity of both non-Muslim and Muslim communities that were subject to relocation, dispossession, and death. Although the seeds of this agenda were first sown in the imperial capital, the course and implementation of the CUP's harshest domestic policies matured and expanded in reaction to the provincial socio-economic conditions of regions like the South Marmara. Furthermore, what happened in the South Marmara demonstrates the limited results achieved by the deportations. A look through this more provincial lens emphasizes the agency of the local population in resisting this violent intervention of the state and adds greater clarity to the faulty mechanisms that the Ottoman government relied upon to enact its plans.

BOYCOTTS AND REFUGEES: THE CUP'S FIRST STEPS

For the Committee of Union and Progress, the Balkan Wars were a painful tutorial in the dangers facing the nation. Within a few short weeks, the armies of the Balkan states succeeded in completing the work that domestic insurgents had started two decades earlier: the complete partition of Ottoman Macedonia. For a time even the security of Istanbul seemed unsure as the Bulgarian army advanced east across the Thracian plain. Although the towns and villages of the South Marmara were left unscathed by the fighting, the battle lines rested only a few kilometers across the sea.[4]

Security and stability in northwestern Anatolia weighed heavily on the minds of the Young Turks immediately after the fighting ended. The sheer size and speed with which refugees began to arrive in Bursa, Çanakkale, and elsewhere overwhelmed the ability of imperial and local authorities to address the consequences of the crisis. As facilities established by the Ottoman government and the Red Crescent Society grew to capacity, American missionaries also joined the effort to care for refugees and suffering natives alike. Jeanie Jillson, a missionary reporting from Bursa, reported that her group had distributed food to 10,672 people in the Bursa region during the spring of 1913 (with the numbers of refugees still growing by twenty to twenty-five individuals a day).[5] Meanwhile, letters and messengers from villages like Yenice outside town arrived with frantic requests for food.[6]

In certain places the arrival of Muslim refugees led to violence. Several official and printed stories from Çanakkale and Gelibolu tell of hundreds of displaced Albanians evicting local Greeks from their villages and stealing at will.[7] A final resolution to this first refugee crisis remained elusive two years after the close of the Balkan Wars. The crisis would prove to get far worse once war again was declared in 1914.

The CUP drew still deeper lessons from the Balkan Wars. More than the failure of the Ottoman army to mobilize and defend the empire, many observers saw treason at the heart of this tragic defeat. Local Christian civilians and armed bands in Macedonia had aided the onslaught of the Balkan States. The eviction of hundreds of thousands of Ottoman Muslims from Macedonia and Kosova entailed the forfeiture of countless homes and hectares of land to the Christian victors. Ottoman Christian subjects still under Istanbul's rule were not immune to blame. Through their stranglehold on the Ottoman economy, Anatolian Greeks were accused of financing the construction of the Greek warship responsible for blockading the reinforcements vital to Macedonia's defences.[8] Albania's secession from the empire added further to the sting of defeat. The complicity of both Christian and Muslim Albanians in establishing an independent Albanian state in November 1912 confirmed to many in the government the duplicity and seditiousness of their former countrymen. As CUP rule took hold after the winter of 1913, the perceived implications of these lessons learned were soon translated into new state policies in the South Marmara.

From the collection of imperial directives, anecdotes, and studies available to us, we can infer a general line of reasoning encased within the CUP's approach to the South Marmara after 1913. The same lethal admixture that had contributed to the fall of the Ottoman Balkans could be found in this region so dreadfully close to the capital. Rum and Armenian communities riddled the South Marmara's landscape. Their economic primacy, backed by the West, mirrored that of Christians in pre-war Macedonia. Added to the dormant threat of Christian sedition was the influx of tens of thousands of Albanians into the towns and villages of the region. Although the vast majority of these newcomers were undoubtedly Muslims (and therefore potentially dependable citizens), the state could not readily count upon their loyalty and their domestic tranquillity. If the integrity of Istanbul's control over the South Marmara was to be maintained, a new, quite radical approach towards these three polities had to be engendered. By 1914, the CUP implemented a two-track solution to deal with the dangers posed by the presence of such large numbers of Armenians, Greeks, and Albanians: economic prohibition and forced relocation.

Through the summer of 1914, an informal boycott of Greek and Armenian businesses and goods began to gather momentum in the South Marmara.

Championed by newspapers both in the capital and in the provinces, the boycott represented one measure in a series of new economic priorities established by the CUP state. In the wake of the Balkan Wars, proponents of state reform heralded the construction of a new 'national economy' based upon Muslim investment, ownership, and production. In bypassing the services and goods offered by non-Muslims, a mobilized Muslim public would help ensure the economic solvency and political security of the empire in the years to come.[9]

In urban neighbourhoods and rural locales throughout the South Marmara, the boycott assumed violent dimensions. Economic conditions in 1914 were already showing signs of strain from the fallout of the Balkan Wars, as silk factories closed and commerce across the sea slowed to a crawl.[10] With a public boycott now in effect, British and American observers declared that Christian peasants, particularly Rum, were physically prevented from harvesting cocoons or bringing vegetables to market.[11] Police officers in Bursa interdicted Muslim and Christian patrons frequenting Greek stores. Armed gangs in the city, reportedly comprising mostly Circassians, torched shops and beat customers and merchants alike when found in violation of the embargo.[12] Although it was not an official policy of the imperial government, British consular officials identified local offices of the CUP as the primary centres orchestrating the campaign.

The beatings and burnings that accompanied the boycott of 1914 appear to be signs of still broader goals favoured by Istanbul. Through the summer of 1914, hundreds of Orthodox Christians from villages in the immediate interior poured into the coastal towns of Mudanya, Bandırma, and Çanakkale.[13] Refugees and inhabitants from a series of villages around Bursa told one British officer touring the region of an ongoing pattern of attacks that summer. Bands of Muslims, some of them residents of neighbouring villages, menaced and robbed their settlements, in some instances murdering and raping innocent civilians.[14] In the aftermath of this violent summer, many Greeks chose to leave their homes for good. American missionaries in the field related several anecdotes to their superiors regarding the 'removal' or migration of Greek and Armenian families to Istanbul and America.[15] In turn, the threat of injury and failing businesses led to the utter collapse of Protestant church communities in Karacabey and Bandırma.[16] Greece was the preferred choice of many Rum vacating their homes. Although Athens may have had a hand in compelling emigrants to seek better fortunes in Greece, the CUP, as one British observer put it, appeared intent upon 'driving the Greeks' out of the region.[17]

Ottoman government sources later claimed that 163,975 Greeks migrated to Greece from northwestern Anatolia during the years immediately preceding the First World War. Yet, according to state officials, those who left did so of their own volition (either to join the Greek army or to resettle on the Greek mainland).[18] A more recent study suggests that the forced migration of Rum from the South Marmara was related to a more general Ottoman attempt at an 'exchange of population' with Greece. Talks between Istanbul and Athens over the issue carried on through the first half of 1914. An agreement appeared to have been imminent until the outbreak of world war.[19]

As the embargo and relocation of non-Muslim progressed through the summer of 1914, Istanbul initiated a string of new policies towards Albanians living in western Anatolia. According to British consular reports in Edirne, recent Albanian refugees from the Balkan Wars were expelled to eastern Anatolia after a rash of petty thefts and acts of brigandage were attributed to Albanians in Vize.[20] In Izmir, Albanians who did not possess Ottoman citizenship were ordered to leave or apply for citizenship.[21] Even Albanians employed by the Ottoman government or who had long resided in Izmir and Edirne were singled out for relocation. In Edirne watchmen and shepherds were offered land for cultivation in Aleppo or 'given the option' of returning to their point of origin.[22] Similarly, the British consul of Izmir reported that several Albanians working in the civil courts, the post office, the customs house, and other civil servants were transferred, released, or arrested for anti-CUP activities.[23] Through the intervention of prominent Albanian delegates, Britain, Russia, and France agreed to extend temporarily some degree of protection to Albanians residing in Ottoman territory.[24] Archduke Ferdinand's death and world war effectively made Western involvement in the affairs of Albanian immigrants a moot point. A much broader policy of displacement for Albanians and many others in the South Marmara would soon follow.

'TEHCIR' FOR ALL: REASSESSING THE WARTIME DEPORTATIONS

For the inhabitants of the South Marmara, the Great War came calling in February 1915 with the Royal Navy's first attack upon the Dardanelles.[25] In light of the shock of the Allied bombardment and the ensuing landing on the beaches north of Çanakkale, residents close to the straits had prepared for the worst.[26] In Istanbul, the news added still more weight to what appeared to be a mortal crisis facing the Ottoman state. After the disastrous battle of Sarıkamış months before, Russian forces rapidly gained ground in the east. In early February, Ottoman forces were beaten back from the Suez Canal. Meanwhile the British Indian Army pushed north through central Iraq, easily occupying Basra in November. The inherent weaknesses and underdevelopment within the Ottoman economy and transport infrastructure only aggravated the situation, as the quantity and flow of provisions from Istanbul and its environs to the men at the front slowed to a trickle.[27] As a region encompassing multiple sea and rail hubs connecting the capital to the Anatolian interior, and now becoming a new front in the war against the Allies, the South Marmara assumed even greater strategic importance to the survival of the Ottoman Empire.

The inner circle of the Committee of Union and Progress had debated the repercussions of a grand war long before Istanbul had entered the conflict on the side of the Central Powers. Among the concerns addressed by leading members of the CUP was the possible Armenian response to an invasion of the east. Despite the initial rapprochement between the CUP and Armenian nationalists during the Revolution of 1908 in the name of 'Brotherhood and Unity', the shocking loss of the European provinces and the displacement of tens of thousands of Muslims from the Balkans heightened suspicions that a mass uprising among Armenians was looming. Growing contact between Russian forces and Armenian dissidents before the outbreak of war appeared to confirm this fear. Rather than see another integral portion of Ottoman territory cleaved from the empire, CUP was determined to pre-empt the worst through the utilization of 'grim measures'.[28] As we will see, these measures not only encompassed the historical Armenian lands of eastern and central Anatolia, but also included the scattered Armenian communities found along the southern Marmara coast.

Several prominent scholars have argued that the deportation of Anatolian Armenians was premissed upon three distinct ends: first, it would eliminate an unruly portion of the Ottoman population that would never reconcile itself to Muslim rule; secondly, the deportation of non-Muslims would create a 'Turkified' space that would allow the Ottoman government to extend its influence to the Turkic east;[29] and thirdly, it would result in an opportunity to assume control over property left behind and would create greater prospects for Muslims within the manufacturing and trading sectors of the Ottoman economy.[30] The thread that ties these three goals together, as Taner Akçam, Vahkahn Dadrian, and others have contended, was a virulent Turkish nationalism. Having infiltrated the ranks of the Young Turk elite soon after taking power, this nationalism could not reconcile itself with the presence of Armenians, or other non-Muslims, within the confines of the Ottoman state.[31] The cancer simply had to be removed.

Little in the way of archival sources exists regarding the internal debate and ultimate intentions regarding the liquidation of the Armenian population.[32] While the transcripts of the Istanbul Military Tribunal of 1919 shed some light on both the execution and the resistance to the deportations of Armenians in Yozgat and Trabzon, little is known about the interaction between the Committee for Union and Progress and the bureaucracy, let alone the manner and degree to which local officials carried out the deportations throughout Anatolia.[33]

From the perspective of the South Marmara, CUP policies towards Armenians were intertwined with aims that were more operational in nature than ideological. The logic encased within state directives from this period emphasizes, above all things, the need for security within this critical region. Fear of a possible Armenian uprising was only one component driving imperial domestic policy in the South Marmara. Sedition among native Greeks, perceived imbalances within the economy, the swarms of impoverished refugees, and the violence wreaked by local gangs (primarily composed of Muslim immigrants) were equally treacherous hazards confronting Istanbul's hold over this vital region. Mass deportation represented a comprehensive solution to the instability inherent in the South Marmara. Blind adherence to an ardent Turkish nationalism cannot fully explain why the Young Turks cast both Muslims (Turkish-speaking or otherwise) and Christians in the same sinister light. More importantly, nationalism cannot substantiate the intrinsic inconsistencies, loopholes, and failures that accompanied the deportations. As we will see, incongruities found in the CUP's approach to the South Marmara were in fact the product of necessary accommodations that resulted from their encounters with the local population.

Armenians were not the first to be ordered out of their homes. Five days before the issuing of the Deportation Laws of 1915 (*Ahar Mahallere Naklolunan Eşhasın Emval Düyun ve Matlubat-ı Metrukesi Hakkında Kanun-ı Muvakkat*) and three months after the Allied landing, interior ministers initiated a large-scale transfer of Çanakkale and Gelibolu Greeks to the environs of Karesi. Orders sent in secret stipulated that any area of Rum resettlement in Karesi had to be further than 'an hour from the coast line'.[34] The transfer of population from the Gelibolu front was soon followed by a more general policy of resettlement, under the direction of local military authorities, encompassing the Rum population from the islands and shores of the South Marmara basin.[35] Greeks from Gemlik, Mudanya, Erdek, Karacabey, Kirmasti, Orhanlı, and numerous other villages and towns were sent to the interior, with some transported as far away as Kayseri and Çorum.[36] The South Marmara also served as a way station for tens of thousands of Rum expelled from the north shore, as well as the Greek border regions in the *vilayet* of Edirne.[37] As with the deportation of Armenians from the region, few official figures exist as to the number of Rum uprooted from the South Marmara.[38] During the entire campaign, it is estimated that at least 100,000 Rum were deported to the interior from northwestern Anatolia alone.[39]

The deportations deepened the wounds brought on by the boycott of 1914. The suddenness of the orders did not allow Rum deportees time to pack even the most essential items for their trip to the interior. Bursa and its surrounding villages were once again transformed into massive centres of refuge and relief. Many Greek families streaming in from the Marmara coast, families that had previously managed to avoid the worst of the embargo, were reduced to poverty. Ottoman officials did place a few lucky families in the homes of deported Armenians.[40] Starvation and disease would kill an unknown number of people without recourse to shelter and aid.[41] Some of the young men among the deportees were drafted into the army.[42] As recruits believed to be too untrustworthy for front-line duty, most Greeks, as well as Armenians, taken into the army were assigned to labour battalions (*amele taburları*). If not worked to death, many soldiers in these units became victims of outright massacre during the course of 1915 and 1916.[43]

Town criers in Adapazarı broke the news of the deportation orders to Armenians in July of 1915.[44] With little time to gather any of their belongings, Armenians living in Adapazarı and İzmit were ushered to the local train station, where they waited for three rainy nights in makeshift tents.⁴⁵ Similar commands were issued a month earlier to the west in the province of Karesi, where the Armenian population of Balıkesir was first ordered to relocate to villages and towns just outside the city limits.⁴⁶ Three weeks before their departure, Armenian inhabitants in the small town of Bahçecik were visited by the organizer of the deportations of the region, İbrahim Bey. With gendarmes at his side, he threatened to flog all those who refused to hand over any weapons and ammunition. After a thorough search of local homes and a church, İbrahim found nothing.⁴⁷

Ottoman authorities repeatedly justified their actions with claims that a rebellion in the İzmit/Adapazarı area was forthcoming. Although hundreds of miles from the Russian front lines, Minister of War Enver Paşa and Minister of Interior Talat Paşa contended that Armenians had planned their rebellion in coordination with an expected Russian landing to the north on the Black Sea. Talat's memoirs, as well as other wartime publications, offered evidence of escalating guerrilla activity on the provincial border between Bursa and İzmit, as well as the discovery of hidden weapons caches throughout the region.⁴⁸ Several secret telegrams do confirm the arrest and deportation of Armenian nationalists in Bursa and İzmit in 1915 and 1916, as well as a few cases of Armenian 'bandit' activity (reports filed *after* the deportations had commenced).⁴⁹ Conversely, seditious activity among the Greeks of the South Marmara at any point during the war went largely unreported.⁵⁰

But Arshag Dikranian, age 10, was no bandit. When the trains arrived in Adapazarı, he remembered them being filthy with manure and without bathrooms. Arshag and thousands of others were then transported along the rails via Eskişehir or on foot to Konya, the primary way station for Armenians deported from western and central Anatolia.⁵¹ Packed among tens of thousands of other Armenians from various points, Armenians from the South Marmara met a variety of fates. Some Armenians, such as Arshag's family, were fortunate enough to remain in Konya or be resettled in villages outside town.⁵² Many more were marched overland further south to camps located near Aleppo or Mosul. Survivors from the environs of Adapazarı tell of horrific experiences similar to Armenians deported from other portions of Anatolia. Rape, execution, loss of family, starvation, and abduction were among the many hardships and calamities that awaited deportees in the camps.⁵³ Aghavni Guleserian, a young girl at the time of deportations, was among those who experienced the very worst of life in exile, yet still lived to return to her native Adapazarı. 'Be happy that we are burying her,' Aghavni's father said to her at the death of her grandmother, 'because we don't know who will bury us.'⁵⁴

The deportation of Armenians from the South Marmara continued well into 1916, with communities in and around Bursa and Çanakkale among the last to be ordered out.⁵⁵ According to missionary accounts, some Armenians refused to submit or leave. When the order was announced in the village of Çengiler, outside Bursa, the population refused. In response, authorities purportedly separated the men from the women and killed most of them.[56] Thousands of other Armenians, rather than openly resist, went into hiding in the mountains. American missionaries estimated that about 5,000 Armenians from Adapazarı, İzmit, and Bahçecik managed to save themselves this way with the help of contacts in town.[57] The American Board of Commissioners for Foreign Missions did their best to protect their converts. Despite official assurances, Protestant Armenians, as well as students, teachers, labourers, and nurses attached to the Americans, were among those exiled to the south and east.[58]

Istanbul attentively followed the progress being made in each of the provinces, repeatedly requesting updates from local officials.[59] Well after the supposed completion of operations, state interior ministries made consistent demands for the identities and numbers of Armenians and Greeks deported, the destination of the deportees, the number of those waiting to be deported, and the number of soldiers available to supervise their transport.[60] Istanbul was vigilant in its oversight of the operation, chiding local authorities when 'treasonous' Armenians were overlooked, when deportees attempted to return, or when the process simply broke down.[61]

Still, it is clear that the deportation of Armenians and Greeks was not a 'final solution', to borrow a mixed metaphor. Special exemptions were made for non-Muslims who were employed by the state or possessed trade or technical skills valuable to the war effort, as well as those who 'posed no threat'. Dispensations were also issued to Armenians who served as members of parliament, military and health officers, and those holding passports issued by the Central Powers or neutral states.[62] Although the exemptions extended to Protestant and Catholic Armenians were often ignored, Armenians who had recently converted to Islam were allowed to remain and were not subject to persecution.[63]

In the removal of Rum from the South Marmara, Ottoman officials appeared deeply concerned not to anger the Greek government in Athens, for fear that it might join the Entente.[64] As a result, Ottoman officials were watchful of complaints from the provinces regarding poverty and acts of violence and vandalism against Rum communities.[65] Istanbul also gave permission to the Rum Patriarchate to distribute aid to impoverished communities and allowed it to conduct independent 'tours' of depressed areas.[66] Most interestingly, specific areas in the South Marmara, such as Biga, appear to have been spared from any sort of deportations.[67] In this case, as well as others, it is not clear by what criteria Greeks and Armenians were allowed to stay.[68] Nevertheless, Ottoman officials made clear that the exemptions listed above could be rescinded if excused Rum and Armenians were found to be 'treasonous'.[69]

On 10 June 1915, the CUP decreed that all property left by deportees was to be registered and protected by the Ottoman government or auctioned off and the profit held in credit. This law was succeeded three months later by a temporary act stipulating the confiscation of all property in order to repay outstanding debts of the deportees.⁷⁰ In a telegram dated 4 July 1915, the Commission for the Settlement of Tribes and Refugees issued two separate sets of regulations (*talimname*) to the *vilayet* of Hüdavendigar regarding the protection of abandoned Rum and Armenian property respectively.⁷¹ In the months that followed, a confusing pattern of compliance and indiscretion emerges from the pages of internal Ottoman correspondence. Authorized by the Commission for the Settlement of Tribes and Refugees, as well as by the military high command, local 'Abandoned Property Commissions' (*Emval-ı Metruke Komisyonu*) and 'Liquidation Commissions' (*Tasfiye Komisyonu*) oversaw the protection and auctioning of vacant or forsaken goods and pieces of land.⁷²

The handling of abandoned property did not arise first during the First World War. The issue appears to have emerged initially during the Balkan Wars, when an estimated 33,317 homes were left abandoned by Rum emigrating to Greece. After the First World War, it was reported that another 90,000 homes were left abandoned by deported Greeks alone.⁷³ Istanbul appears to have kept track of the amount and location of abandoned property, as well as the profit gained from the auctioning of this property.⁷⁴ In several cases though, local officials were accused of abusing this system through such acts as auctioning to lower bidders and illegal trading of property.⁷⁵ Irrespective of the legality of actions taken by local agents, Istanbul clearly indicated that any transfer of property was to favour Muslims. As a result, specific directives emanated from the capital requiring that Muslim refugees be settled on vacated land and be allowed a certain share of abandoned goods.⁷⁶ This policy was also facilitated by the fact that many officials in the Abandoned Property Commissions were also placed in charge of settling refugees.⁷⁷

Istanbul's approach to abandoned property facilitated a collective solution of two problems that had lingered since the Balkan Wars. The acquisition of movable goods on farms and businesses by recently founded Muslim companies helped to complete the process begun during the boycott of 1914 and served further to 'strengthen the culture of trade among Muslims' that was so crucial to building a national economy.⁷⁸ Expropriation of Christian land also held the added bonus of supplying the tens of thousands of refugees who remained without homes or work since 1912. As a result, all property formerly associated with local Rum and Armenians appeared up for grabs. Ottoman officials even made a direct offer to the American Board of Commissioners in order to buy the ransacked remains of Bythinian High School in Bahçecik/Bardezag. The director back in the United States turned down the offer, knowing that a final sale meant condoning the complete eradication of the town's Armenians.⁷⁹

By 1916, the depth of the South Marmara's refugee problem had intensified to a new order of magnitude. The onslaught of Russian forces in the east induced perhaps hundreds of thousands of refugees to relocate to the environs of the capital.⁸⁰ Although the recent availability of appropriated land certainly served to offset this crisis, the Ottoman government was not prepared to give all Muslim refugees *carte blanche* to resettle in the South Marmara. In the midst of the massive outflow and inflow of peoples from the South Mamara, the CUP chose to exploit this chaotic moment of opportunity to restructure the demographic dimensions of the region's Muslim population as well. Among the primary groups to receive the attention of the state in this programme of social re-engineering were Muslim Albanians.

At the start of the First World War, Albanians continuing to cross the frontier were forbidden to settle in several key 'restricted areas' (*menatık-ı memnua*). These restricted districts—namely, Istanbul, Aydın, Edirne, and Hüdavendigar *vilayet*s, as well as the *liva*s (counties) of Çatalca, Kale-i Sultaniye, İzmit, and Gelibolu—were not only viewed as geo-strategically valuable, but were also regions already awash with Albanian immigrants.[81] Instead, newly arriving Albanian refugees were to be transported to Ankara or Konya. From there, officials were instructed to settle Albanians in the environs of these two central Anatolian towns or to dispatch them further on to Sivas, Diyarbekir, Ma'muret-ül-aziz (Elazığ), Kayseri, Adana, and elsewhere.[82] In the last stages of the war, this policy was extended to Albanians previously settled in the South Marmara. In this shift in CUP policy, the Albanians of Kale-i Sultaniye, Karesi, and İzmit, as well as Gelibolu, were particularly targeted.[83] Even local Albanian law enforcement officials in Lapseki appeared to have been swept up in this programme.[84] Yet this order was amended with certain exemptions, such as allowing small numbers of Albanians to settle with family members in İzmit.[85]

In correspondence emanating from Istanbul and the provinces, clear limits were set as to what constituted an undesirable Albanian and what was to be done with those who were to be accepted and resettled. In a general guide (*talimname*) outlined in 1917, the CUP attempted to systematize Albanian entrance and settlement in the Ottoman lands along six guidelines:

1. Albanians who rebelled or caused disorder in hastening the dissolution of the Ottoman government and Sultanate in Rumeli, aided enemy states, known to be hostile to Ottomanism and to Turks, or are seen as political or security threats are not to be accepted into the Ottoman lands.

2. No non-Muslim Albanians are to be accepted in the Ottoman lands.

3. Albanians are forbidden in the *vilayet*s of Istanbul, Aydın, Edirne, and Hüdavendigar, as well as the *liva*s of Çatalca, Kale-i Sultaniye, İzmit and Gelibolu. Both single [Albanians] and Albanians with families are not to be accepted for settlement here. Henceforth, only those who had registered in these regions with the authorities, who have acquired land and property through purchase, those who brought property from outside with them, and who are not dependent upon family [are permitted].

4. Albanians who are to be transported outside of the forbidden areas are to be scattered and to reside and be settled among other different races (*diğer*

ırklarla karışık). Albanians, especially tribal people, being settled as either families or as individuals in both forbidden and acceptable regions are not to be allowed to congregate.
5. Albanians who are given permission to settle in forbidden areas will be settled only after an examination by officials.
6. Albanians accepted in the Ottoman lands are dependent upon administrative inspection and their settlement must be approved by local officials.[86]

In subsequent orders reaffirming state policy in 1918, central authorities added that Albanians 'possessing "foreign personal qualities" regardless of their origin [were] not permitted long term residence' and their registration and settlement were 'not to be deferred'.[87] Upon the 'scattering' (*müteferrikan*) of these immigrants into small communities in central and eastern Anatolia (where the local Albanian population would not exceed 10 per cent), it was implicitly stated that the ultimate goal was to eradicate the Albanian 'national language and their customs'.[88]

Fuat Dündar, in his highly innovative study of the First World War, has convincingly demonstrated that Albanians were among many Muslim groups targeted for resettlement throughout the Ottoman Empire. Under the guise of security and cultural concerns, tens of thousands of settled and unsettled Kurds, Arabs, Roma, Bosnians, Georgians, and Circassians were forcibly scattered in regions outside their traditional milieu.[89] Dündar draws a direct link between this wartime effort and past policies instituted under Sultan Abdülhamid II bent on settling and assimilating so-called 'tribal peoples'.[90] Like other policies intended to increase Istanbul's presence in the provinces, the Young Turks embraced Hamidian social re-engineering efforts, but chose to amplify the scale and breadth of state intervention to include large portions of the empire's Muslim population.

What is striking about Istanbul's approach to Albanian immigrants and settlers is not the policy in and of itself, but rather the way in which the Committee for Union and Progress conceived of Albanians as a segment of Ottoman society. While seemingly not posing a mortal threat to the state's security to the same degree as Greeks and Armenians, the first item of the 1917 *talimname* underscores the general distrust of Albanians after the creation of an independent Albanian state. It is this correlation between Albanianness and the independence movement at the turn of the century that arguably influenced the prohibition of Christian Albanians, who played an influential role in the establishment of the Republic of Albania.[91]

But what about those who spoke Albanian and possessed Albanian 'customs'? These Albanians were seemingly trustworthy enough to enter the state's borders, but menacing enough to place them at a distance from sensitive areas. But what made the 'Albanian' and his 'customs' so dangerous that the government sought to micro-manage their settlement in Anatolia? In several documents prescribing deportation to the interior (including the 1917 *talimname*), Albanian involvement in acts of banditry ('rebelled or caused disorder') and violence ('political or security threats') is asserted as a deciding factor in their removal.[92] By placing them in small groups among the diverse communities of Anatolia, the Albanian 'predilection' to band together and commit acts of violence would seemingly be mitigated. Yet with the prohibition against those 'hostile to Ottomanism and Turks', one can assume that those who were admitted to the Ottoman lands after 1914 were not simply politically 'loyal' Albanians; it suggests that they were at least somewhat conversant in imperial, Turkish-speaking Ottoman culture. In emphasizing the eradication of language and 'custom' as the paramount goal in settling Albanians (a goal also associated with Bosnian and Kurdish immigrants and refugees), the Young Turks reveal their notion of the ideal citizen: Turkish-speaking, Muslim, and loyal to the state. This is in direct, yet implicit, opposition to the recalcitrant 'Albanian': wild, violent, and antithetical to the state and its institutions. As a region already identified as a magnet for Albanian settlement well before the Balkan Wars, the South Marmara proved to be a setting unsuited for moulding loyal Albanians.

The stipulations placed on Albanian immigration and settlement also reveal the limits of the CUP's confrontation with Ottoman society. With regard to preventing the return of Albanian settlers to areas deemed off limits, Ottoman administrators were compelled to either resist or tolerate local inconsistencies. This is particularly apparent in the third, fifth, and sixth items of the *talimname* of 1917, or in the settling of Albanians in İzmit and other forbidden areas. By exempting landowners or individuals who had previously obtained residency permits from local officials, the CUP acknowledged the local influence of certain displaced Albanians in the South Marmara. These caveats also stand in recognition of the verdicts of native administrators who may or may not have knowingly allowed Albanians to settle in the South Marmara regardless of the wishes of the central government.

But who were these 'Albanians' who were allowed to settle or remain in the South Marmara, and who were those banished to the east? The answer to this question may lie in the similarities and differences between the Young Turk elite and the common immigrant in the aftermath of Macedonia's fall. At all levels of the CUP were men from Üsküp, Köprülü, Priziren, Manastır, Ohri, Selanik, Prishtina, and other towns and villages throughout the Albanian-speaking lands of the Ottoman Empire. They were men who spoke Albanian, had Albanian-speaking relatives, or at the very least knew Albanians from the marketplace, from school, or from military service. However, especially after the retreat of the Ottoman Third Army from Rumeli, the men of the CUP became dependents of the capital, leaving their provincial culture behind them. It is here that one sees both the commonalities and the dissonance between these two poles. Both were settlers from the same land, but the Young Turk and the common Albanian were divided by the cultures of the elite and the plebeian. In other words, the Albanians who were allowed to settle in the South Marmara were at the very least not hostile to the culture of the centre. More pointedly, they were familiar with members of the Ottoman bureaucracy or at the very least conversant with the *şehirli*, or urban culture, that the elite represented. For those who possessed neither of these qualities, their passage east was probably assured.

We see evidence of this policy at work in the South Marmara through a handful of documents from both Hüdavendigar and Karesi. In mid-September 1917, the governor of Hüdavendigar, Hakkı Bey, reported that 440 individuals (or 99 households) had settled in the town and county of Kirmasti after the Balkan Wars. They were identified as Albanians from the three former Macedonian provinces of Manastır, Selanik, and Üsküp who were working as traders or agricultural labourers. They were largely counted as visitors (*misafir*) since they had yet to be permanently settled according to the desires of the central government. Hakkı Bey notified the Interior Ministry that he had decided to transfer and scatter the Albanians to the north and east, to the environs of Ertruğul, Gemlik, and Orhangazi.[93] Talat Paşa and the Interior Ministry in part agreed with the governor's actions, stating that it was worrisome that peoples from Manastır, Kosova, and Salonika were forming dense communities around Bursa. Henceforth, it was declared, no one from the former Ottoman provinces of Manastır, Üsküp, Selanik, and Kosova would be allowed to settle in the forbidden areas.[94]

The Interior Ministry and the governor of Hüdavendigar did differ on one important point. In the original report sent in mid-September, the *vali* recommended that *all* Albanians from the two counties of Karacabey and Kirmasti be deported (*kaldırmak*) to the eastern interior, regardless of whether or not they lived in villages or on farms.[95] Many of these refugees, it was explained, had now taken up work as bandits and were wrecking security in the region.[96] He further went on to suggest a similar policy towards Circassians and Georgians in the region, whose acts of brigandage posed a serious threat. After their deportation, property once belonging to the North Caucasians could then be distributed to other peoples (*unsur*).[97] The Interior Ministry rejected this, stating that only those Albanians who did not own property were eligible for deportation.[98]

The Interior Ministry's attempt to dilute and scatter the Albanian diaspora in the South Marmara was not without acts of resistance. In the *kaza* of Edremit, to the west of Balıkesir, Albanians had gathered together in villages outside town and were resisting law enforcement officials. Albanians from one village, the report emphasized, had fought an incursion of gendarmes into their village during the pursuit of an eight-man gang of paramilitaries who killed one of their comrades. The region was saturated with Albanians, the report went on to state, much like other areas in Anatolia.[99] A second report documented the apprehension of sixty Albanians who had fled from an assigned area of settlement in Adana. Taken into custody in Bursa, the group, mostly families hoping to join their relatives in town, were later returned to Adana. Like the Albanians from Kirmasti, the detainees were overwhelmingly from Macedonia.[100]

The forced settlement of Albanians in Anatolia shares many features of the CUP's policy towards non-Muslims. It is clear that the CUP perceived the physical concentration of Albanians, Greeks, and Armenians in the South Marmara as inherent threats to the stability of the Ottoman state and therefore had to be broken up. Unemployed Albanian 'vagrants', or *serseri* in Turkish, were particularly feared as a source of instability, since they were often recruited into bandit gangs and other paramilitary groups (although, as we will see later, many of these poor, unemployed Albanians were at times protected from on high precisely because they were employed as paramilitaries).

All three deportation agendas were carefully managed, with particular emphasis on tracking and cataloguing the status of deportees.[101] Still, archival documents also acknowledge that administrators did allow for certain exemptions and the personal discretion of local officials in the provinces. Resistance was evident at various levels. Yet the deportation of Albanians differed dramatically from that of Ottoman Christians in one distinct way. While the large presence of these three groups in the South Marmara posed a grave danger to the Ottoman state, it appears that the Young Turk government held open the possibility that certain Albanians could be reformed and engineered into loyal citizens. In other words, the CUP was able to formulate a process by which an Albanian who spoke little to no Turkish or was 'unaccustomed' to the cultural norms of the CUP state could adapt to their new homes and, with time, become 'Turks'. No such plan or expectation appears to have been dreamt of in regards to non-Muslims. Instead, the Young Turk regime appears to have seen no means of mitigating the threat posed by Greeks and Armenians, save deportation.

The exclusion of North Causasians in the South Marmara from the Interior Ministry's policy of deportation is curious, however. Like Albanians, Circassians constituted a large portion of the population of the South Marmara. They were also at times identified as almost a criminal class, since North Caucasians were often seen as sources of banditry and other paramilitary activity. Yet the Unionist policy of resettlement was more narrowly extended to Circassian immigrants in the empire. After 1915, both Circassians and Chechens from Jordan and Syria, as well as recent refugees from the fighting in the Caucasus, were forcibly transferred to Urfa, Maraş, and Elazığ for resettlement.[102] Later in the war, Istanbul mandated that Abkhazian refugees from Ordu be settled among 'Turks' in villages to the east of Adapazarı. There the Abkhazians, who were perceived to be particularly 'difficult to punish' since they were accustomed to living in mountains and forests, would pose less of a security threat.[103] In the rest of the South Marmara, though, there appears to have been no such effort at relocating migrant or settled North Caucasians. This could in part be due to the fact that Circassian emigration to the Ottoman Empire was negligible during the war years. But events during and after the First World War suggest that the

CUP had other motives in excluding Circassians from their grander agenda of resettlement.

THE CONDEMNED COME HOME: THE RETURN OF NON-MUSLIMS AND ITS IMMEDIATE AFTERMATH

The scene was an Easter service in Adapazarı in 1919. At the Protestant church in town, still standing after lying dormant for nearly four years, a dense crowd gathered to celebrate Christ's resurrection. The crowd, made up largely of Armenians, had packed the church in increasing numbers each Sunday. Each dressed for the day in their threadbare best clothing. The force and conviction with which the liturgy was celebrated deeply moved the lone American present. The message of this day marking Jesus' resurrection was not to be found in the sermon, the anonymous observer professed, but was embodied 'in the very presence of the congregation'.[104]

The war had ended seven months before this account was written. Before Istanbul's final admission of defeat, the political fortunes of Ottoman Armenians and Greeks had begun to turn. On 18 October 1918, Talat Paşa issued a decree allowing the return of exiled Armenians to their homes. The complete annulment of the 1915 Deportation Laws was inked on 4 November, three days after Enver, Talat, and Cemal fled the country.[105] These legislative acts came in addition to the establishment of the Istanbul Military Tribunal and the admission of guilt by several high-ranking officials for wartime atrocities.[106] Between November and December 1918, Armenian and Rum parliamentary representatives openly aired the complaints of their constituents and their communities as a whole.[107] Meanwhile, the Greek Patriarchate of Istanbul as early as October had begun to take steps of its own to ensure the return and resettlement of the Rum population in the South Marmara and elsewhere.[108]

Soon after an armistice was agreed upon at Modros in October 1918, foreign troops would occupy strategic locations through the empire. Having followed the plight of Ottoman Christians from afar since the first years of the war, representatives of the British government now stationed in the South Marmara soon turned their attention to the Greek and Armenian refugees beginning to trickle back home. Their first observations are worth reporting at length.

Between April and November 1919, officers from the British High Commission undertook a series of tours in the South Marmara. As fact-finding missions related to the status of Christians in the region, the primary focus of these tours was the environs of İzmit and Adapazarı (from where the bulk of Armenians were deported). In other tours conducted in and around Bursa, Gemlik, Bandırma, and Balıkesir, British reports relate a similar pattern of results. According to two separate reports (one comprising British-collected figures, the other comprising Ottoman figures), anywhere between 2,761 and 5,800 Armenians in Adapazarı (out of a reported total of either 26,000 or 17,240) had lived to return by June 1919.[109] That spring, 1,800 Armenians, out of a pre-1915 population of 11,300, returned to the environs of İzmit.[110] In Bahçecik, only 1,500 out of some 12,500 returned from their exile in northern Mesopotamia.[111] In Gemlik, only twenty or thirty Armenians out of 400 survived to return home.[112]

As for the Rum population further west, British observers tell of areas where virtually no deportations took place (such as in Artaki, Susurluk, and Bandırma) and areas of near total expulsion (particularly among the island communities on the Marmara Sea).[113] An impoverished Greek community survived the deportations in Bursa, whereas the town's prominent Armenian families were virtually decimated.[114] Whatever the numbers of those who returned, it appears that the Ottoman state aided at least in part in the transport and feeding of both Greek and Armenian refugees returning to areas around Bursa, Biga, Mudanya, Gemlik, Orhangazi, and Yeniköylü.[115]

Upon returning home, both Armenians and Greeks were confronted with the issue of their abandoned property and possessions. For some, there was simply no home to which to return. British and American sources claim that between 28 and 34 per cent of the Armenian homes in İzmit had been left uninhabitable.[116] Similar numbers were seen in Adapazarı.[117] Through several long winters, the locals who had remained had broken down door frames, fixtures, walls, and furniture for firewood. Armenian factories remained closed while Muslim businesses remained open. Valuables looted from skeletal Armenian homes, churches, and schools could still be found in the local bazaar even at war's end. According to one American report, government offices in Adapazarı unabashedly printed official correspondence on stationery with the header 'Armenian Girls' High School'.[118]

In order better to remedy this crisis in housing and speed the return of abandoned property, the Ottoman government sanctioned the creation of 'mixed commissions' comprising Greek, Armenian, and Muslim representatives drawn from their respective local communities.[119] The British officers touring the area recorded various results among these commissions, reporting abysmal returns in Bandırma, Bursa, and Mudanya but total or near total success in areas such as Bilecik, Karacabey, Kirmasti, and İzmit/Adapazarı.[120] During this period, the central government in Istanbul encouraged this process of restitution.[121] By October 1919, a new Ottoman directive was circulated, comprising a set of guidelines governing the sale and return of Christian property and authorizing village guards (*bekçi*s) to carry out the restitution of abandoned homes and goods.[122]

Many Armenians and Greeks who had either managed to avoid deportation or returned from exile remained determined to re-establish their lives in the towns and villages they had long called home. An unknown number, having found their houses stripped of their possessions or fixtures, chose to move on to the bigger cities of Istanbul, İzmit, or Bursa. Relations between returnees and their Muslim neighbours varied from place to place. In some areas, such as Armutlu, located between İzmit and Bursa, local Muslims attempted to look after the property left behind by those sent away. In Yalova and Biga, however, Muslim refugees occupying abandoned Christian homes refused to be evicted.[123] Tensions among Muslims were high in Adapazarı as hundreds of Armenians came back to reclaim their former lives. One missionary described the situation in the spring of 1919 this way:

> The Turks are not pleased. Their consciences are too unpleasantly active for them to enjoy seeing the people they have robbed. . . . They had lived rather happily on the whole with their Armenian neighbors formerly but after the deportations, which were ordered from above, the return of the people they have so grossly wronged is a constant irritation. Now they say, 'Next time they won't return.' But they recognize clearly that they have done wrong. A year or so ago there was a rather serious fire in the business part of the city but one owner of large warehouses in the path of the fire was very calm and confident that the fire would not touch his property. On being questioned by his friends how he could remain so calm he said, 'The fire won't touch *my* warehouses because there isn't a thing in them stolen from the Armenians.' And set it did not.[124]

Throughout the South Marmara, local Muslim hostility, first brought on by guilt, resentment, and poverty, would grow sharper with the increasing permanence of foreign occupation.

Despite the resilience of the survivors who had returned home, it was hard for many in the region to escape the conclusion that Armenian and Greek life in the South Marmara had been virtually destroyed. Even American missionaries expressed doubts that the region's Christian communities would ever recover from the blow dealt them during the war.[125] For many who had been close to the wartime government, the damage done by the deportations (let alone the policies that had preceded the Great War) was not enough. More than the nation's defeat on the battlefield, the fact that non-Muslims returned with the intention of taking back their property and lives underscored the Unionist government's central failure during the war. The presence of foreign troops, a force that supported non-Muslim claims, served further to burn this realization into the collective consciousness of the remaining Young Turks. As winter turned to spring in 1919, many of those who had pledged their loyalty to the CUP and the Ottoman nation would not sit idly by and wait to see how things would turn out. In short order, echoing calls to resist slowly reverberated throughout the South Marmara.

3

In the Company of Killers: Crime, Recruitment, and the Birth of the National Movement in the South Marmara

Towards the end of May 1919, Captain Selahettin boarded a ship in Istanbul destined for the port city of Bandırma. After a brief passage across the Sea of Marmara, Selahettin and his companion found the town in an uproar. Eight days earlier soldiers from the kingdom of Greece had landed in Izmir. Reports of massacres abounded in the Ottoman press, as did fears of Greece's annexation of the Aegean coast. The current Ottoman government meanwhile had done virtually nothing to thwart the invasion and occupation of Anatolia by other Western Powers. With the departure of the principal wartime leadership days after the Ottoman surrender, power now resided in the hands of Sultan Vahdeddin and other former opponents of the Committee of Union and Progress. Sitting Grand Vizir *Damat* Ferid, himself a long time adversary of the Young Turks, ordered the nation and its military not to contest foreign troops wherever they might be found. With the news of Izmir's occupation beginning to sink in, many of the town's officers and notables had come to believe that the port of Bandırma would fall next.[1]

Selahettin's trip to Bandırma was in direct contravention of Istanbul's edict. Only days before his departure from the capital, he had volunteered to serve as the aide-de-camp of Bekir Sami (Günsav), a former teacher at the military academy who had commanded an elite unit on the Iraqi front during the war. Together the two had come to Bandırma to call upon one of the most powerful families of the region to participate in a covert effort to drive the Greeks back across the Aegean. Somewhere between 22 and 23 May 1919, Bekir Sami and Selahettin came to the family home of Çerkes Reşit in the neighbouring village of Emreköy. Although Reşit was not at home, his father, Hasan, was there to greet the two men. Bekir, a former schoolmate of Reşit's, took the occasion to explain to his host the immediate dangers posed by Greeks.[2] The nation, Bekir declared, was calling on Reşit in this time of peril. As the evening drew to a close, one of Reşit's in-laws kissed Bekir's hand and foot and agreed that their family's assistance would be forthcoming.[3]

The success of the resistance movement envisioned by Bekir Sami, Selahettin, and their comrades depended upon the allegiance of Çerkes Reşit and his family.

Reşit was one of the founding members of the Committee of Union and Progress, an experienced operative of the state's covert service and a close associate of many of the most influential figures of the empire. But Bekir Sami did not simply desire the moral support of this politically connected provincial family. Rather, what he coveted most was the services of the family's criminal network based in the South Marmara. Within weeks of their meeting, the aid the family promised would materialize in the form of hundreds of paramilitaries ready to serve at the behest of the resistance movement taking shape in the region.

This nexus occupied by the CUP, provincial gangs, and network politics is crucial for our understanding of the slow drift towards intercommunal violence in the South Marmara during the war years. It is a phenomenon that strikes deep into the empire's past and is an intrinsic trait that applies to regions in and beyond northwestern Anatolia. Since the founding of the Committee of Union and Progress in 1908, criminals and party officials had intermingled and formed an institutionalized *mélange* within the imperial apparatus. The Ottoman clandestine service, the *Teşkilat-ı Mahsusa* (Special Organization), embodied this alliance that incorporated both the capital and the provinces. Once removed from power, the remnants of the CUP turned again to its alliance with local paramilitaries as a means to reverse their collective fortunes and undo their greatest failures (namely, the imminent partitioning of the state and the return of deported non-Muslims from exile). This chapter traces the local and transnational origins of the South Marmara's 'culture of paramilitarism' and explores the roles which gangs, bandits, and assassins played in first fomenting the violence that followed the Ottoman surrender at Modros.

A dangerous, yet obvious, paradox plagued this time-tested relationship between the overworld Ottoman state and Anatolia's criminal underworld. In tying provincial paramilitaries so closely to the arms of the state, the Young Turks (as well as their predecessors) lent their authority to local elements whose priorities did not always match the party's. At the expense of the CUP's grander designs to ensure the security of the empire, banditry and other forms of violent crime in turn became endemic to areas of paramilitary recruitment. Worse still was the possibility that the relationship between the state and local toughs could be renegotiated, disregarded, or severed. The Circassian diaspora, as we will later see, comprised a key component within this troubled affiliation in the South Marmara.

KILLER PATRIOTS: CIRCASSIANS AND THE ORIGINS OF THE OTTOMAN CLANDESTINE SERVICE

Bandits, private militias, and local strongmen had long provided Istanbul with ready repositories of potential soldiers, bureaucrats, and statesmen in times of need. The early modern Ottoman state arguably depended upon the likes of such less than noble figures as Ali Paşa of Jannina, *Abaza* Hasan Paşa, Mehmet Ali, and many others for the survival of the empire during the crises of the eighteenth century.4 Although representing a new generation of professionally trained and progressively minded officers and officials, the Committee of Union and Progress could not ignore the expediency and capabilities of provincial bandits or private militias residing in their midst. The provinces of Ottoman Macedonia, the adopted birthplace of the party, provided the Young Turks with their first introduction to the utility of local paramilitaries.

On the 2 August, Ilinden (or Saint Elijah's Day), 1903, the central Macedonian province of Manastır exploded in rebellion. Within days, hundreds of guerrillas organized by the Internal Macedonian Revolutionary Organization (*Vutreshna Makedonska Revoliutsiona Organizatsija*, or VMRO) seized control of scores of villages around the provincial capital and openly declared the establishment of a united Macedonian republic. The uprising was a devastating spectacle of intercommunal violence. Throughout southern Manastır, Greek and Muslim civilians alike were subject to attacks by the VMRO. In response, Ottoman officers and landowners organized vigilante groups in order to aid the military in crushing the revolt.5 The use of these *başıbozuk* or irregular forces continued to escalate in the aftermath of the Ilinden Uprising as local Muslim (particularly Albanian) notables contested the activities of Macedonian, Greek, Vlach, Bulgarian, and Serb insurgents in the region. Although the recruitment of landless and unemployed men into local gangs (or *çetes*) was a practice that pre-dated the 1903 revolt, this new emphasis upon paramilitary warfare progressively helped to transform formerly criminal networks into political confederations.

For the officers who established the first clandestine CUP cells in Macedonia after 1906, the rising tide of Muslim paramilitarism was doubly beneficial. In comprising a natural series of local allies in their war against the Christian insurgents, Muslim gangs through their services added an armed component to the drive to unseat Abdülhamid II. Thus many cell members, such as (Resneli) Ahmet Niyazi, undertook concerted efforts to secure the loyalties of provincial notables and their armed gangs in anticipation of the rebellion to come.6 Hanioğlu places particular emphasis on the role of Albanian paramilitaries in providing the backbone for the CUP's push in 1908 (going as far as to say that Albanians understood the Young Turk Revolution as being an 'Albanian enterprise'7).

In the years that followed the Young Turk Revolution of 1908, the CUP did not abandon its reliance on provincial paramilitary groups. With the spread of regional party offices and the rise in party membership, the Unionists correspondingly expanded their influence among local gangs. *Çerkes* Reşit's ascendancy within the CUP, for example, thus entailed the rise of his own personal militia, which in 1919 reportedly controlled the entirety of the Bandırma district.8 Such men, as one parliamentarian noted, were soon counted among the CUP's most loyal constituents.9 Under the sponsorship of CUP patrons, many young paramilitaries entered the gendarmerie or the army and then were charged with fighting guerrillas in Macedonia or policing unstable portions of Anatolia.

The collapse of Ottoman forces stationed in Macedonia in 1912 marked a radical turn in the relationship between the CUP and their paramilitary allies. With the partition of western Thrace seemingly imminent, Enver Paşa, newly appointed to the position of Minister of War, commissioned the formation of a clandestine unit to save the two provinces of Dedeağaç and Gümelcine from foreign occupation. Under the direction of two Circassian officers, Eşref Kuşçubaşı and Süleyman Askeri, the new unit would engage in a direct campaign of subversion against the Bulgarian army in Thrace. With the aid of specially recruited operatives (particularly several prominent Circassian paramilitaries from İzmit and Adapazarı) the 'Special Organization' (*Teşkilat-ı Mahsusa*) attempted to organize local notables into forming an 'Islamic Republic of Western Thrace'.

The Special Organization's failure to continue resistance efforts in western Thrace did not lead to the termination of this clandestine unit. With the outbreak of world war, this clandestine service was instead revived, enlarged, and given several new mandates. Research by Taner Akçam and Vahakn Dadrian has critically documented the essential role which the *Teşkilat-ı Mahsusa* played in executing the deportations, boycotts, and massacres directed at Ottoman Christians during the First World War. Enver Paşa, overall commander of clandestine operations, also assigned to the Special Organization the job of raising tribal troops among the Arabs, instigating rebellions in Italian, British, and Russian colonial territories, and spreading the call of jihad to more distant Muslim lands.

Of those officers who have been identified or who have admitted to participating in the Organization's operations during the First World War, one cannot help noticing the sizeable numbers of 'non-Turks' comprising the *Teşkilat-ı Mahsusa*. In particular, one is struck by the inordinate number of Circassians placed in positions of power within this secret body. In addition to the two founding officers of the organization, we know that numerous Circassian men populated various ranks within the clandestine service. Several of these men, such as Rauf Orbay, Ahmet Anzavur, (Maan) Ali, *Çerkes* Davut, Şah İsmail, Şükrü (Yenibahceli), Mehmet Fuad (Çarım), as well as *Çerkes* Reşit and his brother Ethem, would become pivotal figures in the South Marmara during the war years.

The majority of Circassian agents appear to have served in the army, mostly while stationed in the Caucasus. From the handful of documents that have been garnered from the Ottoman archives, as well as from the proceedings of the Istanbul War Crimes Tribunal, we know that North Caucasians were secretly, yet specifically, requisitioned throughout Anatolia (and in particular the South Marmara) to serve as 'raiders' or 'marauders' (*çetecis*) in the east.[10] The testimony presented before the Istanbul Military Tribunal reveals some details of this policy in the South Marmara. In a telegram written by Musa Bey, the governor (*mutasarrıf*) of Karesi, the following observations were made with regard to the conscription of 'paramilitaries' in the *liva* of Balıkesir:

> As said in a communication which arrived to the *mutasarrıf* a week earlier from the Interior Ministry, the requisitioning of men has begun. The enterprise is being undertaken as far as those two hundred individuals wanted who can work as paramilitaries (*çetecilik yapabilecek*), who are prisoners and Circassian. . . . Of the Caucasian races, only Circassians exist in Karesi. There are no Lezgi, Chechens or Georgians. There is practically no one who speaks Russian or who knows and who has travelled in the Caucasus. Those that can be found are those who possess the desire, good character, courage and [physical] build and who have not entered into the military. It is possible to acquire several hundred—three hundred, four hundred—Circassians like those [who have the qualities previously mentioned] if they are being sought for belligerency (*muhariplik*) or paramilitary action [*çetecilik*] at either the front or at the rear of the army. If a limited number of individuals are being sought for propaganda purposes, there exist five to ten men who can speak and negotiate with the Caucasian villages. . . . These individuals, whose names and places of origin are listed, are well-respected and are able to negotiate.[11]

As Taner Akçam and others have argued, these were the bands, formed by and accountable to the CUP, which proved to be the primary instrument of the Ottoman government in carrying out the massacres of Armenians in eastern Anatolia.[12]

But this document alludes to more than the violence inflicted upon the civilian population of eastern Anatolia and the Caucasus or who was responsible for such acts. Correspondence of this type reveals that local administrators, in this case Musa Bey, were acutely aware of the kind of men wanted for such an operation and where and through whom such men could be attained. In other words, the men chosen to take part in such a suggestive task as 'paramilitary action' were not acquired at random; they were known, either through reputation or recommendation, and thus came under someone's jurisdiction or authority.

Table 3.1 presents an attempt to explain in part the nature and implications of this recruitment process. The sixteen Caucasian men listed served at various levels in the Ottoman military and administration (including the *Teşkilat-ı Mahsusa*). All would later play prominent roles during the War of Independence in the South Marmara. In the first three sections (A, B, and C) are individuals who served in the Special Organization yet ended up on different sides of the War of Independence. The last group (D) is composed of four North Caucasian men who did not serve in the *Teşkilat-ı Mahsusa* but who nonetheless were closely connected to prominent Circassians in the Special Organization and the National Movement. Among the men listed, no one linguistic, ethnic, or 'tribal' affiliation predominated. They were Abkhaz, Adige, Osset, and Ubıh and were largely born in the Ottoman Empire. The table demonstrates a clear series of gradients in terms of place of birth, education, and post-war political affiliation. In short, there is no one 'mould' that typified the 'Circassians' of the Special Organization. What the table does indicate are the informal networks and linkages between

Table 3.1 Class, ethnicity, and the clandestine service

Name	Ethnic origin	Place of birth	Father's profession	Education	Military/bureaucratic service	Post-war affiliation
A.						
(Ç'ince) Hüseyin Rauf Orbay	Abkhaz/Osset(?)	Istanbul	Governor, Senator	*Deniz Harbiye*	Balkan Wars/Libya *Teşkilat-ı Mahsusa*	Nationalist
(Çarım) Mehmet Fuat	Ubıh	Aleppo	Public prosecutor	*Mülkiye*/abroad	Kaymakam of Bornova, Balıkesir, Gönen, etc. *Teşkilat-ı Mahsusa*	Nationalist
(Yenibahçeli) Şükrü	Ubıh	Istanbul	Colonel	*Harbiye*	Balkan Wars *Teşkilat-ı Mahsusa*	Nationalist
B.						
(Sencer) Eşref Kuşçubaşı	Dagestani or Ubıh(?)	Istanbul	Sultan's falconer	*Harbiye*	Balkan Wars/*Teşkilat-ı Mahsusa*	Nationalist/Loyalist
(Sencer) Hacı Sami Kuşçubaşı	Dagestani or Ubıh(?)	Istanbul	Sultan's falconer	*Harbiye*	Balkan Wars/*Teşkilat-ı Mahsusa*	Nationalist/Loyalist
(Pşevu) *Çerkes* Reşit	Adige	Bandırma	Notable	*Harbiye*	Balkan Wars *Teşkilat-ı Mahsusa*	Nationalist/Loyalist
(Pşevu) *Çerkes* Ethem	Adige	Bandırma	Notable	*Rüşdiye*	Balkan Wars/*Teşkilat-ı Mahsusa*	Nationalist/Loyalist
C.						
(Maan) Ali	Abkhaz	Abkhazia/Düzce (settled)	N/A	N/A	Gendarmerie/Balkan Wars/*Teşkilat-ı Mahsusa*	Loyalist

(Maan) Şirin	Abkhaz	Abkhazia/Adapazarı (settled)	Notable(?)	Rușdiye	Balkan Wars/*Teşkilat-ı Mahsusa*	Loyalist
(Sügünlü) Çerkes Davut	Adige(?)	Kırmasti or Manyas(?)	N/A	N/A	Bandit/Gendarmerie/*Teşkilat-ı Mahsusa*	Loyalist
(Ançok) Ahmet Anzavur	Adige	Circassia/Biga (settled)	N/A	N/A	Gendarmerie/*Teşkilat-ı Mahsusa*	Loyalist
Şah İsmail	Adige (?)	Gönen	N/A	N/A	Landowner/Labourer Bandit/*Teşkilat-ı Mahsusa*	Loyalist
D.						
Bekir Sami (Kundukh)	Osset	Istanbul	Bureaucrat	*Mülkiye*/Abroad	Governor of Aleppo, Bursa, Van, Beirut	Nationalist
Bekir Sami (Günsav Zarakho)	Ubıh	Manyas	Notable(?)	*Harbiye*	Balkan Wars/First World War (Iraq, Caucasus)	Nationalist
Yusuf İzzet (Met Çanatuka)	Adige	Yozgat/Eskişehir (?)	Notable(?)	*Harbiye*	Instructor/First World War (Caucasus)	Nationalist
(Bigʻ) Ahmet Fevzi	Ubıh	Düzce	Notable(?)	*Harbiye*	Instructor/First World War (Caucasus)	Nationalist

these warriors. Their various journeys taken to state service speak to the kinds of roles they played within the Organization as well as their respective allegiances after the First World War.

The men in groups A and B were individuals born and groomed for power. Sired by powerful fathers, all but one attended the finest schools the empire had to offer: the *Harbiye, Deniz Harbiye*, and the *Mülkiye*.[13] Each had strong connections to the highest levels of the Committee for Union and Progress, with Eşref and Rauf playing critical roles in its founding.[14] As soldiers and clandestine operatives in the *Teşkilat-ı Mahsusa*, there were entrusted with the most vital operations of the war. Şükrü commanded an elite unit on the eastern front.[15] Rauf Orbay was withdrawn from combat and served as a delegate for the Ottoman Empire at the Treaty of Brest-Litovsk and later during the negotiations of the Modros Armistice.[16] The two enigmatic brothers, Eşref and Sami, were assigned to sensitive operations in the Arab lands and Central Asia.[17]

Military service and politics brought them to one another's attention. Hard combat in Iran, Macedonia, Iraq, or the Caucasus made these veterans close comrades and served to widen their circle of acquaintances and friends. Çerkes Reşit, an odd character within this group, epitomizes the deep ties forged by these old hands. While born to a notable, although by no means highly distinguished, Circassian family from the port city of Bandırma, Reşit attended the *Harbiye*. Soon after graduation he lashed his professional fortunes to Eşref Kuşçubaşı and the nascent CUP. In 1908, he joined Eşref in establishing one of the first CUP cells in Izmir.[18] Reşit later went on to fight in Libya and in the Balkan Wars along-side Rauf Orbay, and became a seminal member of the *Teşkilat-ı Mahsusa*.[19] Strangely, there is no record of Reşit's service in the First World War.

Although not members of the Special Organization, the prominent men of group D attended classes, socialized, and shed blood with their counterparts in the clandestine service. In certain cases, their mutual interests extended to political affairs in the North Caucasus. Three of the men, Rauf Orbay, Bekir Sami (Kundukh), and Yusuf İzzet, were active members of the *Şimali Kafkas Cemiyeti* (The North Caucasian Association), a group composed of prominent North Caucasian immigrants committed to the liberation of Circassian lands under Russian rule.[20]

The remaining five individuals listed in the table, in part C, in many ways stand apart from the likes of Rauf, Yusuf İzzet, and Eşref. They were born in various localities within the confines of the South Marmara. Whereas Şirin was the child of a local landowner, the latter four men, Ahmet Anzavur, (Süngülü) Çerkes Davut, Şah İsmail, and (Maan) Ali were seemingly born without any notable credentials. Of this group, only one (Şirin) had a middle school education, and all of these men may have been functionally illiterate. In the cases of Ahmet Anzavur, Davut, and Ali, who had no formal education to speak of, the gendarmerie served as a springboard into the *Teşkilat-ı Mahsusa*.

Their collective prowess as men of violence brought them into the fold of very influential figures. Ali and Şirin were noted guerrilla fighters who served under Eşref Kuşçubaşı in Macedonia and Bulgaria before joining the very first manifestation of the *Teşkilat-ı Mahsusa* in 1913.[21] Anzavur, an ageing captain of the gendarmerie, was recruited at the outbreak of the war by Yusuf İzzet, an acquaintance he made through the *Şimali Kafkas Cemiyeti*.[22] Davut, on the other hand, was a bandit in the environs of Bursa, before joining the *Teşkilat-ı Mahsusa*.[23] During the war he was recruited by *Çerkes* Mehmet Reşit (a former comrade of Eşref), the *Teşkilat-ı Mahsusa* operative who, as wartime governor of Diyarbakir, was responsible for numerous atrocities against the local Armenian population.[24]

The sketches of these men from the *Teşkilat-ı Mahsusa* suggest that their shared ethnicity was only one node by which the Organization was formed and operated. While their shared heritage of exile and diaspora may have helped bring them to one another's attention, it is clear other factors drew them together and later pulled them apart. The *Teşkilat-ı Mahsusa* was an organization defined by personal networks. At the top were highly educated men of privileged birth. They were thus familiar with the political culture of Istanbul and were intimates of the most powerful individuals and families of the empire. Such men, like Rauf Orbay, *Çerkes* Reşit, and Eşref Kuşçubaşı, served as magnets of recruitment for less distinguished Circassians from the provinces. This group comprised individuals with less refined backgrounds than their superiors. However, these 'men of the provinces' were not simple lackeys for the *Teşkilat-ı Mahsusa* or the CUP at large.

As a body operating outside the traditional confines of the Ottoman military, the *Teşkilat-ı Mahsusa* needed men who did not need to be trained and who could 'live with weapons in their hands' (to use the words of *Çerkes* Ethem).[25] While not explicitly stating that recruitment was the primary function of such individuals as Ethem or Ahmet Anzavur, Hüsamettin Ertürk says specifically that Circassian 'privates and officers' from Gönen, Adapazarı, and Kandıra were a source for Special Organization forces in Iraq.[26] Considering what is known about their backgrounds, men like Ethem, Ahmet Anzavur, and even Reşit possessed the sort of 'skills' and 'pedigree' to gather foot soldiers wanted by the *Teşkilat-ı Mahsusa* for their war in the Caucasus (men 'who can speak and negotiate with the Caucasian villages', as the previous document put it). Their background as men rooted in the provinces yet familiar enough with the capital made them reliable middlemen with the ability to tap provincial militias as sources of military manpower. These credentials allowed them to find men like Davut, Ali, and Şah İsmail. These latter figures were the paramilitaries required by the Special Organization and were men who could also provide conduits to personal retainers, criminals, or other marginal characters.

Taking the telegrams read before the Istanbul Military Tribunal also into consideration, the ties linking Circassian managers and fixers within the Special Organization epitomize the extent to which patronage networks were woven from the capital into the provinces. More than supplying an expedient (if not stopgap) means to fulfil military and extra-legal ambitions, the North Caucasians of the *Teşkilat-ı Mahsusa* helped attach local communities to the Committee of Union and Progress. In rendering their services to the state, co-opted provincial notables hoped, nay expected, to benefit from this system of patronage. It is here that the terms of this relationship became stickier.

But what can be said of other so-called 'ethnics' within the organization? How did they fit into this hierarchical relationship of leadership and mobilization? Fewer clear references to Albanians can be found in accounts related to the *Teşkilat-ı Mahsusa*. Among those Albanians who have been identified in this study as figures within the War of Independence, only four, Eyüp Sabri, Kazım (Özalp), *Kara* Arslan, and Yahya *Kaptan*, are confirmed members of the Special Organization.[27] Of the four, only Eyüp actively agitated among his ethnic 'kin' . However, his actions were restricted to attempting acts of subversion in Albania and in Macedonia (an enterprise that eventually landed him in prison in Malta at the hands of the Allied powers).[28] Available source material does suggest that Albanians (most notably from Kirmasti) were a possible source of recruitment for the *Teşkilat-ı Mahsusa*. Balkan refugees overall are reported to have constituted an important source of recruits for the paramilitary formations utilized on the eastern front.[29] But from what can be gleaned from the few records available to researchers, the 'Albanian' officer and the 'Albanian' fighter of the *Teşkilat-ı Mahsusa* are largely absent by name. Considering the size of the Albanian community, particularly in the South Marmara, why were North Caucasians assuming more notable positions of power within the base of the Special Organization? To put it another way, why do we know more about the origins and roles of Circassians in the Special Organization and less about Albanians?

The reason for this disparity between Circassians and Albanians may reside in the differences between these diasporas within the Ottoman Empire and in the South Marmara in particular. While there is no doubt that the number of Albanians living in the remaining Ottoman lands numbered in the tens or hundreds of thousands, it was nonetheless a community in tremendous flux between 1914 and 1918. The refugee crisis of the war years served only to splinter the Albanian-speaking community of Anatolia as small groups of individuals and families settled in places like the South Marmara. While there is some evidence that Albanians may have previously settled among people from similar regions or towns, the CUP, as previously demonstrated, made a conscious effort to limit the 'congregation' of Albanians and carefully vetted the settlement of wealthy Albanians in Anatolia. During the First World War, Albanians in the provinces largely became a people without notables. The elite Albanian-speaking Ottoman Muslims of Rumeli, be they officers, bureaucrats, or landowners, were left with few options in the aftermath of the Balkan Wars. While those hailing from places like Tirana, Shkrodra, or even Kosova had the option of turning to the newly formed Republic of Albania, those residing in Greek or Serbian Macedonia had no home or local government that desired their services. Thus the Albanian elites that arrived in Anatolia during the war became rootless, having left their local networks of kin, comrades, and business relations behind them in the Balkans. What remained for many of these men was the CUP and the Ottoman state, institutions that were served by friends and colleagues with similar backgrounds and beliefs. The emergence of stalwart Albanian officers like Kazım (Özalp) and (Köprülülü) Hamdi lay not in their ability to mobilize men or spreading propaganda, but in their loyalty to party and state. This stands in stark contrast to the Caucasians of the South Marmara, whose established networks between local elites and the centres of power in Istanbul remained undisturbed throughout the Balkan Wars and the First World War.[30] It was these ties to the state, and not to the party and its ideology, that condemned many Circassians in the aftermath of the War of Independence.

UNDER THE REIGN OF GUNMEN: PARAMILITARISM AND INSTABILITY IN WARTIME SOUTH MARMARA

Long before white flags were hoisted or waved from the Ottoman front lines further south, the fortunes of those who remained at home in the South Marmara loomed stark and dim. In the two years before the Ottoman surrender at Modros, affairs in the towns and villages located between Adapazarı and Çanakkale ebbed painfully and without signs of improvement. Indeed, some farmers and factory owners would reap murderous profits from the starving masses.[31] More often than not, though, shortages of food, fuel, and animals claimed an untold number of lives among settled, displaced, and deported communities alike. Beginning in 1917, hordes of deserting soldiers came marching through the region. Of the more than 500,000 men escaping disease and the advancing Allies, thousands of deserters joined the masses of refugees taking up residence in the South Marmara in the hope of receiving some form of assistance from the capital.[32]

With no aid appearing on the horizon, banditry supplemented what the state could not. Before 1917, official reports of bandit activity are few in number. As early as January 1917, Ottoman authorities reported that bandits had begun 'operating openly' on roads leading to Adapazarı.[33] By November the *vali* of Hüdavendigar and the *mutasarrıf* of Karesi were called to coordinate and aid their gendarmes in the pursuit of 'bandits and deserters' in the two provinces.[34] In the eleven months preceding the signing of the Modros Armistice, reports from around the South Marmara heralded a deluge of incidents involving armed men on the roads.[35]

In part, this rise in brigandage was blamed upon the increasing numbers of bands made up of military deserters.[36] Despite orders issued by the Ministry of War to military commanders to execute anyone caught deserting, officers themselves appear to have taken part in acts of violence committed by bandit-soldiers.[37]

In this guise local officers and officials were chided for their 'incompetence' and corruption, colluding with bandit leaders, misappropriating of money, and committing acts of torture or simply behaving 'indifferently'.[38] Although the needs of the military required taking mounted gendarmes into the army in 1915, local and imperial officials repeatedly called for more troops and gendarmes to be stationed in the region and raised the serious issue of desertion even after the signing of the armistice.[39]

But blame for this seeming epidemic of lawlessness cannot squarely be placed upon the heads of those fleeing the front. Soldiers who resigned themselves to flight found a readily prepared niche in local gangs that had pre-existed the outbreak of war. Government documents and contemporary accounts tell of numerous rural outfits that accepted deserters into their ranks.[40] The plague of desertion, in other words, did not signal a new turn away from tranquillity to instability. The arrival of deserters served instead to uncage native criminal syndicates throughout the South Marmara, tipping the balance of regional power in their favour.

Successive waves of mobilization and recruitment did not turn every man in the South Marmara into a soldier. From the sanctuary of the highlands and outlying villages of the region, the lure of smuggling, theft, kidnapping, and murder for hire remained ever present in the face of foreign invasion. From their mountain hideouts outside Çanakkale, Zeybeks and other Türkmen muled contraband tobacco down towards the coast.[41] An Albanian bandit named *Arnavud* Rahman ran a long-time extortion racket from the village of Değirmencik, just outside the seaside town of Karabiga.[42] Weddings proved ready-made events for extortionists of various shades. With the weakening and reassignment of the local gendarmerie units, livestock, cargo, and people moving along the open roads between Biga, Gönen, Adapazarı, and Bursa provided easy marks for raiders and kidnappers.

Control over these avenues of trade and vice did not pass without disagreement or conflict. As the war lurched into its final years, violence between rival paramilitary groups escalated throughout the region. One well-known case occurred in Biga in 1918, when a Greek deserter named Artin assassinated and overthrew his gang's commander. The brother-in-law of the murdered Halil Pehlivan, *Çerkes* Neş'et, in turn hunted down Artin and personally executed him before his sister. In the wake of Artin's death, Neş'et's gang of Circassian riders took the opportunity to expand the scope of their raiding at the expense of wealthy villages. When this proved too much to swallow, local notables and officials in Biga sought the aid of a Pomak militia leader named *Kara* Hasan to take down the rambunctious Circassians. Hasan's men, with the backing of county administrators and gendarmes, ultimately succeeded in putting an end to *Çerkes* Neş'et's raiding. With the deed done, officials appeared to have awarded the more benevolent Pomaks with the right to extort at will, so long as violence was not used.[43]

This sort of collusion between gangs, police, notables, and administrators prevailed in other parts of the South Marmara. Further west in the towns of

Karamürsel and Değirmendere, Georgian paramilitaries under the command of the Yetimoğlu family menaced farms and villages along the Gulf of İzmit.⁴⁴ The owner of one tobacco farm, Nurettin Bey, responded by recruiting and harbouring Albanian militiamen to protect his own property and carry out counter raids. While village leaders or *muhtars* had a hand in supporting the Yetimoğlus, Nurettin Bey himself was a political force to be reckoned with. In addition to being the former *kaymakam* of İzmit, sources also identify him as a close relative of then Interior Minister Talat Paşa.⁴⁵ Nurettin's chief retainer, *Arnavud* Kazım, would later become a loyal fighter for the National Movement.⁴⁶

An even more complicated and politically charged contest centred on the twin counties of Karacabey and Kirmasti. Since 1909, rival factions of Albanian and Circassian notables vied for the right to plunder, and indeed rule, the two districts. Albanian paramilitaries and notables held the upper hand in this struggle for more than a decade, defying the advances of Circassian gangs as well as the intervention of the local administration and the gendarmerie. The fighting reached boiling point at war's end after one notorious Albanian *çete* leader named *Deli* Hürşid stole fifty horses from one of the wealthiest Circassian families in the village of Canbaz. The bitter feud that followed this incident was to have a profound impact upon both the region and the empire itself.⁴⁷

Two and half months before the Modros Armistice, Istanbul declared a general amnesty to all military deserters and bandits in Karesi, Hüdavendigar, and Kale-i Sultaniye provinces.⁴⁸ With a disintegrating army and a gendarmerie stripped to the bone, amnesty was the last card the government had to play. Many outlaws and brigands came in from the cold to accept the government's absolution.⁴⁹ *Kara* Hasan, for one, paraded his sixty followers into Biga and ceremoniously turned himself in to local authorities. With the ability now to walk the streets of the small market town freely, Hasan established himself in a local *han* and engaged in a regime of extortion through his band of toughs.⁵⁰ While ensuring that banditry was kept to a minimum outside his mini-fiefdom, Hasan still reserved the right to muscle the wealthy figures, bridal parties and businessmen of the town.⁵¹

As winter turned to spring in 1919, other rival paramilitary networks in the South Marmara replicated *Kara* Hasan's takeover of Biga. When the *kaymakam* of Karacabey retired in the first half of 1919, a Circassian, Osman Bey, was appointed to the position of administrative representative (*kaymakam vekili*). Local Albanian notables in town strongly disapproved of Osman's appointment and immediately moved to unseat the Circassian. One notable with deep pockets and friends in Istanbul, (Gostivarlı) İbrahim, contracted the feared assassin *Deli* Hürşid to patrol the outlying villages of Karacabey openly in the company of armed men. Osman got word of this threat against his person and acquired the services of a Dagestani *çeteci*, (Keliyanlı) Zekeriya, to subdue the Albanian insurgency against him. Events came to a head on the evening of 17 June 1919 when Zekeriya and three of his companions were ambushed near his home. Zekeriya escaped with his life, but two of his companions and an innocent bystander peering from a window were killed in the clash. Following the attempt on Zekeriya's life, Osman was forced to flee to the hills after receiving further written death threats. At this point (Gümülcineli) İsmail Hakkı, the anti-Nationalist governor of Hüdavendigar, intervened in the conflict and appointed an Albanian artillery captain, (Debreli) Ziya Bey, to the post of administrative representative of Karacabey.[52] In truth, though, gunmen ran the county.

The collapse of law and order in places like Biga, Karacabey, and Değirmendere was symptomatic of a much larger crisis hanging over the future of the empire. Defeat at the hands of the Allies brought with it the decapitation of the Committee of Union and Progress. The ruling triumvirate of Enver, Talat, and Cemal Paşas, fearing their arrest and prosecution for war crimes, slipped out of Istanbul on a German submarine days after the war ended. Surrender at Modros virtually sealed the partition of the Ottoman Arab lands, a feat guaranteed by force of British arms. The terms of defeat, which included a condition stating that Allied soldiers could travel throughout the hinterland of Anatolia and occupy any strategic point that 'threatened the security of the Allies', seemed to condemn the rest of the empire, including Istanbul, to partition.[53] Society would suffer the worst of fates. One veteran of the war would later describe life after the war in this way:

It was like there wasn't an orphan or woman who was not widowed at a young age or a living mother in every house who did not weep over giving at least one martyr [şehit]. It is as if my beautiful towns and villages were turned to ruin and wiped from the map. Crowds of maimed men formed. An apparently healthy man was simply never met.[54]

With the wolf at the door, the remnants of the Committee of Union and Progress were neither ambivalent nor supine in the face of the dangers facing the state and their own grip on power. Before the party's defeat was even realized, a concerted and organized effort to resist the impending occupation of Anatolia and reinstate party rule was decided upon. Local paramilitaries, central to the CUP's hopes for their political survival, would again be called upon to provide the foot soldiers needed for the struggle to come.

TURNING BACK THE CLOCK: ORIGINS OF THE TURKISH NATIONAL MOVEMENT

The day 19 May 1919 is the 'stunde null' or zero hour of contemporary Turkish historiography. It is the day on which Mustafa Kemal (Atatürk) landed at Samsun, where he would assume command of the Ninth Inspectorate of the Ottoman army in Erzurum. It is the point in history when Atatürk placed himself at the centre of the resistance movement that led to the defeat of the

Allied occupation of Anatolia and the founding of the Turkish Republic. He was, according to his own words, both the inspiration for the movement against foreign occupation and the engine that drove this movement forward.

Erik Jan Zürcher, in his innovative study of the Committee of Union and Progress during the Turkish War of Independence, has done much to demolish this cardinal dogma of Turkish historiography. Zürcher maintains that Enver Paşa and the inner circle of the CUP had laid contingency plans in 1918 to establish a resistance movement in the Caucasus should the Ottoman Empire be defeated and occupied.[55] While this resistance would be under the command of Enver's uncle and brother, Halil Paşa and Nuri Paşa, in Azerbaijan, steps were also taken to store and conceal large caches of arms throughout Anatolia. According to Ertürk, the Ottoman clandestine service, the *Teşkilat-ı Mahsusa*, would remain intact and direct the Anatolian theatre of the Ottoman resistance.[56]

Enver's plans took a detour during the six months immediately following his departure from the empire. No liberation army led by either Halil or Nuri emerged from the Caucasus. Instead, organized acts of resistance to the Allied occupation of Anatolia instead proceeded piecemeal in a select group of provinces on the territorial margins of Anatolia. By the spring of 1919, violence had erupted in Kars, Urfa, Batumi, Adana, and Edirne, territories that by no coincidence also shared a common history of intercommunal violence in the years leading up to the end of the war.[57] In the South Marmara, British troops established a small garrison in the port town of Çanakkale. A contingent of British troops formally occupied İzmit on 19 May 1919, four days after the Greeks landed in Izmir.[58] Elsewhere, British and French forces placed small detachments of soldiers at major railway junctions and harbours and sent officers to conduct informal 'tours' of the interior.[59] With the reports of the first clashes in the South Marmara in January 1919, resistance fighters did not target these foreign troops. The sole victims of this initial wave of violence in the region were instead Armenians and Greeks returning from exile.

A majority of Turkish commentators and scholars almost unanimously represent Ottoman Christians as the chief domestic catalysts that engendered not only the War of Independence but also the human catastrophe that ensued following the Ottoman defeat in 1918. In introducing the subject, historians have often cited the plans of the Armenian and Greek governments to partition Anatolia as crucial to understanding the provocations of both Greeks and Armenians.[60] These plots, some historians go on to say, were manifested in an outbreak of Greek banditry and paramilitary activity.[61] In the eyes of many Turkish commentators, including Mustafa Kemal, the Greek *Megali Idea* and other such nationalist agendas represented the convictions of all Christians in Anatolia.[62]

The historical record only partially substantiates this claim. Acts of brigandage and murder carried out by Greek and Armenian paramilitaries were reported in the environs of Erdek, Adapazarı, Bahçecik, and Kandıra during the six months following the Modros Armistice. One particularly feared gang of Rum villagers operating north of İzmit reportedly made it clear that their intention was to 'destroy the Turk'.[63] Both British and Ottoman sources tell of a rising tide of Greek nationalist and irredentist sentiments in urban centres like Bandırma and Balıkesir. While Lieutenant Hadkinson, a relief officer attached to the British High Commission, tells us of some 'bad Armenian characters' among the bandits operating around Adapazarı (a fact confirmed by local Armenians as well), sources concerning Christian gangs or paramilitary groups in the South Marmara between November 1918 and May 1919 are by no means overwhelming or pandemic.[64]

From their offices and private parlours in Istanbul, former members of the now disbanded Committee of Union and Progress were laying the groundwork for their own offensive in the South Marmara. In October 1918, Enver and Talat convened a meeting that would transform the character and responsibilities of the Ottoman clandestine service. It was decided there and then that the *Teşkilat-ı Mahsusa* would be placed under the directorship of *Kara* Kemal and *Kara* Vasıf, close allies of Talat Paşa, and tasked with supplying and maintaining future resistance fighters. The *Karakol*, as the Special Organization was later renamed, would be staffed with loyal CUP operatives, many of whom had ties and experience with provincial militias. At the behest of *Kara* Kemal, (Yenibahçeli) Şükrü, a former Circassian Special Organization operative, was ordered to recruit and maintain pre-existing Muslim gangs in the İzmit theatre of operations.[65] Together with other high-ranking Young Turks (such as Fuat (Çarım) and (Kıbrıslı) Sırrı, two experienced bureaucrats with established ties with the *Teşkilat-ı Mahsusa*), as well as loyal gendarmes, local officials, and former guerrilla leaders, the *Karakol* bands established a wide swathe of territory under their influence, stretching from Adapazarı to the Istanbul city limits.[66] Professional ties again played a role in recruiting local *çete* leaders. Three of the principal paramilitary commanders in İzmit, Sadık Baba, *Kara* Arslan, and Yahya Kaptan, were former comrades of either Süleyman Askeri or Eşref Kuşçubaşı.[67]

By April 1919, British officers reporting from İzmit were disturbed by the violent trends they were witnessing in their district. The rampant paramilitary activity along the roads and in villages to the west of İzmit, according to their interlocutors, bore the hallmarks of the CUP. British observers in İzmit also understood that local law enforcement officials were assisting in supporting and engineering this campaign.[68] Many attacks staged by these bands appeared to have been scripted to send a message to the Christians of the province. In one instance, Albanian gunmen tied a Greek merchant to a tree and cut off his ears, telling him that they could kill him but that they wanted him to go and complain to the British and the French. The same fate also befell two Greeks from Pendik who were told to 'hand [your ears] to your friends the English, whom you cheered so loudly in Pendik the other day. Perhaps they will help you.'[69] Ottoman sources partially support these conclusions reached by the British. In March, a group of about a hundred Armenians returning to Karacabey were set upon and robbed by a gang of Muslims along the town's streets. An Armenian who petitioned the government for redress identified the organizer of the attack as the head of the local chapter of the CUP, Osman Bey, as well as an Albanian accomplice.[70] Very similar attacks were reported in Armutlu and in the Değirmendere/Karamürsel region. In the latter district, the Yetimoğlu family, with the support of local officials, was held responsible for a series of attacks on Armenians.[71]

Fahri Can, a doctor and an organizer of the first *Karakol* gangs in İzmit, categorically declared in his memoirs that the focus of (Yenibahçeli) Şükrü's campaign was to combat the activities of Christian paramilitaries and nothing more.[72] Yet official British and Ottoman testimonies speak of no open clashes between the *Karakol* gangs and armed Christian factions. The overwhelming civilian toll during the first stages of this conflict reflects three fundamental realities that defined the South Marmara at this time. In the wake of the army's collapse following the November armistice, no Ottoman force could or was willing to challenge the British soldiers taking up positions in İzmit and other portions of the South Marmara. Meanwhile, Armenian and Greek refugees had begun to trickle back into the region under the protection and assistance of foreign troops and aid workers. Some of these Christians, it appears, could not tolerate the political and economic status quo and therefore formed militias or supported the partition of the state. Naturally, none of the activists involved in the *Karakol* could tolerate these new twists in the region's affairs. By targeting civilians, Muslim paramilitary groups and their CUP handlers were simultaneously striking at both the occupation and the return of the deportees.

AFTER IZMIR: CONTRIVING A MILITARY/BUREAUCRATIC RESPONSE

Events on the morning of 15 May 1919 radically changed the polarity and urgency of the *Karakol* resistance. The landing of Greek troops on Izmir's harbour front signalled a new and more ominous phase in Anatolia's post-war evolution. Whereas the fighting in Urfa and İzmit had remained largely localized, the Ottoman press interpreted the arrival of Greek soldiers as the beginning of a much wider war against a force with unbounded territorial ambitions. Reports of massacres of Muslim civilians and the joyous demonstrations seen in Rum neighbourhoods after the landing further galvanized the Muslim public. Mass rallies in the capital, as well as in towns throughout the South Marmara, called for an end to the atrocities and the expulsion of the Greek expeditionary force.[73] Instead, the government of *Damat* Ferid pre-emptively attempted to suppress any resistance to the Greek forces by threatening to prosecute all violators as mere bandits.

Damat Ferid's opposition to armed resistance had little to do with the occupation in and of itself. Having only recently wrestled control of the state from the CUP, Ferid was well aware of Unionist efforts to rearm and recover their authority. In the lead up to May, CUP members and affiliates assembled in Izmir in anticipation of the Greek landing. Notable political and social figures from Bursa, Balıkesir, Edremit, Gönen, Burhaniye, Bandırma, Ayvalık, and Erdek actively participated in such events launched by the Ottoman Defence of Rights Society of Izmir (*İzmir Müdafaa-i Hukuk-u Osmaniye Cemiyeti*) and others. Balıkesir soon became the most vocal centre of opposition to the Allied occupation in the South Marmara. It was the seat of the most outspoken nationalist newspaper in the region, *Ses*, or The Voice. Published by the son of two prominent native families of Balıkesir, Hasan Basri (Çantay), *Ses* was an outspoken organ of Turkist, nationalist, and Islamist sentiment even before the Ottoman defeat in the First World War.[74] Its role as a forum for both ideological and political cheerleading for the Young Turk agenda earned the paper even greater prominence during the first two years of the Turkish War of Independence.

More than just issuing rhetoric, the CUP first readied a military response in advance of the Greek invasion. Testimony from various key figures present in Izmir suggests that Unionist elements worked diligently in the days before the landing to draw up plans for an armed front along the Aegean hinterland. Army officers (notably Kazım (Özalp) and Celal Bayar) appear to have worked in collaboration with prominent local business and intellectual leaders with strong CUP ties (namely, Mustafa Necati, Hüseyin Ragıp Nurretin, Haydar Rüştü (Öktem), and Halit (Moralızade)) up until the night of 14 May in order to smooth the transition from protest to military action.[75] A critical node used to convene military and provincial officers during the first stages of this plot were the offices of the *Türk Ocağı*, an intellectual institution that had in many ways been synonymous with the CUP regime. Influential notables like Halit (Moralızade), Mustafa Necati, and Hüseyin Ragıp Nurretin would utilize the Izmir chapter of the *Türk Ocağı* to host the inaugural meeting of the Ottoman Defence of Rights Society of Izmir in March 1919.[76]

During the eight days following the invasion, Kazım (Özalp), a twice-decorated division commander, toured several pivotal towns along the Aegean and within the Marmara interior and had already begun to mobilize gendarmes, reserve officers, religious figures, and journalists to prepare for action.[77] At the same time officers and bureaucrats like Captain Selahettin and Bekir Sami (Günsav) arranged to make their way from Istanbul and across the Marmara Sea. By 23 May, Bekir, Kazım, Rauf Orbay, and several others met in Bandırma to agree on overseeing operations against the Greeks.[78] From 23 May on, a united front against the Greeks began to take shape in the Aegean. By 12 June forces organized by Kazım (Özalp) and Bekir Sami began to form a defensive perimeter around the towns of Ayvalık, Bergama, Akhisar, and Soma.[79]

Military force alone could not defeat the Greeks. A simultaneous effort to organize and channel the energies of civilian activists and supporters commenced almost immediately following the Greek invasion. In the South Marmara the early resisters relied upon two figures, both possessing deep ties to the CUP, to initiate and manage what would become an unofficial 'Nationalist' bureaucracy. The first of these characters was Vasıf (Çınar), who met with Kazım (Özalp) in Bandırma within days of the landing. As a member of the *Türk Ocağı* (through which he became involved with the Ottoman Defence of Rights Society of Izmir) and later the publisher of the Nationalist newspaper *İzmir'e Doğru* (*Towards Izmir*), Vasıf appears to have been a natural linchpin in constructing the National Movement. Kazım and other members of the Nationalist command structure were clearly aware of the fact that Vasıf offered access to intellectuals, CUP sympathizers, and their retainers organized among the various branches of the *Türk Ocağı* found in the Aegean and the South Marmara. With his establishment of *İzmir'e Doğru*, Vasıf became the *Kuva-yı Milliye*'s official spokesman in western Anatolia, faithfully printing statements on its behalf.[80]

The second figure to bring the bureaucratic wing into line was Hacim Muhittin (Çarıklı), a CUP loyalist who had previously held bureaucratic postings in Gönen, Izmir, and Balıkesir. Based in Istanbul at the time of the Greek invasion, Hacim ultimately decided to depart for Bandırma in order to join the struggle.[81] The most intriguing aspect of this decision lies in the fact that it coincided with a series of meetings with *Kara* Vasıf, the co-founder of the *Karakol* Society. While he does not explicitly state the nature of his relationship with Vasıf, Hacim's journal entries between 3 and 9 June show that he met with the former *Teşkilat-ı Mahsusa* officer more than once and suggest that Vasıf may have influenced his decision to go to the South Marmara.[82]

After an initial effort to raise troops in Bandırma, Gönen, and Manyas, Hacim settled in Balıkesir on 27 June 1919. While continuing to deliver addresses and raise troops and money in this Nationalist stronghold, Hacim quickly situated himself among a group of local organizers who had campaigned on the behalf of the resistance since the middle of May. In addition to Vasıf (Çınar) and Kazım (Özalp), this nascent group of Nationalists largely included notables native to Balıkesir, including (*Keçeci*) Hafız Mehmed Emin, Mehmed Vehbi (Bolak), Abdülgafur *Hoca*, and (Zarbalı) Hulûsi.

A month later, between 26 and 30 July 1919, Hacim and his associates in Balıkesir convened a congress of notables tasked with forming a response to the Greek invasion.[83] In a twenty-nine-point programme, the National Congress of Balıkesir declared the establishment of the Rejection of Annexation Committee of the National Movement (*Hareket-i Milliye Redd-i İlhak Heyeti*), a committee dedicated to 'the saving of the fatherland'. To achieve this goal, the congress stated that it would establish separate steering committees devoted to organizing, financing, and supplying recruits from each county in the region for the construction of a regular army (an army that would not condone paramilitarism or *çetecilik*).⁸⁴ The costs of this enterprise were to be shared equitably among the major urban centres in the South Marmara and the northern Aegean, with the *kaza* of Balıkesir paying the lion's share of the expenses.⁸⁵ The decisions agreed upon by the Balıkesir Rejection of Annexation Committee were confirmed and expanded upon by a subsequent meeting in Alaşehir one month later and another three congresses in Balıkesir between September 1919 and March 1920. In the wake of these meetings, Nationalist sympathizers endeavoured to establish other local branches of the *Redd-i İlhak* Committee throughout the Marmara basin.

Despite Mustafa Kemal's later admission that the National Movement was a rebellion driven by a collective desire to establish a new order in Anatolia, no document authored by the *Redd-i İlhak* or any other Nationalist organization suggests such intentions.⁸⁶ Instead, one sees repeated assertions that the movement under way was committed to the total physical and political expulsion of the Greek army.⁸⁷ The National Movement championed these goals in the name of all 'Muslims and Turks' in Anatolia. As one statement put it, 'The barbarous Greek attacks and crimes perpetrated upon our Anatolia have brought to pass a true and firm national movement among the Muslims and Turks in this realm.'⁸⁸

The meta-narrative of the War of Independence has accepted this representation as an elementary conclusion. But this combination of nationalist and sectarian language is curious. As a phrase that appears repeatedly in the lingo of the resistance, how is the pairing of 'Muslim' and 'Turk' to be understood? As two sides of the same coin? As separate or independent groups? Most importantly, what is the relationship between these two identifiers?

The appropriation of the term 'national' is perhaps the most suitable point of departure in trying to understand the ideological notion and perceptions of the *Kuva-yı Milliye*. The word 'national' at first glance seems to denote the obvious: a state-wide movement that would be all-embracing, representing the aspirations of the populace at large. But the Ottoman Turkish terms 'nation' and 'national' (*millet, millî*) share a loaded history. Beginning with the Gülhane Decree of 1839, the *millet* became a much worked-over concept in Ottoman political philosophy. With the rise of the Young Turks, *millet* had largely ceased to describe the political and social structures governing the non-Muslim subjects of the Otttoman Empire. Instead, the appellation *millî* became a reference to the *vatan*, the Ottoman fatherland, an entity that no longer recognized sectarian difference among its citizens.⁸⁹

The events leading up to the deportations of 1915 altered the meaning of nation once again. With Greek and Armenian 'treason' increasingly accepted as the rule and not the exception, Islam became even more critical to the meaning of citizenship and loyalty in Ottoman political life. The Greek invasion solidified this role of Islam as an identifier within the lingo of state and society. With their departure to Anatolia in May 1919, both Mustafa Kemal and Rauf Orbay echoed this position. In a joint supposition submitted to the Interior Ministry, the two declared that there was something holy about their national struggle (*mücahede-i milliye/cihad-ı milliye*). In committing themselves to this sacred task, Rauf asserted that there was 'an honourable, religious and active blood boiling beneath Istanbul's wilted face'.[90]

The Nationalists in the South Marmara largely shied from this sort of dramatic language. It is only among those members of the *ulema*, such as Abdülgafur *Hoca*, that one sees such vivid appeals to Islam and state.[91] At certain times, Islam, when used as a function of the movement, assumes the form of the state and the Nationalists' legitimate relationship to its institutions. The goal of the *Kuva-yı Milliye*, a group comprising soldiers, officials, and citizens, was to save the state and thus, by extension, was a struggle to save the sultan-caliph, who had ruled the Ottoman lands since the time of Gazi Osman.[92] More often than not, Nationalist rhetoric employed Islam in a descriptive sense. Islam, in other words, is taken to be a dominant characteristic of the population of Anatolia, thereby delimiting Anatolia as a Muslim land.

The invocation of Islam presented not only a system of powerful political and cultural symbols, but also constituted a legitimate discourse that could be readily recognized and understood by all. The resistance's identification with Islam transformed the National Movement into a sacred duty for the community of believers. Those who fought under the *Kuva-yı Milliye* became *mücahidler* (a term that generally denotes a champion or hero in the name of Islam). By virtue of this fact, the fight to drive the Greeks out of Anatolia could be seen to constitute, in the words of Rauf Orbay, a struggle for the faith (*cihad*). The invocation of Islam also held a deeper political significance. As a movement that had from the beginning defied the wishes of Sultan Vahdeddin and the Istanbul government, the Nationalist Movement was aware that its struggle had transgressed the line between devotion and rebellion. The *Kuva-yı Milliye* consequently chose to represent its cause as a struggle in defence of Islam, the sultan-caliphate (as opposed to the sultan-caliph himself), and his lands. This argument rested upon shaky rhetorical ground, as the Nationalists placated their audience in the name of the caliphate (*hilafet*), the throne (*taht*), and the Islamic world (*alem-i İslam*).

Hand in hand with this particular use of Islam is the utilization of the term 'Turk' as a legitimizing factor within the struggle of the *Kuva-yı Milliye*. The National Movement's use of this ethnic marker appears to reflect a conscious decision by the *Kuva-yı Milliye* to appeal to the occupying powers (as well as the world at large). In the spirit of the Wilsonian Principles, the congresses at Balıkesir and Alaşehir repeatedly asserted that the province of Aydın (as well as the rest of Anatolia) had been from time immemorial 'Turkish and Muslim' and therefore should be guaranteed the rights and protection of the Great Powers.[93] The Nationalist press carried this trope even further in the form of daily editorials and open letters. Through allusions to history, population statistics, and international precedent, journalists such as Vasıf (Çınar) and Hasan Basri (Çantay) openly used their journals (*İzmir'e Doğru* and *Ses*) to proselytize their solemn conviction that Izmir, and indeed the rest of Anatolia, was 'Turkish and Muslim'.[94] Rarely does the epithet 'Turk' appear alone.

Within this matrix of language and identity, Islam is *the* essential discursive modifier. One could not address Anatolia in purely ethnic terms without qualifying this sentiment through the evocation of Islam, the supposed universal characteristic of the land and its people. The tension underlying the surface of the Nationalist discourse again suggests the unresolved relationship between the CUP (as both a party and a collective of men sharing similar social, educational, and philosophical traits) and the Muslim population at large. In addition to the ongoing ambiguity over the meaning of Turkishness at this point in time—did it refer to the state (*devlet*)? Did it refer to the race (*ırk*)?—a more fundamental question emerged: Could people be addressed as Turks if they did not believe (or one might say did not know) they were Turks?[95]

Be that as it may, these questions remained unresolved through the first two years of the conflict. After the National Congresses in Sivas and Erzurum, the structure of the *Kuva-yı Milliye* became increasingly centralized under the control of Mustafa Kemal. After the meeting at Sivas in September 1919, the *Karakol* was abruptly closed down.[96] Thereafter all resistance organizations established in Anatolia and Thrace were compelled to submit themselves to the authority of Mustafa Kemal's own organization, the Defence of Rights Society of Anatolia and Rumeli (*Anadolu ve Rumeli Müdafaa-i Hukuk Cemiyeti*).[97] As the circle of leadership grew narrower, the formulation and distribution of the National Movement's message in turn was increasingly consolidated in the hands of Mustafa Kemal. While challengers to Mustafa Kemal's authority continued within the ranks of the resistance into 1921, the provincial Nationalist military and bureaucratic leadership ceded whatever autonomy had been afforded them since the first days after the Izmir landing. Those who wished to be considered loyal henceforth were to follow the lead of Mustafa Kemal and no one else.

The speed with which this assortment of local and national figures were able to organize a coherent force to combat the Greeks again sheds light on the CUP's role in giving life to the National Movement (alternatively called *Haraket-i Milliye* or, in more recent accounts, the *Milli Mücadele*). With high-ranking officials like Rauf Orbay in the lead, civilian activists and army officers in the South Marmara had at their disposal a variety of supporting actors (journalists, merchants, clerics, local officials, landowners, fellow officers, and paramilitaries) to facilitate, finance, or, at the very least, not hinder the building of this movement.[98]

There remains the question of who was at the absolute head of this movement in the spring of 1919. As we have seen, the building of armed resistance groups pre-dated the occupation of Izmir and was the result of perceived local threats (which in the case of the South Marmara were manifested through both the British occupation and the return of Armenians and Rum from exile). Yet during the long winter of 1919, many of the most powerful men of the Ottoman

Empire, men including Rauf Orbay and Mustafa Kemal, remained uncertain as to what exactly was to be done. Clearly there was no one commander or central committee in existence before May 1919. By May, however, this situation changed. Rauf Orbay and a collection of other officers and officials (including Mustafa Kemal, Kazım (Karabekir), Esat (Işık), İsmail Canbolat, and *Kara Kemal*) did have a plan to resist a Greek invasion and knew individuals capable and reliable enough to organize and lead in the defence of Anatolia. But as summer turned to autumn, Mustafa Kemal would leave few with doubts about who was in charge.

Even before Bekir Sami embarked for Bandırma on 21 May 1919, both the commanders and the lieutenants of this movement were confronted with the question of who would fill the ranks of their resistance army. With only a limited grip on provincial authority, the founders of the National Movement were forced to contrive alternative sources of manpower.

ÇETECILIK: ARMING THE MOVEMENT

On 17 September 1919, four days after the emerging Nationalist government met in Sivas, a general directive ordering the raising of 'national detachments' (*milli müfreze*) was sent out to a select group of towns in the South Marmara. The directive was addressed to various chapters of the Defence of Rights Society, a collective body that would form the nascent bureaucracy of the National Movement. According to the directive, two separate types of detachments were to be formed. The first type, 'stationary' (*sabit*) detachments, would be responsible for defending their native villages and towns from 'bandits' and 'non-Muslim *çetes*' attempting to foment revolt. The second type would comprise 'mobile detachments' (*seyyare müfreze*), which would be mobilized should the army be in danger. Three specific restrictions were placed upon the formation of these detachments: first, no non-nationals (*gayr-ı milliye*) could join; second, anyone associated with 'revolutionary or rebellious activities' (*haraket-i ihtilaliye*) was forbidden from joining; and third, the *Kuva-yı Milliye* would not take any Muslim or non-Muslim band, of any size, that commits crimes or acts of brigandage or engages in blood feuds (*intikamcılık*). This last prohibition was repeated a second time in mentioning the raising of mobile detachments (since later it was these groups that would do most of the fighting against the Greeks).[99]

This directive found within the files of Bekir Sami (Günsav) is one of the few pieces of evidence that outlines the composition and duties of the National Forces while under arms. The raising of these detachments was certainly a combined effort, involving the participation of Nationalist sympathizers from both inside and outside the imperial army and bureaucracy. In this regard the Defence of Rights Society (*Müdafaa-i Hukuk Cemiyeti*) and the Rejection of Annexation Society (*Redd-i İlhak Cemiyeti*) were crucial pivots upon which the *Kuva-yı*

Milliye enforced its rule. Throughout the war they would serve to shadow, and at times usurp, the powers and prerogatives of the regular Ottoman bureaucracy run from Istanbul.

How these local committees functioned remains somewhat of a mystery. Few foot soldiers and operatives within the *Kuva-yı Milliye* have left us any account of the individuals, politics, and construction of these local chapters.[100] One area where some evidence as to how these local committees were organized and run is the town of Bilecik, which attracted a great deal of attention from Bekir Sami (Günsav). Bekir Sami personally visited the town in mid-October over concerns relating to the loyalty of local North Caucasians to the National Movement.[101] Days after this visit, on 27 October 1919, five men from the town established a chapter of the Defence of Rights Society.[102] This committee in Bilecik was the fifth Nationalist body to be established in the *sancak* of Hüdavendigar in the autumn of 1919, having been preceded by the creation of committees in Yenişehir, Karacabey, Bursa, and Mihaliç (Kirmasti?).[103] Bekir Sami kept a close eye upon the Bilecik organization during its first month (it was often referred to as the 'National Movement Committee' (*Haraket-i Milliye Heyeti*)), warning it not to raise money or troops from the population.[104] Instead, the task of recruitment was entrusted to a regular army officer, Rıfat Bey, who directly approached the notables of the town to raise troops on the behalf of the *Kuva-yı Milliye*.[105] Rıfat was a constant presence in all the meetings of the committee over the following week, meetings that supposedly included Muslims, Christians, and Jews.[106] However, the main participants in these meetings appear to have been local Muslim notables, as well as former members of the CUP. One former Unionist by the name of Ahmet (Mercimekizade) arrived at a meeting with a contingent of guests from the town of Söğüt, 25 kilometres to the south and east of Bilecik.[107] The British coincidentally knew Ahmet and his supporters by reputation. During the war, he had reportedly murdered thirty Armenians and had aided in the deportations from Bilecik.[108]

Beyond a cursory glance, the September directive is intrinsically misleading. The Nationalists cast a wide net in the South Marmara in their drive to find and enlist men willing to serve in the National Forces. Units within the regular Ottoman army, despite prohibitions to the contrary, were assigned to the Aegean front lines within days of the Greek invasion. Retired officers and local draft offices in the region were also tapped for supplying small numbers of recruits for military service.[109] Nationalist officers even relied on their own initiative, through such methods as press gangs and recruits arriving from the capital.[110] For this purpose, refugees fleeing the advancing Greeks served as a ready well of recruits.[111]

The most glaring contradiction found in the September directive is its stern warning against the use of criminal gangs in fighting the Greeks. Historical precedent alone flies in the face of these regulations. During the First World War, paramilitaries and known criminals like Çerkes Reşit and others were sought after for service in the Special Organization. The realities of the post-armistice era did not change the parameters by which Nationalists identified and contracted the services of provincial militiamen. Then working as a member of the last Ottoman parliament, *Çerkes* Reşit was among the founding members of the *Karakol*. With the backing of Rauf Orbay, he had even gone as far as to protect his brother Ethem from legal prosecution after he kidnapped the son of the *vali* of Izmir, Rahmi Bey, in February 1919.[112] In May 1919, Ethem was charged with the task of commanding a large 'Mobile Force' of Circassian riders that was promised during the meeting between Bekir Sami (Günsav) and Reşit's father. The connection between the *Kuva-yı Milliye* and local paramilitaries did not end with Reşit's family.

After the ascendancy of *Kara* Hasan's gang in the town of Biga, one secret Nationalist agent succeeded in persuading the Pomak gang leader to declare his allegiance to the *Kuva-yı Milliye*.[113] Other active criminals and gunmen from Bursa and Balıkesir, including many seasoned veterans of the *Teşkilat-ı Mahsusa*, were approached and recruited during the months following the Izmir landing.[114]

In the period after the invasion, Nationalist efforts in İzmit continued unabated. Under the stewardship of *kaymakam* Ali Suat, *Kıbrıslı* Sırrı and Fuat (Çarım) situated their administrative base of operations in a schoolhouse in the centre of Adapazarı.[115] In the meantime, Nationalist leaders endeavoured, like their counterparts to the south and west, to give their forces the appearance of a regular army. This attempt to both legitimize and expand the İzmit front was galvanized with the arrival of Eşref Kuşçubaşı to the area in the spring of 1920. According to British sources, Eşref was released around this time from his imprisonment in Malta, where he had been interned since 1917.[116] Despite his absence during the critical months leading up to the founding of the *Kuva-yı Milliye*, Eşref's family remained very much involved in the activities of the Nationalists. Between May and June 1919, Eşref's brother, Ahmet Kuşçubaşı, was instrumental in supplying both arms and money to *Çerkes* Ethem's Mobile Forces.[117] Upon returning to Istanbul from prison, Eşref purportedly established contact with (Yenibahçeli) Şükrü (a Circassian classmate of his from the *Harbiye* and a member of the *Teşkilat-ı Mahsusa*) and became involved in the activities of the *Karakol*.[118] According to İlyas Sami Kavanoğlu, Eşref and other Nationalist leaders of North Caucasian origin (who had been largely based in the Black Sea region) were sent to secure İzmit and Adapazarı as a potential base of support and recruitment among the many Circassian, Laz, Georgian, and Abkhazian communities there.[119]

What is intriguing about Eşref's involvement in the National Movement in the İzmit area is the assumed connection that he, his family, or others like them would have with the North Caucasian communities of the region. Eşref, in his memoirs and his interviews with Philip Stoddard, is silent and misleading on this issue. Hüsamettin Ertürk states that Eşref's main directive was to assuage the fears of the Abkhazian and Circassian communities who were still personally and emotionally tied to the sultanate.[120] While it was rumoured that Eşref had some family relations (purportedly his former slaves) in İzmit, it is not clear exactly in what capacity he or his relatives would be negotiating with the locals.[121]

More broadly, Eşref's arrival in İzmit strikes at the degree to which ethnicity coloured the identification and management of prospective paramilitaries. In accordance with previous practices laid out in the formation of the Ottoman clandestine service, immigrant groups like the North Caucasians of the South Mamara were specifically targeted for recruitment. Yet, in order to secure the loyalties of so-called 'ethnic' paramilitaries, the Nationalists employed a corresponding 'ethnic' figure, one who hopefully had some sort of personal connections with the community in question, as their primary interlocutor. In the case of Circassian recruits, it is probably no accident that Bekir Sami (Günsav) and Rauf Orbay were involved in enlisting the support of individuals like Reşit and Ethem. Similarly, Rauf's brother-in-law, Aziz Bey, accompanied Hacim Muhettin during his negotiations with Circassian notables in Gönen and Manyas.[122]

The recruitment of Albanians appears to have followed a similar logistical path. In a report from the spring of 1920, Bekir Sami (Günsav) assured Mustafa Kemal that Albanians in Bursa and Kirmasti were on the Nationalist side. Many Albanian landowners and policemen had given 'immense amounts' of money and weapons to the cause, as well as 'a big commitment, to the *Kuva-yı Milliye*'. Kazım (Özalp), who was from Macedonia and possibly of Albanian extraction, testified that Albanian paramilitaries in these two counties were skilled in the art of guerrilla warfare through their previous work for 'the government and the army' (possibly alluding to their involvement in the Special Organization).[123]

The combined efforts of officers, notables, and officials did produce and equip an army for the National Movement by the late summer of 1919. Yet the size of this ragtag army of bandits, reserve officers, gendarmes, and imperial troops remains unknown. According to Bekir Sami's own accounting, the 56th Ottoman Division in Bursa, which would see hard fighting in both 1919 and 1920, numbered fewer than 400 men in the summer of 1919.[124] Most Nationalist detachments and *çete*s remained small throughout this period. In November 1919, only fifteen men, mostly gendarmes and police, could be extracted from the town of Karacabey.[125] It was explained that in the case of Karacabey, as well as in Bilecik, Gönen, Manyas, and Adapazarı, many members of the local elite (*eşraf*) simply refused to help.[126] As the summer of 1919 turned to autumn, the National Movement found itself increasingly caught between local elites and communities that often refused to help and nominal allies who were not fully trustworthy. Despite the ability to manipulate or outright control many of the levers of local administration, the Nationalists failed to grasp the fact that large factions of society were beginning to turn their backs on them.

4

The Politics of Revenge: The Rise and Fall of the Loyalist Opposition in the South Marmara

Vivian Hadkinson could sense that things around Gemlik were not right. As chief relief officer for the British High Commission in Istanbul, he had been around the South Marmara and had witnessed the tumultuous sea changes racking Gemlik and other towns in the region. Only small parties of deported Armenians and Greeks were returning home week by week. Gangs were proliferating to the point that local residents could hardly leave their homes and travel down the road without being robbed. Nationalist activists had taken up residence in Gemlik and were now operating in the open.[1]

Of the bleak contours found in Hadkinson's report to his superiors, one qualification stands out. Fear and discontent were indeed brewing among local Muslims, but it was the Nationalists who garnered the most reaction. In Gemlik they were demanding high taxes to support a local militia that had recently been established. When locals, hard pressed after the carnage of the last war, refused to submit their dues, Nationalist officers stripped them of their firearms.[2] Visits to other towns seemed to suggest that public dissatisfaction with the National Forces was not restricted to Gemlik. The new taxes and heavy demands being placed upon the population, Hadkinson argued, led to disillusionment among many. People were 'sick of war' and were generally not willing to take up arms 'however well they may be paid'.[3]

There were foreboding signs visible from the Nationalist camp as well. By the autumn of 1919, officers at the front lines in the Aegean and towards the rear had to contend with units that were either under strength or unruly. A unit of Circassian cavalry promised to Hacim Muhittin (Çarıklı) arrived at the front from Manyas with only thirty-eight riders out of an initially estimated 200 recruits.[4] Another Circassian detachment recruited from Gönen lasted only a few months before returning home. Upon returning to Gönen, the men and their commander, Mehmet Aydemiroğlu, vowed henceforth to oppose the *Kuva-yı Milliye*.[5]

To the north and east, supposed pro-Nationalist Georgian and Abkhazian paramilitaries, including the Yetimoğlu gang, were known to be looting large quantities of money and property from villagers and townspeople around İnegöl and Bilecik.⁶ Perhaps the most notorious offenders allied with the National Forces were the men of *Çerkes* Ethem's Mobile Forces. According to various sources, Ethem and his brother Reşit's tenure at the Aegean front was marked by several violent outbursts, including threatening the lives of fellow officers, stealing money, and rampaging through the towns of Salihli and Akhisar.⁷ Even Bekir Sami (Günsav), commander of the National Forces in Bursa, was compelled to ask his counterpart in Çanakkale if one thieving paramilitary who robbed in the name of the *Kuva-yı Milliye* was indeed under their command.⁸

Although the Nationalists had bottled up the Greek expeditionary force along the Aegean coast, a perfect storm of opposition began to coalesce over towns and villages between Balıkesir and İzmit in the autumn of 1919. In truth, provincial tensions and discontent were present in this portion of the South Marmara before the First World War. Yet the pre-war problems of mass migration, social inequality, and crime became amplified in the post-armistice era as greater Nationalist interference and prospects for yet another war appeared more imminent. Rising tensions would prompt the palace and anti-Unionists in the capital to lend support to anyone contesting the Nationalist presence in the region. Localized clashes between provincial rivals would give way to outright attacks upon the *Kuva-yı Milliye*. A broad coalition of malcontents formed as the pace of rebellion rose exponentially into 1920. In this fight for their very lives, the Nationalists would succeed in suppressing this challenge at the expense of murdering many of those they claimed to be defending.

This chapter takes up the meteoric rise and fall of what one might call the 'Loyalist' opposition in the South Marmara. On the one hand, this period features the seemingly sudden emergence of the sultan and the influence of his supporters in the region. Like the National Movement, a complex web of political interests and social networks bound together a loose clique of Loyalist insurgents in their attempt to forestall the activities of the *Kuva-yı Milliye*. Documentary evidence amply supports contemporary claims that interests closely linked to the palace, as well as Great Britain, played a pivotal role in helping to finance, organize, and incite popular outrage against former members of the CUP.

On the other hand, this period of insurrection in the South Marmara speaks to forces and fears exclusive of the plots hatched in Istanbul. In many ways the outbreak of intercommunal violence stands as a collective act of revenge by a variety of marginalized members of Ottoman society against those allied with the former CUP regime. The official leader of the Loyalist offensive, a retired gendarme by the name of Ahmet Anzavur, embodies many of the tensions that would both define and propel the insurrection through the spring of 1920. Circassians, and to a lesser degree Albanians, filled the ranks of this revolt by the hundreds and the thousands. In sorting through contemporary reports and correspondence, it is clear that Anzavur and his followers were not simple imperialist 'tools' or 'backward reactionaries' blinded by their devotion to the sultan. 'Loyalism' in the South Marmara was a phenomenon grounded in the rage and hardship experienced by thousands of individuals victimized by CUP rule.

THE LOYALIST CONFEDERACY: THE SULTANATE AND THE OPPOSITION TO THE *KUVA-YI MILLIYE*

The legacy of opposition to the *Kuva-yı Milliye* is an ironic twist within Turkish historiography. Considering the breadth of literature related to the emergence of the National Movement, the very notion of factionalism among the Turkish Republic's predecessors begs an embarrassing question: If Mustafa Kemal and his National Movement spoke for all 'Muslims and Turks' in Anatolia, why would some 'Muslims' and some 'Turks' seek to defy him? While historians have not shied away from this issue, works dealing with this period choose to treat the opponents of the National Movement as anomalies to be approached and justified within the context of the Ottoman/Republican transition. Many historians first point to the disparities and isolation among the numerous 'uprisings' (*isyanlar*) that erupted between 1919 and 1921. Studies of the opposition to the *Kuva-yı Milliye* particularly address the 'minority' elements found within internal uprisings, often stressing their 'tribal' (such as the Milli tribe near Urfa),[9] 'ethnic' (such as the Kurdish/Alevi uprising of Dersim),[10] or 'regionalist' (usually associated with the opposition organized around Yozgat by members of the Çapanoğlu family of notables)[11] attributes. The historiography of the last eighty years has depicted these movements as expressions of those unreconciled with the changes sweeping the land, and therefore outside the mainstream. Within this formulation the actions of Ahmet Anzavur and others like him are labelled as reactionary or backward (*irticai/gerici*). These men are seen, in other words, as motivated by short-term gains over the long-term good of the nation. More pointedly, the Muslims who chose to rise up against the Nationalists were joining with the other principal traitors of the period: Greeks and Armenians. The Republican historical establishment has not gone so far as to lay ultimate blame for the movement solely upon these provincial opponents. Blame has also been placed at the feet of those occupying much higher positions of power: namely, the imperial government in Istanbul and its foreign benefactors.[12]

While a rigorous portrayal of the politics of the capital stands outside this study, it is important nonetheless to broach Istanbul's role in engendering the resistance led by Ahmet Anzavur in the South Marmara. At the apex of the Loyalist opposition, both contemporary observers and historians have portrayed two men as the most central orchestrators: Mehmet VI Vahdeddin and his most loyal grand vizir, *Damat* Ferid *Paşa*. Beneath these two men was a constellation of former officials, intellectuals, and provincial notables and bureaucrats who represented and promoted the political interests of a variety of civil organizations and private agendas. While the forces garnered by these various actors are often portrayed as part and parcel of the fallout of war and the resulting collapse of Ottoman political authority, it is clear that the roots of the Loyalist movement extended beyond the Great War and the occupation of Anatolia.

Between 1908 and 1913, the Committee for Union and Progress was confronted with several political factions fiercely opposed to its rise to prominence. The pre-eminent antagonists to the CUP were those aligned with the sultanate. While it initially appeared that the *saray* was able to dispose of the CUP with the so-called counter-revolution of 1909, the Young Turks rebounded quickly from their base in Ottoman Macedonia. Upon the retaking of the capital by the Unionist Action Army (*Hareket Ordusu*) on 24 April 1909, Abdülhamid II was deposed by the Ottoman parliament. The overthrow of Abdülhamid, coupled with the declaration of a CUP dictatorship four years later, radically reduced the power of the sultanate both as an institution and as a faction of powerful political figures bound by marriage and service.

The departure of the CUP troika in 1918 breathed new life into this opposition. Mehmet VI Vahdeddin, who assumed the throne in 1918, made no secret of his desire to restore the authority of the sultanate.[13] Yet, without any direct medium with which to approach and mobilize the Ottoman public on his behalf, Mehmet VI was forced to seek alliances with political parties and organizations still loyal to himself and the Ottoman throne. He found this ally in the form of the resurrected Liberal Union Party (or more precisely, the Liberty and Understanding Party, *Hürriyet ve İtilaf Fırkası*).

The first embodiment of the Liberal Party came into being soon after the establishment of the second Ottoman parliament in 1908. Despite winning a commanding majority within the *meclis*, the CUP, through its aggressive policies of centralization, drove many of its previously loyal supporters to abandon the party. By 1911, dissidents in the empire found their voice in the creation of the Liberal Union or Liberal Entente Party, an organization founded by a group of Muslim and Christian parliamentarians, army officers, and journalists from Rumeli, Anatolia, and the Arab lands.[14] Its 'big tent' policies magnified the Liberal Union's mongrel disposition, uniting religious conservatives, disgruntled constitutionalists, and nationalists of various shades in their shared antipathy to the CUP.[15] The party reached the height of its power in the elections of 1912, only to be pushed aside by the Bab-ı Ali coup a year later. Although the party was never officially outlawed during the war period, an unknown number of Liberal political leaders were exiled or assassinated upon the orders of the CUP regime between 1914 and 1918.

Among those Liberals who would reach their political nadir during the First World War was *Damat* Ferid Paşa, the very first general secretary of the Liberal Union. Although highly educated and fluent in Western languages and culture, Ferid's status as a close ally of the palace earned him little respect in CUP circles. The outbreak of the Balkan Wars and the rise of the CUP dictatorship further marginalized Ferid and his party. Throughout the First World War, Ferid would serve in the Ottoman senate and was noted largely for his personal museum within the confines of his mansion on the Bosphorus.[16] The resurgence of the sultanate under Mehmet VI heralded Ferid's return to power. On the recommendation of Ahmet Tevfik (Oktay) Paşa, Mehmet Vahdeddin's son-in-law and grand vizir during the winter after the Modros Armistice, *Damat* Ferid was appointed *sadrazam* on 4 March 1919. He would serve several times as grand vizir during the War of Independence, and came to be known as the sultan's most active proponent.[17]

The popular base supporting these two men was an eclectic mix of civil organizations grounded in the politics of the capital. Among the most prominent of these groups was the Association of the Friends of England in Turkey (*Türkiye'de İngiliz Muhibleri Cemiyeti*). The organization was the brainchild of Sait Molla, the son of a prominent *ulema* family, who had once worked in the Ottoman High Court of Justice (*Şura-yı Devlet*).[18] Through various offices based in neighbourhoods throughout Istanbul and a series of daily newspapers (including Sait's own *Türkçe İstanbul*), the Friends of England endorsed the creation of a British mandate in Anatolia and promoted the notion of a more Anglophilic Ottoman education system.[19] The organization also purportedly supplied more dubious services to the Liberal government as an intelligence asset on behalf of Great Britain and as a conduit of arms and money for Loyalist paramilitaries (including Ahmet Anzavur).[20] Similar roles were played by the *Nigehban Cemiyet-i Askeriyesi* (or the Sentry Society), a group comprising middle-ranking officers loyal to the sultanate,[21] and the Advancement of Islam Society (*Teal-i İslam Cemiyeti*), an organization founded by the *şehyülislam*, Mustafa Sabri Efendi.[22]

Within days of becoming grand vizir, *Damat* Ferid Paşa moved to assert Loyalist authority in the South Marmara through the naming of (Gümülcineli) İsmail Hakkı to the post of *vali* in Hüdavendigar. As a founding member of the Liberal Party, İsmail Hakkı was at one time *Damat* Ferid's closest lieutenant.[23] As *vali* of Hüdavendigar, İsmail elected to form his own *çete*s in order to protect his personal interests in the provincial capital of Bursa.[24] The Nationalists would go on to accuse him of hindering the *Kuva-yı Milliye* (particularly after he arrested and exiled several Nationalist sympathizers from Bursa) and of bringing deported Armenians and Rum back into the district.[25] Upon hearing of the arrival of Bekir Sami (Günsav) in Bursa as commander of the National Forces in the region, İsmail Hakkı fled the city and returned to Istanbul.[26]

Anti-Unionist appointees also made an impression in the province of İzmit. In March 1919, *Arnavud* Mahmud Mahir, a former gendarmerie officer, was named *mutasarrıf* of İzmit. On his watch, Greek and Armenian paramilitary activities reportedly escalated, leading Rıfat Yüce, a local journalist, to accuse the Albanian governor of collaboration with both the Christians and the British occupying forces.²⁷ That winter, Rıfat, with eleven other private citizens and former CUP officials, was brought before the Istanbul Military Tribunal on the charge of committing war crimes, and was later deported to Malta.²⁸ After Mahmud's dismissal in April, another former gendarme, Ahmet Anzavur, filled the position of governor. He too would work closely with local Christians and the British, and was decidedly against the National Movement.²⁹

Yet none of these officers was successful in stemming the growth or influence of the National Movement. Their collective failure to further Loyalist interests in the South Marmara administratively illustrates the critical weakness of the imperial government. Unlike the CUP-turned-National Movement, İsmail Hakkı and others did not possess a deep well of provincial resources (specifically in the form of loyal notables, bureaucrats, gendarmes, or merchants). The Liberty and Understanding Party, as an organization that had been decimated by the CUP during the First World War, simply lacked such a base within the Ottoman bureaucracy and in society to compete with the Unionist's own political machine.

It is important to note that these differences between the capabilities of the CUP and those of the sultan's supporters were not simply structural in nature. Rather, what separated the two reflects an even more profound rupture within the political elite of the Ottoman Empire. If one compares even briefly the dominant Loyalist and Nationalist personalities of the period, one finds profound generational and regional differences defining these two blocks. The Loyalist sympathizers of the post-armistice years were by and large older than their Unionist rivals. While there were several individuals, like *Damat* Ferid, İsmail Hakkı, and *Arnavud* Mahmud, who came from the Balkans, there is no single association, be it regional or otherwise, that might have drawn these men closer to one another. Rather, so-called Loyalists represented several generations of political losers from various walks of life. The continued dominance of the CUP coalition (on both a national and a local level) in a sense wedded the sultanate to anti-Unionist dissidents. In pooling their resources, these two vestiges of antebellum Ottoman authority still possessed the money and the gravitas to empower those who sought to defy the resurgence of the CUP. Precisely who would comprise the Loyalist ground troops was another matter.

BLOOD FEUDS: THE PRELUDE TO REBELLION

At first glance, reports circulating among the Nationalists in September 1919 seemed to indicate that a political contest was beginning to brew around İzmit. Late that summer, a man by the name of *Çerkes* Bekir Sıtkı was wandering among the villages between İzmit and Adapazarı and meeting with Circassian elders. The man, later identified as a former member of the clandestine service and a native of Gönen, purportedly told people that Mustafa Kemal was seeking to unseat the sultan and name himself *padişah*.³⁰ With the financial backing of agents associated with the Liberty and Union Party, several other notorious men aided Bekir Sıtkı's autumn propaganda campaign. Two of the men, Hikmet and Kazım, were notorious *çeteci*s from the region (one having stood trial for murdering the grand vizir at the time of the Bab-ı Ali coup).³¹ Another, (Çule) İbrahim Hakkı, was a member of the Ottoman parliament who had recently returned from exile in Cairo.³² Still others included prominent members of the Bağ, Berzeg, and Çule families.³³ According to Nationalist officials, all those accused of participating in this 'reactionary movement' (*irticai haraket*) were North Caucasians.³⁴

The emergence of these first counter-revolutionaries signalled a pattern to be replicated elsewhere in the South Marmara. Men unrelated to the CUP or the *Kuva-yı Milliye* were initiating a parallel campaign of propaganda and paramilitary recruitment in the region. Money from Istanbul financed this offensive, with Sait Molla's Friends of England Association supposedly leading the way.³⁵ Some were former members of the clandestine service, a fact that was striking, since some, like Bekir Sıtkı, were once intimates of some of the most prominent members of the National Movement.³⁶ Even more noticeable were the seemingly exclusive roles played by Circassians in fomenting anti-Nationalist sentiments. Contemporary sources from this period, however, fail to ask several key questions: What was driving local leaders to welcome anti-Nationalists into their midsts? Why were former servicemen from the *Teşkilat-ı Mahsusa* turning their backs on some of their former comrades? And why were so many leaders involved in this conspiracy in İzmit and elsewhere North Caucasian immigrants? The answers to these questions allude to much broader, complex trends found throughout the South Marmara.

A series of events in Gönen were among the first indications that the Nationalists were unwelcome in significant portions of the region. Lying roughly 150 kilometers north of Balıkesir, this county, with its numerous North Caucasian villages and neighbourhoods, suffered tremendous losses during the Great War. At least 290 men from the county had offered up their lives for the sake of the empire at the Gallipoli, Romanian, and Egyptian fronts.³⁷ Violence between local Circassian paramilitaries and their rivals in the neighbouring province of Biga added to the strains of loss and economic hardship. Tensions would peak with *Kara* Hasan's triumph over *Çerkes* Neş'et's gang during the closing months of the war. Circassian notables smarted from both the injuries caused by the victorious Pomaks from Biga and the official support lent to *Kara* Hasan.³⁸ Non-Circassians in turn rued the habitual raiding of North Caucasians like Neş'et and his men. When Hacim Muhittin arrived in the county in June 1919, he found the region thoroughly divided. Although once a centre of recruitment for the Special Organization, Gönen's North Caucasian notables refused to unite and join the National Movement.³⁹ Hacim was greeted by a similar cold reception in the nearby village of Manyas, another dense centre of Circassian immigrants.⁴⁰

The few Circassian riders from the county that did heed Nationalist appeals did not stay loyal for long.

Violence between rival paramilitary groups flared in other portions of the South Marmara during the Nationalist summer recruitment drive. In Değirmendere, Albanian bands clashed with Laz and Georgian paramilitaries under the Yetimoğlu family.[41] In late September, fighting between Circassian and Bosnian gangs broke out in Burhaniye on the Aegean coast.[42] Although these outbreaks proved to be only minor distractions to Nationalist officers, they foreshadowed a greater explosion in Karacabey in October.

The Modros Armistice brought no peace to the counties of Karacabey and Kirmasti. Following the Albanian coup against Osman and the appointment of (Debreli) Ziya to the post of deputy administrator in Karacabey, Albanian notables solidified their supremacy over the political affairs of the county. On 25 July, a retired Albanian general, Galip Paşa, hosted a meeting between the head of the Liberty and Understanding Party office in Karacabey, *Yağcı* Mahmud (Mahmud the oil-maker), and (Debreli) Ziya. There it was agreed that an independent, state-financed militia would be formed under the command of the notorious *Deli* Hurşid in order to 'maintain security' in the county.[43]

The militia quickly took up its duties, openly patrolling the streets of Karacabey and extracting money from members of the urban *eşraf*. The reign of Hurşid's band soon extended outside Karacabey. In August, the Albanians attacked the coastal village of Kurşunlu, a small but wealthy trading port with a large Rum population. In the midst of the fighting between local village guards and Hurşid's gang of thirty-five militiamen, five houses and a school were destroyed.[44] In surveying the damage, one reporting officer scornfully noted, 'This is a Turkish government. It is not an Albanian government.' Even (Debreli) Ziya had to admit, while confiding in one British officer, that total anarchy reigned in his county.[45]

Circassian notables in Karacabey and Kirmasti followed Hurşid's bloody campaign with a worrying eye. Under the leadership of (Canbazlı) Hakkı, whose horses were stolen by Hurşid in 1918, a coalition to end Albanian rule in Karacabey promptly took shape. Even the Circassian mayor of far-off Manyas, Said Efendi, signed on as a vocal supporter of the endeavour. After an exchange of delegations between the Albanian and Circassian factions produced no results, both sides prepared for an armed showdown. According to one official account, a combined force of 200–300 Albanians under the command of *Deli* Hurşid and his associate *Kasap* Hüseyin (Hüseyin the Butcher) was assembled with the aid of Karacabey's gendarmerie.[46] The Circassians meanwhile found two valuable allies among the many returning veterans of the *Teşkilat-ı Mahsusa*. One, a bandit named *Çerkes* Davut, had participated in the liquidation of Diyarbakır's Armenian population during the war. The other, Şah İsmail, had been an early recruit in *Çerkes* Ethem's Mobile Forces, but had deserted the front after one of Ethem's men burned down his house in a personal dispute. All told, the Circassians themselves mustered a posse of 200 men.⁴⁷

War finally broke out between the two coalitions on the grounds of Galip Paşa's plantation near Karacabey on 15 September 1919. For hours on end, a force of eighty Circassian riders battled Hurşid's contingent of twenty-five men and forced the Albanians to withdraw with heavy casualties. In the days following, Circassians cornered the remaining militiamen and killed Hurşid in the village of Akçeköy. His bullet-ridden body was then transported by donkey to Karacabey, where it was thrown in front of the entrance to the government offices of the town.⁴⁸

In the aftermath of the battle, a nominal peace was declared. While Circassian bands continued to maintain a dominant presence in the region, two detachments of regular army troops from Bandırma and Bursa were sent to Karacabey to maintain order.⁴⁹ The two factions then resumed talks in order to bring about the return of the political status quo, this time convening in the presence of both regular army officers and British representatives. A deputy of Yusuf İzzet Paşa, commander of the regular Ottoman forces in Bandırma, stated in one report that two *Kuva-yı Milliye* officers were dispatched particularly to influence the Circassian factions to lay down their arms.⁵⁰

The fighting did not cease, however. Through October, victorious columns of Circassians from as far away as Manyas, Gönen, and Bayramiç rode out west to Karacabey and engaged in a massive campaign of plunder. The Circassians first targeted the plantation of Galip Paşa, who had given refuge to *Deli* Hurşi's men a few weeks earlier.⁵¹ On 9 October, 300 riders from Manyas attacked a homestead at Torum Çiftlik near Kirmasti, stealing animals and property from the farm.⁵² Throughout this campaign, the primary victims were Albanian landholders. In a letter addressed to the Interior Ministry, Recep Bey, the owner of Marmara Çiftlik, a farm located near Karacabey, detailed the theft of 127 heads of ox, 11 buffalos, 17 stallions, and 480 sheep. The value of this loss, in Recep's estimate, totalled some 19,100 lira in stolen property. In presenting his calculations, this Albanian emphasized that he was a law-abiding citizen who was blessed with good fortune and wealth. Recep also made a point in declaring himself an 'Albanian but one that had been raised in the Turkish lands'.⁵³

After the pillaging of Albanian farms, (Gostivarlı) İbrahim, one of the Liberty and Understanding Party's representatives in Karacabey and an early backer of *Deli* Hurşid, began to lobby the government for restitution of all stolen property.⁵⁴ This demand was evidently heard by the highest-ranking authorities in the empire. Through the autumn and winter of 1919, Ottoman officials amassed a complete tabulation of all stolen property, as well as a list of those accused of theft in the aftermath of the first clashes in Karacabey. According to the official calculation, thousands of animals and hundreds of household items, worth a total of 85,680 lira, were to be returned to their rightful owners.⁵⁵ Ottoman officials were particularly sensitive in the case of Galip Paşa, who, despite his role in initiating the conflict, was repeatedly mentioned as a principal beneficiary of this programme of restitution. While there was some resistance to the government's insistence of restitution, the final tabulation seems to confirm that the majority of articles stolen were returned to their owners.⁵⁶

By the beginning of November, things appeared to have begun to quiet down after two months of hostilities. In the last week of October, Bekir Sami (Günsav) and the new *vali*, Ebubekir Hazım Efendi, personally visited Kirmasti and met with Circassian notables in the town. In his report to Ali Fuat (Cebesoy), commander of the Twentieth Corps in Ankara, Bekir Sami noted that some forty people had been arrested for crimes committed during this period. As for the *çete* leaders, Bekir Sami admitted that none had been apprehended. He pointed out, however, that the Circassians involved in the fighting were 'influential and were [made up of] ruffians' who were supporters of the *Kuva-yı Milliye*.⁵⁷ In a report posted earlier that day from Bursa, Bekir Sami explained to the commander in Çanakkale, Şevket Bey, that there was no 'Circassian–Albanian issue (*Çerkeslik-Arnavudluk meselesi*)' in the region and that Circassian notables in the region would definitely support the National Movement.⁵⁸

Within two weeks of these statements, fighting again flared in Karacabey, this time between regular troops and Circassian paramilitaries. On the night of 4 November, *Yarbay* (Lieutenant-Colonel) Rahmi, commander of the 174th Regiment based in Bursa, arrived in Karacabey with the commander of the Karacabey gendarmerie, Şükrü Bey, and a detachment of soldiers.⁵⁹ Rahmi Bey had been ordered to the town to gain information on ongoing tensions between Albanians and Circassians in the district. Ironically, the two officers stayed the night as the welcome guests of Galip Paşa, who resided in the centre of town. The following day, Karacabey was also visited by a group of well-known militia leaders, Şah İsmail, (Canbazlı) Safer, and his brother Rüstem. An uneasy standoff then ensued. The Circassians, together with an accompanying band of *çeteci*s, openly strolled the streets of Karacabey with their arms, an act that had been forbidden since the first clashes back in September.⁶⁰

The soldiers who had escorted Rahmi into town apparently took exception to this open display of rebellion and resolved to arrest the militia leaders. When one soldier attempted to arrest Safer in a local café with a bayonet, the Circassian and his brother opened fire and mortally wounded the soldier and another bystander. The fighting then spilled into the streets, leading to a pitched, thirty-minute battle encompassing the entire town core. Şah İsmail and his accomplices fled after driving some sixty soldiers into Galip Paşa's townhouse, but not without taking several officers and men hostage. Following the battle, Şah İsmail rode out to Canbaz, where he was joined by (Canbazlı) Hakkı and *Çerkes* Davut. The Circassians proceeded to write three ultimatums addressed to Şükrü himself, demanding the payment of a small 'tax' as well the return of any animals or men left behind in the town. If payment was not rendered, the three warned, the Circassians would attack the town and burn it to the ground. Eventually the demands were met and the captives let go. According to official sources, no effort was made by either *Yarbay* Rahmi or Şükrü Bey to apprehend the three Circassians or their followers. This did not preclude Rahmi, however, from ordering the confiscation of property owned by some locals suspected of supporting the militias.61

The Karacabey/Kirmasti blood feud was a profound turning point in the South Marmara's journey to mass civil violence. Bekir Sami was correct in one sense when he said that there was no 'Albanian–Circassian issue' in the region; neither side fought the other simply on the basis of its ethnic allegiance. The gross acts of murder and larceny committed by local *çeteci*s were manifestations of a deeper political conflict over the right to rule the two counties. Even the pillaging of Albanian farms had a political component, since it would naturally entail the destruction of the economic base that enabled the likes of Galip Paşa and (Gostivarlı) İbrahim to hold sway over the region. For Said Efendi and Şah İsmail, as well as the foot soldiers in their private armies, the conflict was an economic boon during a time of shortages and instability. One could go as far as to say that the original Circassian objection to *Deli* Hurşid's activities had less to do with the destruction of Korşunlu than with the question of who should monopolize the right to pilfer.

A crucial contradiction, however, defined the Nationalist approach to this crisis. Certainly the fighting highlighted a grave trend in the region. Why would Muslims, in the face of the Greek invasions, kill and steal from one another? At a time when the *Kuva-yı Milliye* still hungered for loyal (particularly trained) recruits, Bekir Sami and other officers could not push too far in bringing offending Circassians or Albanians to justice. To do this would mean placing several men, particularly veterans of the clandestine service (arguably the backbone of the National Movement), behind bars. Yet the economic injuries caused by the raiding North Caucasians could not stand. An economic status quo had to be maintained if the loyalty of local notables (regardless of their ethnicity) and the material support they supplied were to be secured.

Many Circassians did not see things in this light. With the return of the stolen property and the propping up of their Albanian rivals, defeat had indeed been snatched from the jaws of victory. More importantly, the violence around Karacabey and Kirmasti underscored an essential dilemma confronting Circassians, as well as others, in the region. Many North Caucasians from Gönen, Karacabey, and other corners of the South Marmara had served faithfully as the CUP's covert operatives during the Great War. Upon their return home from the front, they soon discovered that the state had compensated them and their families with starvation and dead relatives. Now the *Kuva-yı Milliye* (obviously still the CUP with a new set of uniforms) was demanding more sacrifices and another term of service. Particularly after the Karacabey fiasco, which meant a stark reversal not only to many Circassian notables but also to their foot soldiers who gleaned spoils from the conflict for themselves, both veterans and civilians were caught between their loyalties to their former commanders, comrades, and statesmen and the discontent of the population.

There is strong evidence that there was another, more ominous, factor that tipped the balance of Circassian rage against the Nationalists. As the prospects of revolt appeared more imminent, two notables from the environs of Manyas journeyed to Bursa to meet with Bekir Sami (Günsav) on behalf of other local leaders. The two influential men raised a number of issues with Bekir Sami, but their principal question was by far the most dramatic. In Bekir Sami's version of the story, the delegation voiced its concern that the *Kuva-yı Milliye* was imminently seeking to deport Circassians, 'like the Armenians', from their villages.[62] In another version, the two men's line of questioning was more blunt: Were the 'Turks' going to destroy the Circassians because of their 'unity (*ittihad*)' and 'solidarity (*ittifak*)'? The two men, *Kel* Hüseyin and Hasan Tahsin, assured the colonel that the majority of Circassians were still loyal, but were in danger of becoming divided.

Bekir Sami's memoirs are vague as to the answers he gave the two Circassians. Hacim Muhittin would only add that whatever the answer was, Bekir Sami was a patriotic and trustworthy comrade.[63] The fact that Bekir Sami forwarded a synopsis of this meeting to Mustafa Kemal, Ali Fuat (Cebesoy) (commander of the Twentieth Corps in Ankara), and Colonel Şevket (commander of the Bosphorus straits) reflects the seriousness with which this incident was viewed.[64] Together with the fact that the meeting took place *among* Circassians suggests that the threat of deportation was more than a passing rumour. In any case, the implications of this incident lead to two important questions: What led these Circassians to believe that the Nationalists would deport or destroy them? And, most intriguing of all, what does this statement mean in relation to the popular conceptions of the deportation of non-Muslims during the First World War?

To answer these questions, we must again loosen ourselves from the sectarian confines with which the wartime deportations have been understood and related historically. The wartime deportations were massive operations, encompassing tens of thousands of Muslim *and* Christian participants and victims. This mass of humanity did not comprise isolated individuals; they were, after all, the children, neighbours, comrades, business associates, and rivals of individuals living throughout the South Marmara. Many of the most feared and esteemed figures within the Circassian diaspora aided in sending Armenians and Greeks on their way east. Still others were responsible for filling mass graves with these innocent civilians.[65] Even where there were no direct relations to be had, Circassian living in the South Marmara could not have been immune to the sight of thousands of Armenian, Greek, and even Albanian deportees flooding the roads. The deportations of the First World War were, in short, a mass experience for all who lived through it.

The reference to the 'unity' and the 'solidarity' of the Circassians suggests to us an innate understanding of the communities in which these two men lived and which they represented. To be a Circassian in the South Marmara (and throughout the Ottoman lands) meant that one shared in the common experience and heritage of exile and displacement from the Caucasus. Most of the North Caucasians found within the villages and towns of the South Marmara lived within tightly knit communities in which where their language, customs, and manner of dress formed symbolic bonds among them. Relationships that were forged among and between Adige, Abkhazians, Georgians, and Chechens often extended beyond their immediate surroundings, not only to other villages and towns but to the capital as well. North Caucasians in turn often went to war together, established businesses with one another, and married into each other's families. Coupled with this was the martial potential found within the Circassian paramilitary networks based in the South Marmara, an element that brought them to the forefront of imperial policy and war making.

Kel Hüseyin and Hasan Tahsin's reference to unity and solidarity also suggests an understanding of the Young Turk perception of the threat posed by Armenians, Greeks, and Albanians in the South Marmara during the First World War. The danger underlying the presence of these groups was not so much a product of their ethnicity or political sympathies as it was their *physical concentration* within the region. As mass collectives in which Rum tradesmen, Armenian revolutionaries, and Albanian ruffians lived and worked, three groups that clearly threatened the CUP, these compact communities represented bastions of resistance to Istanbul's political or economic influence. The deportations served to break up these concentrations, in order to pave the way for a more centralized administration whereby the CUP could expand its authority over the countryside.

Considering the depth and complexity of the Circassian networks in the South Marmara, Hüseyin and Hasan Tahsin had reason to fear that the same policies would be visited upon them as well. As a source of special recruits into the *Teşkilat-ı Mahsusa*, Circassians in the South Marmara were spared any attempt towards resettlement during the war (as seen in the correspondence between the *vali* of Hüdavendigar and Istanbul in 1917). The chaos and political reshuffling following the Modros Armistice further unsettled the political and social positions of many Circassians, as paramilitary violence and economic inequality heightened intercommunal tensions to new levels. In the wake of the feuding at Karacabey, imperial administrators ceased to view locally appointed Circassians and Albanians as trustworthy. No Albanian or Circassian employed in an official capacity, one imperial memorandum declared, could be 'free from suspicion (*zandan azade kalmamakta*)' and eventually all must be replaced by 'Turks'.[66] In December 1919, the Interior Ministry stipulated that Turkish law enforcement officials and civil administrators be employed in Albanian, Circassian, and Georgian villages in order to improve security and to regularize local government.[67] These swift changes in administration were accompanied with a selective round of deportations among Albanians involved in the fighting.[68] At the same time, once respected avenues of political negotiation and advancement, such as the *Teşkilat-ı Mahsusa* and the sultanate, were gradually closed down, discredited, or co-opted by a revamped Unionist organization, the *Kuva-yı Milliye*. One could assume that for Hasan Tahsin and Kel Hüseyin, all these shifts in the local winds left many questions as to where Circassians fitted in this new scheme of things.

In a collection of essays published after the War of Independence, Hasan Çantay noted in retrospect: 'During that time, Circassian and Albanian bandits fought one another as enemies. But the two nations also did not refrain from their atrocities and torment of helpless Turkish villagers.'[69] What is particularly revealing in this statement is Hasan's allusion to 'atrocities' on Turkish villagers. Within the pages of the reports related to the violence in Karacabey and Kirmasti, there is no specific mention of a terror campaign against Turkish villages. This statement nevertheless expresses a belief that the violence exposed a fundamental difference between these two immigrant populations and the 'Turks' of the empire. Çantay confirms the formulaic stereotype that we have encountered before: (assimilated) Turks and (unassimilated) Circassians and Albanians. His highlighting of bandits (*şakiler*), however, takes this characterization one step further. Rather than localize the difference between these three groups as the result of some ethnic character flaw, Çantay adds that this also had a socio-economic dimension. In an essay he wrote in 1918 on 'The Banditry Question', he stated quite pointedly that bandits target the wealthiest villages and constitute a threat to the honour and livelihood of both the state and the honest citizen.[70] By extension, Hasan Çantay's indictment of Albanians and Circassians seems to suggest that they were also the economic losers of the region, a group that had to be controlled lest they destroy the economic foundation of the state.

'PROTECTOR OF THE GOVERNMENT AND SLAVE TO THE SHARIAH': RECONSIDERING THE RISE OF AHMET ANZAVUR

Considering his physical state and his pedigree, (Ançok) Ahmet Anzavur did not look the part of a great imperial commander. Born in the Caucasus at some point before the great exodus of 1864, he was by all accounts an old man in the autumn of 1919. He was functionally illiterate, but had spent most of his professional career as a captain in the gendarmerie. It may be said that he owed everything to the palace. His appointment to the gendarmerie came at the intercession of his sister, a consort of Abdülhamid II. Years of loyal service earned him luxurious gifts from the sultan and a townhouse in his adopted home of Biga. The CUP, however, cut him loose after the overthrow of Abdülhamid II in 1909. Ahmet Anzavur returned to duty only upon the recommendation of a high-ranking Circassian general, and served briefly as an inspector in the *Teşkiat-ı Mahsusa*. At war's end, Anzavur was to be found at home in Biga among his collection of racehorses.

The growing divide between Istanbul and the Nationalists of inner Anatolia halted Ahmet Anzavur's slow crawl to obscurity. Although the nature of his relationship with Sultan Vahdeddin appears murky, both Loyalists and Nationalists recognized that Anzavur was held in high regard in the capital and that his allegiance rested with the palace. He was appointed governor (*mutasarrıf*) of İzmit in the spring of 1919 and was repeatedly rumoured to be high on the list for the governor's chair in Karesi. The Nationalists feared Ahmet Anzavur. But before the autumn of 1919, there was little indication of his absolute intentions and capabilities.

That mystery formally ended on 25 October 1919. Before a crowd of Circassians gathered at a racetrack in Manyas, Ahmet Anzavur delivered his first of many addresses to the local inhabitants of the South Marmara. According to a telegram from the head of the Gönen chapter of the *Müdafaa-ı Hukuk*, *Müftü* Şevket Efendi, Anzavur declared to those who had gathered that he was assembling an army to march on Balıkesir in order to arrest (or kill) Nationalist commander Hacim Muhittin (Çarıklı).[71] This threat was soon followed by two telegrams from Anzavur, the first to the sultan and the second addressed to Karesi *mutasarrıf* Ali Rıza. The first telegram, written on behalf of those living in the towns of Manyas and Aşklar, accused the *Redd-i İlhak*, despite its attempt to oust the Greeks from Aydın and to block the formation of an Armenian state in the east, of attempting a coup against the *padişah*. While Anzavur conceded that many simple-minded individuals (presumably Muslims) were misled into following the Nationalists, the prospect of a *Redd-i İlhak* putsch against the caliph and his state represented an assault on the entire Islamic world. Defeating the Nationalists therefore became a matter for all believers.[72] In his second telegram to Ali Rıza, Anzavur declared that the 'founders and administrators' of the *Kuva-yı Milliye* were in fact the same Unionists who had for years grown wealthy while 'the poor nation shed their blood and saw their homes destroyed'. The sultan, Anzavur explained, understood that the people had lost patience with the opportunism of the Unionists and was now gathering an imperial force to save the nation. He specifically called upon the Balıkesir chapter of the Defence of Rights to refrain from its activities and to unite behind the sultan's army, a force that would demand no monetary support from the people of Karesi.[73]

Nationalists in Istanbul, Balıkesir, and Bursa understood the threats and accusations embedded within these telegrams and immediately moved to counter Anzavur's actions. It emerged early on that among the men rumoured to have met with Anzavur was a suspected member of the *Nigehban* Association, Captain Ali Kemal.⁷⁴ In addition to his activities with this known anti-Nationalist organization, *İngiliz* Ali Kemal, an Albanian, was also aide-de-camp to Kiraz Ahmet Hamdi Paşa, commander of the Fifth Corps and a personal attendant of Sultan Vahdeddin.⁷⁵ His association with Ahmet Anzavur confirmed the Nationalist suspicions first garnered from Bekir Sıtkı's activities in İzmit and Adapazarı that the Istanbul government was laying the foundations for a military response to the National Movement.⁷⁶ Still, Hacim Muhittin feared that British forces might look upon a 'spilling of blood between Muslims' (*beynel'islam bir kan dökülmesi*) as an invitation to expand their occupation of the region.⁷⁷ This was a sentiment also shared by Mustafa Kemal, who directed Kazım (Özalp) and *Çerkes* Ethem to avoid bloodshed in settling the matter.⁷⁸

Ahmet Anzavur swiftly demonstrated that his threats were not hollow. During the first two weeks of November, he and a cohort of faithful followers criss-crossed the provinces of Karesi and Hüdavendigar, attacking government offices and soldiers, delivering speeches, and gathering more men to his side.⁷⁹ Circassians in Karacabey, Kirmasti, Gönen, and Manyas flocked to meet the aging gendarme by the hundreds. North Caucasian *çeteci*s fresh from their conflict with the Albanians of Karacabey, such as Şah İsmail, *Çerkes* Davut, and others, soon joined up with Anzavur.⁸⁰ Small groups of Çetmi, an indigenous group related to the Alevis of eastern Anatolia, pledged their allegiance to the gathering army.⁸¹ Angry politics made strange bedfellows out of former enemies. Despite a previous case of bad blood, (Gostivarlı) İbrahim and other Albanians in Kirmasti joined the ranks of *Çerkes* Davut's gang in a mutual understanding to bring down the *Kuva-yı Milliye*.⁸²

Seeing that bloodshed was imminent, Kazım (Özalp) commissioned one of his trusted lieutenants, (Köprülülü) Hamdi, to meet with Ahmet Anzavur to negotiate an end to hostilities before the shooting began. At the meeting, Hamdi offered Anzavur the opportunity to take part in the defence of the Aegean in exchange for a cession of hostilities.⁸³ Anzavur's immediate response is not known; however, he did purportedly agree to meet with Hacim Muhittin the following day. But when the morning arrived, Anzavur never showed.⁸⁴

Within days of the failed meeting, official Nationalist communications began to describe Ahmet Anzavur as the leader of 'a movement to shatter the peace (*harekat-ı asayiş-şikenaneleri*)' and a threat to the *Kuva-yı Milliye*.⁸⁵ In reducing Anzavur to the role of a mere criminal, the Nationalist leadership in the South Marmara, Ankara, and the capital also labelled the Circassian as nothing more than a tool (*alet*) of the British, the sultan, and the Liberty and Understanding Party.⁸⁶ Anzavur's movement, Ali Fuat (Cebesoy) would claim, was clearly 'abetted by the very highest circles in Istanbul'.⁸⁷

Consternation within the Nationalist camp further swelled as the number of Circassians answering Ahmet Anzavur's call to arms grew. Whispers of a growing 'Circassian-Turkish issue (*Çerkes-Türklük meselesi*)' swirled in reports and news accounts in early November.⁸⁸ Initially Bekir Sami (Günsav), himself a native of Manyas, dismissed the idea that his people were turning their backs on the National Movement. He stated in a report on 19 November that 'The Ahmet Anzavur incident is absolutely not a Circassian issue. Ahmet Bey has not seduced any of the Circassians. Right now there are only ten to fifteen people at his side. I cannot believe that he will be able to create a mass movement (*umumi bir hareket*) from the districts of Manyas and Gönen when as many as forty people joined him from Susurluk.'⁸⁹ Later, in an especially revealing moment of desperation and distress, Bekir Sami confided in his commanding officer and fellow Circassian, Yusuf İzzet, his perceptions of the gravity of this moment:

On 22 October 1919, I went in conjunction with the *vali* [Ebubekir Hazım Bey] to Karacabey and Kirmasti in regards to Ahmet Anzavur and the Circassian Question. At that time I saw some of the leaders of the Circassians who were seduced by Anzavur and influenced by such propaganda as 'the *Kuva-yı Milliye* will deport the Circassians.' A certain portion of the Circassians was simply carried away by such contrary ideas about the *Kuva-yı Milliye*.

While looking to my own feelings, it must be kept in mind that there are between six and a dozen Circassians who are in the vanguard of the *Kuva-yı Milliye*.

During the course of his encounter with the locals of Karacabey and Kirmasti, Bekir Sami purportedly addressed his fellow immigrants as follows:

The National Forces are strictly concerned with an independent Turkey. We are grateful to the Ottomans who graciously accepted those Circassians who abandoned the Caucasus in the name of religion and all things sacred. I declare that it is necessary to condemn all actions that are not becoming of Circassian national history. At this time I am an Ottoman regimental commander, but I request of you, Circassians, as co-nationals and co-religionists, who love their nation, do not partake in any incident that is against the state. Do not partake in pillaging, stealing or any evil act resembling these things. I say to you, support the *Kuva-yı Milliye*! The Circassian notables who have listened to me speaking of these things have agreed and sworn allegiance. I submit [this to you] to rouse your energies and attention, so that henceforth our people, our co-nationals, do not become the instrument of a corrupt man.⁹⁰

Bekir Sami's framing of Ahmet Anzavur within the context of the Circassian diaspora and Circassian identity is a curious one. The report is in a sense an acknowledgement of the influence that Ahmet Anzavur had within North Caucasian circles in the South Marmara. Yet, if his pleas to Circassians are to be accepted as genuine, Bekir Sami appears to have consciously avoided the communal nature of Circassian anger and resistance to the *Kuva-yı Milliye*. According to this line of thinking, an act of brigandage or an attack on townspeople is not a local matter inspired by local events, but a political crime, a crime against the state. It is in this regard that Bekir Sami's argument takes a very interesting turn. By citing the heritage of exile from the Caucasus and imploring Circassians to remember the generosity of the Ottoman state, Bekir clearly attempts to play on the heartstrings of his 'co-nationals'. In short, supporting the *Kuva-yı Milliye* is the duty of a good Circassian and is befitting of their noble history of fealty to their adopted land. But there is an obvious gap within this argument. Did the *Kuva-yı Milliye* necessarily represent or embody the same Ottoman state that gave shelter to Circassian refugees in the middle of the nineteenth century? More importantly, did this matter?

Anzavur and the *Kuva-yı Milliye* finally came to blows on 15 November 1919 near the village of Demirkapı, just north of Balıkesir. The battle lasted two days, with Anzavur's forces, now called the Army of Mohammed (*Kuva-yı Muhammediye*), suffering the most casualties.[91] Over the following days Anzavur's forces retreated north through Susurluk, where they were hotly pursued by (Köprülülü) Hamdi. By 20 November, the Nationalist detachments following Anzavur were joined by *Kara* Hasan's Pomaks, as well as a detachment of cavalry lead by *Çerkes* Ethem.[92] The fighting continued for another two weeks, as the two sides clashed in a series of engagements in Gönen, Manyas, Karacabey, Biga, and Susurluk. After a big battle between Anzavur's Circassians and a mixed detachment composed of Nationalist regulars and *Kara* Hasan's *çete*, Anzavur, his son Kadir, Şah İsmail, and *Çerkes* Davut, disbanded and scattered among the villages and towns of Kale-i Sultaniye, Karesi, and Hüdavendigar.[93]

With winter setting in, the *Kuva-yı Milliye* turned to a man of considerable gravitas to help convince Anzavur's followers to lay down their arms. Of all the Circassians who had come to the aid of the Nationalists in the South Marmara, (Big) Ahmet Fevzi Paşa arguably represented the very height of the pre-CUP Ottoman military establishment. In addition to being an Abkhazian immigrant from the district of Düzce, his service to the state was long and storied.[94] Having arrrived in the South Marmara ostensibly to 'admonish' Circassians for the violence of the previous month, he toured the environs of Manyas and Gönen in order to win back support for the *Kuva-yı Milliye*.[95] The tour was a failure. Ahmet Fevzi later told Kazım (Özalp) that the people of Manyas appeared to be biding their time for another opportunity to rise up.[96]

Ahmet Anzavur, for his part, appeared undaunted, despite his initial reversals. In January, he posted two conciliatory letters to *Kara* Hasan, each attempting to explain to his Pomak rival the greater danger posed by *Kuva-yı Milliye*:

It is known by everyone that orderliness is the most important duty of the state and nation, since everywhere that one finds perfect security, [one finds] the justice of Islam. . . . [Koca Suleyman, an unidentified elder] . . . has explained that the wicked Unionists and Free Masons are the ones who have brought forth the marauding and banditry to this Islamic government for the last ten years. He curses these people. They have violently effected this situation, [even] calling you a bandit. . . . In the time when the children and women of martyrs were eating grass and earth and dying of hunger, [the Unionists] took official possession of their homes. In the time when those traitors in the military offices were having helva and lamb feasts, they were taking houses as bribes from *Musevi* Nesim [Nesim the Jew] and others. . . . I wish to try all of those who pray five times a day so that they will be accountable to God. . . . Have recourse to the *müftü* and take the correct fatwa. Do not assist one individual from those intractable Muslims. I ask this: who is it that denied to us the religious sacredness of the exalted peace of the Prophet and the Qa'aba to which Muslims pray? Who is it that cast Muslim children into the sea at the Straits of Çanakkale? Who is it who destroyed these children in the Caucasus Mountains, in the deserts of the Arab lands, in Iran, in Janinna and in the mountains of Romania? Are they not the young Free Masons who today gave documents to a hundred thousand Muslim women and girls in Istanbul and made them into prostitutes? Currently there can categorically be no other party other than the Party of Mohammed that can save our Muslim brothers. . . . I shall pursue those vile men who have besmirched the caliph and the Muslim state. I shall be a protector of the government and a slave according to the just decrees of our Shariah.[97]

The language used above provides a fairly complete encapsulation of the reasoning and rhetoric invoked by Ahmet Anzavur. Here the Committee for Union and Progress, and its unnamed successor, the *Kuva-yı Milliye*, takes centre stage as the sole culprits responsible for the nation's ills. But in Anzavur's summation, this body of 'Unionists and Free Masons' denotes something more than just a political party. Rather, his evocation of the CUP seems to implicate a much larger circle of characters taken from day-to-day life in the South Marmara. If we include previous statements in this equation, the CUP comes to encompass a broad list of partisans and patsies, including landowners, recruiters, bureaucrats, quartermasters, traders, foreigners, and bandits.[98] These were the men who, as Anzavur eloquently put it, condemned the mothers of dead soldiers to devour grass while they grew fat. Through this description of both the CUP and the physical state of the South Marmara, Anzavur paints his revolt as an act of vengeance aimed at those truly responsible for the hardships incurred by immigrant Circassians, Pomaks, Çetmi, Albanians, and others like them.

Anzavur's use of Islamic imagery suggests an even starker base of comparison between himself and the National Movement. In what appears to have been a carefully chosen set of phrases, Anzavur appears to tell *Kara* Hasan that the Committee of Union and Progress's moral culpability extends beyond the economic ruin of the nation; he points a finger at the CUP as a clique of Free Masons who have defied the will of the Islamic world by slandering and taking up arms against the exalted Islamic government in Istanbul. While statements such as these appear to testify to the political (or rather holy) legitimacy of his position, Ahmet Anzavur's depiction of the CUP as a clique of Free Masons adds the connotation that the Unionists are nothing more than outsiders. In certain ways, this accusation reflects the popular understanding of the origins of the party in Salonika, an environment where Free Masons, Ottoman nationalists, and Westernizers of various shades are said to have mixed in the city's harbour front cafés. If placed within the context of the tight-knit communities of the South Marmara, however, the perceived distance between Anzavur's accusations and reality may not have been great. As a group that wore Western clothes, drank alcohol, and attended school in Istanbul and the provincial capitals, many Unionist 'Turks' in both town and country stood out among the masses of people who continued to wear traditional dress, speak in dialect, and never learn to read. This must certainly have been true of Ahmet Anzavur, an immigrant whose age and lack of education denied him entrance into Young Turk circles. When seen in the larger socio-economic context of the South Marmara, Anzavur's juxtaposition of the *Kuva-yı Milliye* and the CUP presents an effort to highlight the differences between urban, upwardly mobile Nationalist supporters and the more traditional elites of the villages.

As the long winter of 1920 turned to spring, Anzavur prepared for his second attack upon the Nationalists. Again he used his position as an emissary of the sultan and a noted member of the Circassian diaspora to fan populist rage. Meanwhile, Nationalist countermeasures served only to expand the ranks of the Loyalist insurgency.

In the first week of January 1920, former Edremit *kaymakam* Hamdi (Köprülülü) arrived in Biga with his aide-de-camp (Dramalı) Rıza Bey and forty mounted troops.[99] Through the course of 1919, Hamdi Bey had already begun to establish himself as a leading commander within ranks of the *Kuva-yı Milliye*. Since the armistice, Hamdi had been active in the resistance campaign in western Anatolia. After Izmir's occupation in May, Hamdi took part in the fighting along the Ayvalık front and became a close associate of Kazım (Özalp), a fellow native, possibly Albanian, of his hometown in Macedonia.[100] As the newly appointed military administrator of Biga, Hamdi's first task was to negotiate the dissolution of *Kara* Hasan's band. Despite *Kara* Hasan's cooperation with the Nationalists, Hamdi demanded the surrender of the Pomak's weapons, stating that there could not be 'two roosters in the henhouse'.[101] Hasan instead chose to stall Hamdi, assuring him of his loyalty while refusing to disband his militia. Soon thereafter Hamdi arrested the Pomak along with the majority of his band.[102]

(Köprülülü) Hamdi's consolidation of Biga under Nationalist control was closely followed by a general effort at acquiring new arms and recruits for the *Kuva-yı Milliye* from the area. This was in part supplied through Hamdi's daring raid on the Akbaş arms depot, a large cache of decommissioned arms located near Çanakkale.[103] But this celebrated exploit of Hamdi's leadership represented an isolated endeavour within the Nationalists' much larger enterprise within the Biga area. Between February and March 1920, Hamdi and his entourage toured the villages surrounding Biga, taking arms and conscripts to be sent to the Aegean front. Village *muhtar*s were also recruited as tax farmers and required to raise a set sum of money from their constituents every week for the Nationalist cause.[104] These efforts towards building a Nationalist base in Biga subsequently earned Hamdi the ire of many of Biga's residents. With the arrest and imprisonment of *Kara* Hasan, the *Kuva-yı Milliye* inadvertently fused together two groups that had previously been at each others' throats: Pomaks and Circassians. Having lost their advocate at the hands of the Nationalists, the surviving members of *Kara* Hasan's band and other Pomak dissidents found common cause with many Circassians in Biga, Gönen, and elsewhere. At the fulcrum of this new paramilitary alliance was the now famous anti-Nationalist, Ahmet Anzavur.

On Monday morning, 16 February 1920, gunfire rang out in the streets of Biga as the vanguard of Anzavur's motley army entered the town. Witnesses watched as 'men of every sort of dress, immigrants, Circassians, Pomaks and others . . . a group with firearms, all villagers' gathered in front of the government offices, kissing and greeting one another.[105] As the town fell into the hands of the insurgents, Hamdi is said to have been at the city's gendarmerie offices. Upon hearing the sound of gunfire, he and his second-in-command, Kani Bey, rushed to the weapons depot outside town. The few men accompanying them refused to carry out Hamdi's orders to return to the town, saying that they would not fire upon their fellow citizens. Instead, Hamdi dispatched his executive officer to the town jail with orders to execute *Kara* Hasan. Kani promptly carried out the order, mowing down Hasan and thirteen others in cold blood.[106]

Upon hearing the news of Hasan's death, the villagers occupying the town square took matters into their own hands and attacked Kani Bey's house. The officer initially managed to escape from the house with the assistance of a neighbour, but was eventually cut down by the mob's bullets.[107] Hamdi meanwhile fled Biga, hoping to link up with a detachment of gendarmes in nearby Yenice under the command of another Nationalist sympathizer, (Dramalı) Ali Rıza. Along the way, however, a party of Pomaks cornered the officer. The Pomaks then bound Hamdi, beat him with sticks, and broke his neck. In addition to Kani and Hamdi, the rebels killed another twenty gendarmes and other sympathizers that day.[108] Before a howling crowd in Biga, the leader of the Pomak rebels, *Gavur* İmam Fevzi, would declare that (Köprülülü) Hamdi had tried to snap off the necks of the people, but it was now he who had had his neck snapped.[109]

Anzavur and his swelling army of thousands consolidated their great victory in Biga over the following month. A committee of three local notable business and paramilitary leaders convened in order to coordinate dissidents in the town. Three days after Biga was occupied, Nationalists dispatched a former regional inspector from Çanakkale, Simah Rifat Bey, to plead with the townspeople to return to the fold. After Simah's appeal in the centre of town, a crowd of Circassians shouted back, 'We don't want the *Kuva-yı Milliye!*'[110] In the middle of March Circassians and Pomaks again joined together to beat back a Nationalist column of 500 men sent to retake the town. Anzavur personally led the defenders into action, many of whom carried only axes or sticks.[111]

The news continued to get worse for the Nationalists. After their second defeat in Biga, several officers attached to the regular army and scores of men retreating towards Gönen deserted in mass.[112] A similar incident was reported days later in Kirmasti, where virtually an entire regiment deserted with their weapons.[113] Anzavur meanwhile seized upon the *Kuva-yı Milliye*'s failure at Biga and gathered more men from the surrounding areas to march on Gönen.[114] In the face of the impending attack, still more soldiers from the regular army in Gönen deserted their positions. According to the explanation given to Rahmi Bey, who commanded the National Forces in Gönen, fifty-four deserting soldiers declared that they 'would not open fire on the people (*halk*)', and in turn joined the resistance.[115] On 4 April, the combined forces of Ahmet Anzavur and Gavur İmam, numbering between 2,000 and 3,000 men, entered Gönen after meeting little resistance.[116] An orgy of looting and executions followed. Gönen and several outlying villages were sacked. Even homes belonging to Circassians who had not supported Anzavur were torched during this period.[117] By 6 April, Bandırma, Karacabey, and Kirmasti fell to the Army of Mohammed in rapid succession.[118]

With Anzavur's men pushing towards Bursa, Edremit, and Balıkesir, Nationalists in the South Marmara knew that they were staring into the abyss. Rumours of assassination plots against the top leadership circulated.[119] Despite Bekir Sami's directives to punish 'idiot' Circassian beys 'with extreme prejudice' (*en sert şekilde cezalandırılmasını gerekiyor*), a substantial portion of once loyal North Caucasians were lost to the National Movement.[120] British reports go further in suggesting the scope of Circassian defiance. Contacts made by officers in the field foretold coordinate assaults against the *Kuva-yı Milliye* by previously unengaged Circassian *çeteci*s in İzmit (under (Çule) İbrahim Hakkı) and Yalova. The Laz *ulema*, the report continued, would follow Anzavur's lead, and even Armenians based in the capital would join in the rising.[121] With words and with a bit of money, London wagered on Anzavur's success.

Among Istanbul's Albanian elite, however, the mood was different. The report declared that Albanian notables in the capital were largely neutral regarding the conflict and viewed it as one simply between the government and the Nationalists. But *Damat* Ferid's government expressed the hope that two prominent Albanian generals, *Kara* Sait and Nazif Paşas, could be used to turn the tide in Istanbul's favour. The grand vizir also placed hope in the work of *İngiliz* Ali Kemal, who was said to have a good deal of influence among young officers. If the word was given, one British observer declared, these Albanians would also take part in 'annihilating' the *Kuva-yı Milliye*.[122]

This understanding of the Albanian diaspora's role in aiding and prosecuting Anzavur's rebellion, even if it contains only a kernel of truth, underscores many of the comparative paradoxes between Albanians and Circassians. On the face of things, many Albanians in the South Marmara shared the same grievances as the Circassians, Pomaks, and other groups among Anzavur's host of rebels. Yet both documentary evidence and the accounts provided by contemporary observers tell of only piecemeal support among Albanians at this point. Considering the prevalence of paramilitarism among the Albanian communities of Karacabey, Değirmendere, and İzmit, as well as the relative strength and influence of the Albanian elite in Istanbul, this fact seems to run contrary to expectations. Why, at the threshold of rebellion, would Albanians appear to stand aside?

The answer to this question may lie in a combination of factors. One should consider the fragmentation of the Albanian diaspora of the South Marmara in comparison to the density and cohesion of many Circassian communities. Many Albanians were newcomers to the region and were without extensive social networks. Circassian rebels, by contrast, were descendants of refugees who had put down roots in the South Marmara decades in advance. The epicentre of the revolt, the triangle between Biga, Gönen, and Manyas, was a region that Ahmet Anzavur was well familiar with. Within these counties only a few Albanians were found scattered among the heavily populated Circassian and Pomak villages. Perhaps the written historical record is for some reason intentionally biased in highlighting the roles of Circassians. Or perhaps there is some element of the conflict that is still hidden from the view of the contemporary observer, such as a new or continuing dispute between the two sides on the scale of the Karacabey blood feud. It is not clear.

In this dark hour for the *Kuva-yı Milliye*, a familiar face came to the rescue. Çerkes Ethem was again called upon to break up Anzavur's rebels and was given command of 2,000 men gathered from throughout the Aegean front.[123] On 16 April, at Yahyaköy, a village located on the road between Kirmasti and Susurluk, Anzavur met a resounding defeat.[124] Nationalist troops from Bursa meanwhile pressed westward against Çerkes Davut and other Loyalists in the Kirmasti and Karacabey region. On 19 April, Ethem reclaimed Bandırma for the *Kuva-yı Milliye*.[125] The fall of Bandırma marked the steady disintegration of the Army of Mohammed. Gavur İmam, who had been ordered to move against Balıkesir, was driven back to Biga by Kazım (Özalp) and Ethem's second-in-command, Parti Pehlivan.[126] From Gönen, Anzavur purportedly raged against the grand vizir, *Damat* Ferid, and demanded that a new Minister of War be appointed in order to resupply his forces.[127] It was not to be. Before the end of April, Ahmet Anzavur boarded an English ship docked in Karabiga's harbour and departed for Istanbul.[128] His forces meanwhile, as after the first uprising, simply melted back into the landscape.

With Anzavur gone, the *Kuva-yı Milliye* reasserted itself in the South Marmara with a fury. Çerkes Ethem, along with his brothers Reşit and Tevfik, took the lead in mopping up the rebels.[129] The leaders of the revolt in Biga were hung in the town square.[130] Other public executions of Anzavur supporters were carried out in Lapseki and Kirmasti.[131] Although details are limited, the people of Gönen and Manyas suffered considerable acts of retribution, including executions, forced exile, and destruction of property.[132] Nationalist officers supposedly also threatened the Christian population of Biga with deportation for their support of the Loyalist rebellion. Members of the town's Muslim population opposed this action, however, threatening to abandon Biga themselves if the deportations were carried out. With that, the Nationalist authorities abandoned their plans.[133]

A VILLAGE SAINT'S LAST ACT: THE İZMİT UPRISING AND THE DEATH OF AHMET ANZAVUR

On the heels of Anzavur's defeat at Yahyaköy, a second revolt enveloped villages and towns east of Adapazarı. Tensions appear to have suddenly exploded on 13 April when a Circassian and Abkhazian mob shot two *Kuva-yı Milliye* officers on the outskirts of Düzce.[134] As in Biga two months before, a crowd of thousands then marched on the town and established a *de facto* government under (Berzeg) Safer and (Maan) Koç, two Circassians who were earlier associated Bekir Sıtkı's Loyalist circle.[135] Among Safer's lieutenants was (Maan) Ali, a founding member of the *Teşkilat-ı Mahsusa* and an early compatriot of Eşref Kuşçubaşı.[136] Within a week of Düzce's occupation, a wave of duplicate assaults swept across the northern half of the province, with the towns of Bolu, Hendek, Mucur, Girede, and Beypazarı falling in rapid succession.[137] On 23 April, a committee headed by (Karzeg) Sait, a Circassian notable from Adapazarı, attempted to meet with rebels from Hendek in order to resolve the crisis without further bloodshed.[138] When the two sides met in a village on the road between the two towns, the insurgents shot Sait and his companion dead.[139] Thereafter Adapazarı also fell under the influence of the rebels.[140]

A similar series of Nationalist missteps preceded this outbreak. According to Rifat Yüce, Eşref Kuşçubaşı, then a commander on the İzmit front, proved highly unpopular among both the moneyed classes of Adapazarı and the local Circassian and Abkhazian elite.[141] Like the condemned (Köprülülü) Hamdi, Eşref demanded high taxes from Adapazarı's notables, extracting 100,000 liras from one merchant family alone.[142] By mid-April, local civic leaders in Adapazarı had had enough of Eşref Kuşçubaşı. It is at this point that (Karzeg) Sait convened a committee to negotiate his departure. Interestingly, this group of notables included individuals who openly advocated an end to the *Kuva-yı Milliye*'s occupation of the town, including (Maan) Şirin, another former *Teşkilat-ı Mahsusa* officer of Abkhazian extraction.[143] The Nationalist headquarters in Ankara also demanded that Eşref leave the city immediately and be replaced by a regular army officer. Claiming that the son of the sultan's falconer was stealing from the population, Sait declared Eşref nothing more than a guerrilla (*komiteci*).[144] After some wrangling, Eşref did vacate Adapazarı, leaving the command of Nationalist forces in the region in question.[145]

This confusion in the upper echelons of the *Kuva-yı Milliye* created an opening for the Loyalist opposition. On 9 April, rebels burned a bridge on the road between Adapazarı and Hendek. Just before leaving his post, Eşref declared this an act of rebellion and called upon local gendarmes to break up the rebels. Instead, the commander of the gendarmes fled and left the region in Loyalist hands.146

According to the papers released during the deliverance of Mustafa Kemal's *Nutuk*, the Nationalist government immediately recognized the gravity of the situation in Düzce and ordered the rebellion to be crushed.147 The capture of Düzce, Adapazarı, Hendek, and Beypazarı had effectively closed the road between Istanbul and the Anatolian interior. Although the capital had fallen under an official British occupation since March, Istanbul was still a vital source of men and material for the National Movement. Moreover, the spread of the Loyalist opposition to Düzce and Beypazarı threatened the security of Ankara and the end of Mustafa Kemal's government itself. Through the month of May, Nationalist detachments pulled in from İzmit, Zongudak, and the Black Sea gradually moved against the resistance, taking back the region almost village by village.148 On 23 May, *Çerkes* Ethem arrived in the town of Geyve fresh from mopping up the remnants of the Anzavur uprising. Ethem's Mobile Forces then moved east against the heart of the rebellion, taking Adapazarı and Sabanca without a fight.149 Along the way, he ordered the destruction of villages that had been declared in league with the Loyalists.150 On 26 May, he entered the town of Düzce and promptly executed both (Berzeg) Safer and his Abkhazian associate, (Maan) Koç. The third leader of the Düzce rebels, (Maan) Ali, meanwhile had managed to flee the town.151

With the outbreak of revolt in Düzce, *Damat* Ferid's government decided to intervene. On 18 April, the government announced the creation of its own army, the *Kuva-yı İnzibatiye* (The Disciplinary Forces), a body with the express purpose of 'doing away with the organization carrying the name the *Kuva-yı Milliye*, which had forcibly impeded government officials from carrying out the state's laws'.152 Composed of more than 1,000 unemployed soldiers from Istanbul and officers loyal to the *Nigehban*, this new Loyalist force, under the command of Süleyman Şefik Paşa, arrived in İzmit on 4 May.153 However, after a meeting on 26 April, it was announced that Ahmet Anzavur (now elevated to the rank of *paşa*) would have his own command in the region.154 With some 500 men brought by him from Biga, Anzavur arrived in İzmit four days after the *Kuva-yı İnzibatiye* came into town.155

Ahmet Anzavur's contribution to the Loyalist campaign around İzmit was brief and dismal. In more than a week of fighting with both the Nationalists and the local population, Anzavur suffered a broken leg and withdrew his men to Istanbul. The *Kuva-yı İnzibatiye* lasted a few weeks longer, but was ultimately forced to retreat by the end of June. For roughly a year after his last defeat, it is unclear what became of the old man. At some point he returned to the environs north of Biga, again collecting a small band of devoted followers. In May 1921, a group of pro-Nationalist paramilitary leaders got wind of Anzavur's movements and decided to put an end to the former rebel. The arch-conspirator in this group was later revealed to be *Arnavud* Rahman, whose gang had held sway over the environs of Karabiga since the First World War. Rahman's men ambushed Anzavur outside Karabiga and killed him. After the deed was done, the old Loyalist was decapitated.[156] He was later laid to rest in a cemetery in the modern village of Cihadiye, outside Biga. The inscription on his headstone read as follows:

Here lies the honored Anzavur Paşa, commander of the Army of Mohammed. Having worked selflessly in the name of [his] religion, nation and home, he was killed in a brutal fashion by the *Kuva-yı Milliye*. He leaves behind a wound that will not be forgotten by the nation.[157]

In the year after his death, local Circassians transformed Anzavur's grave into a site of religious pilgrimage. Sufferers of malaria and other ailments are reported to have travelled to his resting place in order to gather dirt from around his grave, rubbing it on their faces and eyes and ingesting it with water. When the war ended, the local administrators took custody of the grave. Under orders from his superiors, one official personally took the headstone and defaced its inscription.[158]

The uprisings seen between November 1919 and April 1920 were not to be replicated in the South Marmara for the remainder of the Turkish War of Independence. Neither would a figure with the stature and influence of Ahmet Anzavur emerge from this region. The onset of the Greek occupation would again change the socio-political dynamics of the South Marmara, broadening the means of resistance to the National Movement along with it. Henceforth, the resistance would take the form of *de jure* collaboration with the occupying powers, further deepening the crisis in the region.

5

Separatism, Violence, and Collaboration in Bandit Country: The South Marmara during the Greek Occupation

A relative calm had passed between storms in Ezine. True, the town, located on the northern lip of the Aegean between Çanakkale and Ayvacık, did see its share of terror before the armistice of 1918. In the wake of the Allied attack upon the Dardenelles, Ottoman authorities used the region as a repository for native Rum exiled from Çanakkale.[1] Yet the county of Ezine remained a fairly sleepy place during the war years. Anzavur's bloody revolt passed over the county's inhabitants with only a few murmurs of discontent.[2] The county's scattered pockets of Circassians, Albanians, and Turkmen remained quiet while districts kilometres away burned.

Life in Ezine went into arrest after vanguard elements of the Greek army entered the county during the summer of 1920. Upon Athens's orders, members of Ezine's elite were rounded up, threatened, imprisoned, or exiled to the Greek mainland.[3] Rather than keep the peace, Greek troops and irregulars regularly fleeced the population of its food, livestock, and money. Villages such as Sarıçalı suffered repeated attacks by Greek authorities, leading to the death or incarceration of several civilians.[4] Ottoman gendarmes who remained at their posts laboured on ambiguously under the occupation, while some local Christians assumed critical roles as allies of the Greek troops.[5]

As the occupation progressed, Ezine became a shooting gallery for the region's warring factions. Although cut off from the bulk of the National Forces, several men emerged during the ensuing months to take up the standard of the Ankara government. Men such as Sadık, *Arnavud* Aziz, and Abdülrahman formed armed bands and took to the hills in defiance of the Greek invasion. Occasionally the two sides came to blows outside the towns of Bayramiç, Ezine, and Ayvacık.[6] More often than not, paramilitaries like Sadık and Aziz busied themselves by robbing helpless travellers or extorting goods and animals from Muslim and Christian villagers alike.[7] In Ezine, as well as in many other counties and towns in the South Marmara, the onset of foreign occupation served to blur the lines between friend and foe. Ideological and political absolutes often disappeared under the rule of paramilitaries and occupying armies. Instead, each faction would judge local loyalties individually and in accordance with a loose set of metrics.

At this critical juncture in the war, Armenians, Greeks, and Circassians were forced to make a critical choice. Although the Greek occupation allowed non-Muslims a reprieve from the renewed threat of extermination, many continued to struggle with the effects of the deportations. Some attempted to stay on and forge new lives out of what remained of the old. Many gave up and left Anatolia for ever. Still others signed on with the occupying forces and seized the moment to exact a bloody revenge upon their erstwhile Muslim neighbours.

The Circassian dilemma was different but no less dramatic. Although the *Kuva-yı Milliye* had indeed been defeated and driven from the region in the summer of 1920, those who had supported the Loyalist opposition remained wary of a final outcome. Escalating paramilitary violence and the uncertain future over the political status of Anatolia would push former rebels to craft a new consensus among themselves. By the end of 1921, several former stalwarts of the Loyalist movement put forward a radical solution to their past grievances: independence. It was a desperate move, one that thousands of Circassians would ultimately pay dearly for.

In surveying this two-year period of the War of Independence, we see the South Marmara's 'culture of paramilitarism' at its full height. Rather than catalogue an almost endless list of atrocities and counter-atrocities, this chapter strives to define and analyse the tactics and motivations of the various parties working to determine the final outcome of the conflict. At the apex of this struggle were the competing statist visions of the three major factions: the Nationalists, Great Britain, and the Kingdom of Greece. Each of these groups in turn sponsored acts of mass murder, ethnic cleansing, rape, theft, and separatism in order to strengthen their hand in consolidating the region. Yet, on the ground, provincial detachments and militias coloured the conflict with their own ambitions, transforming the South Marmara into a checkerboard of civil strife. When the fighting formally ended in September of 1922, Nationalist brutality had won the day.

THE ONSET OF OCCUPATION: GREECE, BRITAIN, AND NON-MUSLIMS

The defeat of Ahmet Anzavur and the *Kuva-yı İnzibatiye* at the end of June 1920 did not signal the end of the troubles facing the National Movement in the South Marmara. Rather, it was clear to Kazım (Özalp) and Bekir Sami (Günsav) that Greek forces on the Aegean front were preparing a major offensive. According to Kazım, Greek aircraft appeared above Nationalist defences at an increasing rate after 15 June. Meanwhile Greek spies and reconnaissance columns were stepping up their probes.[8] On 22 June, Greek forces launched a massive attack all along the Western lines and routed the *Kuva-yı Milliye*, whose numbers in the Aegean had dwindled with the spring uprisings.⁹ Seven days later, the Greeks had swept into Balıkesir, taking 1,500 prisoners and several heavy weapons.¹⁰ In the face of an imminent collapse, both Kazım and Bekir Sami attempted a controlled withdrawal from the region and re-established a second line of defence outside Bursa. Meanwhile both the Greeks and the British took advantage of the confusion, taking both Bandırma and Mudanya by sea.¹¹ Renewed fighting in Karacabey further hampered the Nationalist defence of the region as former supporters of Ahmet Anzavur attacked soldiers fleeing from the front.¹² On 8 July Bursa fell into Greek hands without any resistance. Four days later, British forces re-entered İzmit. Greek troops continued to push east of İzmit during the following months, aided in part by local Circassian partisans. On 4 September a lone force of Circassian rebels expelled Nationalist guerrillas from the town of Sabanca.¹³

Greek and British forces soon moved to secure the internal security of the South Marmara following the June offensive. From town to town, Greek officers recalled members of the local Ottoman gendarmerie and placed them under Greek supervision. While Ottoman gendarmes and police officers were allowed to continue some of their duties throughout the region (although in certain areas Ottoman gendarmes were disbanded altogether), the Greek and British military assumed most law enforcement responsibilities in the South Marmara. Greek soldiers were garrisoned in every major administrative centre, while British troops (in part composed of South Asian units) stationed themselves in the coastal towns of Çanakkale, Lapseki, Karabiga, and Mudanya. The *sancak* of Kale-i Sultaniye itself was officially divided in half among the British and Greek occupation forces, with the two acquiring law enforcement responsibilities respectively in the northern and southern portions of the province.¹⁴ Greek security personnel would also be bolstered by the presence of gendarmes brought in from Greece and by officially sponsored paramilitary bands raised from local population.¹⁵

The June offensive seemed to mark the complete realization of Greece's *Megali Idea*. Irredentist circles in Athens had indeed informed previous designs in Macedonia and Thrace during the Balkan Wars. Territorial acquisition, based on a pan-Hellenist vision of the Aegean and Black Seas, compelled Greece's entrance into the First World War on the side of the Allies. Compensation for this service came in the form of a territorial stake in western Anatolia, sandwiched between British and Italian claims.

By 1920, Italy abandoned its territorial rights in Anatolia, leaving the British as the sole check upon Greece's imperial appetite. London meanwhile tentatively endorsed their position in Anatolia; control over the Dardenelles and Bosphorus straits remained a British strategic priority. Yet the British commitment to the future of Anatolia was not open-ended. Grander imperial prerogatives and strains in Iraq, India, and Ireland begged still greater attention from Whitehall.

Resting somewhere between the interests of these two powers were the remaining Armenians and Greeks of Anatolia. As Christians and, to a degree, former dependants of the Western Powers, British and Greek forces viewed Armenians and Rum living in the South Marmara and elsewhere as natural allies. For the locals, however, the harsh realities of the post-deportation years appeared to have relegated broader Greek and British goals to the rear. Physical survival trumped all other concerns.

The passing of Anzavur and his insurrection appear to have mattered little to Armenians and Rum in the South Marmara. This was a Muslim fight over the future of a state that still appeared uninterested in the plight of its Christians. Trouble emerged only with the resurgence of the *Kuva-yı Milliye*'s military fortunes. Some Christians found themselves displaced a second time after the Nationalists regained the upper hand against the Loyalists. In Adapazarı, American missionaries reported a general campaign of extortion levied against the people of the town. Summary execution awaited those who could not or would not pay.[16]

The presence of Greek troops could only partially reverse the effects of the deportations. In one noted case, Athens oversaw the resettlement of 500 Christians in three villages situated outside the port town of Karabiga.[17] In most cases, however, the integrity of non-Muslim life continued to deteriorate. Thousands of Rum and Armenian survivors abandoned their villages to take up residence in the larger towns of Istanbul, İzmit, and Bursa.[18] A select few who could, like Arshag Dikranian and Aghavni Guleserian, eventually made their way to the USA.[19] Meanwhile, American missionaries reported only a partial resumption of their pre-war activities. Schools like the Girl's Boarding School in Bursa reported brief increases in attendance among Armenian, Greek, and Muslim students.[20] Many students were the orphans of deported or dead parents.[21] Despite the lack of trained ministers, a resurgence of interest in Protestant services in the town of İzmit gave Mary Kinney, an American missionary who had worked in both Anatolia and Egypt, hope for the future. Her optimism did not extend to Adapazarı or Bahçecik.[22] Those towns, including large sections of Bursa, were now almost entirely inhabited by Muslims.

For Christians in the South Marmara, one significant thing had changed: the Nationalists were now gone. Greek troops arriving in the region saw to it that practically anyone linked or associated with the CUP regime was neutralized before they could organize against the occupation. Hundred, perhaps thousands, of Muslim notables were arrested, beaten, killed, or deported to Greece.[23] As the summer of 1920 turned to autumn, the South Marmara increasingly took on the look of Greece proper. Blunt force backed this transformation. When the Greek king Alexander died in late October 1920, occupation authorities in Biga demanded that Muslim business-owners close their shops upon pain of injury and imprisonment.[24] Store fronts in Balıkesir were required to display Greek flags and Greek signs.[25] Troops brought in from the Greek mainland often exercised their domination over the Muslim population perniciously. Although some corners of the South Marmara, such as Bursa, remained quiet, Muslims living in small villages like Sarıçalı and market towns like Gönen and Biga became frequent victims of theft and assault.

As the occupation took on a permanent veneer, Greece presented the surviving Christian population of the South Marmara with an open door to serve in the ranks of the local administration and security personnel. In 1921, Greek authorities sponsored a local Armenian man to serve as *kaymakam* of Kirmasti (despite the absolute decimation of the county's Armenian population).[26] Thousands of other Armenians and Greeks joined up to serve as auxiliaries in the new security force. Native Christian collaboration did not escape the notice of the Nationalist press in Ankara. In early March 1922, one paper reported that 2,000 Greek and Armenian civilians from Bursa, Bandırma, and İzmir volunteered that month to join the Greek army.[27] According to Rıfat Yüce, the former CUP sympathizer who had been tried and imprisoned by the Istanbul War Crimes Tribunal, the Greeks marshalled a force of 700–800 Rum and Armenians drawn from the environs of Bilecik alone.[28]

Whether officially licensed or acting independently of Greek command, Christian paramilitaries garnered a gruesome reputation. One incident that stands out is the assault on Ali Al-Sabah, a small village of 150 households near the port of Mudanya. According to a report submitted by the Ottoman gendarmerie, a band numbering 500 Christians from the neighbouring villages of Yalı Çiftlik, Valideler, and Dereköy set upon Ali Al-Sabah on 10 May 1921. After gathering up the townspeople in the village mosque, the bandits proceeded to rape the women and girls in front of their families. With the people bound and locked within the mosque without food or water, the band then began to pillage the town, stealing money and more than 800 animals. After fleecing the village, the Christians purportedly attacked another settlement near Bursa, again stealing money and property.[29]

Violent incidents involving Christian gangs proliferated well beyond the environs of Mudanya. The most serious and organized cases of Christian paramilitary violence occurred to the north of Bursa during the summer of 1921. After failing to dislodge Nationalist troops further east along the İnönü River, Greek forces decided to stage a slow, strategic withdrawal from the Yalova/Gemlik peninsula.[30] Between April and June 1920, news of attacks on Muslim civilians in this region poured into the Ottoman Interior Ministry.[31] In the midst of the Greek pull-out, a total of twenty-seven villages were razed in the two *kaza*s of Gemlik and Yalova (fourteen in Yalova alone).[32] Orhangazi, a town with a population of 4,500, was partially burned down.[33] The towns of Yenişehir and Armudlu were also directly targeted by occupation forces and burned to the ground. In Armudlu, women were methodically raped.[34] The violence around the Gulf of İzmit continued well into the summer, only trickling off by August of 1921. In the town of İzmit itself, famed historian Arnold Toynbee, then a reporter for the *Manchester Guardian*, asserted that up to 300 people, mostly men, from two Muslim neighbourhoods had been executed by Greek troops. Their bodies were then interned in a mass grave outside of town.[35]

Muslim refugees from the Yalova/Gemlik peninsula streamed into Istanbul and Bursa, putting even greater strain upon state and foreign agencies tasked to treat the masses of refugees from the Great War and the initial Greek landing in Izmir.[36] Officials circulated a standard questionnaire in the Davut Paşa refugee camp in Istanbul, asking victims to detail their lives and their attackers. Written answers submitted to the Interior Ministry reveal that the refugees were both rich and poor and had plied various professions. A significant number of refugees, particularly those who owned large tracts of land, had worked as merchants and boatmen. There were also a number of local officials, army officers, religious figures, tradesmen, and store-owners. Even women who had been widowed were driven from their homes. The range of personal losses was much greater for refugees arriving from Değirmendere (a town with a population of between 1,000 and 1,200 people), totalling a value of 2,700 lira for one farmer to 220,000 lira for the owner of a large farm.[37] The vast majority of these men and women, rich or poor, had left their homes with few or no personal belongings.

Statements gathered by Ottoman officials reveal, somewhat strangely, a fairly low number of casualties in this campaign of destruction. Of the 177 people responding to the questionnaire, only twenty-eight individuals responded that they had family members harmed during the Greek occupation. In total, only thirty-five were reported to have been killed, wounded, beaten, or missing. This is in line with the observations of Arnold Toynbee, who declared that 'one to two murders were sufficient in driving away the population' of a given village.[38] A mixed commission of British, Ottoman, and French officers reported that only twelve to twenty-five individuals were killed or wounded after Greek forces attacked the village of Karacaali.[39] Yet the nineteen refugees from this village reported to officials in Istanbul that only three people of out their extended families had died.[40]

Informants in the Davut Paşa camp were generally vague in identifying their attackers, overwhelmingly stating that they were either 'Greek soldiers', 'native Greeks (*yerli Rum*)', or 'Armenians'. Despite the fact that the refugees of Armudlu did not name their attackers, Toynbee claimed that 100 men from five separate Rum villages had repeatedly victimized the town.[41] Still, he emphasizes throughout his account of the South Marmara during 1921 that the refugees he encountered were fearful of future retribution should they return to the region.[42]

The breadth of these attacks seems to suggest that the counties comprising the Yalova/Gemlik peninsula—namely, Gemlik, Yalova, and Orhangazi—as well as the Karamürsel/Değirmendere area, were the focus of an organized campaign directed and executed by the Greek authorities. Toynbee, in reporting his findings to the Inter-Allied Commission (a body established to investigate war crimes in the region), affirms this suspicion.[43] If this is in fact true, it must be asked why this region in particular was the focus of such a bloody ordeal. How is it that a town like Armudlu, as opposed to say Biga or Lapeski, bore the brunt of such deliberate acts of violence? The answer to this question may lie not simply in the Greek military and political strategy of 1921, but in the demographic make-up of the region and the effects of the wartime deportations.[44] According to the Ottoman census of 1914, Muslims living in the *kaza*s of Yalova and Orhangazi comprised only 36 and 34 per cent of the respective populations. Gemlik meanwhile possessed only a slight majority population of Muslims (57 per cent). During the war, however, this differential may have changed radically. One British official touring Gemlik in 1919 estimated that 90 per cent of the town comprised Rum not deported in 1915, while whole villages in outlying areas were exiled with only an hour's notice. He also estimated that most Armenians deported never returned, and that a substantial percentage of the property held by deported Greeks and Armenians in the Gemlik area was either sold or given to Muslim refugees.[45]

Although principally organized by the Greek military command, native Christians made a profound mark on this collective act of violence and retribution. Most Christian irregulars involved in the ethnic cleansing of the Gemlik–Yalova–İzmit region, Toynbee notes, were not professional paramilitaries. They were instead shepherds, charcoal-burners, merchants, factory-owners, and shop-owners, individuals who had previously been on friendly terms with their Muslim neighbours.[46] This being the case, it is arguable that both Greek and local non-Muslim paramilitary forces in the region took advantage of the chaos and discontent to exact a fearsome revenge.

'THOSE WHO STAY WILL BE DESTROYED BY OUR HANDS': THE NATIONAL MOVEMENT UNDER OCCUPATION

The fall of Balıkesir was a bullet to the National Movement's central nervous system. As we have seen, the capital of Karesi was a cornerstone of the Nationalist resistance in western Anatolia and among the first cities to provide a base for the administrative and propaganda components of the *Kuva-yı Milliye*. Combined with the loss of Bursa, Balıkesir's capture served to close off physically the southern basin of the Sea of Marmara to the National Movement. Beginning in the spring of 1921, the Nationalist leadership holding out in Ankara appointed İbrahim Ethem *Akıncı*, a former bureaucrat and lawyer from Balıkesir, to form a guerrilla army that would carry on the Nationalist resistance in the South Marmara. İbrahim Ethem, who had been appointed in November 1920 to the position of *kaymakam* of Demirci in the *kaza* of Sındırgı, was a longtime Nationalist proponent who had joined the movement soon after the occupation of Izmir.[47] By October of 1921, İbrahim gathered a group of ten subordinates who would lead an organized guerrilla campaign against the occupying forces.

The eleven men agreed to abide by a set of regulations laid out in accordance with Ankara's wishes. Each detachment (*müfreze*) within this small guerrilla army would have a standardized chain of command and set uniforms.[48] The regulations issued by İbrahim Ethem also state that the detachments would not seize animals, money, or other property from local villages, or accept food or shelter from the population.[49] More pointedly, Nationalist guerrillas were forbidden to have any contact with local Christians, be they hostile or not, even to the point of prohibiting any trade between the detachments and Christians merchants.[50]

Repeatedly, İbrahim Ethem declared to both the Greeks and the population at large that his detachments were not bandits and that the National Movement would henceforth have nothing to do with brigandage.[51] His men would not stir up violence between Muslims or accept the support of anyone known to cause friction among Muslims.[52] These specific declarations are clear acknowledgements of the failures of the *Kuva-yı Milliye* during its first years in the South Marmara and the heavy-handedness with which the local population was taxed and abused. On both counts, the regulations laid down by İbrahim Ethem would ring hollow.

The most striking element in İbrahim Ethem's memoirs is the prominence of sectarian rhetoric within the statements issued by his detachments. While he adopted unconditionally the main Nationalist line that the war was one to 'save the state' from foreign occupation, İbrahim Ethem and his lieutenants repeatedly asserted that the enemy they were facing were 'unbelievers' (*gavurlar*).[53] In corresponding with Greek commanders opposing him in the field, İbrahim Ethem stated on several occasions that Anatolia was a land of 'Muslims and Turks' and that victory would be achieved in the killing of Greeks and Armenians.[54] One letter to a Greek commander in Sındırgı underscored as much:

We are not bandits. We are committed (*memuruz*) to killing Greeks (*Yunanlı*) and murdering the native Rum who took up arms with the Greeks and shot at and attacked our honourable nation. Let us speak openly with one another: The Rum comprise only 5 per cent of Anatolia. The remainder is Muslim and Turkish. Now in such a wide land with such a majority of population, what is the point of the Greeks remaining? For what purpose? Are you saying that ninety-five people should surrender to five people? . . . I request that you do not reply, and take my final advice. Soon the Greeks will flee or those who stay will be destroyed by our hands.[55]

In another letter to the Greek commander of the occupation forces in Balıkesir, İbrahim Ethem suggested this difference between Muslims and Christians:

We have all the ammunition and clothing we need. We can get coffee, sugar and various other things from the village grocers. At the most, it is possible to get information [from them] on your forces and movements. Muslims and Turks will not do this but it is natural that we do and will take advantage of Rum and Armenians this way. Because money makes everything in the world and especially in the Christian nations (*milletlerinde*), it plays the biggest role. Because in wasting and spending so much money, you have your monuments, bars (*meyhane*), theatres, cinemas, brothels, gambling houses and promenades. You must not generate hostility in our [town of] Balıkesir with such displays.[56]

This passage seems to follow the recognizable tension found in wartime, with the virtuous challenger contrasting himself with the weak and corrupt opponent. But viewed in the context of the evolving relationship between non-Muslims and the Ottoman state (especially under the CUP), the statements above seem to signal the final manifestation of a long simmering conflict. With the Greek army occupying most of western Anatolia, the gloves were now off. There would be no compromise between the Nationalists and the occupiers. The only solution in the eyes of İbrahim Ethem and his lieutenants was not only to drive the Greeks from the land, but to punish every traitorous native Christian in the process. Not only were all Rum and Armenians traitors in action or in waiting, İbrahim Ethem somewhat cryptically suggests that Christians were themselves inherently corrupt and decadent (an opinion he may have arrived at before the war). The conclusion that one must draw is clear: If the state was to survive, the Christian cancer had to be cut out entirely.

İbrahim Ethem chose the mountains around the *kaza* of Sındırgı, just south of Balıkesir, as the base for his guerrilla campaign in the South Marmara. Beginning in the early summer of 1921, İbrahim Ethem could count on a growing number of *çeteci*s assigned to him from the regular army. Many of these men were veterans of the Nationalist defence of the Aegean front, while others were local notables who appear to have equipped their own men from the region. The names of many of these men are well known: Parti Pehlivan, *Arnavud* Arslan, *Sarı* Mehmet, (Bakırlı) Mustafa, and *Arab* Ali Osman. In a lengthy report from the General Commander of the Gendarmerie dated 11 October 1921, several other *çeteci* leaders are listed as being active partisans for the National Movement in the Karesi area. What is interesting about this list is not so much the names of the individuals on it or the number of men they led, but the fact that for many of the entries, the ethnic make-up of their bands are also given. The men led by *Arnavud* Arslan, for example, a native of Balıkesir, comprised not only Albanians, but also Circassians and Turks. In another band, both Turks and Yörüks are cited as the main ethnic groups.⁵⁷ This interest in the make-up of these bands confirms once more the importance of ethnicity in the minds of law enforcement officials. Whether this information told them something of the relationship between these bands and certain communities in the region or the behaviour of a specific band is unclear. Yet this sort of characterization of these paramilitary groups reminds us of the inherent diversity on both sides in this conflict. As we have seen with the paramilitary bands and notables who joined Ahmet Anzavur, the men within the *Kuva-yı Milliye* were drawn from diverse ethnic backgrounds. Yet without any information or testimony on the recruitment of these men, it is difficult to say for certain what compelled them to join the Nationalist side.

Arguably the most celebrated and influential of the paramilitary leaders was Parti Pehlivan. Having split from *Çerkes* Ethem with thirty-three of his men, Pehlivan Ağa, as he was called colloquially, reconstituted his forces under İbrahim Ethem.⁵⁸ Among his first assignments (one not recorded in his commanding officer's own memoirs) was an attack on a village outside Bigadiç in April 1921. After routing Greek forces in the area, his men killed eight inhabitants of the town, including two Rum, one Armenian, and five Muslims.⁵⁹ Later that November, Parti Pehlivan was implicated in an attack on a village three hours outside Balıkesir, where he purportedly executed one Ottoman officer and burned down his house.⁶⁰ The paramilitary campaign carried out by Parti Pehlivan in Karesi also attracted a good deal of retribution from Greek security forces. As a result of daily clashes between Pehlivan Ağa's men and Greek and Ottoman forces in the environs of Sındırgı and Bigadiç, the Greek authorities burned down villages in the region and then arrested the *kaymakam* and *müftü* of Sındırgı, as well as thirty Muslim notables and a number of Ottoman gendarmes.⁶¹

These first two examples of Parti Pehlivan's activities again attest to the fact that the Nationalist effort in Karesi and elsewhere (such as in Ezine) was as much a war on the population at large as it was against the Greeks. In addition to seizing property, Parti Pehlivan and other *çeteci* leaders loyal to the *Kuva-yı Milliye* undertook a concerted policy of disciplining the population in cases of collaboration or theft. One incident that stands out occurred on 25 October 1921 when a gang of six Çetmi robbed property and money from a village called Kırca in the *nahiye* of Mecidiye, near Balıkesir.⁶² A day later, İbrahim Ethem sent four columns under the command of Parti Pehlivan and *Arab* Ali Osman after the bandits. In a battle that lasted two hours, İbrahim states that three of the Çetmi were killed (one deliberately executed) and 'several' were wounded.⁶³ During the following month, İbrahim and his men executed several other Çetmi bandits for similar crimes and warned other villages not to partake in any theft in Turkish villages.⁶⁴

These clashes between the *Kuva-yı Milliye* and the Çetmi in the *kaza* of Balıkesir suggest another side to the sectarian character of this conflict. On the one hand, the Çetmi were treated as harshly as any Muslim found collaborating with the occupation forces. On the other hand, the fact that their heterodox beliefs were cited in speaking of the Çetmi raises the possibility that the war against the Greek occupation was not confined to the Muslim/Christian divide. It seemed to matter little that the Çetmi were 'Turks' in the absolute ethnic sense of the word. Criminal actions by some amplified the malignance of their collective religious unorthodoxy and provincial mannerisms.[65] This sort of collective criminalization differed little from that of provincial Albanians and Circassians as perceived by Ottoman law enforcement officials and the urban elite; they were law-breakers and inherently seditious.

Yet certain exceptions to this notion of ethnicity, sectarianism, and recalcitrance applied to the Çetmi can still be found within Ottoman sources. One case that stands out concerns the activities of one independent bandit leader from Karesi, *Boşnak* (Bosnian) Karabulut İbrahim. Based around the town of İvrendi, west of Balıkesir, Karabulut İbrahim's band of Bosnian and Çetmi paramilitaries was implicated in several acts of brigandage during the autumn of 1921.[66] Even after one such attack that netted Karabulut İbrahim 4,500 lira from a local member of the *eşraf* named Hacı Şükrü, Greek efforts to arrest or destroy his band proved fruitless.[67] A report from İbrahim Ethem dated 20 February 1922 declared Karabulut İbrahim someone who 'committed acts of brigandage as a profession' and who was not officially aligned with the National Movement.[68] Yet at war's end, İbrahim's allegiances changed. In September, with the Greek forces now in retreat, the Bosnian submitted his men to the disposal of the *Kuva-yı Milliye* and took part in some of the final battles of the war.[69] Loyalty to the National Movement, in this case, seems to have absolved İbrahim and his band of Çetmi and Bosnians not only of their past crimes, but also of any suspicion due to their ethnic character.

Absolution for 'ethnic' or criminal behaviour extended to other paramilitaries willing to fight under the Nationalist banner. *Arnavud* Aziz, Sadık, and other *çeteci*s operating in Kale-i Sultaniye, despite their flagrant acts of violence against the local Muslim population, were counted among those loyal to İbrahim Ethem and the National Movement.[70] Outside Biga, *Arnavud* Rahman, whose paramilitary activities began during the First World War, continued to pledge his loyalty to Mustafa Kemal. Together with a Roma *çeteci* named *Çingene/Kıbti* Ali (Ali the Gypsy), Rahman waged a low-level insurgency against both occupying troops and the local population. The two launched at least nine deliberate attacks, mostly by ambush, against Ottoman, Greek, and British security forces in the environs of Biga.[71] As with the bands found in Ezine, the activities of these gangs included seizing property and demanding money from local Muslim notables.[72] The effect of this campaign is difficult to gauge, especially since the clashes appear to have resulted in few casualties among the Greek, Ottoman, and British forces in the area (only four in total). While the damage incurred by the security personnel may have been consciously under-reported, the insurgents themselves also suffered a limited number of casualties and arrests.[73]

Greek and British troops were not the only collective force standing against the ongoing Nationalist efforts in the South Marmara. In the wake of foreign occupation, many former supporters of Ahmet Anzavur took up Greek offers to serve in the local security force. Their collaboration with the British and Greek forces in a certain respect presents a continuum between the rebellions of 1919/20 and the occupation. Yet, as time wore on, notable members of the North Caucasian diaspora in the South Marmara, who formed the core of Anzavur's insurrection, would move beyond the means and goals of the Loyalist movement. The onset of foreign occupation shattered the possibility of return to some antebellum status quo. A new consensus among dissident Circassians emerged, leading to a dramatic political and rhetorical turn in the anti-Nationalist resistance in the South Marmara.

FROM REBELS TO COLLABORATORS: CIRCASSIAN PARAMILITARISM AND THE GREEK OCCUPATION

After recovering from the broken leg he suffered outside İzmit, Ahmet Anzavur returned to the South Marmara and joined his son Kadir, whose own band dwindled to a fraction of its previous strength during the spring uprising of 1920. Greek authorities welcomed Anzavur's arrival in the region and offered to integrate his Circassian riders into the ranks of the occupation. With the blessing of the Greek authorities, Kadir and his men freely patrolled the outlying villages of Karabiga, extracting 40–100 lira from each village to protect it from the likes of *Çingene* Ali and *Arnavud* Rahman.[74] In January 1921 one of Ahmet Anzavur's men was even appointed to the position of aide-de-camp to the Greek commanding officer in Biga.[75] In April 1921, however, Anzavur himself was cut down outside of Karabiga, killed at the head of his men by a group of Nationalist conspirators aligned with *Arnavud* Rahman.

Following his father's death, Kadir swore revenge upon all those who played a role in the plot. One of his first targets was a village notable from Örtülüceli, near Karabiga, who surrendered only after Kadir threatened to kill all the inhabitants of the village. The man, Müminin Selman, was then taken to the hills south of the town and murdered.[76] In May 1921, Kadir and a mixed detachment of Circassian and Greek troops cornered *Çingene* Ali and his men outside Biga, leaving two Nationalists dead and Ali and his brother Osman wounded.[77] Two months later, Kadir stormed into the town of Karabiga with twenty men and assassinated the captain of the local Ottoman gendarmerie unit, Vehbi Bey.[78]

Circassian violence and collaboration with the Greek occupation remains one of the most unexplored chapters in the history of the Turkish War of Independence. Past and contemporary scholars of the period have often shied away from the topic, claiming, as in the case of the Anzavurist rebellion, that Circassian 'treason' was the work of a small number of reactionaries.⁷⁹ This assertion is in part true: a relatively limited number of North Caucasian immigrants actively supported the Greek administration in Anatolia. But to discount this phenomenon as isolated or insignificant obscures the broader impact and implication of the roles played by Circassians during the war years. The Greek occupation of the South Marmara marked a dramatic turn among North Caucasian dissidents. As former rebels recovered from the Nationalist suppression of 1920, the Greek occupation opened a window through which a new provincial order could be fashioned.

According to a report by an unnamed British officer, the mood towards the National Movement in Bandırma immediately after the Greeks entered the town was sour:

The general impression I obtained from my stay in Panderma [Bandırma], July 2ⁿᵈ to July 8ᵗʰ, was that the Nationalists had no popular backing at all in the Panderma-Manias [Manyas]-Balikesir [Balıkesir] area. Indeed their exactions made them most unpopular with all the elements in the country. The farmers and small owners who during the war had made more money than ever before, and resented the forced contributions levied on them by Kemalist leaders, often, it is believed, without the consent of the Angora Government. This resentment expressed itself more strongly than would otherwise have been the case when the Kemalists began to burn houses, flog people and deport women and children. This severe policy was inaugurated after the suppression of the Anzavur movement, which thus obtained more sympathy than it might otherwise have gained. Anzavur was not highly esteemed at Panderma but the suffering not only of his followers but of persons who were merely suspected of Anzavurism or who had had relations among the Anzavur faction aroused general indignation. Further it should be remembered that the villages in the Panderma hinterland contained a large number, perhaps a majority, of people who were non-Anatolian, Pomaks, Cherkese [sic], Tatars, etc. These were altogether a more independent people [than] the true Turks and resented ill treatment much more.⁸⁰

The British observer goes on to state that the Greeks sought to curry favour with the population at large by opening up communication and trade with Istanbul, a channel previously closed off to the population during the uprisings, and by not exacting further acts of revenge against the previously warring factions.⁸¹

In a second testimonial written a year later by the commander of the Manyas gendarmerie in April 1921, the reporting sergeant opens his account of the contemporary political situation by stating, 'The Ottoman government categorically has no influence in this district, which is in part Circassian.' He blames this state of affairs squarely upon the rule of the Circassian notables and in particular a group of 'tyrants' (*mütegallibeler*) led by (Anzavuroğlu) Kadir. Under Kadir's governance, the entire population, and in particular Turkish villages, lived in a state of imprisonment. According to the commanding sergeant, the houses of 'poor Turks' would be attacked every two to three days and their oxen would be stolen. The same went for Christians living in the environs of Manyas, who, according to the sergeant, existed in a continual state of anxiety and terror. 'Even the slightest opposition', the commander went on to say, 'will bring forth evil consequences.'[82]

Both of these accounts reflect the degree to which portions of the North Caucasian community had become disgruntled, yet empowered, during the aftermath of the Greek offensive of June 1920. From the beginning, authorities within the Greek occupation saw an opportunity to capitalize on the alienation felt among Circassians. In July 1920, a British official stationed in Bandırma reported that he assisted a Greek captain by the name of Gerontas in meeting with Circassian notables in the Manyas area. Their primary interlocutor was Şah İsmail, one of Ahmet Anzavur's chief lieutenants. According to the deal struck between them, the Greeks promised to allow the return of certain local notables from Istanbul and to facilitate the transfer of individuals deported by the Nationalists and rescued by advancing Greek forces. Şah İsmail and the other Circassians in turn swore to police the behaviour of Circassian paramilitaries in the region and not to take part in acts of vengeance upon the Nationalists remaining in the region (save three who were suspected of raping Circassian women). Most importantly, the Circassians agreed to supply 200 horsemen to the Greek occupation authority.[83] It is unknown how many North Caucasians ultimately entered the service of the Greeks. By war's end, Nationalist and British estimates of Circassian involvement in the Greek occupation at any one time ranged from 300 to 700 men.[84] As we will see, the actual numbers throughout the South Marmara may have reached the thousands.[85]

İbrahim Ethem and other leaders of the National Movement in Karesi were acutely aware of the role being played by these Circassian collaborators. In a memorandum dated 31 March 1922, İbrahim Ethem saw this phenomenon in the most crass of terms. Those Circassians joining the Greeks, he argued, were driven by a desire to 'crush the Turks', as well as by the opportunity to 'fill their purses'. These were Circassians who insisted upon driving forward the lingering 'Turkish-Circassian issue', which was a slander to Islam. Worse still, the Circassian paramilitary units now being formed in Izmir and elsewhere were also composed of Rum and a small number of Armenians.[86] Together, these heavily armed *çetes* were to be an instrument for the execution of Greek atrocities, with licence to burn down villages, rape women, and rob and execute Muslims.[87] In a war that seemed clearly defined along sectarian lines, Nationalists simply could not understand why Muslim Circassians could throw in their lot with the Christian invaders and their co-religionist allies in the provinces. In a Circassian village south of Balıkesir, İbrahim Ethem openly lectured the population for failing to support the *Kuva-yı Milliye*. 'You are either a Muslim or an infidel,' he exclaimed; 'I cannot understand [how] one remains between the two.'[88]

Without any kind of testimony from these Circassian collaborators, one can only speculate as to their views of this confessional divide. Yet, if we trace the origins of this resistance back to summer of 1919, it can be argued that it may not have mattered much at all. What was in question for Circassian notables and their dependants was the political and social future of their communities, not the integrity of Islam. This is not to say that this was a nationalist uprising on the part of Circassians. On the contrary, the evidence available suggests that collaboration with the Greeks was only a continuation of the organized localist resistance ignited by Ahmet Anzavur. Be it fighting Albanian gangs in Kırmastı or Nationalist irregulars in Gönen years earlier, the question of fighting fellow Muslims did not deter Circassian notables or their retainers from pursuing their provincial objectives. The spilling of blood between Muslims was instead of grave concern to Nationalists, who continually tried to maintain a veneer of unanimity through the invocation of Islam. Thus the question of being either a Muslim or an infidel served as a rhetorical instrument both to explain deviations from the Nationalist cause and as a cudgel to intimidate Circassians into the fold.

To the north in the İzmit and Adapazarı region, the nature of Circassian collaboration was similar. Reports beginning as early as April 1921 declared that gangs of Abkhazians, Greeks, and Armenians were working together with Greek authorities in pillaging Muslim villages around İzmit and Adapazarı.[89] In June, these reports became more precise, with details emerging that these mixed units were not only raiding villages, but also robbing travellers, merchants, and refugees on the İzmit/Istanbul road.[90] Circassian irregulars were also implicated in the massacres conducted after the Greek pull-out from İzmit on 28 June 1921.[91]

The North Caucasians were led by (Çule) İbrahim Hakkı, an early anti-Nationalist activist who had apparently survived the Nationalist counter-attack after the uprising in the summer of 1920. While serving as the *mutasarrıf* of İzmit between April and November 1920, İbrahim continued to menace the *Kuva-yı Milliye* and provide assistance and intelligence to the British.[92] Even after being removed from office in November, he continued to patrol outlying areas and obstruct the activities of the new *mutasarrıf*, Abdülvehab.[93] Greek occupation authorities gave İbrahim Hakkı free rein in his activities, allowing him to become the *de facto* leader of the North Caucasian community of İzmit and Adapazarı. According to a report circulated within the Ministry of the Interior, İbrahim was the central figure within a group of twenty-nine paramilitary leaders in the region. Unlike the Circassians who allied themselves with the Greek occupation in Karesi and Kale-i Sultaniye, this cabal of men was comprised not simply of local notables, but of many individuals who had served or were continuing to serve within the regular Ottoman provincial administration, including gendarmes, bureaucrats (both imperial and local), and military officers. While most of the names do not possess any ethnic epithets, most appear to be either Circassian or Abkhazian, with several of the leaders related to either the Bağ or the Maan families (although one Bosnian was listed among them). While often mentioned together in similar reports, the names of Armenian or Rum *çete* leaders do not appear.⁹⁴

Of the men mentioned among the twenty-nine anti-Nationalist paramilitary leaders in the region, one of them was in fact the *kaymakam* of the *kaza* of Adapazarı, (Maan) Mustafa Namık. An Abkhazian by birth, Mustafa Namık was the son of an immigrant family that had settled in the village of Kayalar after the Russo–Ottoman War of 1877–8. As a wealthy landowner and former captain in the Ottoman gendarmerie, he was an early supporter of (Karzeg) Sait.⁹⁵ Following the Greek occupation, Mustafa Namık was appointed to the position of *kaymakam* in Adapazarı, a position he obtained with the support of then *mutasarrıf* İbrahim Hakkı. His collaboration with Greek authorities, it was later claimed, was in part facilitated by his wife, a local Rum who had converted to Islam.⁹⁶ Newspaper articles and Interior Ministry reports from 1921 claim that after leaving office, both Mustafa Namık and İbrahim Hakkı engaged in a campaign to 'destroy the Turks' (*Türkleri imha etmek*) in the environs of İzmit and Adapazarı. With the assistance of the former police chief of İzmit, *Çerkes* Fuat, the three men amassed hundreds of North Caucasian riders and proceeded to pillage the homes of many of the wealthiest landowners of the region.⁹⁷ In late 1921 Mustafa Namık was arrested while in Istanbul and put on trial for murder and arson. In December 1921, an Istanbul court found him not guilty of these charges, yet ruled that he was guilty of treason and sentenced him to death.⁹⁸ Authorities in the British High Commission in Istanbul later intervened and secured his release.⁹⁹

The most striking aspect of Mustafa Namık's story and the stories of other North Caucasian paramilitaries is the evolving agenda of the Circassian resistance in the South Marmara. While at times assisted by Greek troops and local Christian irregulars, it appears that this collection of Adige and Abkhazian militants continued to maintain a degree of autonomy of action. The same can also be said of *Çerkes* Davut in the environs of Kirmasti, who, with the apparent consent of the Greek authorities, was purportedly running the county like a *derebey* or a great lord of old.¹⁰⁰ Yet, unlike in the period of rebellion that marked the years 1919 and 1920, the land had been largely emptied of Nationalist administrators and *çete*s. The war carried out by these paramilitary leaders during the Greek occupation instead focused upon the civilian population, particularly its wealthiest members.¹⁰¹ Whether or not the victims of İbrahim Hakkı and *Çerkes* Davut were Nationalist sympathizers is immaterial.¹⁰² An essential feature of this conflict throughout the South Marmara was the disciplining of the population. Nationalist, anti-Nationalist, and Greek occupational forces sought to make sure that all civilians, in particular the most prominent or affluent, were made aware of who was in charge and the price of disloyalty. There is also the possibility that the Greek occupation paved the way for the redistribution of the wealth among the poor Circassians and Abkhazians who followed their leaders into battle. From all appearances, the call to 'destroy the Turks', if this is indeed what *Çerkes* Fuat and İbrahim Hakkı had said, entailed the looting of property of village and town notables who had enough property to be shared among the gangs. This current within the activities of Circassian *çete*s was one that was apparently shared by local Christians who also took up arms at this time. Both parties, one way or another, had lost everything and held a common desire to retrieve what was once theirs.

RESISTANCE BY ANOTHER MEANS: THE MOVE TOWARDS CIRCASSIAN SEPARATISM IN THE SOUTH MARMARA

In January 1921, *Çerkes* Ethem, who had saved the *Kuva-yı Milliye* from certain disaster on multiple occasions during the first two years of the conflict, completely broke with the National Movement. After an ongoing dispute over the integration of his forces into the regular army and the absolute leadership of Mustafa Kemal, Ethem's forces rose in rebellion against Ankara and were defeated outside of Kütahya. He and his two brothers, Reşit and Tevfik, then retreated through Karesi, finally seeking the sanctuary of an allied Circassian *çeteci* in the *nahiye* of Manyas.[103] On 2 February, Ethem and his few remaining troops, mostly Circassians, surrendered to Greek authorities.

Çerkes Ethem's break with the *Kuva-yı Milliye* is the subject of numerous books that have been published over the last several decades.[104] The central theme of most of them is the political intrigues within the Nationalist camp and the factors that led Ethem and his two brothers to choose 'treason' over the National Movement. This infighting among the Mustafa Kemal's chief lieutenants largely falls outside the parameters of this study, as it had very little to do with the way in which the war had begun to progress in the South Marmara. The one way in which *Çerkes* Ethem's insurrection does reflect the course of events in İzmit, Biga, Kirmasti, and elsewhere is the degree to which 'Circassianness' had become politicized during the later stages of the War of Independence.

While the *Kuva-yı Milliye* was still populated by officers and men of North Caucasian descent, Ethem's break with the Nationalists pushed the Circassian issue to the fore. Shortly after İsmet (İnönü) took command of the western Nationalist front in 1920, his head veterinarian had this to say about Ethem's forces:

[The number of] Circassians in the Mobile Forces (*Kuva-yı Seyyare*) is increasing. [Ethem] gives a great deal of privilege to the Circassian officers and privates. In their opinion, the other officers are nothing. Yet from the beginning to the present, are not the majority of people killed or had their blood spilled by the Mobile Forces under command of Ethem Bey Turks?[105]

Soon after Ethem surrendered his command to the Greeks, Sarı Mehmet, a lieutenant of İbrahim Ethem's and a former comrade of Çerkes Ethem, lamented: 'The Circassians are the ones who have brought disaster upon us. While we were fighting they would do nothing other than sell their homeland. Now they are corrupt to the basest level, surrendering to the Greeks while they fill up their saddlebags. The penalty for them is the bullet.'[106] The sentiment expressed in these statements reflects attitudes prevalent in the past, not only about Ethem, but about Circassians overall: Circassians steal and are self-serving; they are seditious, and they kill Turks. This opinion, however pervasive, also appeared at the most local of levels.[107]

The statements and actions of İbrahim Hakkı and his men in İzmit also indicate that 'Turkishness' and 'Circassianness' were acquiring new political connotations in certain circles within the provincial North Caucasian elite. In the winter of 1921, we receive a strong indication of what ethnic identity meant to at least some of the most powerful Circassian notables in the South Marmara, as well of what political direction this group was leaning towards under the Greek occupation.

On 24 November 1921, a group of twenty-two Circassians met in a coffeehouse in the middle of Izmir. They were largely drawn from towns and counties around the South Marmara: Adapazarı, İzmit, Karamürsel, Kandıra, Bilecik, Geyve, Bursa, Gönen, Erdek, Bandırma, and Balıkesir. There were also representatives from areas further afield, such as Hendek, Düzce, Manisa, Aydın, Eskişehir, and Kütahya. Many of the men who came were individuals who were at the forefront of the Circassian resistance, while others may have remained in the background of the uprisings of 1919 and 1920. Even Çerkes Reşit, who was once a central figure in the *Kuva-yı Milliye* and the Committee of Union and Progress, took part in the meeting, as well as his brother Ethem.[108] At the end of the meeting, the group of men, now calling themselves representatives of the Association for the Strengthening of Near Eastern Circassian Rights (*Şark-ı Karib Çerkesleri Temin-i Hukuk Cemiyeti*), released a document entitled 'The General Statement of the Circassian Nation to the Great Powers and the Civilized World'. It reads as follows:

The authorities signed below are the representatives of the Circassian people of western Anatolia, which is today under the Greek occupational army, [and in particular of] Balıkesir, Bandırma, Erdek, Gönen, Biga, Kirmasti, Mihaliç [Karacabey], Bursa, İnegöl, Yenişehir, Aydın, Manisa, Izmir, Eskişehir, Kütahya, Afyonkarahisar as well as İzmit, Adapazarı, Hendek, Düzce, Bolu and their environs. They are also the founders of 'The Association for the Strengthening of Near Eastern Circassian Rights' [which is] sanctioned by the Greek government. This meeting, which is in the form a congress, undertakes its national rights as a minority based on the national rights as determined by the national principles accepted and declared by the Great Powers at the end of the Great War. The representatives ask for their national demands with the declaration that the Circassians will seek refuge under the Allied Great Powers, who agreed among themselves to force the acceptance [of these rights] of the losing states, and its partners, in particular the Greek government.

The population of Circassians today residing in Anatolia is at the very least two million. Circassians defend and maintain their national traditions through language, customs, feelings and civilization. . . . They are in the contemporary family of civilizations and are a part of the white race and the distinguished Aryan family. . . .

Upon the collapse of the Arab government and upon the decision of the Egyptian government in Cairo, Circassians were continuously in the governments that were established in the Arab lands, North Africa and Syria for three centuries. In the Caucasus, which is their national homeland, the Circassians formed a republic [which was] independent administratively and politically. They are the famous fighters [who] continuously fought for twenty years against the Russian Empire, under the administration and command of the well-known Sheikh (*şeyh*) Shamil, who saw the danger of the Russian invasion.

A population of two million Circassians from the northern and western Caucasus, which was composed of three million people, was suspicious of [Russian actions] and bit by bit emigrated to Turkey (at that time the Sublime Porte extended a protective invitation). The one million people that stayed in the North Caucasus have to today grown to a population of three million according to Russian statistics.

According to calculations, the two million Circassians who emigrated to Turkey would have risen to a population of between three to six million. Unfortunately, today it is closer to two million. The reason why is this: It is extremely clear that there were tragedies in transport as a result of mismanagement, which is impossible for the Ottoman government to deny. As a result of being sacrificed to these catastrophes, Circassians have been denied four million of its population.

Thirteen years before with the institution of constitutional rule, the Turkish administration became bereft of correct policies. Now filled with feelings [stemming] from Turkishism and Turanism, Turkish administrators followed at this unique moment in history a false policy of terrorism, by means of Turkification, towards the various Ottoman nationalities. With the destruction of the nationalities and the destruction of the vital security of non-Turks, the Circassians were stirred with a just grievance coming from a 'pure desire of self-preservation'. Because of these continuous calamities, Circassians have [moved towards] a national goal of self-preservation and commit themselves to armed resistance against the mass murder of the Circassian nation.

Because of this, Circassians have lost thousands of their precious children. Their property and animals have been stolen and their villages burned. In short, Circassians have been and continue to be in a state of defiance in this war despite being allotted no sanctuary and the destruction and seizure of their property.

However, it is not [the case] that Circassians did not join the world war either as commanders or as soldiers with their farm animals. But like various other nations, they were forced by their feelings and by the law. Nevertheless a very small portion of Circassians joined the Anatolian revolutionaries (filled with false feelings) right after the ceasefire. Mustafa Kemal [says] his movement supports the foundation of the sultanate, yet the Kemalists are seen and understood as a movement against humanity and with false policies. Regretfully, a very small number of Circassians have entered into the service of this movement.

Circassians in the Sublime Porte, which continues to support the caliphate, are especially working together with the Kemalists. Despite this self-sacrifice, [the Porte] still neglects Circassians. After not seeing that they will be saved, Circassians decided correctly and naturally to join the Greek army, which promises to preserve them, in the occupation zone. (There is no doubt that Albania and the Arab States similarly sought foreign saviours well before). These Circassians, who have struggled for a year and a half and who have saved thousands of innocent Muslims and non-Muslims from mass murder, should be praised for their services.

The understanding Greek government, which is included in the highest levels of civilization and humanity among nations, recognizes no difference among Circassians, Armenians and especially Rum. It has provided for the welfare of Circassian immigrants and refugees in the form of substance and settlement.

It is fitting to remember, with thanks and with kind words, those who aid and extend trust to our countrymen taken as prisoners of war, those under the submission of Kemalist oppression and to the Circassian people living in areas under the administration of the military occupation since the days the Greek government set foot in Anatolia.

As a consequence of these kind actions, the Circassians hope and request that, because of their convictions, they be included in the understanding of civilization and their legal and human rights be defended. These things have been [discussed] face to face between the Circassians, which is a secular nation, and the Rum peoples.

The goals of this petition are:

A. Recognition of our national existence.
B. To make known that the secular Circassian nation lives in constant danger.
C. To advance the demand that the Circassians wish to live as an element of peace under Greek protection in order to protect the Circassians of the Near East from the sins of the Turkish administration. [This is in response to] the Ottoman government which was a warring and tumultuous element in Europe and the Near East, both within and without, which denied a competent, modern and civilized administration and which collapsed because of the mismanagement of the sultan over the last three hundred years. [This continued with] the constitutional government, which stood in the place of the Ottoman government, which insisted, under the extreme Turkists, that it did not recognize the human rights of non-Turks in Anatolia. This is an impossible denial of the truth according to the civilized world.

As a consequence, our congress requests a statement to the petitioners, who expect action with impatience, regarding the acceptance of our demands which are national [in nature] according to the Allied Great Powers and their partners.

1. The application of the laws regarding the guarantee of human rights to minorities to all Circassians, laws that were accepted and proposed among the states following the war and that was to be brought into the Near East.
2. The imposition of protection under the civilized Greek government [and] of the desired [fulfilment] of the predestined unity of the Circassian nation with the Rum nation, which has been agreed upon. The Greek government hopes by force to [further] the progress and development [of these two nations].

3. The rendering on an indemnity from the Turkish government to the Circassian nation for all the damages incurred. . . .
4. The participation of our representatives in the peace conference in order to negotiate our national demands.[109]

After completing their petition, the following individuals undersigned the document.

Adapazarı representative—(Bağ) Talustan Bey
İzmit representative—(Çule) İbrahim Bey
İzmit representative—(Çiyo) Kazım Bey
Hendek representative—(Bağ) Osman Bey
Düzce representative—(Maan) Ali Bey
Düzce representative—(Hamete) Ahmet Bey
Kandıra and Karasu representative—(Maan) Şirin Bey
Yalova–Karamürsel representative—(Ançok) Yakup Bey
Bilecik representative—(Bağ) Rifat Bey
Eskişehir representative—(Bağ) Kamil Bey
Geyve representative—(Çule) Beslan Bey
Bursa representative—Harunelreşit Efendi
Biga representative—(Ançok) İsa Nuri Bey
Gönen representative—(Lampez) Yakup Efendi
Gönen representative—Hafız Sait Efendi of the Regional Committee
Erdek representative—(Şahabel) Hasan Bey
Bandırma representative—(Neçoku) Hasan Bey
Bandırma representative—(Brau) Sait Bey
Bandırma representative—(Berzek) Tahir Bey
Balıkesir representative—(Bazadoğ) Sait Bey
Manisa representative—(Pşev) Reşit Bey
Aydın representative—(Kavaca) Hüseyin Bey
Kütahya representative—(Açofit) Sami Bey[110]

This document is a dramatic piece of evidence in both its composition and its objectives. Traditionally, however, its meaning within the historiography of the Turkish War of Independence has been marginalized. Tarık Zafer Tunaya, the famous Turkish historian, first brought this to public attention in 1952 in his work on the development of political parties during the late Ottoman/early Republican period. In summarizing the goals and reasoning behind the creation of the Near Eastern Circassian Association, Tunaya argued that this organization was an extension of the 'Circassian issue' first reared by Ahmet Anzavur and *Çerkes* Ethem (in other words, by the enemies of the National Movement). More importantly, Tunaya points out that the demand for autonomy, which is implied in the document, was only a ruse that concealed the imperialist machinations of the Kingdom of Greece and Great Britain, since both powers offered moral support to this separatist organization.[111]

In defending and confirming the dogmas of Turkish national history, Tunaya is in part correct in his analysis of this congress in Izmir. There was certainly a connection between the Circassian resistance first kindled by Ahmet Anzavur and the men who convened to write (or at the very least approve) this document. Some of the participants were indeed among the first engineers of this struggle: İbrahim Hakkı, (Maan) Ali, (Maan) Şirin, (Bağ) Talustan, and (Berzek) Tahir. Since the meeting was held in Izmir, there is also no doubt that the occupying powers played a role in facilitating the meeting.

Beyond these points, however, this petition had real implications for the Circassian communities that these men claimed to represent. This document demonstrates the radical shift in the thinking of many anti-Nationalist leaders, men who had personally led local Circassian immigrants into battle against the *Kuva-yı Milliye* since the start of the conflict in 1919. What this document implies is the degree to which the onset of the Greek occupation had changed both the parameters under which their struggle would be waged *and* the meaning that Circassianness would assume in this new political environment.

There are two key elements that define the composition of this statement by the Near Eastern Circassian Association. The first is the reciting, and rewriting, of North Caucasian history. The second is the presentation and defence of the association's demands. While corresponding roughly to the first and second halves of the petition, the two elements play off one another throughout the piece.

The use of history in this document does not serve some perfunctory purpose; rather, it forms a key justification for the association's argument. The main themes of this history in many ways reflect the historical arc inherent in the traditional writing of Ottoman history: a nation with noble origins that was laid low by catastrophe. In an overture to its European audience, the petition emphasizes that these feats were accomplished not by an Oriental or degenerate people, but by white Aryans. This reference to race and colour serves as a clear message to the European reader: we are inheritors of the same civilization, making our culture and history no less noble or worthy of your respect. The use of race in this petition likewise draws a contrast with other peoples of the Middle East: namely, the Arabs, who were collectively viewed as the bastard offspring of a rich civilization.[112]

This history reaches its crescendo, as the petition continues, in the mass exile of the Circassians from their homeland. The moment of disaster occurred not with the deportation, but with their arrival in the Ottoman lands. At first this took the form of the Ottoman government's mismanagement and incompetence, which resulted in the death of a vast numbers of refugees (and by extension, it seems, millions of unborn Circassians). Ottoman incompetence was then followed by outright maliciousness when the Committee of Union and Progress (which goes unnamed throughout this document) undertook a policy of Turkification. These 'false policies' apparently continued to manifest themselves in the post-war period under the auspices of Mustafa Kemal's National Movement. Thus, it seems, the Circassians faced an impossible choice between the corruption of the Ottoman sultan and the destructive intentions of Mustafa Kemal.

This discussion of the contemporary political predicament that confronted the Circassians is accompanied by a startling allusion to mass murder and theft on the part of the CUP regime. Further, it is a reference also to the suffering of Christians in the empire. Considering the audience, this rhetorical tact may be an attempt to play upon Western perceptions of the Ottoman Empire after the deportations of Armenians in 1915. As a calamity that attracted considerable attention in the Western press during the First World War, this pairing of the plight of non-Muslims in Anatolia and that of Circassians would have been an effective tool in furthering the agenda of the association (even though, ironically, many of the allies of the organization were known to have aided in the deportations).

The message to be gleaned from this abstract of Circassian history boils down to the tradition of resistance and defiance by the peoples of the North Caucasus. Just as Sheikh Shamil saw the dangers of Russian imperialism, so the framers of this document identified the National Movement as a mortal threat to their existence. The strength and conviction of this resistance, it is argued, demand both recognition *and* action from the Great Powers of Europe. The authors raise an interesting point in this regard. By seeking the protection of Greece and the attention of the Great Powers, they cite the precedents of Albania and the Arab lands, who, they claim, sought independence through foreign intervention. There were, in other words, past precedents, where similar demands were extended and granted. The means and manner in which these pleas were raised are striking. In citing both the historical and the legal basis for their demand for protection, the Association for the Strengthening of Near Eastern Circassian Rights demonstrates a keen awareness of its audience and the contemporary international consensus.

In laying their claims, the authors of this document understood that there was a higher power to which they could appeal: international law. Thus the policy of Turkification and the violence of the Kemalist movement were more than acts of cruelty and inhumanity; they were violations of the 'civil and political rights' of the Circassian 'minority'. Their demand for protection, and by extension separation, was a direct allusion to the twelfth point of Woodrow Wilson's Fourteen Points. The passage reads in part: 'The Turkish portion of the present Ottoman Empire should be assured a secure sovereignty, but the other nationalities which are now under Turkish rule should be assured an undoubted security of life and an absolutely unmolested opportunity of autonomous development.'[113] For this reason, the Near Eastern Circassian Association specifically requested that their existence as a minority in Anatolia be recognized, in turn justifying their claim for 'autonomous development'. This claim was similarly extended by the Society for the Advancement of Kurdistan (*Kürdistan Teâli Cemiyeti*), which claimed that Kurds too formed an indivisible nation within Anatolia.[114]

These rhetorical devices that pepper the document further betray an astute comprehension of the post-Versailles imperial order. The petition's framers understood that a legalistic argument alone would not validate their claim. The appeal had to be written using the same diction employed by the Great Powers in dealing with 'the Orient'. Like some long lost tribe or Anatolian Prester John, the Circassians of this congress presented their people as no less the successors of European traditions and institutions. They were racially and culturally superior to their Turkish oppressors, yet forced to live under the latter's corrupt rule. Their devotion to Islam did not prevent them from meeting with their Rum and Armenian neighbours on an equal footing, since each desired re-entry into the European family of nations. In short, it was a humble request among distant kin. For good measure, Greek and French translations of the document were distributed both in Anatolia and to various governments in Europe.[115]

It is difficult to reconcile the desires and the words of the Association for the Strengthening of Near Eastern Circassian Rights and the writings and statements of the resistance in 1919 and 1920. The differences between the two periods are fundamental and profound. By November 1921, it is clear that these men who had once supported Ahmet Anzavur no longer desired to turn back the clock to the antebellum status quo. The Ottoman Empire seemed destined for partition, if not outright collapse. They wanted to be no longer local notables under the patronage of an imperial court, but architects of what would become their own state. In turn, they graduated from Ahmet Anzavur's provincial populism. In abandoning the broader Loyalist coalition, the Near Eastern Circassian Association erased the contribution of Pomak, Albanian, Çetmi, Turkish, Kurdish, and Bosnian supporters from both the history of the uprisings and the future of the South Marmara. Now there was no further need of Ottoman and Islamic symbolism. The social and economic injustices of the Young Turk regime could no longer be rectified under the good graces of the Istanbul government. Nor could the basis for any just settlement be meted out under the time-tested and indigenous principles of Islam. A new political and rhetorical regime had to be established if the resistance was to continue.

There are only scraps of evidence suggesting that the work of the Association for the Strengthening of Near Eastern Circassian Rights extended into the South Marmara. According to anecdotes relayed to Fahri Görgülü, a similar congress was organized in Balıkesir at some point between 1921 and 1922.[116] At one meeting in July 1921, 169 Circassian village notables offered to give up their Ottoman citizenship and to form a cavalry unit for the Greek occupation (although the Greek government purportedly turned the offer down).[117] Another man interviewed by Görgülü, a former gendarme from Kirmasti who had worked under the Greek occupation, claimed that disciples of the Near Eastern Circassian Association were meeting clandestinely in town soon after the Izmir congress.[118]

One key issue raised by Tarık Zafer Tunaya remains unanswered: Did Greece or Great Britain play any role in the creation of this organization and its agenda? The answer appears obvious, since the meeting was held in Greek-occupied Izmir in the first place. But does this mean that the demands of the Circassians were disingenuous or that the men who met in Izmir were willing puppets of the occupiers? Two dispatches found in the British Public Records Office offers some answers to these questions. One from October 1920 reads as follows:

Non-Turkish Muslims are being treated with certain attention and politeness, and the Circassians especially have been won over to a certain extent by the Greeks. They are given greater facilities for travel and trade, etc. Greek policy has been explained by diverse [sic] non-Greek sources as follows:-

(a) It is purely opportunistic [sic] and will have no equal [sic] when the Greeks leave.
(b) The admission of Circassian settlers on the frontier of Ionia is being contemplated. They would replace the Turks in the border villages like the Cossacks in the North Caucasus.
(c) The creation of pro-Greek sentiment is desired among the Muslim minorities in the hope that they will call upon Greece to be their intercessor with the League of Nations which is charged with the protection of 'minority rights'.

Informant personally favours the last explanation. Circassians in Bursa, Pandirma and Ismidt [İzmit] stated that there was a growing desire for autonomy on the part of the Circassians, and to concentrate near the Greek sphere, i.e. the Manias–Balikesir region. If England did not care to protect them, Greece might do so, and their good opinion of the Greeks had increased, but they were sick of the Turks.

Informant received the impression that by their cruel tyranny, the Nationalists had alienated the sympathies of many of their fellow countrymen. So far as the clever and more courageous Circassian elements were concerned, this policy had been a particularly grave blunder from which the subtle and politic Hellenes may derive great advantage.[119]

Almost a year and a half later, a second report was submitted, this time by Sir Harry Lamb, Representative of the British High Commission in Izmir, regarding the question of Circassian status in Anatolia. Lamb stated to his superiors that he had met İbrahim Hakkı soon after the convening of the Circassian congress and was given a copy of the organization's petition. İbrahim reiterated the main demands of the Near Eastern Circassian Association and contended that the ideal solution was the creation of a British protectorate over some region of northwestern Anatolia where Circassians could be gathered together. Failing this, the Circassians would also accept the protection of 'Europe', as represented by the League of Nations, or of the Kingdom of Greece. İbrahim Hakkı also informed Harry Lamb that Greek diplomatic representatives abroad were undertaking the Circassian cause and that their case would be presented to the other members of Allied Powers.[120]

The British response to these demands was less than enthusiastic. Sir Horace Rumbold, Head of the British High Commission in Istanbul, categorically stated that the Circassians deserved no special treatment as a 'racial minority' in Anatolia and that Greek protection was an impossibility since many Circassians lived in territory not under their control. Despite the fact that he had no 'special sympathy' for the self-serving Circassians, he did agree with Lamb that some consideration had to be given to North Caucasians in İzmit, since they had supported British forces in the region. Desk officers back in London were also sceptical of İbrahim Hakkı's intentions, with one commenting on the side that it was 'pretty clear that [the association's statement] is Greek propaganda'. All seemed to agree that 'nothing special' could be done for the Circassians, and that ultimately they (as well as Greeks and Armenians) had to rely upon a general governmental amnesty in the war's aftermath.[121]

Even in the absence of Greek archival sources, these two documents do shed some light on the relationship between Greece, Great Britain, and the Near Eastern Circassian Association. It appears that some Circassian notables in the South Marmara decided very soon after the last of the Loyalist uprisings to seek some sort of autonomy. Harry Lamb's report suggests that this conviction among the Circassian delegates who met in Izmir was indeed genuine. But it also appears that the Greeks had a hand in the process from the beginning. Most intriguingly, as the first document suggests, it seems that the Greeks may have had a 'Circassian policy' even before they had pushed into the South Marmara. Whatever the case, it was clearly in the interest of the Greek occupation to seek local Muslim allies in securing their position in Anatolia. The real question that remains unanswered is who in fact crafted the association's statement? Was it the 'illiterate' İbrahim Hakkı or another Circassian? Was it a Greek administrator? Or a combination of the two? It may not in the end matter all that much; the Association for the Strengthening of Near Eastern Circassian Rights demanded autonomy and protection, and the Greeks supported them in this claim.

The *Kuva-yı Milliye* responded quickly to the statement issued by the Circassians in Izmir. On 28 November 1921, a group of Circassian intellectuals, officers, and notables gathered in Beşiktaş, just north of Istanbul's old quarter, to release a statement countering the demands of the Near Eastern Circassian Association. The group was led by two men who typified the Circassian establishment in Istanbul: (Big) Ahmet Fevzi, who had attempted to convince Circassians in the South Marmara to end their revolt in the winter of 1919, and *Deli* Fuat, the old mandarin of the *Şimali Kafkas Cemiyeti*. The group told the crowd that gathered that the Association for the Strengthening of Near Eastern Circassian Rights was composed of 'good-for-nothings' (like Şah İsmail, Çerkes Reşit, and his brother Ethem).122 The association, it was claimed, was composed of only 'ten to fifteen men from Bandırma', and that the Greeks forced them to write this statement and brought them into Izmir for this purpose alone.123 *Hakimiyet-i Milliye*, the official newspaper of the National Movement, which first reported the existence of the association through a source in Düzce, called these defenders of the *Kuva-yı Milliye* in Istanbul beloved Circassians (*aziziyeli Çerkesler*).124 The message from Ankara and from Circassian supporters in Istanbul was nearly identical: these Circassians were the minority, and in reality there was no 'Circassian issue' to speak of in Anatolia.125 True Circassians were still grateful to the Ottoman state, and would never join with the enemy and take up arms like the traitors in Izmir.

At this stage in the progression of the War of Independence, such statements were solely for the consumption of the party faithful. The fact that the Nationalists could count on the support of several ageing Circassian officers from Istanbul meant little in terms of the underlying resistance among Circassians in the South Marmara. The gulf between the pro-Nationalist Circassians of Istanbul and local Circassian notables in Adapazarı and Gönen was too wide to be bridged. What mattered for the *Kuva-yı Milliye* (as well as for the anti-Nationalists in Izmir) was the illusion of solidarity.

No such debate was taking place among Albanians in Anatolia. More pointedly, the Albanian diaspora is noted only for its absence during the occupation years. At the local level, the Albanian alliances that were once so influential in places such as Karacabey, Kirmasti, and Karamürsel/Değirmendere are barely mentioned save at the end when Albanian bands were reported to have played a role in evicting Çerkes Davut's band from Kirmasti.126 Even the Albanian diaspora in Istanbul presents itself as an indifferent party within the occupation. For the Albanian Mutual Aid Society (*Arnavud Teavün Cemiyeti*), the only émigré organization representing the interests of Albanians in Anatolia, attention was drawn more towards affairs in the Balkans in 1921 and 1922, during which time the Kingdom of Yugoslavia (with Serbia in the lead) pushed ahead in its war of expansion against Albania.127 The neglect shown by the 'Albanian Colony in Turkey' towards its fellow Albanians in Anatolia may in part be the result of the nature and make-up of the party, since it was established primarily as an organization of Albanian expatriates committed to issues in the Balkans as opposed to the Ottoman Empire.128

As we have seen, there were clear differences between the development of the Albanian and North Caucasian diasporas at the provincial level. The distinct manners in which the two groups came to settle in Anatolia had a profound effect on organizational abilities both within the communities themselves and in the relationship between the state and provincial notables. The little that we know about the Albanian Mutual Aid Society reveals that it continued to have a strong connection with the Balkans, either through personal contacts, financial relationships, and/or nationalist impulses. These bonds between the Albanian elite in Istanbul and the Balkans ultimately appeared to have superseded any interest in Albanian immigrants' affairs in the Anatolian hinterland. Like the colonies established in Bucharest, Geneva, Cairo, and Boston, the Albanian elite in Istanbul was more concerned with issues in the homeland than in the fading heart of the Ottoman Empire.

Any and all separatist aspirations in the South Marmara came to a crashing halt during the summer following the Izmir congress. In September 1922, Mustafa Kemal's forces counter-attacked along the Sakarya front to the east of Eskişehir, and within a matter of days drove the Greeks across the Aegean. The rout was swift and total. Greek soldiers stationed in Bursa ran and swam for their lives in the face of the Kemalist onslaught. Thousands of Armenian and Rum civilians and collaborators followed in tow.[129] Columns of armed and unarmed North Caucasians, fearing the worst, made their way across the Marmara Sea by way of Çorlu and Tekirdağ, to find safety only on the other side of the Greek frontier.[130] Most of the members of the Association for the Strengthening of Near Eastern Circassian Rights fled along with them, as did many of the infamous Circassian *çeteci*s such as Davut and Kadir.

War did not end formally following Mustafa Kemal's grand entrance into Izmir on 9 September. Sporadic fighting and diplomatic wrangling continued well into the new year. The South Marmara's physical and economic recuperation took still longer. For most non-Muslims living along the Marmara's southern shores, the ensuing peace was accompanied by one last great horror: total banishment. Under the stipulations laid out in the Treaty of Lausanne in 1923, all Rum in the region were forced to pack what possessions they could and board ships bound for the Greek mainland and permanent resettlement. Small numbers of native Greeks, as well as Armenians, circumvented the order by relocating to Istanbul. In their wake, whole villages and city quarters became ghost towns for a second time in less than a decade. Old homes were again distributed to newly arriving Muslim refugees and migrants or were broken down into firewood.[131]

In the next, and final, chapter, I wish to depart somewhat from the traditional line of inquiry into the war's effect upon Anatolia's population. Several fine scholars have recently documented and described the state of non-Muslims during the immediate post-war era in rich detail. Although it is true that Rum and Armenian life persisted in the South Marmara in the years following Lausanne, it is clear that the weight of multiple acts of deportation and disenfranchisement reduced these two communities to a mere shadow of their former selves. I intend, instead, to close by looking more closely at the war's effect upon Albanians and North Caucasians in the South Marmara and beyond. Although much of the following chapter discusses matters well beyond the purview of the war years, it is only after the closure of the War of Independence that the Nationalist (now Republican) government fully addressed issues related to North Caucasian and Albanian resistance and recalcitrance. As will become clearer over the next chapter, the Turkish state continued to grapple with several complex local, as well as transnational, challenges posed by Circassian and Albanian migrants in the South Marmara. This confrontation between governmental and provincial forces, which had begun during the Young Turk period, remained unresolved well into the reign of Mustafa Kemal (Atatürk).

6

Settling Accounts: Circassians, Albanians, and the Founding of the Turkish Republic

The year following Mustafa Kemal's entrance into Izmir is the quintessential moment of redemption in Turkish historiography. On 1 November 1922, the Grand National Parliament in Ankara abolished the Ottoman sultanate, ending nearly six centuries of rule under the descendants of Gazi Osman with the stroke of a pen. A formal peace would be signed with Greece after months of negotiations at Lausanne on 24 July 1923. Two weeks after the treaty, the Allied Powers turned over Istanbul to the Nationalists, marking the final departure of occupation armies from Anatolia.[1] On 29 October, the Grand Turkish National Assembly announced the creation of the Republic of Turkey, a state that would encompass most of the territories claimed by Mustafa Kemal in his National Pact of 1920.[2] The administration of this new state fell to Mustafa Kemal's own party, the People's Party (*Halk Fırkası*, later the Republican People's Party, *Cumhuriyet Halk Fırkası*), which had been established two and half months before the republic was declared. It is from this point that Turkish historians have begun to tell the story of Anatolia's rebirth under the reforms of this single party. With the darkest hours in the past, Mustafa Kemal could now, in the words of Andrew Mango, 'concentrate on the job of fashioning a new Turkey'.[3] Victory, in other words, seemed total.

Upon closer inspection, the realities of this crucial period do not appear to have been so clear-cut. Opposition to Mustafa Kemal and his People's Party was manifest even before the proclamation of the Turkish Republic. By the summer of 1923, Mustafa Kemal had forbidden the reconstitution of the Committee of Union and Progress or the fielding of any opposition party in the June parliamentary elections.[4] Coupled with the declaration of the Turkish Republic and the abolition of the caliphate (accomplished in March 1924), the old guard of the National Movement (particularly men such as Rauf Orbay, Kazım (Karabekir), Ali Fuat (Cebesoy), and Adnan (Adıvar)) feared that they too would be forced aside by Mustafa Kemal and the supporters of his expanding dictatorship. In November 1924, these former stalwarts of both the National Movement and the CUP joined together to form the Progressive Republican Party (*Terakkiperver Cumhuriyet Fırkası*), an organization that expressly opposed the authoritarian tendencies exhibited by Mustafa Kemal and his People's Party.

This effort, however, proved short-lived. The outbreak of the Şeyh Sait Rebellion in the southeastern province of Diyarbakir in February 1925 allowed the Kemalist parliament to assume new dictatorial powers, powers used in June to ban the Progressive Republican Party.[5] One year later, after a supposed assassination attempt on Mustafa Kemal, the Progressive leaders were arrested as co-conspirators and charged with attempting to revive the CUP.[6] Seventeen men were condemned to death for their part in the plot, and several others, including Rauf Orbay and Adnan Adıvar, were sentenced to long prison terms.[7] The message gleaned from the trial's proceedings is clear. Despite the fact that its infrastructure and personnel had given life to the National Movement, the CUP as a party had no place in the Turkish Republic. While the men who comprised both the People's Party and Progressive Republican Party had both emerged from the ranks of the CUP, loyalty would be counted only in terms of one's acceptance of Mustafa Kemal's sole authority. Anything deviating from this recognition of Kemalist rule would stand as treason.

This chapter expands the scope of this narrative of transformation, violence, and retribution in looking at the South Marmara during the first years of Republican rule. The end of the war not only brought a new administration to the region, but also heralded a total physical and demographic reconstitution of its cities and towns. The Greek occupation and the Nationalist counter-attack left many of its cities and villages completely destroyed and in urgent need of repair. While towns like Bandırma, Adapazarı, and Orhangazi were rebuilt, a new wave of immigrants flooded the region after the 'Great Exchange' of populations (*Büyük Mübadele*) between Turkey and Greece in 1923. In the South Marmara and elsewhere, thousands of Rum were deported to Greece and then replaced by Muslims from Macedonia, the Epirus, Crete, and western Thrace. This new wave of settlers did not end with the exchanges, as thousands more from Yugoslavia, Bulgaria, Cyprus, Romania, and the Soviet Union continued to arrive in the South Marmara through the following decades. By the time of Atatürk's death in 1938, much of what had been Ottoman society in the new provinces of Çanakkale, Balıkesir, Bursa, Kocaeli, and Sakarya had disappeared and been replaced by the new cultural and political norms created by the Kemalist state.

It is at this point in the history of Albanians and North Caucasians in the South Marmara that the trail largely turns cold. Sources are few and far between, and those that do exist often deliberately avoid any mention of the presence of 'non-Turkish' Muslims in Anatolia. This chapter presents an attempt to locate Albanians and Circassians in the first years of the Turkish Republic just before they disappeared altogether from official and popular consciousness. In lieu of further excavation of the personal lives of the members of these diasporas, it is my intention to focus more on the consequences of the War of Independence in the South Marmara and how Kemalist policies towards North Caucasians and Albanians fitted within the grander schemes of the young Republic.

KILLING ANZAVUR'S GHOST: REPUBLICAN POLITICS AND THE END OF CIRCASSIAN RESISTANCE IN THE SOUTH MARMARA

In September 1922, the Nationalists retook the town of Gönen for the second time in two years. Unlike in the spring of 1920, it is unclear to what degree the Nationalists were able to mop up the Circassian resistance that fought to defend the town with their Rum allies.[8] Little is known about the immediate aftermath of the war in the South Marmara. It has been suggested recently by one journalist that in Susurluk alone, the National Forces executed thirty-three members of the local *eşraf* for collaboration.[9] If *Çerkes* Ethem's 1920 campaign of retribution after the Anzavur uprisings served as any kind of precedent, it is likely that mass executions and other forms of collective punishment were commonplace following the Greek withdrawal.

The capture of Izmir did not end the war in the South Marmara. Almost immediately following the Nationalist victory, a new guerrilla resistance reared itself in the environs of Balıkesir. In late November 1922, a party of men, numbering between twenty-five and thirty individuals, landed on the shores near the town of Ayvalık. They were ferried ashore on Greek vessels, yet were led by a former Ottoman gendarmerie officer, Mehmet Ali, who had served in Manyas during the War of Independence. Mehmet Ali's men were divided into two columns. One, under the command of a Yörük by the name of İsmail *Efe*, was sent towards Izmir, and the other, led by Çallı Kadir *Efe*, was directed towards Manyas.[10] The latter band first met resistance from local Nationalist forces at Dikili, just south of Ayvalık, where Mehmet Ali was wounded and captured. The remaining men, now under the former Nationalist and close friend of *Çerkes* Ethem, Takiğ Şevket, turned north towards Manyas, where they were again beaten and scattered by local gendarmes.[11]

Mehmet Ali's raid was the first of at least five incursions made by paramilitaries armed and supported by Greece. The second was carried out in April 1923, when a band of between twenty and thirty men arrived at the village of Dalyan İskelesi near Bayramiç. Led by a former partisan of Ahmet Anzavur, *Kel* Aziz, the band got as far as Bayramiç before being defeated by a detachment of gendarmes. The third, and perhaps the largest, of the incursions occurred in May 1923. At the head of this group of up to seventy men was Anzavur's oldest son, Kadir, and *Kanlı* Mustafa, his long-time lieutenant from Biga.[12] The men purportedly attempted to land on shore with the intention of taking Biga, but were ambushed on the beach by an armed government contingent lying in wait for them.[13] Kadir survived the ambush but was wounded in a second clash while entering the town of Çanakkale.[14] He was transported to Bayramiç for medical treatment and then executed for treason.[15] Two other groups of paramilitaries would land on Anatolia's shores in August 1923 and in 1927 respectively.[16] Both of these later invasions would fail just as miserably.

This effort certainly had its roots before the Battle of Sakarya, beginning with the arming of the first Circassian paramilitaries after the Greek offensive in early summer of 1920. Yet, with the war at an end, this relationship between the Greek government and its North Caucasian supporters at first appeared to have become strained. According to a Greek report found by Emrah Cilasun, both *Çerkes* Ethem and his brother Reşit told their Greek hosts that it was their intention to kill Mustafa Kemal and replace him with Enver Paşa. Despite their promises to prepare their Circassian supporters for a campaign against the Nationalists, both Reşit and Ethem remained in contact with Ankara and did little in the way of bringing their armed retainers into the struggle. In addition to their difficulties with these two brothers, the Greeks were also forced to contend with the reluctance of İbrahim Hakkı and his followers in the Near Eastern Circassian Association, who seemed more willing to negotiate their future with the British and the French than with the 'small and poor' Kingdom of Greece.[17] To top it all off, there were initial signs that the faction led by Ethem and his brother would not associate with İbrahim Hakkı, who did not support the two men's commitment to Enver Paşa and a pan-Islamic struggle.[18]

This bickering that followed the Greek retreat from Izmir gave way to discussions of more pressing matters, as it became clear that thousands of North Caucasians, as well as Rum, Armenians, and other dissidents, had fled Anatolia and were seeking refuge in territories still held by Athens. According to Rıza Nur, a high-ranking member of the Nationalist government in Ankara, some 12,000 North Caucasians, mostly Abkhazians, fled from the environs of Adapazarı alone.[19] British officials, in anticipating a Greek pull-out from Anatolia, projected in the spring of 1922 that a minimum of 90,000 Rum (50,000 of this number being the relatives of men under arms) and around 30,000 Circassians would have to be evacuated from their homes for fear of acts of retaliation carried out by a victorious Nationalist army.[20]

The main destination for many of these Circassians was the island of Midilli (Lesbos), just a few kilometers off the coast of Ayvalık. There some 5,000 men, women, and children, many of whom were from the İzmit/Adapazarı region, had settled under the leadership of *İngiliz* İbrahim Hakkı.[21] During the following months, İbrahim Hakkı vigorously pleaded with the British High Commission to take an interest in their plight. In a letter to Lieutenant Vivian Hadkinson dated 2 October 1922, he wrote:

For years we acted in the interests of England and attracted upon us the tremendous hatred of the Turks. We took arms, without any condition, and fought against Kemalists, with the firm belief that we were serving justice and humanity. When the English and the Greeks withdrew their forces from [the] Ismidt region we were obliged to follow their example, leaving behind all property and extensive estates. . . . We naturally expect that the British Authorities should run to our aid in such a narrow circumstance, as we did once when they needed our armed help.[22]

The primary concern for İbrahim and his followers on Midilli was the issue of resettlement. The party most receptive to İbrahim's demands was Vivian Hadkinson, who had been the primary British agent in the South Marmara since 1919. Beginning in November 1922, Hadkinson had proposed sending the Circassians to Palestine, Iraq, or India, should hostilities resume following the Greek pull-out from Anatolia. Almost immediately, the idea of resettling the Circassians from İzmit in Palestine was excluded from the realm of possibilities.[23] In January 1923, India was also taken off the list, with one officer lamenting the fact that it was 'a bit hard luck on the Greeks to hold on to the Circassians indefinitely'.[24] By the spring of 1923, only two other possible areas of resettlement remained: Cyprus (İbrahim Hakkı's personal choice) and Iraq.[25] As far as Iraq was concerned, the British Foreign Office initially seemed to favour the idea, so long as no additional expenses were incurred.[26] The British High Commission in Athens promoted the plan, saying that a body of Circassian cavalry would be useful in providing for security in Iraq. However, financial and bureaucratic concerns again ended any further consideration of the matter. Not only was the defence of Iraq a matter for the Air Ministry, but the Foreign Office was adamant in its position that no further money be spent on the North Caucasians.[27] İbrahim Hakkı continued to press for their transfer to Iraq until March. In one dispatch from Vivian Hadkinson, it was asked whether or not there was some philanthropic society which could help fund the settlement of Circassians in Iraq. İbrahim even went as far as to say that his followers were happy to work as agricultural labourers, and that they would have a lot in common with the Kurds, the predominant population of northern Iraq.[28] In the end nothing appeared to have come of any of these plans.

Throughout the winter of 1922/3, the situation among the Circassian refugees in Midilli grew worse. The Greek government at one point cut off all funds for İbrahim Hakkı's retainers, leading to shortages of food and shelter on the island.[29] While American missionaries eventually took up the slack, the state of the displaced North Caucasians on the island continued to be poor into March 1923.[30] That month İbrahim Hakkı received more bad news when British authorities informed him that no Circassian representatives would be allowed at the peace negotiations in Lausanne. Again, neither the Greek government nor the British government was willing to provide funds for bringing such a representative to Switzerland. Instead, Circassians in Anatolia, as well as those now abroad, would have to rely upon the amnesty clauses in the forthcoming treaty.[31]

With no place to go and no voice in the diplomatic process, Circassian refugees on various islands in the Aegean and in western Thrace had few options left. In several British dispatches, it was made clear that the refugees were prepared to fight or do anything that would help bring down the new Kemalist government.³² As early as November 1922, Greek authorities were readying many of the Circassians residing in their territory for that very purpose.

It is not clear who first engineered the incursion conducted by Mehmet Ali in November 1922. Yet Greek, English, and Ottoman documents categorically demonstrate that covert operations had begun to take shape on the island of Midilli by April 1923. According to British documents, some 1,400 Circassians (as well as other individuals, including Armenians and Rum) were being trained on the island. The plan called for the Greek military eventually to ferry as many as 600 guerrillas at a time to the Anatolian mainland. Mehmet Ali's assault appears to have been the first step in this effort, which, despite having been unsuccessful, was reported to have gathered 1,700 men to his side during his brief incursion.³³ The later two attacks would have more of an official air. According to Ottoman documents, the guerrillas arrested and executed after the attacks of April and June 1923 were organized under the auspices of a Greek-supported organization entitled the Ottoman Revolutionary Committee of Anatolia (*Anadolu Osmanlı İhtilal Komitesi*). In their brief tour of the South Marmara, Kel Aziz and (Anzavuroğlu) Kadir distributed formal written statements declaring an open revolt in the region.³⁴

The British, for their part, took a particularly curious stand on the conduct of this organization. While recognizing that this offensive was in violation of the terms of the Mudanya Armistice, both London and the British High Commission in Istanbul and Athens approved the covert operation. The consent given by the British Foreign Office (which was accompanied by an indirect order to deny any involvement with the plan) came also with the realization that the plan was destined to fail and that the Circassians would most likely be sent to their deaths.³⁵

What is interesting about this brief, but desperate, campaign is the collection of men who organized and led these insurgents. The commanding officer of this covert force was none other than Eşref Kuşçubaşı, who had fled to Greece with *Çerkes* Ethem and was now helping to engineer the campaign with funds gathered from Berlin and Switzerland.³⁶ This revelation is most striking for the fact that Eşref not only failed to mention it in his own recollections of his actions during the War of Independence, but there is seemingly no record of exactly when and why Eşref turned against the National Movement altogether.³⁷ The British High Commission Office also name *Çerkes* Ethem as one of the executive organizers of this campaign, even though Ethem was known to be sick and most probably in Germany at the time.³⁸ Together with these one-time leaders of the National Movement was a rogues' gallery of former Loyalists, including Kadir, *Kanlı* Mustafa, and *Çerkes* Davut, to name only a few.³⁹ The nascent Turkish government in Ankara understood, however, that it was Ethem and Eşref who were the real threats, and called upon the national and local governments to be on guard against rebellion or revolution (*ihtilal*).⁴⁰

The concerns of the Kemalist government extended beyond the thousands of Circassian refugees who were encamped on Greek islands in the Aegean.[41] They were also aware that there were 3,000 armed Circassians, as well as Armenians and Rum, who had taken up positions just across the Turkish frontier in western Thrace.[42] The consequences of the threat posed by these Circassian refugees did not translate, however, into an outright confrontation with Greece. Instead, Ankara's countermeasures were focused upon the South Marmara, and upon the *kaza*s of Gönen and Manyas in particular.

The first signs of the troubles to come occurred immediately after the Mehmet Ali raid, when the village of Mürüvetler, near Manyas, was dismantled, and its inhabitants deported to eastern Anatolia.[43] The motivation for this action, as Mehmed Fetgerey Şoenu explains, was the fact that Takığ Şevket was a native of the village. Following *Kel* Aziz's attack on Bayramiç in April 1923, the Interior Ministry posted the following declaration on the doors of mosques in the region:

1) Any village that supplies, gives shelter to any person who is from the bandits (*şakiler*) in the Anatolian Revolutionary Society will be dispersed to the interior of Anatolia.
2) It will be the responsibility of the villages, and not the government detachments, for the battles and the burning of villages that will come with the hiding of the above-mentioned individuals.
3) 200 lira will be given to those who facilitate the arrest of those individuals and information regarding the areas where those people are hiding.[44]

The incursion made by *Kanlı* Mustafa and (Anzavuroğlu) Kadir proved to be the last straw. Between 28 May and 21 June 1923, local authorities ordered the dismantling of a total of thirteen villages in the counties of Gönen and Manyas.[45] Approximately 3,775 North Caucasians were deported with only a limited amount of time to prepare for the journey east.[46] Between June and November 1923, Circassians from another thirty villages were then subject to deportation orders, leading to the removal of another 5,825 men, women, and children from Gönen and Manyas.[47] The families from the first thirteen villages were ultimately scattered to Malatya, Kayseri, Sivas, Ulukışla, Niğde, and Van.[48] Mehmet Fertgerey Şoenu, the Circassian activist who first documented the Gönen deportations, is silent, however, on the final destinations of the Circassians of the later thirty settlements. Nevertheless, Şoenu repeatedly mentions that even among the first round of deportees, only North Caucasians were sent into exile. Their non-Caucasian neighbours were allowed to stay on in the region and settle where they pleased.[49] Both groups of Circassians were also forced to sell their property to whomever they could at a moment's notice, naturally at cut rates.[50]

The only document supporting Şoenu's account of the Gönen and Manyas deportations is a brief directive sent to the governments of Niğde and Malatya, requesting that the Circassians sent to their provinces for 'political reasons' be settled on abandoned lands (most probably lands abandoned by either Rum or Armenians).⁵¹ An anthropologist who visited the village of Keçidere (near Gönen) in the mid-1950s confirms the veracity of these deportations.⁵²

Mehmet Fertgerey Şoenu published his account of the Gönen and Manyas deportations in a pamphlet he entitled 'A Second Petition to the Grand National Turkish Parliament and the Greater Turkish Conscience Regarding the Circassian Question' (*Çerkes Mes'elesi hakkında Türk Vicdan-ı Umumisine ve Turkiye Büyük Millet Meclis'ne İkinci Arıza*). He sent copies of the pamphlet to every member of the parliament, but it is unclear what the immediate result was. One scholar has suggested that Rauf Orbay secured the return of these Circassian exiles within a year or two years following the deportation.⁵³ Many of those who did return found their houses ransacked or destroyed, forcing them to build anew.⁵⁴ Şoenu for his part paid dearly for his appeal to the parliament. Although he escaped going to jail, he was no longer permitted to publish anything further in Turkey, and died in Istanbul at the age of 41.⁵⁵

Şoenu's observations are of interest not only for the valuable information they provide regarding North Caucasians in the South Marmara, but also for the manner in which he discusses this human tragedy. There are two themes that dominate Şoenu's account of the deportations. The first theme is Şoenu's firm belief that Circassians were wrongfully blamed for any wrongdoing during the first year of peace. Circassians, he claims early on in his pamphlet, were even greater victims of the Ottoman Revolutionary Committee in Anatolia, and they would never join such an organization of 'dumb, deaf and blind individuals'.⁵⁶ On the contrary, Circassians remained loyal during both the First World War and the War of Independence, and the collapse of stability in the South Marmara was the fault of the central government (who pulled out the region's gendarmes during the First World War) and a select group of tribes (*aşiretler*) who were against the government.⁵⁷ In pointing to these dissident 'tribes', Şoenu emphasizes that Circassians comprised the minority of counter-revolutionaries and law-breakers. In totalling up the number of *çeteci*s who invaded the South Marmara between November 1922 and May 1923, Şoenu argues that only fifteen Circassians were found among the 70–150 men captured. The rest, in Şoenu's words, were made up of 'Yörüks and Turks'.⁵⁸

The second and even more profound theme concerned the labelling of the government's actions in Gönen and Manyas and why the Circassian deserved such a fate. For Şoenu, what had occurred was clear: the deportation of the Circassians from the South Marmara was a *tehcir*, the same infamous term applied to the deportations of Rum and Armenians. The term *tehcir*, according to Şoenu, meant not only to be exiled from one's home but also the physical abuse (to the point of death) that accompanies it. The Circassians of Manyas and Gönen, he argues, would agree with that definition.⁵⁹ The underlying cause of the deportation was the growing impression throughout Anatolia that Circassians were traitors, bandits, and rebels.⁶⁰ Şoenu recalls that during the time of Abdülhamid II, the word 'freedom' was a term feared by many people. Now, he argues, people came to abhor the word 'Circassian' with the same bitterness as the term 'sultanate'.⁶¹ Terrible propaganda was being directed against the Circassians, and 'on every tongue came the words "traitorous Circassians (*hain Çerkes*)!"'⁶² Still, many Turks believed that there was no 'Circassian Question (*Çerkes meselesi*)' and that their deportation (*tehcir*) and mass murder (*taktil*) were impossible.⁶³

There is something truly central to the Gönen and Manyas deportations that Şoenu does not wish to confront: the legacy of Ahmet Anzavur. Throughout his pamphlet, Şoenu argues that the deportations occurred in response to the activities of the Ottoman Revolutionary Committee of Anatolia, and that Circassians had been targeted because of the unfair association between North Caucasians and treason. He makes no direct reference to the uprisings of 1919 and 1920 or to Ahmet Anzavur's connection with the villages that were later subject to deportation. These omissions make it seem, then, that the deportations were almost accidental and that the Circassians of the region were simply the victims of a slander without any basis in reality. If Şoenu's argument is to be taken at face value, why, then, were these three separate incursions and the forty-three acts of deportation that followed confined to such a limited area? More importantly, what were the Ottoman Revolutionary Committee and the Ankara government trying to achieve at this time? Considering the evolution of the War of Independence within this region, the motives of the guerrillas were clear: to revive the resistance begun by Ahmet Anzavur and to drive out the National Forces from the region. The men who were involved in these attacks (Kadir, *Kanlı* Mustafa, *Kel* Aziz, Eşref Kuşçubaşı, *Çerkes* Ethem, and Takığ Şevket) were still fighting the War of Independence. While these individuals may have stood on different sides of the war only a few years earlier, they now shared two common bonds: a desire to destroy the Kemalist state before it took hold in the South Marmara and a shared notion of their collective North Caucasian heritage. In choosing the South Marmara, and particularly the North Caucasian regions north of Balıkesir, as their base for this campaign, they clearly knew, on both counts, from where they could launch this struggle to return to Anatolia.

There were other implications of the deportations that Mehmet Şoenu also seems to have avoided, implications that he may have seen only in hindsight. On 4 April 1924, almost one year after the second group of paramilitaries came ashore near Bayramiç, members of the Grand National Turkish Parliament took up the issue of those Muslim traitors who still remained in the country or who had left following the Nationalist counter-attack in 1922. According to the stipulations of the General Amnesty Agreement amended to the Treaty of Lausanne, all those who had aided either Greece or Turkey during the course of the First World War or the War of Independence were granted immunity from prosecution. Yet others could not be forgiven. The Turkish parliament declared that a select number of Muslim 'traitors to the fatherland (*vatan hainleri*)' be expelled from Anatolia and stripped of their citizenship.[64] The list of 150 names (*Yüzellilikler*) included those of many of the Ottoman state's highest officials, including the former *şeyülislam*, Mustafa Sabri, and former War Minister, Kiraz Hamdi (*Damat* Ferid, Ahmet Anzavur, and *şeyhülislam* (Dürrizade) Abdullah were left off the list since they had died before it was drafted).[65] The list also included thirty-one individuals who had served in local administrations during the War of Independence, as well as another twenty-four former police officers and journalists who had aided the Ottoman or Greek governments in the course of the war.[66] *Çerkes* Ethem, Eşref Kuşçubaşı, and their respective brothers were stripped of their citizenship, along with four other accomplices, for rising up against the Nationalist government in 1921.[67] During the proceedings, one member remarked that *Çerkes* Ethem was still a threat to the state, and that his influence was now extending all over Europe.[68]

Several members of the Near Eastern Circassian Association were also included among the 150, although, strangely, many of the founding members were left off the list.[69] During one sitting of the parliamentary session in which the names of the 150 were read, a list of some twenty-one men from Gönen and six from Manyas were inserted into the minutes.[70] Unlike the others accused of betraying the fatherland, no specific charges were levelled against these individuals. Kütahya representative Ferit Bey generally referred to these men as implicated in 'paramilitary activity (*çete faaliyetleri*)'.[71] In subsequent publications of the list, they would be included along with such individuals as *Çerkes* Davut (the infamous paramilitary leader from Kirmasti) and *Çerkes* Bekir Sıtkı (the Loyalist organizer from Adapazarı). All of these purported traitors were categorized simply under the title of the 'Other Individuals (*Diğer Eşhas*)'. However, considering the company which these twenty-nine men kept, it is reasonable to assume that they were members of the *eşraf* of their respective villages.

Despite the government's silence on the issue of why a total of twenty-nine individuals from Gönen and Manyas (as well as two others from Susurluk and Marmara) were stripped of their citizenship and sent into exile abroad, the points of origin of these condemned men give a clearer indication of Ankara's true intention. Of the twenty-three men from Gönen, twenty represented villages whose populations had been deported to eastern Anatolia (namely, Muratlar, Tuzakçı, Bayramiç, Balcı, Ayvacık, Keçeler, and Keçidere). The remaining three individuals from Gönen were either from the Circassian quarter (*Çerkes Mahallesi*) of the town of Gönen or from the village of Rüstem, which no longer exists. Of the Manyas notables, all six represented villages whose populations were deported in 1923 (Kızık, Hacı Yakup, Değirmenboğazı, and Bolcaağaç).

Taken together, one can only deduce that the combined goal of the deportations and the elimination of the significant portion of the *eşraf* from Gönen and Manyas was to drive a stake through the heart of the North Caucasian community in this portion of the South Marmara. Since 1919 this corner of northwestern Anatolia had been the epicentre of resistance to the National Movement. Many of the notables, paramilitaries, and common citizens of Gönen county continued to resist despite every reversal, be it after the defeat of Ahmet Anzavur or after the end of the Greek occupation. Turkish officials were deliberate in undertaking the deportations in this region. In villages such as Tuzakçı, Üçpınar, Keçeler, Balcı, Çalıoba, and Ayvalık, authorities purportedly did not molest the Albanians, Pomaks, or native Turkish-speakers who also resided there.[72] As with Armenians and Greeks before them, the main target of the government's policy was to attack and cripple the economic and political base of the North Caucasians of Gönen and Manyas. Beyond their physical removal, the deportations stripped them of their property and wealth (if they possessed any). This was then followed by the political decapitation of these communities, should they return from exile. It is important to view this pattern of retribution and political marginalization not simply as an act of revenge. Rather, the repression visited upon North Caucasians in Manyas and Gönen was a well-refined tool of Ottoman, and now Turkish, state building. The advent of the Young Turk government in 1913 had spelled the end of any meaningful negotiations between the capital and populations deemed to be in defiance of the state's project to consolidate and modernize the provinces. The tragedy that befell thousands of Gönen's Circassian population in 1923 would be enacted elsewhere over the coming decades, in Dersim, Diyarbakir, and even Istanbul.

The air of suspicion and repression that surrounded North Caucasians in the South Marmara after the War of Independence was slow to dissipate during the fifteen years of Kemalist rule. Settlement documents suggest that Circassians who had been dispossessed of their land during the Great Exchanges sought the return of their property into the mid-1920s.[73] As late as 1935, Ankara required local administrators in Balıkesir, Kocaeli, and Çanakkale to monitor those Circassians who were known to possess arms.[74]

The persistence of the 'Circassian issue' into the early Republican period may also have been a reflection of concerns over the continuing threat of subversion by North Caucasians living abroad. After the Ottoman Revolutionary Committee of Anatolia moved its headquarters to Bucharest in the winter of 1923, some of its more prominent members, such as Eşref Kuşçubaşı, abandoned the struggle and returned home. Others, such as *Çerkes* Ethem and Eşref Kuşçubaşı's brother, Hacı Sami, chose to remain in exile.[75] In 1927, Hacı Sami and several accomplices secretly landed near the Aegean town of Kuşadası with the purported intention of assassinating Mustafa Kemal. Neither he nor his band of conspirators got far, and were gunned down outside of town.[76] *Çerkes* Ethem and a group of Armenians and Circassians on the Dodecanese Islands in the Aegean purportedly continued to plot violent actions into the 1930s.[77] Ankara's fear of yet another Circassian rebellion compelled it to monitor settled and migrant North Caucasian communities throughout Anatolia for fear that they might aid in other plots planned abroad.⁷⁸

By 1926, Adige and other North Caucasian languages, as well as use of the epithet *Çerkes*, were banned in Turkey.⁷⁹ Arsen Avagyan has taken this argument one step further, stating in his study of the role of North Caucasians in the Ottoman state that the trial against the Progressive Republican Party was not only a direct attack on political opposition in Ankara, but was an attempt to marginalize influential Circassians in the Turkish Republic. He correctly points out that many of those tried and condemned by the Izmir court in 1926, such as Rauf Orbay, were of North Caucasian descent, leading him to believe that the role of Circassians in the Loyalist opposition and the Greek occupation influenced the Kemalist regime to view all elite North Caucasians as a 'special threat'.⁸⁰

Ankara's hostility towards North Caucasians in Anatolia showed other signs of resilience during the Turkish Republic's first years. This is particularly evident with regard to immigration, a political issue that dominated the politics of Turkey throughout the 1920s and 1930s. According to the immigration law passed in 1926, individuals seeking entrance into Turkey were classified under the parameters of a three-tiered system. In the first tier, all those who were of 'the Turkish race' or whose primary 'culture' and 'language' were Turkish were to receive naturalization papers without inspection by officers of the Interior Ministry. This group included Tatars, Turkmen, Pomaks, and Bosnians. North Caucasians (a group that specifically included Circassians (Adige), Georgians, and Abkhazians) meanwhile were relegated to the second tier, meaning that they were allowed to settle in Turkey after obtaining permission from the Ministry of the Interior.⁸¹ Soner Çagaptay suggests that some Circassians were denied entry into Turkey on the basis of being nomadic (*göçebe*), a term often applied to Kurds, Arabs, and Roma (three of the most subversive and undesirable groups according to Ankara's world-view).⁸² Surprisingly, Albanians were placed within the third and final tier, alongside Arabs and Kurds, and were expressly forbidden to be naturalized at all.⁸³

The wording of the Turkish immigration law of 1926 raises two difficult questions regarding Circassians and Albanians in the early Republican era. First, how can the relative laxness of the law regarding North Caucasian immigrants be reconciled with the harsher treatment received by Circassian citizens in places like Gönen and elsewhere? Secondly, and more to the point, why were North Caucasian and Albanian immigrants viewed and managed so differently? The answer to the first question may have something to do with the level and nature of immigration from the Caucasus during the early Republican period. Population statistics from the Soviet Union in 1926 indicate that there were more than a quarter of a million Circassians still residing in the North Caucasus (a number that continued to rise to 1939).⁸⁴ Considering also some of Moscow's more conciliatory policies towards the North Caucasians at this time, a second great migration from the Caucasus, rivalling that of 1864, would not have been possible during the early Republican period.[85] A smattering of Turkish immigration documents from this period also suggest that the numbers of North Caucasians seeking asylum in Turkey was relatively small. One document states, for example, that only 3,441 'Circassians and Turks' from Georgia had sought refugee in the *vilayet* of Kars between 1918 and 1923. In 1921, immigration officials catalogued only six individuals from Dagestan arriving in Kars. By contrast, 9,648 'Turks and Kurds' had crossed the border from Armenia between 1918 and 1923.[86]

Still, regardless of the numbers of North Caucasians arriving in Turkey during the early Republican period, why were Circassian immigrants seemingly given a pass while Ankara barred Albanians outright? Albanians had not risen up en masse in defiance of the National Movement; nor was there an 'Albanian plot' to kill Atatürk.[87] To understand this divergence between Albanians and Circassians during the first decades of the Turkish Republic, one must look at a different aspect of the transition between empire and nation-state. Ankara's policy towards Albanians after the War of Independence was in many ways both the product of Turkey's new position within regional politics and the continuation of policies initiated before the Turkish War of Independence.

THE UNWELCOME PRODIGAL SONS: ALBANIANS AND THE CONTRADICTIONS OF TURKISH STATE BUILDING

In early August 1923, the Turkish Interior Ministry received reports that some 1,200 Albanians had gathered in the Bulgarian capital of Sofia and were seeking entrance into the Turkish Republic. They were largely from the Kingdom of Serbs, Croats, and Slovenes and were living in a dire state of 'poverty and suffering' while waiting to cross into Thrace. They were eventually turned away, although the Ministry requested that Bulgarian officials look after their welfare.[88]

The reporting officer in the case of the Albanians crossing from Bulgaria added an interesting preamble in stipulating the state's denial of entrance to these refugees. He stated flatly that a great number of Albanians were migrating from Albania and Yugoslavia, and that originally they were forbidden to settle in Istanbul, Bursa, and Izmir. Over time, however, the state had found it difficult to settle Albanian refugees permanently in their assigned destinations or to prevent them from seeking residence in these formerly forbidden areas. Therefore, he declared, the National Assembly had decided to forbid the entrance of any Albanian with an Albanian or Serbian passport into the Republic of Turkey. Room had to be made instead for the '400,000 Muslims and Turks' arriving from 'Rumeli', the Ottoman word for the entirety of the southern Balkans.[89]

Although the end of the War of Independence may have opened a new chapter in Anatolian politics through the declaration of the Turkish Republic, it also marked the continuation of a crisis that was now decades in the making. The expulsion of the Allied Powers from Anatolia came at the cost of yet another massive refugee crisis. These new refugees, who had gathered by the tens of thousands in Istanbul and elsewhere, came on the backs of tens of thousands of other refugees and immigrants who had come during the Balkan Wars, the First World War, and even earlier.[90] Matters would only get worse after the signing of the Treaty of Lausanne, which resulted in the arrival of almost half a million Muslims from Greece. Often not noticed in this period is the continued migration of Muslims from other areas of the southern Balkans, particularly from Yugoslavia and Bulgaria. The main question that confronted the new Turkish administration was not simply how to solve the immediate refugee crisis, but on what terms present and future waves of immigration would be received. With the crafting of the republican system of immigration and settlement, Albanians, as a group, would once again be singled out as undesirable.

Ankara's position regarding Albanian immigrants and settlers first came under review at the end of December 1922, a little over a month after the abolition of the sultanate. In the months and years that followed, policy-makers would identify five potential segments of the Albanian population of Anatolia that had to be addressed both now and in the future:

1. Albanians who had been settled in Anatolia before 1918 and were displaced by the fighting between the Greek army and the forces of Mustafa Kemal.
2. Albanians who had been settled in Anatolia before 1918 but had illegally moved to areas considered off limits to them (*menatık-ı memnua*).
3. Albanians living in Anatolia who remained uncatalogued or unsettled throughout the First World War and the War of Independence.
4. Those Albanians seeking to emigrate to Turkey under the auspices of the population exchange with Greece.
5. Those Albanians continuing to migrate from Yugoslavia, Albania, and elsewhere to Anatolia.

The system that was eventually created to deal with these five categories of Albanians was not an entirely new policy, but a recrafting of the original guidelines laid out by the CUP in the summer of 1915. Like the Unionist regulations, Ankara reserved the right to remove, scatter, and resettle Albanians in large numbers in order to restructure the demographic composition of Anatolia. Immigration and Interior Ministry officials would also continue to catalogue recent immigrants and long-time residents and monitor their movements in the country. Yet the Republic's approach to Albanians differed in several important ways from that of its Ottoman predecessors. The paramount difference was the expressed prohibition of new Albanian immigrants into the Turkish Republic, a regulation codified in the immigration law passed in 1926. Conversely, Albanians who had established residence in the Turkish Republic were now allowed to settle in provinces that had once been off limits to them. This change in policy in one sense reflects the new strategic priorities of the republican government after the seat of power had been transferred from Istanbul to Ankara. Thereafter, the South Marmara, which was once designated a restricted zone enveloping the Ottoman capital, lost its status as an area vital to the security of the state, allowing the unreliable Albanians a new freedom of movement in the region. This change in the relationship between Albanians and the South Marmara as a region speaks to the broader vision with which the state now approached Albanians as it sought to integrate them into republican society.

On 21 December 1922, Ankara's Ministry of Health sent out a strangely worded circular to all provinces now incorporated into the Turkish Republic. It requested regional governors to state the number and location of Albanian men and women living in their province, as well as the number and location of 'this year's immigrants' (*bu sene muhacirleri*), referring possibly to the expected Muslim refugees who would be arriving from Greece.[91] It also requested data on the number of immigrants that each province could accept, although it is unclear in the document whether or not the Health Ministry was referring to Albanian immigrants or immigrants in general.[92] The responses received between December 1922 and March 1923 offer great insight into the state of Albanians across Anatolia, as well as the ways in which the political leadership of the various Turkish provinces understood and responded to this issue.

In total, fifteen provinces stated that they had no Albanians either within the central county (*liva*) of the province or in the province at large (Rize, Gümüşhane, Iğdır, Kars, Maraş, Mardin, Van, Silifke, Bolu, Bayezit, Urfa, Muş, Siirt, Yozgat, and Erzurum). Other officials were more demure in their responses, saying they had not settled any Albanians yet (Trabzon, Osmaniye, Giresun, and Zonguldak).[93] The twenty provinces that did respond affirmatively to the government's query provided the statistics shown in Table 6.1.

The statistics provided by these local administrations contain several interesting addendums, omissions, and corollaries. Almost all of the responding provinces, including those who claimed to have no Albanians, sent estimates of the numbers of immigrants they could accept for resettlement (estimates often based on the amount of abandoned property in the province) (see Table 6.2). Some of these provinces, including Antalya, Kocaeli, and Çatalca, explicitly stated that they refused to accept any Albanians, while others (Iğdır and Adana) expressed their willingness to accept Albanians without question. The situation in Adana is an interesting case in point in this series of correspondence. On 24 December 1922, the governor of Adana enclosed in his response an extended estimate detailing the districts in Adana that were willing to accept certain numbers of Albanians and Bosnian refugees. According to the list, the counties of Adana,

Table 6.1 Numbers of Albanians (and Bosnians) in Anatolia by Province, 1922–3

Province	Men	Women	Household	Total population
Antalya	440	400		840 (Bosnians and Albanians)
Denizli	26	26	17	43
Kastamonu	31	36		67
Aksaray			2	
Çarkırı				22
Eskişehir	160	160	92	320
Niğde				16
Izmir[a]				2,594
Çanakkale (Biga)	306	27		333
Çanakkale (Çanakkale)[b]				501
Edirne				2,277
Kocaeli				1,288
Sinop				4
Aydın				262
Adana			369	1,109 (Albanians and Bosnians)
Konya				370
Çatalca				1,501
Kütahya	101	100		201 (settled)
Kütahya	159	172		331 (unsettled)
Muğla				56
Karesi (Edremit)			48	
Tokat				800
Total (minimum)				12,096

Source: BCA 272.11.16.66.1, 4 August 1923.

[a] The Figures for Izmir *vilayet* are as follows: Izmir *kaza:* 830 Albanians, 110 Bosnians; Bayındır *kaza:* 252 Albanians, 112 Bosnians; Foça *kaza:* 625 Albanians, 315 Bosnians; Karaburun *kaza:* 3 Albanians, 150 Bosnians; Urla *kaza:* 107 Albanians, 230 Bosnians; Kuşadası *kaza:* 144 Albanians, 5 Bosnians; Menemen *kaza:* 117 Albanians, 14 Bosnians; Tire *kaza:* 58 Albanians, 25 Bosnians; Çeşme *kaza:* 248 Albanians, 280 Bosnians; Ödemiş, *kaza:* 69 Albanians, 77 Bosnians; Nefer *kaza:* 0 Albanians, 1,132 Bosnians; Bergama *kaza:* 141 Albanians, 67 Bosnians; Total: 2,594 Albanians, 2,317 Bosnians.

[b] The following data were given for the environs of Çanakkale: İrlkirköy *Nayihe*: 75 men, 69 women (unsettled Albanians); Ezine: 17 men, 20 women; Bayramiç: 11 Albanians; Süleymanpaşa *mahallesi* (Çanakkale): 154 men, 156 women.

Kozan, Cebel Berket, and Ceyhan would agree to take thousands of immigrants, while other counties, such as Mersin and Yumurtalık, refused to take any (see Table 6.3).

Governmental reports from Edirne and elsewhere add other interesting details about the nature of the Albanian communities residing in their midst. It was revealed that the Albanian colonies in areas such as Çatalca, Niğde, Kırkkilise, Kastamonu, and Osmaniye were only recently established, largely comprising refugees from Kosova and Macedonia. In Denizli and Niğde, Albanian refugees were by and large working either as merchants or as officials in the local

Table 6.2 Estimates of the numbers of refugees and immigrants that each province could accept

Province	Number of households	Number of individuals
Amasya	400	
Gümüşhane	500	
Denizli	100	
Kars		100,000
Kastamonu	775	
Silifke		4,000
Giresun		5,000
Eskişehir	20,000	
Muş		50,000
Zongdulak	400	
Siirt	3,450	
Çanakkale (Biga)		300 (+250 households)
Çanakkale (Çanakkale)		335 (+100 households)
Kocaeli		2,000–3,000
Aydın	261	
Sinop		3,700
Adana	2,272	
Kütahya	1,050	
Erzurum		3,000–10,000
Tokat		4,790
Rize		Land available
Antalya		Land available
Osmaniye		Land available
Iğdır		Land available
Mardin		Land available
Bolu		Land available
Trabzon		Land available
Urfa		Land available

Source: BCA 272.11.16.66.1, 4 August 1923.

administration.[94] Officials in Kırkkilise paint a somewhat different picture of the Albanians living under their administration. After a rash of bandit attacks on the roads outside town, administrators in Kırkkilise informed both the Interior Ministry and the Representative of Exchanges, Reconstruction, and Settlement (*Mübadele, İmar ve İskan Vekaleti*) that between 5 and 7 per cent of the local population was Albanian in origin. These Albanians, estimated to number around 600 individuals, had arrived during the Balkan Wars or had fled the Balkans for 'political reasons'. The governor explained that many of these refugees were working as wage labourers on the land or in coffee-houses or as innkeepers. None appeared to own property, yet many seemed to be supplementing whatever income they made by robbing people on the road outside town. The solution offered by the Interior Ministry was to deport these Albanians outside

Table 6.3 Statistics for the province in Adana

Name of kaza	Present Albanian and Bosnian residents (households)	Present Albanian and Bosnian residents (individuals)	Possible number of Albanian and Bosnian immigrants (households)
Adana	257	773	32
Kozan	14	49	300
Cebel Berket	20	51	1,320
Ceyhan	57	170	500
Karaisalı	3	6	30

Source: BCA 272.11.16.66.1, 4 August 1923.

the borders of the *vilayet*.[95] Throughout eastern Thrace, local officials voiced similar complaints about Albanians, Bosnians, and other 'destructive' (*tahripkar*) immigrants (see Table 6.4).

One of the most misleading things about the data supplied by these local officials is the actual number of Albanians claimed to be residing in a given province. The various responses recorded by the Ministry of Health suggest that the original question posed in the December circular was interpreted in a variety of ways. In certain cases, such as that of Kars, it appears that the question was interpreted to mean the number of Albanians existing in the province in total. In other cases, such as in Kütahya, administrators supplied the numbers of both settled and unsettled Albanians. Most responses give no such specifics, giving the impression that the number of Albanians living in a province may have been under-reported. Furthermore, as was the case with the number of Albanians living in the South Marmara and elsewhere, the figures offered to the Ministry of Health leave open the possibility that there may have been other 'assimilated' Albanians who were bilingual and long-time residents. As a result, it would be counter-intuitive to suppose that a total of four Albanians resided in the entire province of Sinop, a region that had a long-established Albanian colony.[96] It is also nonsensical to believe local reports that only twelve Albanians could be found in the environs of Karamürsel, the region out of which *Arnavud* Kazım and other well-known Nationalist Albanian paramilitaries emerged (see Table 6.5). On the other hand, considering the violence and destruction wreaked upon this small town during the Greek occupation, there could have been some truth to it.[97]

Further than simply reporting the size and character of the Albanian diaspora in Anatolia, this correspondence in 1923 also served to inform Ankara of efforts to break up and scatter communities of Albanians that had grown too dense. It perhaps comes as no surprise that Ankara's efforts to dilute the number of Albanians in Anatolia were the same as those chosen by the Young Turks almost a decade before: namely, the environs of Istanbul, İzmit, Bursa, and

Table 6.4 Population of Bosnians and Albanians in Edirne province

Name of kaza	Number of men (Bosnian)	Number of women (Bosnian)	Total number (Bosnian)	Number of men (Albanian)	Number of women (Albanian)	Total number (Albanian)
Tekirdağ	198	81	179	44	35	79
Çorlu	26	25	51	25	21	46
Saray	40	42	82	15	40	55
Hayrabolu	186	181	267	5	15	20
Merkete?				105	108	213
Kırkkilise	110	110	220	367	410	782
Lüleburgaz	2	3	5	99	83	182
Babaeski	27	33	60	28	59	97
Vize	142	153	295	194	149	343
Demirköy	78	79	167	85	91	176
Gelibolu	2	1	3	1	5	6
Keşan	4	8	12	14	15	29
Eceabat	2	2	4	24	33	57
Lalapaşa	6	9	15	1	25	26
Havsa	100	90	190	3	3	6
Uzunköprü	(111 Bosnians and Albanians total)					
Edirne	24	25	49	86	81	167
?		2	2	1	13	14
Total	847	859	1,706	1,107	1,181	2,288

Source: BCA 272.11.16.66.1, 4 August 1923.

Table 6.5 Albanian statistics for the province of İzmit

Name of kaza	Albanian total	Albanian (women)	Albanian (men)
Adapazarı	800	400	400
Karamürsel	12	6	6
Geyve	49	22	27
Yalova	69	33	36
İznik	28	12	18
İzmit	330	136	194
Total	1,288	609	679

Source: BCA 272.11.16.66.1, 4 August 1923.

Izmir. Official directives and reports from each of these regions suggest that these former 'restricted areas' continued to possess towns, neighbourhoods, and villages with Albanian populations that exceeded 10 per cent, the officially designated proportion for Albanians living in any given population centre. In addressing their Albanian settlements, the government of Kocaeli (İzmit) would only state that they would not accept any more Albanians in 1923. The *vali* of Bursa meanwhile declared his intention of expelling 180 Albanians from Prishtina outside its borders, in keeping with the restriction against Albanian settlements that surpassed 10 per cent.[98]

The reports from Izmir and Istanbul give greater detail as to the kinds of concerns and challenges confronting Ankara in dealing with Albanians. Of the provinces that responded to the Ministry of Health's inquiry, Izmir claimed the most Albanians.[99] In March 1923, the Ministry of Health demanded that 175 Albanian and Bosnian households in the neighbourhood of Buca, a district on the east side of town with a total of 1,300 households, be removed and dispersed elsewhere. Ultimately about 134 households were removed and replaced by a group of 580 Turks.[100] Similar requests were made from the outlying village of Bornova as well as the towns of Urla and Bergama.[101] By all accounts, the Albanians who lived in these districts were not recent immigrants but had resided in the region for some time. Some, such as the 500 Albanians in Bornova and Buça, were designated as unemployed 'vagrants (*serseri*)' who were squatting on property abandoned by the native Rum.[102] Others, such as those in Bergama, were identified as refugees from Kosova who had been driven from their original settlements in Alaşehir by the Greeks. Ultimately these groups received different fates. Ankara chose not to allow the Albanians in Bergama to return to their homes and instead offered them abandoned Rum property around the town.[103] The group from Bornova, as well as some of those from Buca, were eventually transported further east and settled on Armenian lands outside İsparta and Niğde.[104] The Greek property they left behind was then given to Muslims arriving from Greece.[105]

A different aspect of this policy is seen in Istanbul. The documents posted from the former Ottoman capital tell of the effort to weed through the vast number of Albanians living in the city and decide who would be allowed to stay and who would have to be transplanted further east. On 18 March 1924, the Istanbul offices of the Ministry of Health filed a sample registry of Albanians (as well as other ethnicities) they planned to remove from the city, stating their names, places of origin, dates of arrival in the city, number of family members, and the destinations to which they would like to be sent (see Table 6.6).

Table 6.6 shows that fifteen out of the nineteen families on the list were from southern Yugoslavia (either Kosova or Macedonia), and eleven claimed to be Albanian. For these Albanians, their desired destination was almost uniformly Izmir.

Almost four years later, a similar report was sent to Ankara. Enclosed in this report, however, was a list of individuals and their families registered to stay in the city of Istanbul. As well as supplying their names, places of origin, and dates of entry, this report from 1927 also supplied short biographies of each of the applicants. One immigrant named İbrahim Efendi, for example, had

Table 6.6 Sample migrant registry from Istanbul, March 1924

Name of patriarch or matriarch	Birthplace	Date of arrival	Ethnicity	Number of family members	Destination requested
Salih	Manastır	6 months ago	Turk	5	Izmir
Huseyn	Karafiriye	1920	Turk	3	Izmir
Mehmet	Karacik	1920	Turk	4	Bursa
Zekeriya	Kosova	February 1923	Albanian	5	Silivri (Çatalca)
Arıf	Crete	January 1923	Turk from Crete	2	Izmir
Kaharman	Priştine	January 1923		2	Izmir
Necip	Manastır	1921	Albanian	3	Izmir
Şerif	Gilan	1922	Albanian	2	Izmir
Murad	Priştine	February 1921	Albanian	7	Izmir
Mustafa	Karcik	January 1922	Albanian	3	Izmir
Asad	Sarajevo	January 1922	Bosnian	1	Izmir
Yusuf	Peç	November 1922	Albanian	3	Izmir
İskender	Manastır	March 1923	Turk	5	Adapazarı
Resam	Kucasi	1920	Turk	7	Izmir
Ali	Prilip	1920	Albanian	1	Akhisar
Huseyn	Shtip	1922	Albanian	1	Izmir
Süleyman	Kalkandelen	1922	Albanian	3	İzmit
Abdul	Prilip	1923	Turk	6	Adapazarı
Ayşe	Üsküp	1923	Albanian	5	Izmir

Source: BCA 272.11.16.66.1, 4 August 1923.

arrived in Istanbul from Albania on 5 August 1923. He was originally from Jannina (Yanya in Turkish) in northern Greece, but had lived in exile in Albania during the ten years following the Greek attack upon his home town. Another immigrant by the name of Süleyman was from the northern Macedonian town of Tetova (Kalkendelen). He was a veteran of the Ottoman army during the First World War, but had settled in the Süleymaniye section of Istanbul after he left the service. With his Turkish passport, Süleyman returned to Tetova in April 1924 to retrieve his wife and family, who were both Yugoslav citizens. They returned together in December of that year and then registered with the Istanbul authorities. The report cites the stories of two other refugees, one a 17-year-old from Skopje, who fled in haste to Istanbul in 1926 (possibly because of the paramilitary struggle then raging in Macedonia) and the other a man from Priziren, who had worked as a shepherd in Istanbul ever since he fled Kosova during the Balkan Wars.[106]

These few select documents from Izmir and Istanbul, which constitute only a tiny fraction of the correspondence generated during this period, give some insight into both the complexities of Turkish policy towards Albanians as well as the character of Albanian immigrants and refugees during these first years of the Turkish Republic. The first thing that these documents reveal is the degree to which Turkish officials earnestly attempted to count and monitor the Albanians in their midst. Administrators in both Ankara and the provinces understood where large numbers of recent Albanian immigrants could be found and what percentage of the population they composed. Settlement officials also had a clear knowledge of where 'extraneous' Albanians could be sent and upon what land or in what neighbourhoods they could be placed. Still, as the documents in Istanbul and elsewhere appear to show, Ankara lost track of many Albanians who remained unregistered or unaccounted for through the war years. While the War of Independence and the shift from empire to republic may have caused gaps in Ankara's knowledge of the state of this diaspora in Anatolia, the methods and care with which the republican government approached Albanians was a direct continuation of the practices first conceived by the Committee of Union and Progress.

These documents also show that the Albanian population in Anatolia did not remain static between the First World War and the founding of the Republic of Turkey. Statistics and descriptions found within these government reports demonstrate the various degrees to which Albanian communities throughout Anatolia were affected by this period of war and civil strife. Many Albanians who migrated or were deported to central and eastern Anatolia remained unsettled years after their arrival. Other immigrants immediately blended into their surroundings as officials, merchants, or labourers. Some Albanians eked out a living any way they could and resorted to theft and banditry, reinforcing their reputation as a criminal class. The fighting in western Anatolia and the Balkans forced many to flee more than once in their lives. The documents presented here give some indication that some of these poor immigrants attempted to return home or rejoin their families. Yet the concerns and observations of the Settlement, Health, and Interior Ministry officials are misleading. As in the CUP years before, what worried Ankara most was the potentially, and seemingly inherent, volatile nature of the Albanians living in Turkey. The documents do not, however, give many details about those Albanians who apparently integrated into the Turkish state and society, the professionals, merchants, tradesmen, landowners, officers, and officials. They mattered less than the poor, displaced refugees in Kırkkilise or Izmir, who possessed the ability to do harm to both the state and their neighbours. This blind eye turned towards the more elite segments of the Albanian diaspora again underscores the classist perception of Albanian ethnicity. 'Albanianness' mattered most when an individual did not own land or stole in order to survive.

The continuities between the Ottoman and Turkish systems of governance did not end with their shared notions and methods in identifying and locating Albanian immigrants. As before, Ankara's approach to its Albanian citizenry was beset by one crucial, yet problematic question: who exactly is an Albanian? One of the first pieces of evidence suggesting the degree to which Ankara struggled with this question comes in late 1923 during the continuing talks at Lausanne. During the 19 December session, the Italian representative raised the issue of Albanians in the forthcoming population exchange between Greece and Turkey. On this issue both Ankara and Athens agreed: the Albanians living in Greece were not eligible for the exchange. Greek representative Demetrius Caclamanos assured his Turkish counterpart Rıza Nur that the Albanians in Greece were restricted to the Çamëria region of the Epirus, in the most northwestern portion of the country, and were distinguishable from Turks.[107] Both Rıza Nur and the Turkish government appeared to take Caclamanos at his word and to trust his assurances.[108] Ankara expected a thousand 'Turkish-speakers' from the Çamëria to arrive in Anatolia, who would then be settled in Erdek in the South Marmara, as well as Ayvalık, Menteşe, Antalya, Senkile, Mersin, and Adana.[109] While a portion of the Muslims in this section of the Epirus were claimed by Albania to be their co-nationals, Ankara vowed that they would not accept any Albanians in the population exchanges, only 'Turkish-speakers'.[110]

Yet there were reservations about this aspect of the Great Exchange even during the course of the negotiations. The British High Commission in Athens reported that no standard had been set for what constituted an Albanian, even though there was confusion over whether 'race' or 'religion' was the most determining factor in distinguishing among Muslims. Despite claims that the Albanians in the Epirus inhabited a well-defined region, the British representative at a League of Nations meeting between the Albanian and Greek delegates stated that no registry documenting the number of Albanians living in Greece existed. Greek representative Caclamanos reiterated Athens's position on the Albanians of the Epirus, stating that none would be deported. He went on to claim that out of 200 families in the Çamëria that had been examined by Greek exchange officials, only nine had been disqualified. Albanian representative Benoît Blinishti disputed Caclamanos's guarantees and asserted that Greek officials in the region had told all the Muslims of the Çamëria that they would be deported to Anatolia.[111] To resolve this issue, it was agreed that the League of Nations should establish a mixed commission comprising representatives from Greece, Albania, and a third party to decide who among the potential deportees were Albanians. The British High Commission, however, still appeared wary of even this solution. In the Balkans, one British observer remarked, race and religion had long been synonymous, and there were many Muslims who retained Albanian cultural traits. According to the High Commission, language was not an appropriate metric for deciding between Turks and Albanians, since many were multilingual.[112]

Greek authorities ultimately followed through on the deportation of thousands of Muslims from the Çamëria, together with tens of thousands of others from Larissa, Langada, Drama, Vodina, Serez, Edessa, Florina, Kilkis, Kavala, and Salonika.[113] Between 1923 and 1930, the infusion of these refugees into Turkey would dramatically alter the Anatolian landscape. By 1927, Turkish officials had settled 32,315 individuals from Greece in the province of Bursa alone.[114] It is difficult to say who among these thousands were Albanian. According to Raif Kaplanoğlu, who did an ethnographical study of Bursa in the late 1990s, Albanian refugees from Jannina, Preveza, and Florina did arrive and settle around Bursa.[115] The settlement of these refugees in Bursa and the other provinces in the South Marmara was accompanied by an even larger effort to rebuild the cities that had been levelled during the War of Independence. During the negotiations at Lausanne, the structural losses shown in Tables 6.7 and 6.8 were registered in the South Marmara. Likewise, land, businesses, and 'movable property' were catalogued and redistributed throughout the region. Although Muslims throughout the South Marmara lost millions of Turkish lira in property, property abandoned by Rum and Armenians served to make up some of the difference.[116] In such places as Karamürsel, state efforts to build houses (400 in total) and schools was coupled with the distribution of olive oil factories once owned by Greeks and Armenians to new Muslim owners.[117]

In his final analysis of the population exchange with Greece, Rıza Nur was not fully satisfied with the results he had found. A political activist who had established his credentials in Turkist circles even before the First World War, Rıza Nur was among Mustafa Kemal's most outspoken supporters (and critics) and had served in the Nationalist government throughout the War of Independence. As Minister of Health during most of 1923, he most probably helped oversee Ankara's efforts to count and resettle Albanians. In 1929, he released his multi-volume autobiography, in which he railed vociferously against Albanians, Circassians, and other 'foreigners' whose rival notions of nationalism endangered the state. According to Nur, the population exchange ultimately had the opposite effect from its original intention, as thousands of Albanians sought refuge in Anatolia under the auspices of being 'Turks'.

In discussing his participation in negotiating the Treaty of Lausanne, Rıza Nur had this to say about the prospect of immigrants arriving from the environs

Table 6.7 Structural losses in the South Marmara during the War of Independence (by province)

Name of the sancak	Buildings destroyed (both rural and urban)	Value of losses (Turkish lira)
Bursa	13,668	16,837,000
Ertuğrul	3,235	7,774,000
İzmit	17,728	27,476,597
Karesi	6,385	21,480,495

Source: Lausanne Conference, 676–7.

Table 6.8 Structural losses in the South Marmara during the War of Independence (by town)

Name of town destroyed	Number of buildings destroyed	Buildings existing before the war	Value of losses (Turkish lira)
Bilecik	2,245	Completely destroyed	1,136,000
Söğüt	948	Completely destroyed	2,940,000
Yenişehir	1,187	Half destroyed	5,136,000
İznik	615	648	1,467,400
Karamürsel	830	847	9,106,500
Yalova	232	286	772,960
Mihaliç	905	Completely destroyed	3,364,750
Bandırma	1,305	In very great part destroyed	49,122,000

Source: *Lausanne Conference*, 677.
Note: The monetary value of these losses is exclusive of the general statistics given above.

of Jannina: 'From the regions such as Yanya [Jannina], I did not want Albanians coming to us during the exchange. These types are among the bandits and tyrants in our state and have killed and greatly swindled from our villages. It was even so in earlier periods.... For this reason we placed the clause, "Those to be exchanged are to be Turkish, Muslim and Greek citizens"'.[118] It was to his surprise and outrage when he discovered that Albanians were among those refugees who settled in Ankara and on 'the best lands in Turkey' near Kartal, Pendik, and Erenköy, west of İzmit.[119] In addition to the duplicity of the Albanians of Jannina (who claimed that they were Turks and believers), Nur laid blame on Mustafa Abdülhalik (Renda), a former Nationalist minister who was now governor of Izmir.[120] Nur accused this native of Jannina of not only being in collusion with these restricted Albanians, but also of attempting to relocate and attract Albanians in Turkey to Izmir. According to his contacts in the gendarmerie and other local officials in Bursa, Eskişehir, Konya, and elsewhere, he states that Albanians from throughout Anatolia were illegally taking to the roads, leaving their established places of settlement and finding their way to Izmir. One secret telegram from the Izmir police department purportedly claimed that 'all the Albanians in Turkey are gathering here. It's going to make this place into Albania.'[121] This was all the work of Abülhalik, Rıza Nur argued, who was deliberately seeking out his fellow co-nationals.

Abdülhalik refuted these charges, but Rıza Nur may not have been far off. Settlement documents from Afyon, Izmir, and elsewhere do suggest that Albanians were coming into Turkey illegally and that some Albanians were illegally trying to come to Izmir.[122] Yet his argument that an Albanian governor was responsible for both of these phenomena is far-fetched. The question of whether or not those who came into Anatolia from the southern Balkans were Albanians or Turks pre-dated the Treaty of Lausanne. A single set of criteria for what constituted a Turk or an Albanian still had not been established in 1923, despite the multiple waves of migration and flight between 1878 and 1923 (although, as we have seen from the regulations of 1916, there certainly were loopholes in place in the case of certain individuals identified as Albanian). If the documents pertaining to the negotiations at Lausanne suggest anything, it is that Turkish officials in 1923 simply expected those arriving to be both Muslims and Turkish-speakers. Thus Turkish officials continued to use an ill-defined system established by Ottoman authorities to discriminate between Muslim immigrants, many of whom were multilingual and conversant in both provincial Albanian and urban Ottoman culture.

The questions and consequences of Albanian immigration did not subside with the Treaty at Lausanne or the population exchange with Greece. Overall, the wave of Albanians arriving with the refugees from Greece was small in comparison to a parallel stream of migrants arriving from elsewhere in the Balkans. Between 1923 and 1939, Turkish sources record at least 400,000 immigrants from Yugoslavia, Bulgaria, and Romania arriving in Turkey.[123] It was reported that in the province of Bursa, 9,000 'non-exchangees' (*gayri mübadil*) had been settled by 1927.[124] Of the more than 115,000 Yugoslav citizens crossing the Turkish frontier between 1923 and 1939, both Turkish and Yugoslav sources argue that the majority were Albanian.[125]

The reason for this new wave of migrants from Yugoslavia during the inter-war period was a direct result of Yugoslav state policies aimed at undermining and disenfranchising its Muslim population. At the centre of Belgrade's war against the Muslims remaining in Yugoslavia was the region of South Serbia, an area roughly encompassing portions of the former Ottoman territories of Yeni Pazar (Novi Pazar or Sancak), Kosova, Üsküp (Skopje), and Manastır (Bitola). On 25 February 1919, the Yugoslav government formally abolished the Ottoman system of landholding.[126] The law allowed local administrators the right to break up large estates throughout South Serbia (most of which were owned by Muslims) and distribute the land primarily to Orthodox (largely Serb) families and settlers.[127] This programme of 'agrarian reform' was accompanied by a concerted effort by Belgrade to colonize these lands with Serb peasants. These two measures devastated the economic base of Yugoslav Muslim society. According to one scholar, 381,245 hectares of land was confiscated in Kosova as well as along the plains south and west of Skopje.[128] Within the same period of time, 13,000 families (totalling possibly 70,000 individuals) were settled by the Yugoslav government in Kosova alone.[129]

This pressure on Muslims in South Serbia was reinforced by an active Yugoslav military and paramilitary presence in the region. Armed clashes between local resistance groups and army and gendarmerie units were ongoing throughout the First World War and the first years of the Yugoslav Kingdom.[130] This resistance movement, populated in large part by Albanians from the countryside, came to be known collectively as the *kaçak*s, or the fugitives in Turkish.

Many of its leaders, such as Bajram Curri, Azem Bejta, and Hasan Prishtina, were former Ottoman officers and notables who had resisted Ottoman rule years before. Organized into small local bands, the *kaçak*s staged attacks on the Yugoslav military and gendarmerie throughout the early 1920s, hitting targets in Gostivar,[131] Gilan,[132] Tetevo,[133] Kičevo,[134] Kumanovo,[135] Peja,[136] Prilip,[137] Prishtina,[138] Novi Pazar,[139] and Skopje.[140] According to statistics gathered by the Committee for the National Defence of Kosova, an organization led by Albanian nationalists who supported the *kaçak* movement, 12,371 people had been killed and 22,110 imprisoned by 1921 as result of the violence.[141]

The violence and disenfranchisement facing Muslims in South Serbia forced families throughout the region to flee by the thousands. On the part of the Yugoslav, and largely Serb, forces in the region, the goal was not simply to cleanse Muslims from every arena of public life, but specifically to neutralize Albanians as a segment of Yugoslav society. The 'Albanian problem' of Kosova and Macedonia had been at the heart of Serbian nationalist desires since the late nineteenth century, representing the cancer that had to be removed before the ancient Serb homeland could be fully reclaimed. Vasa Čubrilović, a Serb scholar and one of the architects of Yugoslav policy regarding South Serbia, put it this way:

> The Albanians cannot be repulsed by means of gradual colonization alone. They are the only people who during the last millennium managed not only to resist the nucleus of our state, Raška and Zeta, but also to harm us, by pushing our ethnic borders northwards and eastward. . . . The only way and the only means to cope with them is the use of brutal force by an organized state. . . . It is our fault that since 1912 we were not successful in dealing with them—we did not apply our authority vigorously. We have had no success to assimilate them. If we do not settle accounts with them at the proper time, within twenty to thirty years we shall have to cope with a terrible irredentism, the signs of which are already apparent. They will inevitably put all our southern territories in jeopardy.[142]

Although the programme of 'agrarian reform' had induced many rural Albanians in Kosova and western Macedonia to migrate to Turkey ('moving out of their lands to be with their brothers', as one newspaper article put it), Belgrade's policy regarding South Serbia took a dramatic turn in 1933.[143]

On 28 February 1933, Turkish Foreign Minister Rüştü Aras arrived in Belgrade and initiated the first of several meetings with the Yugoslav Foreign Ministry regarding a mass deportation of Muslims from South Serbia to Anatolia. Aras, along with his Serb counterpart, Milan Stojadinović, negotiated for five years, with the two signing a joint convention in June 1938.[144] The preamble of the pact began with the observation that there was a 'constant tendency' among the 'Muslim Turks' of Yugoslavia, a group that did not appreciate the 'liberal and generous' Yugoslav state, to migrate to Turkey.[145] The two countries therefore agreed to regulate and facilitate a mass migration of this population, numbering 40,000 families, between the years 1939 and 1944.¹⁴⁶ Those eligible for resettlement in Turkey had to fulfil a number of requirements. According to Article 1, they had to be Muslims who spoke Turkish and possessed 'Turkish culture' ('nomads' and Roma were specifically excluded from these criteria, in keeping with Turkish immigration laws). The deportees would be drawn from a series of counties throughout contemporary Kosova and Macedonia, ranging from such regions as Mitrovica, Skopje, Ohrid, Vučtrin, Bitola, Priziren, Veles, and Prilip. Despite the extensive territory covered in the convention, the two parties agreed to limit the transfer to the rural counties and to exempt the Muslim population of the urban centres. The property of the deportees would be liquidated, while their deportation and settlement would be in large part financed by the Republic of Turkey. Their passage to Anatolia would be booked through Salonika and be monitored by a mixed Yugoslav–Turkish commission.¹⁴⁷

Archival materials and printed materials from the period have thoroughly demonstrated that the 1938 agreement is a deceptive and misleading document in both its wording and its spirit. In a memorandum written for the General Staff of the Yugoslav Military (and then presented as a lecture to the Serbian Cultural Society in March 1937), Vasa Čubrilović outlined in vulgar detail the intentions and manner by which these deportations were to take place: 'As we have heard, Turkey has agreed to accept about 200,000 of our deported people initially, on condition that they are Albanians, something which is most advantageous to us. We must comply with this desire of Turkey readily and sign a convention for immigration.'¹⁴⁸ For Čubrilović, Turkey was a natural choice for such a mass migration, since the 'uninhabited and uncultivated lands' of Anatolia and Kurdistan presented 'almost boundless possibilities for internal colonization'.¹⁴⁹ The Albanian population was to be driven out (which in Čubrilović summation, unlike the convention, was to be restricted to Kosova and western Macedonia) by a variety of methods: police harassment, repudiation of land deeds, ill-treatment of the clergy, attacks by Montenegrin paramilitaries (*četnik*s), and other forms of state terror. The Turkish government was also permitted to play a role in instigating Albanians to leave, sending 'agitators' to spread propaganda about the wealth of the Turkish lands and the orderliness of other deportations, from Romania (as well as kindling 'religious fanaticism among the masses').¹⁵⁰ Čubrilović emphasized that the deportation of Albanians could not simply be limited to villagers, but must be expanded to the urban middle class. 'The middle and rich classes make up the backbone of every nation. Therefore, they too must be persecuted and driven out.'¹⁵¹

Mustafa Kemal personally met with Yugoslav officials during the negotiation of this agreement, which was submitted to the Grand Turkish National Assembly.¹⁵² Yet in July 1938, five months before Atatürk died, the parliament refused to ratify the agreement. Before the measure could be reconsidered, the Second

World War intervened.[153] Kosovar scholar Zamir Shtylla argues that Ankara had long been aware of the implications of the agreement. Documents obtained from the Albanian National Archives in Tirana state that Ankara knew that they were receiving Albanian refugees from Yugoslavia and began discussions regarding the deportation of Albanians as early as 1927, a fact that placed the Turkish government in strict contravention of the 1926 immigration law. While Ankara may have attempted to send these refugees to eastern Anatolia, particularly Diyarbakir, Elazığ, and Yozgat, many Albanians ended up in Bursa, Istanbul, Tekirdağ, Izmir, Kocaeli, and Eskişehir.[154] Others were allowed to emigrate to Albania, an arrangement also established with Albanians arriving from the Çamëria.[155]

It is difficult to make absolute sense of the 1938 convention agreement with Yugoslavia and Ankara's policy towards Albanians during the first years of the Republic. How can these two tangents in Turkish state policy be reconciled? How does one ban Albanians from entering the country yet sanction, and even aid, the complete ethnic cleansing of Albanians from Yugoslavia in order to receive them as immigrants? Without access to the Turkish Foreign Ministry archive, it is not possible fully to answer this question. Admittedly, as with previous waves of Albanian migration, it is impossible to know the absolute number of Albanians arriving from Yugoslavia during the inter-war period. Whether one trusts the numbers compiled by Turkish sources (which state that no more than 115,000 immigrants arrived in Turkey from Yugoslavia) or more recent studies by Kosovar and Albanian scholars (which estimate the number of Albanian refugees arriving in Turkey as in the hundreds of thousands), this was not a marginal affair.[156]

Perhaps the best explanation of the contradictions in Ankara's policies towards both North Caucasians and Albanians rests in the complications which the state encountered during this transition from empire to nation-state. Even in 1938, the Kemalist state was still coming to grips with the revolutionary changes that had occurred over the previous two decades. Policy-makers in the capital and in the provinces were compelled to craft decisions in accordance with a new ideology based upon secularism, modernism, and ethno-Turkish identity.[157] Yet realities on the ground intervened.

On the one hand, Ankara believed that it could ill afford to allow 'traditionally' dissident populations the opportunity to undermine the new republic. Internal security was still key. Therefore the rebellious Circassian communities had to be crushed before areas like the South Marmara became fully integrated into the state. Likewise, the thousands of Albanians arriving at the borders of Turkey had to be halted so that the older communities could be consolidated or dispersed. North Caucasians and Albanians had to be monitored and transplanted in order to prevent internal disturbances before they occurred. These steps were only part of the nation-making process undertaken by republican authorities throughout the country. The promise of greater internal security would then permit even greater projects to commence: the building of new health, educational, structural, and architectural regimes commensurate with the ideological ambitions of the Kemalist government.

On the other hand, provincial and international pressures could not be evaded. The waves of Albanian and Circassian refugees could not be stopped. As a result, Ankara sought to play at least a mitigating role in managing their passage to Anatolia, to the point of playing a collaborative role in facilitating the violence perpetrated upon both of these groups abroad. Within the Turkish Republic, Albanians and Circassians still comprised a significant percentage of the population, particularly in a region like the South Marmara. The two groups continued to supply both the Turkish state and society with thousands of labourers, merchants, officials, army officers, intellectuals, and educators. Immigrants new to Anatolia often came to reside among these older settlers, and in turn contributed to the construction of the Republic of Turkey. The transformation of Anatolia into the Turkish Republic also did not remove the limitations upon Ankara's control of the provinces. Local officials and provincial populations continued to resist or negotiate the rules laid down by the centre. In short, contradictions and ambiguities within Ankara's policies towards Circassians and Albanians were both unavoidable and necessary.

Conclusion

One weekend several years past, I boarded an Istanbul bus bound for Bursa. After a three-hour bus ride through the endless suburbs stretching eastward towards İzmit, I arrived this time round to enjoy the relative tranquillity, yet sophistication, that a weekend in Bursa had to offer. On this particular weekend, I took only a day's pause in Bursa and then pressed on a bit further outside town. That Sunday I found myself in nearby Mustafakemalpaşa, formerly known as Kirmasti until local officials changed the name in 1922 in honour of the *Gazi*. A walk through town revealed nothing remarkable. Quaint, grey, and a bit sleepy, Mustafakemalpaşa was like many provincial towns I had previously visited in Turkey. Although my research had guided me to this place, nothing I could see bore any direct reference to the war years I had been writing about. The most prominent testament to war, any war, that I could find was the military cemetery on the far side of the river that bisected the town. Instead of rows of graves memorializing the men lost at Gallipoli or victims of the Greek occupation, the cemetery, lined with fresh, clean crimson flags, bore greater witness to the numerous *şehid*s or martyrs the town had offered up in Ankara's more recent battles against Kurdish separatists to the southeast.

Towards late afternoon I found myself sitting in the courtyard of the central mosque, perched on a chair outside the office of the local *müftü*. A group of curious, concededly bewildered, men formed around me as we talked about why a young American would choose to spend his Sunday in their little town. They nodded approvingly when I told them of my work. I asked the men, somewhat naïvely, if they had heard of the intercommunal violence between Albanians and Circassians that had racked their county in 1919. Each of them, young and old, shook their heads. No idea. One young man, however, enthusiastically responded that there were still Circassians living in the villages outside town (he being one of them). His older relatives still spoke Adige, but he knew only a few words. When I asked about Albanians in the area, I was greeted with more puzzlement. After a brief aside, an older man agreed to take me to see the only Albanian he knew of in the town. After a ten-minute walk past the local market, we arrived at the foot of a tomb of an Albanian-born *şeyh* from the sixteenth or seventeenth century. 'You see,' he said, pointing to the placard on the wall, 'born in Albania'. The violence that had befallen the town only a few generations past, like the tomb of the Albanian *şeyh*, was ancient history for the people I spoke with that day.

Indeed, much has changed in the South Marmara since 1922. Most of the physical scars have long since healed as cities and villages have been rebuilt. Subsequent waves of new immigrant groups have come to settle in the region. Cities like Bursa and Balıkesir, as well as small towns like Bandırma and Sabanca, now house tens of thousands of migrants and refugees from Bulgaria and eastern Anatolia.[1] Homes and property formerly owned by Armenians in small towns like Bahçecik have been bought and resold, with some becoming summer houses for those seeking a respite from the stresses of Istanbul. Rain or shine, as the old adage goes, one can always find an Aussie or Kiwi touring the hallowed fields outside Gallipoli in search of the beaches and trenches where their fathers, grandfathers, and great-grandfathers fought so fiercely. When the sun sets, these same descendants of warriors past are warmly welcomed in the numerous bars, hotels, and restaurants dotting the streets of nearby Çanakkale.

These recent changes have not completely put an end to civil conflict in the environs of the modern South Marmara. In 2001, mobs of armed men attacked Kurdish migrants in the small town of Susurluk after the murder of a young girl was attributed to a man who had recently relocated to the region from eastern Anatolia. Five years before that, a mysterious automobile accident had placed Susurluk at the centre of a political firestorm involving Ankara's involvement with organized crime, drug traffickers, and death squads that had targeted political dissidents. Journalist Zülfikar Ali Aydın, in writing about both of these incidents, was quick to remind his readers that communal violence, gangs, and state oppression had overlapped in Susurluk before. Ahmet Anzavur had marched through the town in 1919 and 1920 with his bands of peasant rebels. After Mustafa Kemal's forces retook Susurluk for good in September 1922, Ankara levied heavy penalties upon all those accused of collaboration.[2]

Aydın's point is well taken. The absence of physical wreckage from the war years does not take away from the profundity of what has been lost or erased. In taking a closer look at the lives of both Muslims and Christians during the years between the Balkan Wars and the founding of the Turkish Republic, I have tried to underscore not only the sheer totality of the transformation witnessed during this period, but the unanimity of the experiences of conflict for those who once lived along the southern banks of the Sea of Marmara.

The period between 1912 and 1923 stands as *the* central turning point in the modern history of Asia Minor. One could go so far as to say that the Turkish War of Independence was particularly as catastrophic, definitive, and transformative an event in Anatolia's history as the Battle of Manzikert in 1071. During this decade of near constant warfare, Anatolia's physical, political, and human landscape was irrevocably altered. What was broken during the war years cannot be reconstituted or put back together again.

The final outcome of the war years appears, for the most part, unequivocal. Emptied city quarters and burned-out villages signalled a near total end to the ongoing existence of Armenian and Greek life in the region. Following a wave of summary executions and forced deportations, opposition among the remaining Muslims of the South Marmara was obliterated, co-opted, or cowed into silence. With the final cleansing of Greeks and Armenians from the territory, tens of thousands of 'Turkish' immigrants were settled in their place. Resettlement and reconstruction efforts allowed Ankara a free hand in redistributing property to loyal Muslim entrepreneurs and settlers, eliminating the economic foundations of previously dissenting groups. The slate, for the most part, has been swept clean.

One must not lose sight of the continuities that span the pre- and post-war eras. The South Marmara, beginning in the nineteenth century, was a site of intense imperial competition. Both the Ottoman government in Istanbul and Western interests committed themselves to capturing the loyalties of the region's inhabitants. Events surrounding the Great War raised the stakes in the South Marmara to an extreme. As factions within the Ottoman government went to war with one another, and foreign troops took hold of the land, competition over local allegiances turned ever more violent.

Fierce fighting between various factions for political control over the state gave way to clashes in both town and country. Very quickly the absolute meaning of this decade of conflict in the South Marmara degenerated as local groups asserted their own prosaic agendas. From the perspective of the battlefield, statist and provincial aspirations became blurred and interlaced. The rhetoric of the period, often adorned with rivalling discourses of legitimacy and authority, cannot hide, upon close inspection, the ultimate vulgarity found in the convictions of the many warring factions. Gross atrocities were unquestionably committed by all.

The political fragmentation in the South Marmara during the war years exacerbated the pre-existing social and economic fault lines of the region. In an atmosphere defined by dire poverty, the weariness of war, and the ever encroaching influence of the state, sectarian and ethnic ties became increasingly politicized and were often interpreted along the shifting scale of consent or opposition. Both foreign and domestic parties tended uniformly to equate Armenian and Greek Christians with either treason or Western interests. As time wore on, the pressures of state violence and the security found in foreign sponsorship arguably forged greater unanimity among the Armenian and Rum communities in the South Marmara. Yet, as one examines the multiple Muslim combatants and civilians involved in the struggle over this portion of Anatolia, neither ethnic nor religious links produced or delineated the formation of monolithic factions. Class and regional associations were often greater factors in swaying the allegiances of Muslim Circassian or Albanian immigrants than the forces of nationalism and Islam. Likewise, the Ottoman and Nationalist governments demonstrated varying degrees of attention and sensitivity towards to the complex identities of these newcomers in negotiating a final outcome to the conflict.

The violence portrayed in this book was often not the work of uniformed, regular armies with defined command structures or regular rules of engagement. Most of the killing, destruction, and theft enacted upon the population of the South Marmara was the result of what I would call 'a culture of paramilitarism'. In part, this aspect of the war years was a by-product of the region's history and the evolution of the modern Ottoman state. Yet, as the conflict escalated after 1919, the multiple parties in competition with one another in the South Marmara readily adapted and promoted the recruitment and formation of irregular militias or gangs. Interestingly, paramilitarism became a feature of both statist forces and what one might call 'subaltern' interests in the region. The utilization of gangs is crucial to an understanding of the blurring of statist and localist desires. We see in the proliferation of local paramilitaries in the South Marmara the convoluted extent to which the War of Independence was in fact a civil war without a clear, binary set of protagonists and antagonists.

In taking stock of the legacy of the war years in the contemporary Republic of Turkey, I am reminded of an important insight of François Furet regarding the French Revolution. The French Revolution of July 1789, Furet argues, cannot be understood in isolation. Rather, one must look at the radical agenda of the French Jacobins at the turn of the nineteenth century as a continuation of the centralizing policies initiated decades before by Cardinal Richelieu and Louis XIV. In other words, although the actors and the nature of the ruling structure may have changed, the monarchical and revolutionary reforms spanning the eighteenth and nineteenth centuries equally contributed to the centralization and consolidation of the French state.[3] One must see the war years and the events described in this book as part of a similar stream of historical continuity. Sociologist Şerif Mardin has suggested that one should look at the War of Independence, and by extension the war years overall, as only one moment during the course of the 'Turkish Revolution', a period of 'indefinite length during which the Turkish political system was transformed'.[4] If one goes back as far as the reign of Mahmud II in tracing the history of this revolution, it is clear that the notion of a unitary, centralized state encompassing Anatolia remained an absolute constant. Although no one may have envisioned a 'Turkish Republic' in the years between 1912 and 1923, a common commitment to a consolidated, unbounded state served to unite the CUP/Nationalist coalition through hardship and defeat. However, internal dissension regarding this process of consolidation and centralization in Anatolia did not vanish with declaration of the Republic. Contestation over the contours, limits, and trappings of the state, particularly at the regional level, continues to the present day.

Meaningful debate over the legacies of the war years, however, is still rarely found in public forums in Turkey. In part this lack of critical discussion is due to the present political significance that issues like the Armenian Genocide hold with regard to Turkey's contentious relationship with the European Union, the United States, and with some of its immediate neighbours. One could also say that a state-imposed climate of historical amnesia, a condition now nearly a century in the making, persists in the country. There are certainly encouraging signs that this erasure of popular memory is being reversed. The Prime Minister's Archive in Istanbul, which houses the official records of the Ottoman Empire, has become increasingly accessible to both native and foreign scholars. Since the 1950s, Turkey has witnessed a growing proliferation of local and national cultural associations among the nation's various ethnic communities. Turks of Albanian and North Caucasian descent have been among the most active participants in this movement.[5] Recent conferences held in Istanbul and abroad, such as those held by the Workshop on Armenian and Turkish Studies (WATS), have helped forge greater dialogue between Turkish and Armenian scholars of the Armenian Genocide. Writers such as Orhan Pamuk and Elif Şafak have done much to bring the country's tortured past to the attention of the public, despite threats of violence and legal prosecution. Each of these trends, I believe, are hopeful signs of a changing consensus in Turkey.

Appendix 1: Cast of Characters

Abdülgafur Hoca A high-ranking member of Balıkesir's *ulema*. He was also a founding member of the Balıkesir chapter of *Redd-i İlhak*.

Abdülhalik (Renda) Bureaucrat of Albanian descent. He was a member of the Kemalist government during the War of Independence as well as after the declaration of the Turkish Republic.

Abdülhamid II Sultan of the Ottoman Empire from 1876 to 1909. He reinstated the Ottoman constitution following the Young Turk Revolution of 1908.

Abdülvehab Bureaucrat. He served as *mutasarrıf* of İzmit in 1921.

Abdurrahman Paramilitary from Ayvacık. He and his band were allied with the Nationalists during the Greek occupation.

Ahmet Anzavur Gendarmerie officer and *Teşkilat-ı Mahsusa* member of North Caucasian descent. In 1919 Anzavur was appointed to the position of *mutasarrıf* of İzmit. With the support of the Istanbul government and British occupational forces, he led three failed uprisings against the *Kuva-yı Milliye* in the South Marmara. He was assassinated outside the town of Karabiga by Nationalist guerrillas in 1921.

Ahmet Esat Tomruk Also known as *İngiliz* Kemal. He was a spy for the Ottoman government and the National Forces. In 1919 he aided in the recruitment of *Kara* Hasan into the *Kuva-yı Milliye*.

Ahmet Kuşçubaşı Brother of Hacı Sami and Eşref Kuşçubaşı, he was also an early supporter of the National Movement. He supplied weapons and refuge to *Çerkes* Ethem's forces in 1919 and joined in *Kuva-yı Milliye* activities in Adapazarı in 1920.

Ahmet (Mercimekizade) Unionist official from Bilecik. He reportedly oversaw the deportation and murders in Bilecik during the First World War.

Ali Suat Officer and bureaucrat. He was appointed to the position of *kaymakam* of Adapazarı in 1920 and aided in Nationalist efforts in the region.

Names are alphabetized according to the first letters in the name (or the epithet) of the individual, irrespective of diacritical marks. Aside from providing basic information regarding the individuals mentioned through the text, this index also gives considerable attention to those who were members of the Ottoman clandestine service, the *Teşkilat-ı Mahsusa*.

Alim Efendi The *müftü* of Manisa. He participated in the Izmir Defence of Ottoman Rights Committee as a representative from Manisa and was among the earliest organizers of the *Kuva-yı Milliye* in the South Marmara.

Arab **Ali Osman Efe** Paramilitary from Manisa. He served under İbrahim Ethem during the Greek occupation of the South Marmara.

Arnavud **Arslan Ağa** Albanian paramilitary from Balıkesir. He served under İbrahim Ethem during the Greek occupation of the South Marmara.

Arnavud **Aziz** Paramilitary from Ezine. He and his band were allied with the Nationalists during the Greek occupation.

Arnavud **Aziz Kaptan** Paramilitary from Karacabey/Kirmasti. He was nominally allied with both the *Kuva-yı Milliye* and Ahmet Anzavur.

Arnavud **Kazım** Albanian paramilitary leader from Değirmendere. First active during the First World War, he joined the National Movement in 1919.

Arnavud **Mahmut Mahir** A bureaucrat of Albanian descent. He was appointed to the position of *mutasarrıf* in İzmit and Kale-i Sultaniye during the War of Independence. In 1923 the Turkish government charged him with collaboration and stripped him of his citizenship.

Arnavud **Rahman** A paramilitary leader of Albanian descent from the environs of Karabiga. Although first active during the First World War, he emerged as a partisan for the National Movement. In 1921 he aided in the assassination of Ahmet Anzavur.

Artin Rum paramilitary commander from Biga. He became a prominent bandit after murdering Halil Pehlivan during the First World War. Soon after, he was executed by Halil's brother-in-law, *Çerkes* Neş'et.

Aziz (Captain) A North Caucasian, he assisted Hacim Muhittin during his first tour of the South Marmara. He later joined *Çerkes* Ethem's Flying Column and represented Saruhan in the Grand National Turkish Parliament in 1920. He was also a brother-in-law of Rauf Orbay.

(Bağ) Kamil A notable of North Caucasian descent from Adapazarı. He was among the seminal leaders of the Loyalist resistance in the İzmit/Adapazarı region. In 1921, he participated in the Near Eastern Circassian Society congress in İzmir.

(Bağ) Taluastan Bey A notable of North Caucasian descent from Adapazarı. He was among the seminal leaders of the Loyalist resistance in the İzmit/Adapazarı region. In 1921, he participated in the Near Eastern Circassian Society congress in İzmir.

(Bakırlı) Mehmet Efe Paramilitary from Manisa. He served under İbrahim Ethem during the Greek occupation of the South Marmara.

Bekir Sami (Günsav) High-ranking officer of North Caucasian descent. In 1919 he was appointed to command the Nationalist Forces in the Bursa area. He helped in the suppression of Ahmet Anzavur's uprising and led the Nationalist withdrawal from the South Marmara in 1921.

Appendix 1: Cast of Characters

Bekir Sami (Kundukh) Prominent bureaucrat of North Caucasian descent. During the War of Independence he was a close ally of Mustafa Kemal (Atatürk). After the war he was accused of treason and left politics.

Benoît Blinishti Diplomat. He represented Albania during the negotiations at Lausanne in 1923.

(Berzeg) Safer Abkhazian notable from Düzce. He was among the first participants in the Loyalist resistance in İzmit. In 1921 he attended the Near Eastern Circassian Society congress in İzmit.

(Big) Ahmet Fevzi Paşa Officer of Circassian descent. After rising to the rank of *paşa* during the reign of Abdülhamid, he became a prominent member of the North Caucasian diaspora in Istanbul. Throughout the War of Independence he stood against Ahmet Anzavur and the Near Eastern Circassian Society.

Boşnak **Karabulut İbrahim Çavuş** Bosnian paramilitary from İvendik. Although originally a non-partisan bandit, İbrahim became an ally of the Nationalist Movement towards the end of the Greek occupation.

Çallı Kadir Efe Paramilitary. He was among the first guerrillas to participate in the Greek-backed incursions into Anatolia in 1922.

(Canbazlı) Safer Circassian notable and paramilitary from Manyas. He was a participant in the intercommunal violence in Karacabey in 1919 and a supporter of Ahmet Anzavur.

Celal Bayar Officer and bureaucrat. He served as a *Teşkiat-ı Mahsusa* agent in the Aegean during the First World War. As one of the first organizers of the National Movement, Celal later rose to become one of Mustafa Kemal's closest allies.

Cemal Paşa Governor of Syria and leading member of the CUP triumvirate government during the First World War.

Çerkes **Bekir Sıtkı** Circassian officer and member of the *Teşkilat-ı Mahsusa*. In 1919 he led the Loyalist resistance in the İzmit/Adapazarı region. We was later stripped of his Turkish citizenship and sent into exile.

Çerkes **Çakır** Circassian paramilitary and soldier from Gönen. During the First World War he served as Enver Paşa's bodyguard and was a member of the *Teşkilat-ı Mahsusa*. He later fought under the command of *Çerkes* Ethem.

Çerkes **Davut** North Caucasian paramilitary leader from Kirmasti. He served in the *Teşkilat-ı Mahsusa* during the First World War. In 1919 he became an ally of Ahmet Anzavur and fought against Nationalist forces in Kirmasti. After the war he supposedly participated in the guerrilla attacks organized by the Greek government in the Aegean.

Çerkes **Ethem** *Teşkilat-ı Mahsusa* officer of North Caucasian descent. As brother of *Çerkes* Reşit, he was among the first military commanders of the *Kuva-yı Milliye*. After serving on the Aegean front, Ethem was charged with putting down the rebellions of Ahmet Anzavur in the South Marmara and the Çapanoğlu uprising in Yozgat. He defected to Greece in 1921 with his brothers and died in exile.

Çerkes Fuat Former police chief of İzmit of North Caucasian descent. He actively collaborated with (Çule) İbrahim Hakkı and Greek occupational forces.

Çerkes Hakkı Circassian notable and paramilitary leader from Karacabey. He participated in the Circassian–Albanian conflict in Karacabey/Kırmasti of 1919. He later became a supporter of Ahmet Anzavur.

Çerkes Hikmet Paramilitary and assassin of Circassian descent from İzmit. During the War of Independence he aided his brother Kazım in organizing the Loyalist resistance around İzmit.

Çerkes Kazım Paramilitary and assassin of Circassian descent. In 1913 he stood trial for the murder of grand vizir Mahmud Şevket Paşa. During the War of Independence he was among the first organizers of the anti-Nationalist resistance in İzmit.

Çerkes Mehmet Reşit Intellectual, bureaucrat, and *Teşkilat-ı Mahsusa* operative of North Caucasian descent. As wartime governor of Diyarbakır, he was responsible for numerous atrocities against the local Armenian population. He committed suicide before being prosecuted for war crimes.

Çerkes Neş'et A paramilitary of Circassian descent from the environs of Biga. At the end of the First World War Neş'et was among the most powerful North Caucasian paramilitary leaders in Biga and was a rival to *Kara* Hasan.

Çerkes Reşit Seminal member of the Committee of Union and Progress, army officer, and member of the *Teşkilat-ı Mahsusa*. Initially among the first organizers of the *Kuva-yı Milliye*, he later fled to Greece with his brother *Çerkes* Ethem in 1921.

Çerkes Said Circassian notable and paramilitary leader. As the mayor of Manyas, he participated in the Circassian–Albanian conflict in Karacabey/Kırmasti of 1919. He later became a supporter of Ahmet Anzavur.

Çerkes Tevfik Circassian officer and brother of Reşit and Ethem. During the War of Independence, he served as a recruiting officer in Gönen. Like his brothers, he initially joined the *Kuva-yı Milliye*, but later defected to Greece.

Çingene or Kıbti Ali Paramilitary of Roma descent from Karabiga. He and his band were allied with the Nationalists during the Greek occupation. In 1921 he aided in the assassination of Ahmet Anzavur.

(Çule) Beslan A notable and gendarme of North Caucasian descent from Adapazarı. He was among the seminal leaders of the Loyalist resistance in the İzmit/Adapazarı region. In 1921, he participated in the Near Eastern Circassian Society congress in İzmir.

(Çule) İbrahim Hakkı Circassian notable and paramilitary from Sabanca. As an anti-Unionist dissident, he was tried for the murder of Mahmud Şevket Paşa in 1913 and fled the Ottoman Empire. During the War of Independence he led the Loyalist resistance in the İzmit/Adapazarı region. In 1921 he chaired the meeting of the Near Eastern Circassian Association. After the war he went into exile and became an advocate for the resettlement of North Caucasians expelled from Anatolia.

Damat **Ferid Paşa** Co-founder of the Liberal Entente and brother-in-law of Sultan Abdülmecit. During the War of Independence he served as grand vizir on two separate occasions. He would come to be known as one of the most loyal partisans of Sultan Vahdeddin.

(Debreli) Ziya Bey Provincial bureaucrat of Albanian descent. His appointment to Karacabey's administration in the summer of 1919 helped instigate the Albanian–Circassian conflict of Karcabey/Kirmasti.

Deli **Fuat Paşa** A field marshal of North Caucasian descent. He founded the Society for Circassian Unity and Mutual Support (*Çerkes İttihad ve Teavün Cemiyeti*). He later founded the *Şimali Kafkas Komitesi* (North Caucasus Committee) in 1914. During the War of Independence, *Deli* Fuat threw in his lot with the National Movement and spoke out against the activities of the Near Eastern Circassian Society.

Deli **Hurşid** Albanian paramilitary leader from Karacabey. He helped instigate the Circassian–Albanian conflict in Karacabey/Kirmasti in the summer of 1919. He was later murdered by Circassian paramilitaries outside Karacabey.

Demetrius Caclamanos Diplomat. He represented the Kingdom of Greece during the negotiations at Lausanne in 1923.

(Dramalı) Ali Rıza Officer and member of the *Teşkilat-ı Mahsusa*. He served as (Köprülülü) Hamdi's aide-de-camp during the Nationalist takeover of Biga. He was later executed after attempting to assassinate *Damat* Ferid.

(Dürrızade) Abdullah Efendi *Şeyhülislam* in 1920. He declared in 1920 that Mustafa Kemal and the *Kuva-yı Milliye* were bandits in open rebellion to the state.

Ebubekir Hazım Bureaucrat and pro-Nationalist. In 1919, he served as governor of Hüdavendigar.

Enver Paşa Officer and founding member of the Committee of Union and Progress. He was Minister of War during the First World War. In 1918 he fled to Russia, where he resided for most of the War of Independence. He died leading a revolt in modern-day Tajikistan.

Eşref Kuşcubaşı Seminal member of the Committee of Union and Progress and founder of the *Teşkilat-ı Mahsusa*. He briefly commanded the National Forces in the İzmit/Adapazarı district, but was removed from command. During his falling out with Mustafa Kemal, he organized and led paramilitary operations in the Aegean under Greek supervision. Later he was accepted back into Turkey and retired in Izmir.

Eyüp Sabri Officer and *Teşkilat-ı Mahsusa* member of Albanian descent. He was a seminal member of the Committee of Union and Progress and participated in the Young Turk uprising of 1908. Although a supporter of the Nationalist Movement during the War of Independence, he was marginalized by Mustafa Kemal (Atatürk's) partisans.

Fahri Can Doctor. He was among the first organizers of the National Forces in İzmit.

Fahri Görgülü Historian from Kirmasti. In 1960 he compiled a history of Kirmasti under the Greek occupation.

Galip Paşa Retired Albanian officer and landowner from Karacabey. He was among the leaders of the Albanian faction in the Albanian–Circassian conflict in Karcabey/Kirmasti. Later he became a supporter of the *Kuva-yı Milliye*.

Gavur İmam Also known as İmam Fevzi. A Pomak immigrant from Bulgaria, he was among Ahmet Anzavur's closest allies during the uprising of 1920.

(Gönenli) Osman Notable from Gönen. He was among the seminal participants of the Balıkesir congress of 1919.

(Gostivarlı) İbrahim Albanian notable from Karacabey. He participated in the Circassian–Albanian conflict in Karacabey/Kirmasti in the summer of 1919. He later became a supporter of Ahmet Anzavur.

(Gümülcineli) İsmail Hakkı Co-founder of the Liberal Entente during the Young Turk period. During the War of Independence he was appointed governor of Hüdavendigar, but fled after the *Kuva-yı Milliye* assumed control of the town of Bursa.

Hacı Sami Kuşçubaşı The brother of Eşref *Kuşçubaşı*. During the First World War he joined the *Teşkilat-ı Mahsusa* and was sent to Central Asia in order to raise a rebellion against the Russian Empire. He was a loyal follower of Enver Paşa and remained in Central Asia throughout the War of Independence. When the war was over, he joined his brother in leading paramilitary activities against the Kemalist government. He was killed during an assault on Kuşadesi in 1927.

Hacim Muhittin (Çarıklı) High-ranking bureaucrat under the CUP and organizer for the *Kuva-yı Milliye*. He was appointed *mutasarrıf* of Balıkesir in 1919 and led the pro-Nationalist Balıkesir congress.

Halil Pehlivan A paramilitary leader of Circassian descent. During the First World War he was active in the environs of Biga.

Halit (Moralızade) A merchant and intellectual from İzmir. He was among the first organizers of the Nationalist resistance in İzmir in 1919.

Harry Lamb British official. In 1914, he conducted several tours of the South Marmara, documenting the plight of Greek refugees in the region. Later he became representative of the British High Commission in Izmir.

Hasan Basri (Çantay) An intellectual and notable from Balıkesir, Hasan Basri was among the first organizers of the *Kuva-yı Milliye* in the South Marmara and the publisher of the pro-Nationalist newspaper *Ses*.

Hasan Tahsin Circassian notable from Manyas. He and *Kel* Hüseyin met with Bekir Sami (Günsav) regarding the possible deportation of Circassians in the South Marmara.

Haydar Rüştü (Öktem) Teacher and intellectual. He was among the organizers of the Nationalist resistance in İzmir in 1919.

Horace Rumbold Diplomat. He was head of the British High Commission in Istanbul during the Turkish War of Independence.

Hüsamettin (Ertürk) Soldier. During the First World War he was among the highest-ranking officials in the *Teşkilat-ı Mahsusa*. After the war he aided in the construction of the *Karakol* network.

Hüseyin Ragıp Nurretin Intellectual from İzmir. He was among the organizers of the Nationalist resistance in İzmir in 1919.

İbrahim Ethem Akıncı Paramilitary, lawyer, and bureaucrat. Throughout the war he served as a bureaucrat throughout Anatolia. In 1921 he was appointed *kaymakam* of Sındırgı and led a guerrilla campaign against the Greek occupation of Balıkesir.

İbrahim Süreyya (Yiğit) Of Abkhazian descent. CUP officer and active organizer in the *Kuva-yı Milliye* in the İzmit region. One-time member of the *Teşkilat-ı Mahsusa*.

İlyas Sami Kalkavanoğlu Soldier. During the Turkish War of Independence he served in the İzmit area as well as in the Black Sea region.

İngiliz **Ali Kemal** Loyalist officer of Albanian descent. He had aided Ahmet Anzavur during the first uprising of 1919.

İngiliz **Kemal**—see Ahmet Esat Tomruk.

İsmail Efe Paramilitary of Yörük extraction. He was among the first guerrillas to participate in the Greek-backed incursions into Anatolia in 1922.

Jeanie Jillson American missionary in the Bursa region during the pre-war years.

Kadir (Anzavuroğlu) Paramilitary from the environs of Biga/Karabiga. Among the eldest of Ahmet Anzavur's sons, Kadir first emerged as a bandit during the First World War. During the War of Independence, he aided his father during the rebellions of 1919–20. He later collaborated with Greek occupation troops and was among the North Caucasian insurgent leaders during the incursions of 1923. He was killed by local security forces.

Kani Bey Nationalist officer. He was (Köprülülü) Hamdi's second-in-command in Biga. He was executed by Loyalist insurgents in February 1920.

Kanlı **Mustafa** Paramilitary from Gönen. He and his band were allied with (Anzavuroğlu) Kadir during the Greek occupation.

Kara **Arslan** Paramilitary of Albanian descent. During the First World War he joined the *Teşkilat-ı Mahsusa* and was among the first Nationalist paramilitary commanders on the İzmit front.

Kara **Hasan** A Pomak immigrant from Bulgaria, Hasan was among the most influential paramilitary leaders from Biga. After being recruited into the National Movement, he fought against Ahmet Anzavur in 1919. In 1920 he was arrested and executed on the orders of (Köprülülü) Hamdi.

Kara **Kemal** Officer and *Teşkilat-ı Mahsusa* member. In 1918 he was charged along with *Kara* Vasif with the creation of the *Karakol* organization, the support network for the *Kuva-yı Milliye*.

Kara **Vasif** Officer and *Teşkilat-ı Mahsusa* member. In 1918 he was charged along with *Kara* Kemal with the creation of the *Karakol* organization, the support network for the *Kuva-yı Milliye*.

(Karzeg) Sait A Circassian notable from Adapazarı. He was assassinated while negotiating with Loyalist insurgents near Hendek.

Kasap **Hüseyin** An Albanian paramilitary leader from Karacabey. He helped initiate the Circassian–Albanian conflict in Karacabey/Kirmasti in the summer of 1919.

Kazım (Özalp) Officer and statesman possibly of Albanian descent. He joined the *Teşkilat-ı Mahsusa* during the First World War. During the War of Independence he commanded the *Kuva-yı Milliye*'s Balıkesir front. He helped in the suppression of Ahmet Anzavur's uprising and led the Nationalist withdrawal from the South Marmara in 1921. He was later one of the commanders of the Nationalist counter-attack of 1922.

(Keçeci) Hafız Mehmet Emin Merchant from Balıkesir. Participant in the Balıkesir congress of 1919.

Kel **Aziz** Paramilitary of North Caucasian descent. After the outbreak of the War of Independence, he became an ally of Ahmet Anzavur. In 1923 he became a leader of one of the Greek-organized incursions into the South Marmara.

Kel **Hüseyin** Circassian notable from Manyas. He and Hasan Tahsin met with Bekir Sami (Günsav) regarding the possible deportation of Circassians in the South Marmara.

(Kıbrıslı) Sırrı Bureaucrat and Nationalist organizer. He was among the first *Kuva-yı Milliye* commanders on the İzmit front. He later participated in the Turkish parliament in 1920.

(Köprülülü) Hamdi Bureaucrat and officer of Albanian descent. At the outbreak of the War of Independence he served on the Aegean front and was later appointed Nationalist commander in Biga. In 1920 he was captured and executed by Loyalist insurgents.

Kürd **Mehmet** Kurdish paramilitary leader and follower of *Kara* Hasan. He became an ally of Ahmet Anzavur in 1920.

(Maan) Ali Gendarmerie officer of Abkhazian descent. He was a founding member of the *Teşkilat-ı Mahsusa*. In 1920, he was a leading paramilitary of the anti-Nationalist uprising in the İzmit/Adapazarı region. He was also a participant at the Near East Circassian Association meeting of 1921.

(Maan) Koç Abkhazian notable from Düzce. He was among the first participants of the Loyalist resistance in İzmit. In 1921 he attended the Near Eastern Circassian Society congress in İzmit.

(Maan) Mustafa Namık Gendarmerie officer, bureaucrat, and landowner of Abkhazian descent. As *kaymakam* of Adapazarı, he actively collaborated with (Çule) İbrahim Hakkı and Greek occupational forces.

(Maan) Şirin Soldier and *Teşkilat-ı Mahsusa* officer of Abkhazian descent. In 1920, he was a leading paramilitary of the anti-Nationalist uprising in the İzmit/Adapazarı region. He was also a participant at the Near East Circassian Association congress of 1921.

Appendix 1: Cast of Characters

Mehmet VI Vahdeddin Nephew of Mehmet V, he reigned as sultan of the Ottoman Empire from July 1918 to November 1922.

Mehmet Ali Gendarme from Manyas. He later led one of the first Greek-organized incursions into the South Marmara.

Mehmet Aydemiroğlu Circassian paramilitary leader from Gönen. During the War of Independence he fought both for and against the National Movement.

Mehmed Fertgerey (Şoenu) Well-known historian and intellectual in the North Caucasian community in Istanbul. During the First World War he served in the *Teşkilat-ı Mahsusa*. After the War of Independence, he published his account of the Gönen and Manyas deportations in a pamphlet entitled 'A Second Petition to the Grand National Turkish Parliament and the Greater Turkish Conscience Regarding the Circassian Question'.

Mehmet Fuat (Çarım) Former bureaucrat and member of the *Teşkilat-ı Mahsusa*, of North Caucasian descent. During the War of Independence he served as the *kaymakam* of Adapazarı and was selected to attend the first Nationalist Parliament in Ankara.

Mehmet Vehbi (Bolak) Long-time bureaucrat in the South Marmara during the Young Turk period, he founded the Balıkesir chapter of the Rejection of Annexation Society.

Müftü Şevket Efendi Notable from Gönen. He was the head of the local chapter of *Müdafaa-ı Hukuk*. In 1920 he was arrested and executed by Ahmet Anzavur.

Mustafa Necati Lawyer, teacher, and administrator. During the War of Independence, he became an organizer for the *Kuva-yı Milliye* and co-founded the Nationalist newspaper *İzmir'e Doğru* with Vasıf (Çınar).

Mustafa Sabri Efendi *Şeyhülislam*. He also was the founder of the Loyalist organization, the Advancement of Islam Society (*Teal-i İslam Cemiyeti*).

Nurettin Bey Bureaucrat and landowner from Değirmendere. He helped support the activities of *Arnavud* Kazım. He was also a relative of Talat Paşa.

Parti Mehmet Pehlivan Long-time paramilitary. Initially he served as a lieutenant to Çerkes Ethem and helped suppress Ahmet Anzavur's uprising. In 1921 he split with Ethem and joined İbrahim Ethem in his campaign against Greek occupation forces in Balıkesir.

Rahmi Bey Wartime governor of Izmir. During the War of Independence, he purportedly abandoned the National Movement and joined the Ottoman Revolutionary Committee.

Rauf Orbay Former Minister of the Navy, member of the *Teşkilat-ı Mahsusa*, founder of the *Kuva-yı Milliye*, and close confidant of Mustafa Kemal (Atatürk).

Rıfat Yüce Journalist from the environs of İzmit. During the War of Independence he was tried for war crimes and imprisoned in Malta. After the war he published a personal history of the İzmit/Adapazarı region during the War of Independence.

Appendix 1: Cast of Characters

Rıza Nur Bureaucrat. Although a member of the Liberal Entente before the First World War, he became a staunch supporter of the National Movement. After the war, he became Minister of Health and a critic of Albanian immigration into Anatolia.

Rüştü Aras Statesman and diplomat. After serving in the Nationalist administration during the War of Independence, Rüştü Aras served as Foreign Minister during the first years of the Turkish Republic. He was also responsible for the negotiated deportation of Albanians from Yugoslavia.

Sadık Paramilitary from Ezine. He and his band were allied with the Nationalists during the Greek occupation.

Sadık Baba A Bulgarian (or possibly Pomak) paramilitary and possibly a member of the *Teşkilat-ı Mahsusa*. He was among the first *Kuva-yı Milliye* commanders on the İzmit front.

Şah İsmail Landowner and paramilitary of Circassian descent. During the First World War he purportedly served with the *Teşkilat-ı Mahsusa*. After splitting with *Çerkes* Ethem, he joined forces with Ahmet Anzavur. In 1921 he was placed on trial for assassinating two North Caucasian notables in Istanbul. He was shot before the sentence was delivered.

Sait Molla Member of the *ulema* and newspaper publisher. He was among the staunchest proponents of the Istanbul government. He founded the Association of the Friends of England in Turkey, which assisted Ahmet Anzavur's campaign against the *Kuva-yı Milliye*.

Selahattin Bey Officer of Albanian extraction. During the War of Independence, he became Bekir Sami (Günsav's) aide-de-camp in Bursa.

Süleyman Askeri Officer of Circassian descent. He was a co-founder of the *Teşkilat-ı Mahsusa* with Eşref *Kuşçubaşı*.

Süleyman Şefik Paşa Officer and bureaucrat. In the War of Independence he served as Minister of War during Ali Rıza's tenure as grand vizir. In 1920 he led the Loyalist army, the *Kuva-yı İnzibatiye*, against the *Kuva-yı Milliye* in the İzmit/Adapazarı region.

Tahsin (Uzer) Administrator and CUP activist, possibly of Albanian descent. During the Turkish War of Independence, he loyally served the Nationalist government.

Takığ Şevket A Circassian paramilitary leader from the village of Mürüvetler near Manyas. He joined *Çerkes* Ethem in the early stages of the War of Independence. He would later be among the first North Caucasian guerrillas to participate in the Greek-run campaign to subvert the Kemalist government.

Talat Paşa Officer and seminal member of the Committee of Union and Progress. He served as Minister of the Interior during the First World War and helped orchestrate the deportation of Ottoman Christians. He was assassinated in Germany in 1922.

Uluğ İğdemir A schoolteacher from Biga. After the war, the Turkish Historical Association published sections of his diary related to the Anzavur uprising of 1920.

Vasıf (Çınar) Teacher, intellectual, and Nationalist organizer from İzmir. During the War of Independence he became the publisher of the pro-Nationalist newspaper *İzmir'e Doğru*.

Vivian Hadkinson British officer and assistant to the British High Commission in Istanbul. Between 1919 and 1922 he conducted several fact-finding tours of the South Marmara.

Yahya Kaptan Paramilitary of Albanian descent. During the First World War he joined the *Teşkilat-ı Mahsusa* and was among the first paramilitary Nationalist commanders on the İzmit front. He was later killed in an inter-Nationalist dispute.

Yarbay Rahmi Bey Officer. He served as regimental commander under Bekir Sami (Günsav) during the War of Independence. He was killed outside Gönen by Ahmet Anzavur's forces.

(Yenibahçeli) Şükrü An officer of North Caucasian descent. He was among the first members of the *Teşkilat-ı Mahsusa* and was a member of the Committee of Union and Progress. He was also among the first organizers of the *Kuva-yı Milliye*'s paramilitary bands. He was later accused of treason after the Izmir affair in 1926.

Yetimoğlu family A family of Georgian paramilitaries in the Karamürsel/Değirmendire region. Although first active during the First World War, they were allied with the *Kuva-yı Milliye* in 1919.

Yusuf İzzet Paşa Officer and intellectual of North Caucasian descent. He was one of the most prominent members of the North Caucasian community of Istanbul. During the War of Independence he was the commanding officer of Nationalist Forces in Bandırma. He was later removed from his command due to suspicions of his loyalty towards the Istanbul government.

(Zarbalı) Hulûsi Merchant from Balıkesir. He was a participant at the Balıkesir congress of 1919. Before İzmir's occupation, Hulûsi attended the Grand Congress of the Ottoman Defence of Rights Society in Izmir.

Zühtü (Güven) Served in the gendarmerie in the South Marmara throughout the First World War and the War of Independence. After retiring, he published his memoirs covering his service in Biga and Ahmet Anzavur's uprisings of 1919–20.

Appendix 2: Glossary of Terms

Abaza Abkhazian.

Adige a term used to describe the largest linguistic group within the North Caucasian diaspora. Often used synonymously with Circassian.

Ağa Master or Lord.

Army of Mohammed (Kuva-yı Muhammediye) the rebel army raised and led by Ahmet Anzavur between the autumn of 1919 and spring of 1920.

Arnavud Albanian.

Bey often used as the equivalent of sir or mister.

Boşnak Bosnian.

Çavuş Ottoman equivalent to the rank of sergeant.

Çerkes Circassian or North Caucasian.

Çete a gang, militia, or paramilitary group.

Çeteci a gangster, militiaman, or paramilitary.

Çetecilik paramilitarism.

Çetmi an Alevi-related Turcoman group found in the South Marmara.

Deniz Harbiye Ottoman Naval Academy

Efendi a gentleman.

Eşraf the notables or the elite of a given district or region.

Harbiye the Ottoman Military Academy.

İmam an Islamic teacher.

Kara black. It is often used to refer to someone's hair.

Karakol a resistance group formed by Kara Kemal and Kara Vasif, two former members of the Special Organization, in the aftermath of the First World War. It was instrumental in forming the National Movement.

Kaymakam the chief administrator of a kaza.

Appendix 2: Glossary of Terms

Kaza a provincial administrative unit organized around a major town. A *sancak* is composed of several kazas.

Kuva-yı İnzibatiye the Disciplinary Forces, the Loyalist army led by Süleyman Şefik Paşa in 1920.

Kuva-yı Milliye the National Forces.

Kürd a Kurd or Kurdish.

Liva the Ottoman equivalent of a county.

Manav An indigenous Sunni Turkish-speaking group found in the South Marmara.

Millet nation or nationality.

Milli Mücadele the National Movement.

Muhacir an immigrant.

Muhtar a neighbourhood official or village head.

Mustasarrıf the governor of a sub-province or *sancak*.

Müdafaa-ı Hukuk Cemiyeti Defence of Rights Committee. One of the predecessors of the central Nationalist umbrella committee, the Defence of Rights Society of Anatolia and Rumeli.

Müftü a judge under Islamic law.

Mülkiye Ottoman Civil Service School

Mülteci a refugee.

Nahiye a district incorporating a large village or small town.

Nutuk the speech delivered by Mustafa Kemal during the annual congress of the Republican People's Party in 1927.

Padişah the sultan of the Ottoman Empire

Paşa a general.

Redd-i İlhak Cemiyeti Rejection of Annexation Committee. One of the predecessors of the central Nationalist umbrella committee, the Defence of Rights Society of Anatolia and Rumeli.

Rum an Anatolian Greek. This is used in opposition to the term Yunan, which refers to a Greek-speaker from contemporary Greece.

Sadrazam Grand Vizir. It refers to the chief bureaucratic officer responsible for the running of the Ottoman government (often compared to the office of Prime Minister).

Sancak a sub-province, below a *vilayet*.

Saray the palace. It is often used in reference to the sultan's palace.

Serseri a vagrant or ruffian.

Tehcir exile. It is a term often used to refer to the Armenian deportations of 1915.

Teşkilat-ı Mahsusa the Special Organization, or the Ottoman clandestine service.

Türk a Turk or Turkish.

Ulema religious class (comprising imams, müftüs, etc.).

Vali the governor of a *vilayet*.

Vilayet The largest administrative unit in the Ottoman Empire, above a sancak. A vilayet was often composed of several sancaks.

Yörük a Turcoman, originally nomadic, group found throughout western and central Anatolia.

Zeybek a Turcoman group found in western Anatolia.

Notes

INTRODUCTION

1. Karesi and Hüdavendigar were two *sancak*s within the larger province (*vilayet*) of Hüdavendigar. The *vilayet* of Hüdavendigar included three other *sancak*s: Ertuğrul, Kütahya, and Karahisar-Afyon. For the sake of historical and narrative continuity, I have omitted any discussion of these latter *sancak*s.
2. The South Marmara has benefited greatly from scholarly interest in the years since the Turkish War of Independence. Still, the dogmas of the *Nutuk* pervade almost the entire breadth of Turkish-language historiography. See Doğan Avcıoğlu, *Milli Kurtuluş Tarihi, 1838'den 1995'e* (Istanbul: Tekin Yayınevi, 1995); Yusuf Çam, *Milli Mücadele'de İzmit Sancağı* (İzmit: İzmit Rotary Kulubü, 1993); Fahri Görgülü, *Yunan İşgalinde Kirmasti (Mustafakemalpaşa)* (Mustafakemalpaşa: Yeni Müteferrika Basımevi, 1960); Orhan Hülagü, *Milli Mücadele'de Bursa* (Istanbul: Emre Yayınları, 2001); Zekeriya Özdemir, *Balıkesir Bölgesinde Milli Mücadele Önderleri* (Ankara: Zekeriya Özdemir, 2001); idem, *Milli Mücadele Yıllarında Balıkesir Cepheleri* (Ankara: Zekeriya Özdemir, 2001); Kemal Özer, *Kurtuluş Savaşında Gönen* (Gönen: Türkdili Matbaası, 1964); Adnan Sofuoğlu, *Kuva-yı Milliye Döneminde Kuzeybatı Anadolu, 1919–1921* (Ankara: Genelkurmay Basım Evi, 1994); Rifat Yüce, *Kocaeli Tarih ve Rehberi* (İzmit: Türkyolu Matbaası, 1945).
3. Taner Akçam, *A Shameful Act: The Armenian Genocide and Turkish Responsibility* (New York: Metropolitan Books, 2006). See esp. ch. 1. Similar conclusions are also reached in Vahakn N. Dadrian, *The History of the Armenian Genocide: Ethnic Conflict from the Balkans to the Caucasus* (Providence, RI: Berghahn Books, 1995). For more of an internationalized perspective on the Armenian genocide see Donald Bloxham, *The Great Game of Imperialism, Nationalism and the Destruction of the Armenians* (New York: Oxford University Press, 2007).
4. Stanford Shaw, *From Empire to Republic: The Turkish War of National Liberation, 1918–1923: A Documentary Study* (Ankara: Türk Tarih Kurumu Basımevi, 2000). Günter Lewy, while acknowledging Ottoman mistakes and inaction, also puts the greater blame on Ottoman Armenians during the First World War. See Guenter Lewy, *The Armenian Massacres in Ottoman Turkey: A Disputed Genocide* (Salt Lake City: University of Utah Press, 2005).
5. Ussama, Makdisi. *The Culture of Sectarianism: Community, History and Violence in Nineteenth-Century Ottoman Lebanon* (Berkeley: University of California Press, 2000); Isa Blumi, 'The Consequences of Empire in the Balkans and the Red Sea: Reading Possibilities in the Transformations of the Modern World' (Ph.D. diss., New York University, 2005); Hans-Lukas Kieser, *Der Verpasste Friede: Mission, Ethnie und Staat in den Ostprovinzen der Türkei* (Zürich: Chronos Verlag, 2000).
6. Gyanendra Pandey, *The Construction of Communalism in Colonial North India* (New York: Oxford University Press, 1990); Ranajit Guha, *Elementary Aspects of Peasant Insurgency in Colonial India* (New York: Oxford University Press,

1991); Stanley Tambiah, *Leveling Crowds: Ethnonationalist Conflicts and Collective Violence in South Asia* (Berkeley: University of California Press, 1997); See also Eric Hobsbawm, *Bandits* (New York: New Press, 2000); Anton Blok, *The Mafia of Sicilian Village, 1860–1960: A Study of Violent Peasant Entrepreneurs* (Oxford: Blackwell, 1974); *idem, Honour and Violence* (Cambridge: Polity, 2001); Richard Slatta (ed.), *Bandidos: The Varieties of Latin American Banditry* (Westport, Conn.: Greenwood Press, 1987).

7. Alan Knight, *The Mexican Revolution* (New York: Cambridge University Press, 1986); Allen Wells and Gilbert M. Joseph, *Summer of Discontent, Seasons of Upheaval: Elite Politics and Rural Insurgency in Yucatan, 1876–1915* (Stanford, Calif.: Stanford University Press, 1996); Paul Vanderwood, *Disorder and Progress: Bandits, Police and Mexican Development* (Lincoln: University of Nebraska Press, 1981); John Hart, *Revolutionary Mexico: The Coming and Process of the Mexican Revolution* (Berkeley: University of California Press, 1997); Ana Maria Alonso, *Thread of Blood: Colonialism, Revolution and Gender on Mexico's Northern Frontier* (Tucson: University of Arizona Press, 1997); Florencia Mallon, *Peasant and Nation: The Making of Postcolonial Mexico and Peru* (Berkeley: University of California Press, 1995).

8. For example, the various names for towns such as Bursa (Prusa in Greek), İzmit (Nicomedia in Greek), and Bahçecik (Bardezag in Armenian) reflect this diversity.

CHAPTER 1

1. İlhan Selçuk, *Yüzbaşı Selahattin'in Romanı, II. Kitap* (Istanbul: Remzi Kitabevi, 1975), 15.
2. Ibid. 38–40.
3. Ibid. 15.
4. Atatürk's own account of his origins bears certain similarities. Although Atatürk claimed to be the descendant of Yörük nomads from Anatolia, Andrew Mango points out that it is not possible fully to substantiate this claim. One distant relative of Mustafa Kemal would later claim that the Republic's founder had a paternal grandfather who was Albanian. See Andrew Mango, *Atatürk: The Biography of the Founder of Modern Turkey* (Woodstock, NY: Overlook Press, 2000), 27–8.
5. For an analysis of how the Young Turk Revolution, as a 'revolution from above', compared with the Russian Revolution of 1905 and the Iranian Constitutional Movement in 1906, see Nader Sohrabi, 'Constitutionalism, Revolution and the State: The Young Turk Revolution of 1908 and the Iranian Constitutional Revolution of 1906 with Comparisons to the Russian Revolution of 1905' (Ph.D. diss., University of Chicago, 1996).
6. Bernard Lewis, *The Emergence of Modern Turkey* (Oxford: Oxford University Press, 1968), 212. Lewis refers this phrase to the emergence of the CUP, yet he makes clear throughout this seminal work that this question (*Bu devlet nasıl kurtarılabilir?*) preoccupied earlier generations of thinkers and officials in the empire.
7. See Selim Deringil, *The Well-Protected Domains: Ideology and the Legitimation of Power in the Ottoman Empire, 1876–1909* (London: I. B. Taurus, 1998); Benjamin Fortna, *Imperial Classroom: Islam, the State and Education in the Late Ottoman*

Empire (Oxford: Oxford University Press, 2002); François Georgeon, *Abdülhamid II: Le Sultan Calife (1876–1909)* (Paris: Fayard, 2003).

8. Erik Jan Zürcher, 'Young Turks—Children of the Borderlands?', in Kemal Karpat and Robert W. Zens (eds.), *Ottoman Borderlands: Issues, Personalities and Political Changes*, (Madison: University of Wisconsin Press, 2003), 279–80.
9. Paul Dumont, 'Said Bey—The Everyday Life of an Istanbul Townsman at the Beginning of the Twentieth Century', in Hans Georg Majer (ed.), *Osmanische Studien zur Wirtschafts und Sozialgeschichte: In Memoriam Vančo Boškov* (Wiesbaden: O. Harrasowitz Verlag, 1986), 1–16; Zürcher, 'Young Turks', 281–2. Zürcher identifies three specific points of origin associated with the founding members of the CUP: Bitola/Ohrid (Manastır/Ohri in Turkish), Salonika, and Prishtina.
10. Saim Sakaoğlu, *Türk Gölge Oyunu Karagöz* (Ankara: Akçağ Yayınları, 2003), 172–3. One of the stock characters from the *Karagöz* shadow puppet plays is the *Çelebi*, the well-spoken gentleman from Istanbul. He is somewhat of a dandy, who is constantly fitted with the height of Ottomanized 'Western' fashion.
11. Resneli Ahmet Niyazi, *Hürriyet Kahramanı Resneli Niyazi* (Istanbul: Örgün Yayınevi, 2003); Zürcher, 'Young Turks', 284.
12. Feroz Ahmad, *The Young Turks: The Committee of Union and Progress in Turkish Politics* (Oxford: Oxford University Press, 1969), 61–4; Hasan Kayalı, *Arabs and Young Turks: Ottomanism, Arabism and Islamism in the Ottoman Empire, 1908–1918* (Berkeley: University of California Press, 1997), 55; Sohrabi, 'Constitutionalism, Revolution and the State', 566–71, 574–8, 593–6.
13. Aykut Kansu, *Politics in Post-Revolutionary Turkey, 1908–1913* (Leiden: E. J. Brill, 2000), 63–4. Rıza Nur, an outspoken anti-Unionist, yet future participant in the National Movement, labelled the CUP 'an empire within an empire' in terms of its control over the bureaucracy and called for its disbandment in 1909.
14. Ahmad, *Young Turks*, 47–57.
15. Erik Jan Zürcher, 'Kosovo Revisited: Sultan Reşad's Macedonian Journey of June 1911', *Middle East Studies*, 35, no. 4 (1999): 26–39.
16. Kayalı, *Arabs and Young Turks*, 91.
17. For an example of the argument for local linguistic rights, see Sami Frashëri, *Shqipëria: Ç'ka Qenë, Ç'është e Ç'do të Bëhet?* (Tirana: Perparim Xhixha, 1999), 58–62.
18. Masami Arai, *Turkish Nationalism in the Young Turk Era* (Leiden: E. J. Brill, 1992); Hakan Kırımlı, *National Movements and National Identity among the Crimean Tatars, 1905–1916* (Leiden: E. J. Brill, 1996); Jacob Landau, *Pan-Turkism: From Irredentism to Cooperation* (London: Hurst Press, 1995); Michael Reynolds, 'The Ottoman–Russian Struggle for Eastern Anatolia and the Caucasus, 1908–1918: Identity, Ideology and the Geopolitics of World Order' (Ph.D. diss., Princeton University, 2003), 154–69; Holly Shissler, *Between Two Empires: Ahmet Ağaoğlu and the New Turkey* (London: I. B. Taurus, 2003).
19. Arai, *Turkish Nationalism*, 73.
20. Mahmoud Haddad, 'The Rise of Arab Nationalism Reconsidered', *International Journal of Middle East Studies*, 26, no. 2 (1994): 201–22; Kayalı, *National Movements*, 113–14. Haddad, while giving a certain degree of credence to the 'Turkification' thesis, adds further details on the way in which the provincial

appointments made by the CUP government aided in their agenda of state centralization.
21. Arai, *Turkish Natinalism*, 3.
22. Şükrü Hanioğlu, *Preparation for a Revolution: The Young Turks, 1902–1908* (Oxford: Oxford University Press, 2001), 296–300.
23. Ibid. 297–8; Kayalı, *Arabs and Young Turks*, 113; Erik Jan Zürcher, 'Young Turks, Ottoman Muslims and Turkish Nationalists: Identity Politics 1908–1938', in Kemal Karpat (ed.), *Ottoman Past and Today's Turkey* (Leiden: E. J. Brill, 2000), 172–3.
24. Şükrü Hanioğlu, *The Young Turks in Opposition* (Oxford: Oxford University Press, 1995), 206. Other revolutions and reform movements occurring worldwide cemented the CUP's commitment to rapid modernization and centralization. Meiji Japan served as an especially brilliant example to the Young Turks as an 'Eastern' people who had transformed themselves from an isolated, backward nation into a global power in less than a century. See Nader Sohrabi, 'Global Waves, Local Actors: What the Young Turks Knew about Other Revolutions and Why It Mattered', *Comparative Studies in Society and History*, 44, no. 1 (2002): 53–6.
25. See Keith Watenpaugh, 'Bourgeois Modernity, Historical Memory and Imperialism: The Emergence of an Urban Middle Class in the Late Ottoman and Inter-war Middle East: Aleppo, 1908–1939' (Ph.D. diss., University of California at Los Angeles, 1999).
26. Kemal Karpat, 'Turkishness of the Community: From Religious to Ethnic-National Identity', in *idem* (ed.), *The Politicization of Islam: Reconstructing Identity, State, Faith and Community in the Late Ottoman State* (Oxford: Oxford University Press, 2001), 369; *idem*, 'Historical Continuity and Identity Change or How to be Modern Muslim, Ottoman and Turk', in *idem* (ed.), *Ottoman Past and Today's Turkey*, 7; Zürcher, "Young Turks", 156–8. The CUP had earlier argued that the 'Turks', while comprising the core population of the empire, were the most economically oppressed group in the Ottoman state. Kemal Karpat repeats this argument, citing it as the foundation of the CUP's Turkist policies. However, Karpat, as well as others, fail to take into account the state-run programmes of social re-engineering (particularly in terms of education and resettlement) as keys to 'making' and 'inventing' the Turkish population of Anatolia.
27. Karpat, 'Historical Continuity', 8–11.
28. There are many different parallels that can be drawn between the Ottoman notion of civic and cultural conformity and other cases around the world. Neil Foley speaks to the socio-political pressures on identity in his study of working-class cotton producers in central Texas. Through this matrix, he investigates the meaning of being white (particularly among the working class), Mexican, and African American. See Neil Foley, *The White Scourge: Mexicans, Blacks and Poor Whites in Texas Cotton Culture* (Berkeley: University of California Press, 1997).
29. Kemal Karpat argues that Turkish identity comes out of two components, the first being the tribal roots of the Turkic peoples of Anatolia and the second being the historical identification between the Ottoman state and the Turkish *volk*. However, in summarizing the origins of Turkism, Karpat also ignores the way in which the

Ottoman government (as well as Ottoman intellectuals) discriminated between the Turkic peoples of Anatolia along sectarian, linguistic, and cultural lines. See Karpat, 'Historical Continuity', 20–6.
30. Ziya Gökalp, *The Principles of Turkism* (Leiden: E. J. Brill, 1968), 17–21.
31. The Zeybek Turkmen are also found as stock characters in *Karagöz*. They are portrayed as rough, imposing characters who are often associated with banditry. See Sakaoğlu, *Türk Gölge Oyunu Karagöz*, 182.
32. Roderic Davison, 'Turkish Attitudes Concerning Christian–Muslim Equality in the Nineteenth Century', *American Historical Review*, 59, no. 4 (July 1954): 844–64.
33. Fikret Adanır, *Die Makedonische Frage: Ihre Entstehung und Entwicklung bis 1908* (Wiesbaden: Steiner Verlag, 1979); Kieser, *Der Verpasste Friede*; Makdisi, *Culture of Sectarianism*; İpek Yasmanoğlu, 'The Priest's Robe and the Rebel's Rifle: Communal Conflict and the Construction of National Identity in Ottoman Macedonia, 1878–1908' (Ph.D. diss., Princeton University, 2005).
34. Fatma Müge Göçek, *Rise of Bourgeoisie, Demise of Empire: Ottoman Westernization and Social Change* (New York: Oxford University Press, 1996), 44–86.
35. Deringil, *Well-Protected Domains*, passim; Nadir Özbek, 'Philanthropic Activity, Ottoman Patriotism and the Hamidian Regime, 1876–1909', *International Journal of Middle East Studies*, 37, no. 1 (2005): 59–81.
36. Göçek, *Rise of Bourgeoisie*, 87–116.
37. Ibid. 140–1.
38. Kemal Karpat, *Ottoman Population, 1830–1914: Demographic and Social Characteristics* (Madison: University of Wisconsin Press, 1985), 3–11. While census data collected by Ottoman officials are tainted with certain recognizable flaws (such as the undercounting of transient peoples), Karpat argues that they present the most comprehensive and reliable statistics in terms of diversity and size of the population at the turn of the century.
39. Again, the vast majority of the Protestant population was found in İzmit, suggesting that these converts were of Armenian origin.
40. ABCFM 16.9.3, vol. 28, doc. 176: 'Report of Nicomedia Sub-Station', 1908.
41. Çam, *Milli Mücadele'de İzmit Sancağı*, 24.
42. Georgios Nakracas, *Anadolu ve Rum Göçmenlerin Kökeni* (Istanbul: Kitabevi Yayınları, 2005), 111.
43. Arshag Dikranian, Interview, Zoryan Institute Oral History Project, conducted on 4 Feb. 1986 in Los Angeles, video recording. Arshag's father had established a lucrative trade in dry goods and fabrics with the help of two brothers who worked as wholesalers in the capital.
44. ABCFM 16.9.3, vol. 28, doc. 151: 'Brousa Field 1904–1905'; ABCFM 16.9.3, vol. 39, doc. 19: 'Brousa', presented by James P. McNaughton, 29 Apr. 1912; Alexis Alexandris, 'The Greek Census of Anatolia and Thrace (1910–1912): A Contribution to Ottoman Historical Demography', in Dimitri Gondicas and Charles Issawi (eds.), *Ottoman Greeks in the Age of Nationalism: Politics, Economy, and Society in the Nineteenth Century* (Princeton: Darwin Press, 1999), 53.
45. Dimitri Gondicas, *The Greeks of Asia Minor: Confession, Community, and Ethnicity in the Nineteenth Century* (Kent, Ohio: Kent State University Press, 1992), 28.
46. ABCFM 16.9.3, vol. 28, doc. 177: 'Brousa Report for the Year 1908'.

47. ABCFM 16.9.3, vol. 39, doc. 19: James P. McNaughton, 'Brousa', 29 Apr. 1912; ABCFM 16.9.3, vol. 39, doc. 51: 'Report of Constantinople 1913–1914', 27 July 1914.
48. Gondicas, *Greeks of Asia Minor*, 98.
49. Ibid. 98–103.
50. ABCFM 16.9.3, vol. 28, doc. 141: 'Bythinian High School and Orphanage for Boys', 15 Mar. 1902. Bardezag, as one missionary noted, was known for the production of timber, horseshoes, and iron fretwork.
51. Nakracas, *Anadolu ve Rum Göçmenlerin Rökeni*, 111.
52. ABCFM 16.9.3, vol. 27, doc. 160: 'Special Committeee re-Brousa G.B.S.', 16 Dec. 1909; Gondicas, *Greeks of Asia Minor*, 98. In Bursa, Greek and Armenian communities were situated respectively to the west and east of the fortress along the banks of the major streams that ran down from the hills.
53. Dikranian, Interview. He comments in passing that his father, while conducting business in both town and countryside, was careful to maintain separate stocks of 'village' and 'urban' clothing for his customers.
54. See Mete Tuncay and Erik Jan Zürcher (eds.), *Socialism and Nationalism in the Ottoman Empire 1876–1923* (New York: Palgrave Macmillan, 1994).
55. The most pertinent question for the purposes of this study is the effect of Armenian groups like the Dashnaktsutiun and Hnchaktsutiun upon the South Marmara in the years leading up to the deportation. Both groups, respectively founded in 1889 and 1886, had a mass following in various urban centres around the empire. Considering the emphasis which subsequent Ottoman and Turkish sources have placed upon the 'devious' activities of organized Armenian nationalist groups in the South Marmara and elsewhere, it would be of interest to see how this primarily urban and intellectual movement was able to mobilize support in places like Adapazarı or Bursa. See Louise Nalbandian, *The Armenian Revolutionary Movement* (Berkeley: University of California Press, 1963); Ronald Grigor Suny, *Looking toward Ararat: Armenia in Modern History* (Bloomington: University of Indiana Press, 1993), 72–93.
56. ABCFM 16.9.3, vol. 51, doc. 233: Reports by Edith Parsons, 16–22 Apr. 1921. Anecdotally speaking, Western observers mention often in passing that the Rum in the South Marmara were nationalists and 'mad' supporters of Greek Prime Minister Eleftherious Venizelos. Yet one could view statements of this sort as symptomatic of the post-war/post-deportation era.
57. ABCFM 16.9.3, vol. 27, doc. 156: 'Needs of the Turkey Missions', 23 Nov. 1908. The following statistics are mentioned in this report: as of 1908, the ABCFM operated 140 churches with 16,000 members, 4,000 pupils attending mission colleges and high schools, 23,000 students in all, 102 ordained and 110 unordained preachers, 784 teachers, 1,100 total native labourers, 305 regular preaching places, 40,000 church attendees, 54,000 adherents, and 305 Sunday schools with 34,000 pupils.
58. ABCFM 16.9.3, vol. 27, doc. 212: Eghia Shamikian, President, Board of Managers of Protestant Boys' School, 'Church Members—Brousa'; ABCFM 16.9.3, vol. 27, doc. 160: 'Special Committee re-Brousa G.B.S.', 16 Dec. 1909; ABCFM 16.9.3, vol. 28, doc. 176: 'Report of Nicomedia Sub-Station', 1908; ABCFM 16.9.3 vol. 51,

doc. 34: Letter to Enoch Bell, from Sophie Holt, Nicomedia Girls Orphanage, 25 Mar. 1920.
59. ABCFM 16.9.3, vol. 27, doc. 160: 'Special Committee re-Brousa G.B.S.'.
60. ABCFM 16.9.3, vol. 27, doc. 156: 'Needs of the Turkey Missions'; 1908; ABCFM 16.9.3, vol. 51, doc. 177: James McNaughton, 'Notes on Brousa Field', McNaughton gave the following advice to future missionaries in Bursa: 'If one wished to work among Moslems there is a large field. There would be very meagre response for years as the people are rather fanatical. It is an old capital and religious center so the people have been slow in responding to the newer appeals. The chief approach to the Moslems would be through education and medical work.'
61. ABCFM 16.9.3, vol. 28, doc. 141: 'Bythinian High School and Orphanage for Boys'.

> [P]upils [to the Bythinian High School] come from every part of the Turkish Empire that is inhabited by Armenians, from the homes of Gregorian priests, Protestant pastors, teachers, businessmen, artisans, farmers, a goodly sprinkling of widows' sons and poor lads of promise supported by Constantinople merchants and other benevolent persons. One Armenian merchant contributes to the support of 5 lads besides his own.

62. ABCFM 16.9.3, vol. 39, doc. 51: 'Report of Constantinople 1913–1914'; ABCFM 16.9.3, vol. 50, doc. 26: Letter to James Barton from John Kingsley Birge, 26 May 1920; ABCFM 16.9.3, vol. 50, doc. 40: letter to James Barton from John Kingsley Birge, 16 July 1920.
63. ABCFM 16.9.3, vol. 28, doc. 177: 'Brousa Report for the Year 1908'; ABCFM 16.9.3, vol. 39, doc 19: 'Brousa' presented by James P. McNaughton, 29 April 1912. It is not clear from the documents what the origin of this conflict was (most probably a conflict between rival notables).
64. ABCFM 16.9.3, vol. 28, doc. 156: 'Report of the Broussa Field 1905–1906'; ABCFM 16.9.3, vol. 51, doc 73: Letter to James Barton from Mary Kinney, 14 May 1921. Mary Kinney had this to say about the Armenian Protestant community in İzmit in 1921:

> I refer to the attitude our Protestant community was taking in regard to the management of the school. The people were under the influence of a few young men who had the Bolshevist point of view and wanted to break away from the leadership of Americans and run things themselves. Their experiment in running a school of their own *might* have taught them the lesson they needed if it had not been that the political situation was so upsetting that they were able to put part of the blame on the Government and so 'save their own face'.

65. ABCFM 16.9.3, vol. 43, doc 89: Letter to James Barton from John Kingsley Birge, 19 April 1912.
66. Thanos Veremis, 'The Greek Millet in Turkish Politics: Greeks in the Ottoman Parliament (1908–1918)', in Gondicas and Issawi (eds.), *Ottoman Greeks in the Age of Nationalism*, 193–206.
67. Arsen Avagyan, *Osmanlı İmparatorluğu ve Kemalist Türkiye'nin Devlet- İktidar Sisteminde Çerkesler* (Istanbul: Belge Yayınları, 2004), 23–36; İzzet Aydemir, *Göç* (Ankara: Gelişim Matbaası, 1988), 64–6; Karpat, *Ottoman Population*, 67.
68. Karpat, *Ottoman Population*, 69; Ehud R. Toledano, *Slavery and Abolition in the Ottoman Middle East* (Seattle: University of Washington Press, 1998), 84. According to Toledano, anywhere between 595,000 and a million Circassians came between 1855 and 1866. Karpat estimates that up to two million North Caucasians,

mostly Circassians, came between 1859 and 1879. After 1879, Karpat approximates the number of Caucasian refugees to be around half a million.
69. Karpat, *Ottoman Population*, 65–6.
70. Ibid. 69; Marc Pinson, 'Ottoman Colonizaton of the Circassians in Rumeli after the Crimean War', *Etudes Balkaniques*, 3 (1972): 73.
71. Kemal Karpat, 'The status of the Muslim under European Rule', The Erichon and Settlement of the Çerkes', in *idem* (ed.), *Studies on Ottoman Social on Political History* (Leiden: E. J. Brill, 2000), 660; *idem, Ottoman Population*, 69. In response, the Ottoman administration established an official General Commission for the Administration of Immigration (*İdare-i Umumiye-i Muhacirin Komisyonu*) charged with the responsibility of cataloguing, monitoring, and settling the tens of thousands arriving at ports of entry throughout the Ottoman Empire. This commission was replaced in the early 1870s by a sub-department under the authority of the Interior Ministry. See David Cameron Cutbell, 'The Muhacir Komisyonu: An Agent in the Transformation of Ottoman Anatolia, 1860–1866' (Ph.D. diss., Columbia University, 2005).
72. Karpat, 'Muslim under European Rule', 664–75; Pinson, 'Ottoman Colonization', 75. Like the numbers for Anatolia, the estimates for the Balkans remain less than exact. Marc Pinson cites a series of statistics, including Ottoman figures: Edirne—6,000 families; Northwestern Bulgaria (Silistria, Vidin, etc.)—13,000 families; Northeastern Bulgarai/Dobruca (Nikopolis, Ruse, Varna, etc.)—10,000 families; Kosova (Prishtina)—42,000 families. It must also be kept in mind that these North Caucasians sent to the Balkans may have included refugees from the Crimea (Tatars, Nogay, etc.).
A great mixture of North Caucasian (particularly Adige and Chechens) and Crimean (Tatars and Nogay) refugees were sent to the *balad al-Şam*. One document cited by Karpat estimated in 1879 that 75,000 people would be sent to northern and southern Syria.
73. 'Čerkezi u Naši Zemli', *Glasnik: Skopskog Naučnog Društva*, no. 1 (1928): 143–53; Noel Malcolm, *Kosovo: A Short History* (London: Macmillan, 1998). Well before the 1999 war in Kosova, a Serb social scientist reported in 1928 that very few Circassians remained in Yugoslavia following the Balkan Wars (most staying in Priziren).
74. Aydemir, *Göç*, 154–5. Ottoman officials certainly monitored the return of North Caucasians to the Russian Empire.
75. BOA.A.MKT.MHM 209/54, 19 Feb. 1861; BOA.A.MKT.MHM 222/84, 7 June 1861; BOA.A.MKT.NZD 372/31, 16 Oct. 1861; BOA.A.MKT.UM 550/10, 26 Mar. 1862; Toledano, *Slavery and Abolition*, 99–102.
76. Pinson, 'Ottoman Colonization', *passim*.
77. Michael Provence, *The Great Syrian Revolt and the Rise of Arab Nationalism* (Austin: University of Texas Press, 2005), 37; Eugene Rogan, *Frontiers of the State in the Late Ottoman Empire: Transjordan 1850–1921* (Cambridge: Cambridge University Press, 1999), *passim*. In the Syrian lands, local militias raised from the recently settled Circassian and Chechen immigrant communities played a predominant role in Istanbul's oppressive policy towards native Druze and Bedouin.

78. Dror Ze'evi, '*Kul* and Getting Cooler: The Dissolution of Elite Collective Identity and the Formation of Official Nationalism in the Ottoman Empire', *Mediterranean Historical Review*, 11, no. 2 (1996): 177–96.
79. Toledano, *Slavery and Abolition*, 102–4.
80. Avagyan, *Osmanli İmparatorluğu*, 99–104; Galip Vardar, *İttihat ve Terakki İcinde Dönenler* (Istanbul: İnkılap Kitapevi, 1960), 30–4, 173–6. Security for Abdülhamid's palace was also staffed with an especially selected group of North Caucasians, as well as Albanians and Kurds. However, absolute loyalty to the sultan and his household appeared to have its limits. Several personal clashes broke out between Circassian and Albanian guards despite efforts by Abdülhamid to show equal favour towards both factions.
81. Sefer Berzeg, *Türkiye Kurtuluş Savaş'ında Çerkes Göçmenleri, Cilt II* (Istanbul: Ekin Yayıncılık, 1990), 12–13.
82. Avagyan, *Osmanli İmparatorluğu*, 132–5.
83. PRO/FO 371/3418/196842, 29 Nov. 1918; PRO/FO 371/3418/209961, 21 Dec. 1918.
84. The settlement of Circassians and Tatars was not entirely fraught with difficulties and conflict. According to a report submitted to the British Foreign Office, local people in the province of Edirne readily welcomed North Caucasian and Crimean refugees in their villages, providing both groups with food and shelter in the initial stages. PRO/FO 881/3065, Jan. 1877.
85. Raif Kaplanoğlu, *Bursa'da Mübadele* (Orhangazi: Avrasya Etnografya Vakfı, 1999), 135. Nedim İpek cites an estimate of 29,886 North Caucasians in the province of Bursa. It is not clear whether or not this tabulation includes those who came after 1878. See Nedim İpek, *Rumeli'den Anadolu'ya Türk Göçleri (1877–1890)* (Ankara: Türk Tarih Kurumu, 1994), 185.
86. The settlement patterns among the Adige in the South Marmara are interesting. Certain counties, such as Biga and İzmit, were settled entirely by one Adige tribe (in this case the Bjeduğ and Abzeh, respectively). In other areas, such as Gönen and Karacabey, Adige settlements were more mixed. However, in the environs of Manyas, which is closely located to Gönen, the vast majority of villages were settled by Ubıh refugees. See Peter Alford Andrews, *Ethnic Groups in the Republic of Turkey* (Wiesbaden: Dr. Ludwig Reichert Verlag, 1989), 385–419.
87. Yalova has a particularly high concentration of Dagestani peoples (particularly Avars). Adapazarı, as well as neighbouring Düzce, Hendek, and Bolu, has a very large Abkhazian presence (although thousands fled the region to Greece after the War of Independence). Pockets of Laz migrants can be found throughout the South Marmara, but in particular in Değirmendere and Karamürsel. Surprisingly, there are few Chechen communities found in the South Marmara.
88. İpek, *Rumeli'den Anadolu'ya Türk Göçteri*, 187–8, 198, 200.
89. Ibid. 200.
90. PRO/FO 371/3418/199234, 3 Dec. 1918; Toledano, *Slavery and Abolition*, 106.
91. Alexander Lopasic, 'Islamization of the Balkans with Special Reference to Bosnia', *Journal of Islamic Studies*, 5, no. 2 (1994): 163–86; Antonina Zhelyazkova, 'Islamization in the Balkans as a Historiographical Problem: The Southeast-European

Perspective', in Fikret Adanır and Suraiya Faroqhi (eds.), *The Ottomans and the Balkans* (Leiden: E. J. Brill, 2002), 235–45.
92. Halil Inalcık, 'Arnawutluk', *in Encyclopedia of Islam*, i (1960): 656. According to İnalcık, at least thirty Ottoman Grand Vizirs (*sadrazam*), the highest officers of the state, and countless generals (*paşa*) and officers in the Ottoman army were of Albanian extraction.
93. It must be emphasized that Islamic practices vary widely among Albanian-speakers. During the Ottoman period, devotion to Islamic brotherhoods (*tarikat*s) was commonly associated with Albanians. In present-day Albania, Macedonia, and Kosova, however, such brotherhoods as the Bektaşis, Mevlevis, and others have begun to vanish.
94. Bernd J. Fischer, 'Albanian Highland Tribal Society and Family Structure in the Process of Twentieth Century Transformation', *East European Quarterly*, 33, no. 3 (Sept. 1999): 281–301.
95. Aleks Buda *et al.*, *Historia e Popullit Shqiptar: Vëllimi i Dytë, Rilindja Kombëtare* (Tirana: Toena, 2000), 17–31; T. Zavallani, 'Albanian Nationalism', in Peter F. Sugar and Ivo Lederer (eds.), *Nationalism in Eastern Europe*, (Seattle: University of Washington Press, 1994), 62–76.
96. For example, see Zeqirja Rexhepi, *Zhvillimet Politiko-Shoqërore te Shqiptarët në Maqedoni, 1990–2001* (Tetova: Tringa Design, 2005), 8–9.
97. For a succinct critique of recent Albanian scholarship, see Isa Blumi, 'Defying the State and Defining the State: Local Politics in Educational Reform in the Vilayets of Manastır and Yanya, 1878–1912', in *idem* (ed.), *Rethinking the Late Ottoman Empire: A Comparative Social and Political History of Albania and Yemen, 1878–1918* (Istanbul: Isis Press, 2003), 103–22; *idem*, 'Recent Studies on Albanian Nationalism at the End of the Ottoman Empire from Turkey and the Arab World', *Balkanistica*, 14 (2001): 139–44; *idem*, 'Understanding the Margins of Albanian History: Communities on the Edges of the Ottoman Empire', in *Rethinking the Late Ottoman Empire*, 83–102.
98. Isa Blumi, 'Locating Fragmented Identities in Switzerland's Ottoman–Albanian Diaspora, 1899–1920', in *Rethinking the Late Ottoman Empire*, 123–34; Bilgin Çelik, *İttihatçılar ve Arnavudlar: II. Meşrutiyet Döneminde Arnavud Ulusçuluğu ve Arnavudluk Sorunu* (Istanbul: Büke Kitapları, 2004), 210–16. The Albanian intellectual community of Istanbul (and to a certain degree Izmir) played a considerable role in the crafting of Albanian nationalist aspirations. The group *Bashkimi* (or The Union), for example, opened offices in Istanbul, as well as in cities and towns throughout Anatolia and the Balkans, promoting the development of Albanian language education, literature, and publishing, as well as political rights.
99. Halil İnalcık and Donald Quataert (eds.), *An Economic and Social History of the Ottoman Empire*, ii: *1600–1914* (Cambridge: Cambridge University Press, 1994), 778–82. The *vilayet* of Selanik, e.g., boasted the highest population density in the Ottoman Empire in 1894, with 74.9 persons per square kilometer.
100. Fikret Adanır, 'The Macedonians in the Ottoman Empire, 1878–1912', in Andreas Kappler (ed.), *The Formation of National Elites*, iv (Dartmouth, NH: New York University Press, 1992), 162–4. Adanır points out several examples of the expanding urban base in Ottoman Macedonia. The town of Üsküp (Skopje) grew from a town

of 10,000 inhabitants in 1800 to a town of 37,000 in 1913. İştip (Shtip), once a small market town of 5000, grew to a population of 20,000 just before the end of Ottoman rule in the south Balkans. Other examples he cites are Manastır (Bitola) 50,000 and Siroz (Serres) 35,000. Of course, Selanik was the major metropolis of the region, with a population of 150,000 in 1912.

101. Burcu Akan Ellis, *Shadow Genealogies: Memories and Identity among Urban Muslims in Macedonia* (Boulder, Col.: Eastern European Monographs, for Columbia University Press, 2003), 28. This point may be the weakest part of her argument. While Turkish was without question the language of administration in Ottoman Rumeli, significant portions of the emerging Albanian nationalist elite endeavoured to promote Albanian as the political and intellectual medium of expression. Greater research needs to be done on the social backgrounds of the Albanian nationalist elite and how they differed from their compatriots who remained loyal to the Ottoman state.
102. Eran Fraenkel, 'Urban Muslim Identity in Macedonia: The Interplay between Ottomanism and Multilingual Nationalism', in Eran Fraenkel and Christina Kramer (eds.), *Language Contact, Language Conflict*, (New York: Peter Lang, 1993), 32.
103. Akan Ellis, *Shadow Genealogies*, 30–2. In an interview carried out in the late 1990s, a long-time resident of Tetevo would describe the process of becoming an urban dweller this way:

> My grandfather was from an Albanian village. His village had been burned down and he migrated to Skopje when he was forty. He spent all his life trying to become a part of the city. My father was born in Skopje, he was a full Skopjean. Neither he nor his father would ever reminisce about his village. They would always deny it with an affirmative sentence about their Skopjan identity.

104. Akan Ellis, *Shadow Genealogies*, 31.
105. Fraenkel, 'Urban Muslim Identity in Macedonia', 33.
106. The blurred line between Albanian- and Turkish-speakers is not an isolated phenomenon. Orthodox Christians too formed a rather amorphous group, with individuals within many multilingual families professing either a Bulgarian, Serb, Greek, or Macedonian identity. The same could also be said for Anatolia. One good example of these blurred notions of identity is Ziya Gökalp, the 'father' of Turkish nationalism. Although he was of mixed Kurdish parentage from Diyarbakır, he came to see himself not only as an Ottoman Turkish-speaker, but also as an ethnic Turk. Other Turkish nationalists, such as Tekin Alp, also came from non-Anatolian Turkish backgrounds.
107. Suraiya Faroqhi, *Towns and Townsmen of Ottoman Anatolia: Trade, Crafts and Food Production in an Urban Setting* (Cambridge: Cambridge University Press, 1984), 271.
108. Yücel Dağlı et al., *Evliya Çelebi Seyahatnamesi (5. Kitap)* (Istanbul: Yapı Kredi Yayınları, 2001), 146, 147.
109. Eyal Ginio, 'Migrants and Workers in an Ottoman Port: Ottoman Salonica in the Eighteenth Century', in Eugene Rogan (ed.), *Outside In: On the Margins of the Modern Middle East* (London: I. B. Taurus, 2002), 136–8.
110. Ibid. 137.

111. Fredrick Anscombe, 'Albanians and "Mountain Bandits"' in *idem* (ed.), *The Ottoman Balkans 1750–1830* (Princeton: Markus Wiener Publishers, 2006), 101.
112. Ginio, 'Migrants and Workers', 141.
113. Anscombe, 'Albanians and "Mountain Bandits"', 87–95.
114. H. N. Brailsford, *Macedonia: Its Races and their Future* (London: Methuen & Co., 1906), 221. During the Illinden Uprising of 1903, a correspondent from the British news paper *The Daily News* lamented that the use of Albanian troops against Christian insurgents was 'as if we were to let loose Ulster on the South of Ireland'. See 'Macedonia Again', *The Daily News*, 7 Aug. 1903.
115. Sakaoğlu, *Türk Gölge Oyunu Karagöz*, 196. The *Arnavud* tends to roll his r's and refers to the main characters affectionately as *mori* (the Albanian word for boy, used similarly to the word *ağabey* or older brother in Turkish). He is always dressed in the white smock worn by a shepherd, with a red hat and a white skirt.
116. Ibid. 196–7.
117. Zürcher, 'Young Turks', 278.
118. Peter Holquist, 'To Count, to Extract, to Exterminate: Population Statistics and Population Politics in Late Imperial and Soviet Russia', in Ronald Grigor Suny and Terry Martin (eds.), *A State of Nations: Empire and Nation-Making in the Age of Lenin and Stalin* (Oxford: Oxford University Press, 2001), 113. Holquist raises a similar point in his discussion of the evolving Russian/Soviet policies towards the North Caucasus. Indeed, ethnicity, crime, and class were intertwined in several different societies.
119. Nathalie Clayer, 'The Albanian Students of the Mekteb-i Mulkiye: Social Networks and Trends of Thought', in Elisabeth Ozdalga (ed.), *Late Ottoman Society: The Intellectual Legacy*, (London: Routledge Curzon Press, 2005), 307–8.
120. Ibid. 308.
121. Tahsin Uzer, *Makedonya Eşkiyalık Tarihi ve Son Osmanlı Yönetimi* (Ankara: Türk Tarih Kurumu, 1979), 1–3.
122. *The Other Balkan Wars: A 1913 Carnegie Endowment Inquiry in Retrospect with a New Introduction and Reflections on the Present Conflict by George F. Kennan* (Washington: Carnegie Endowment for International Peace, 1993).
123. BCA 272.14.75.24.6.21, Sept. 1920.

CHAPTER 2

1. Dikranian, Interview.
2. Ibid. I have not been able to find any reference to this demonstration in either secondary or primary literature. In the interview, he refers to the rally as a celebration of the Armenian alphabet's fifteen hundredth anniversary.
3. Ibid.
4. Aram Andonyan, *Balkan Savaşı* (Istanbul: Aras Yayıncılık, 1999), 483–91.
5. ABCFM 16.9.3, vol. 39, doc. 19: James Naughton, 'Brousa', ABCFM 16.9.3, vol. 48, doc. 33: Letter to Mr Peet from Jeanie Jillson, 10 Apr. 1913.
6. ABCFM 16.9.3, vol. 48, doc. 30: Letter to Mr Peet from Annie Allen, 4 Apr. 1913; ABCFM 16.9.3, vol. 41, doc. 11: Letter to Mr Peet from Annie Allen, 21 Feb. 1913.

7. ABCFM 16.9.3, vol. 48, doc. 156: Anonymous, 'A Disquieting Situation', n. d.; PRO/FO 195/2458/2240, 1 June 1914. Near Çanakkale, Albanian refugees from Kosova were blamed for ransacking Greek villages, leading British officials to demand that the Albanian refugees be evicted from the district. According to one source, the Albanians told the departing Greeks that they were welcome to take their abandoned homes back in Macedonia.
8. Eyal Ginio, 'Port Cities as an Imagined Battlefield: The Boycott of 1913', paper presented at the Eighth Mediterranean Social and Political Research Meeting, Florence, Italy, 21–5 March 2007, 7–9. Many thanks to Eyal Ginio for allowing me to have a copy of this paper.
9. See Zafer Toprak, *İttihad-Terakki ve Cihan Harbi: Savaş Ekonomisi ve Türkiye'de Devletçilik* (Istanbul: Homer Kitabevi, 2003); idem, *Türkiye'de 'Milli Yktisat' (1908–1918)* (Ankara: Yurt Yayınları, 1982).
10. ABCFM 16.9.3, vol. 41, doc. 13: Letter to Mr Bell from Annie Allen, 21 Apr. 1913; ABCFM 16.9.3, vol. 41, doc. 19: Letter to Dr Reverend James Barton from Annie Allen, 22 July 1914.
11. ABCFM 16.9.3, vol. 39, doc. 51: 'Report of Constantinople Station, 1913–1914', 27 July 1914. An American report of the situation in Bursa reads as follows:

   We were informed by creditable witnesses that Greek villagers were not allowed to bring their vegetables to the city to sell, that Greek women were prevented from gathering mulberry leaves for their silk-worms, that when Moslems patronized Greek shops the goods were taken from them by force, the packages torn and the goods injured, and then taken back and the merchant compelled to refund the money; that a policeman was seen beating an Armenian boy for buying bread at a Greek bakery, and that other similar injuries were inflicted on those whose only fault was that they belonged to or patronized the Greek race.

12. Ibid.; PRO/FO 195/2458/3080, 21 July 1914. Some store-owners did not comply, pending written assurances from local officials that they would not be molested.
13. PRO/FO 195/2458/3080, 21 July 1914. Mudanya had reportedly housed 15,000 Greek refugees from the interior by the summer of 1914. Another 500 were found in Bandırma.
14. PRO/FO 195/2458/2240, 1 June 1914; PRO/FO 195/2458/3080, 21 July 1914.
15. ABCFM 16.9.3, vol. 39, doc. 51: 'Report of Constantinople Station, 1913–1914'.
16. ABCFM 16.9.3, vol. 39, doc. 19: Naughton, 'Brousa'; ABCFM 16.9.3, vol. 39, doc. 20: 'Annual Report Brousa Station, 1912–1913'. As the threat of war loomed, the Protestant preacher in Bandırma abruptly fled the town with his family and left behind his school of twenty-five pupils. The school was ultimately abandoned.
17. PRO/FO 195/2458/2240, 1 June 1914; PRO/FO 195/2458/3080, 21 July 1914. In a conversation with Harry Lamb's assistant, Mr Braitwaite, a Greek *muhtar*, privately disputed the Ottoman officers' charge that Greeks planning to emigrate were compelled by Greek propaganda. He claimed instead that the trouble began with the attacks of local Muslim gangs.
18. 'Muhacirler', *Tesvir-i Efkar*, 1 Jan. 1919. According to the report cited in this article, thousands of Rum either emigrated to Greece to join the Greek army during the Balkan Wars or used the Balkan Wars as an opportunity to 'abandon' Anatolia. The following statistics are supplied regarding the numbers of Greeks who left

during the Balkan Wars: Edirne: 50,004; Aydın: 80,766; Çatalca: 6,461; Karesi: 1,551; Kale-i Sultaniye: 11,037.
19. Yannis G. Mourelos, 'The 1914 Persecutions and the First Attempt at an Exchange of Minorities between Greece and Turkey', *Balkan Studies*, 26, no. 2 (1985): 389–413.
20. PRO/FO 195/2458/2160, 28 May 1914.
21. PRO/FO 195/2458/797, 26 Feb. 1914.
22. PRO/FO 195/2458/2160, 28 May 1914.
23. PRO/FO 195/2458/797, 26 Feb. 1914.
24. PRO/FO 195/2458/58456, 26 Dec. 1913.
25. Edward J. Erikson, *Ordered to Die: A History of the Ottoman Army in the First World War* (Westport, Conn.: Greenwood Press, 2001), 79.
26. Zühtü Güven, *Anzavur İsyan: İstiklâı Savaşl Hatiralindan Acı Bir Safha* (Ankara: Tinkiye İş Bankası, 1965), 2–3.
27. For the state of the Ottoman economy and infrastructure before the war, see Erikson, *Ordered to Die*, 15–19.
28. Taner Akçam, *From Empire to Republic: Turkish Nationalism and the Armenian Genocide* (New York: Zed Books, 2004), 143–4; Celâl Bayar, *Ben de Yazdım: Millî Mücadele'ye Gidiş* (Istanbul: Baha Matbaası 1965), 1573.
29. Gotthard Jäschke, 'Der Turanismus und die Jungtürken zur Osmanischen Aussenpolitik im Weltkrieg', *Die Welt des Islams*, 23 (1941): 1–53; Landau, *Pan-Turkism in Turkey*.
30. Akçam, *From Empire to Republic*, 142–3.
31. Akçam, *Shameful Act*, 82–92.
32. The relevance of Ottoman sources in proving or disproving the charge of genocide has attracted more attention with the greater usage of documentary evidence drawn from the Prime Minister's Archive in Istanbul. Over the last two decades, official Turkish bodies have released numerous documentary studies of the 'Armenian Question' (*Ermeni Sorunu*). Through the publication of these Ottoman documents, Turkish scholars, such as Kamuran Gürün, have attempted to bolster Ankara's threefold position regarding the Armenian genocide: first, the deportations were a just and humane response to the Armenian rebellion; secondly, Ottoman authorities took great measures, despite the hardships of the war, to treat Armenian citizens humanely; and thirdly, the bulk of Armenian casualties were the result of a 'civil war' between Armenian revolutionaries and innocent Muslim civilians, the latter of which suffered the greatest loss. This official Turkish thesis has been further complemented by the works of Justin MacCarthy, Jeremy Salt, Stanford Shaw, and, most recently, Günter Lewy. Conversely, Vahakn Dadrian argues that works utilizing Ottoman sources only demonstrate the partiality or, in some cases, the fraudulence found in the Ottoman voice. How, after all, Dadrian asks, can the perpetrators of this crime be trusted? Truly much of the official correspondence that would unlock this controversy was destroyed or sold off after the war (this is particularly the case of the holdings related to the *Teşkilat-ı Mahsusa*). For further reading on the debate over guilt and documentation see Peter Balakian, *The Burning Tigris: A History of the Armenian Genocide* (London: William Heinemann, 2003), 175–96; Başbakanlık Devlet Arşivleri Genel Müdürlüğü, *Osmanlı Belgelerinde*

Ermeniler, 1915–1920 (Ankara: Başbakanlık Devlet Arşivleri Genel Müdürlüğü, 1994); Vahakn N. Dadrian, 'Ottoman Archives and Denial of the Armenian Genocide', in Richard Hovannisian (ed.), *The Armenian Genocide: History, Politics, Ethics* (London: Macmillan, 1992), 280–310; Kamuran Gürün, *Ermeni Dosyası* (Ankara: Türk Tarih Kurumu, 1983), 193–252; Justin McCarthy, *Death and Exile: The Ethnic Cleansing of Ottoman Muslims, 1821–1922* (Princeton: Darwin Press, 1995); Münir Süreyya, *Ermeni Meselesinin Siyası TarihÇesi, 1877–1914* (Ankara: Türk Cumhuriyet Devlet Arşivleri Genel Müdürlüğü, 2001).

33. The Turkish Military Tribunal (*Fevkalade Dar üs-Saadet Divan-ı Harb-ı Örfisi*) represents the only official attempt to prosecute Ottoman officials guilty of war crimes between 1914 and 1918. The transcripts provided in the *Takvim-i Vekayı*, the official newspaper of the state, detail the actions of local officials who organized both the deportations and the mass executions of Armenian men, women, and children in the vicinity of Yozgat and Trabzon. However, the court was unable to establish the degree to which the Ottoman military and civil bureaucracies were complicit in these crimes. Instead, responsibility for the massacres was placed upon the *Teşkilat-ı Mahsusa*, about which few cabinet members or parliamentary representatives had any information. From these transcripts, it becomes clear that the *Teşkilat-ı Mahsusa* had a great deal of influence over the liquidation of the Christian population. However, the trials appear to have avoided the role of the Commission for the Settlement of Tribes and Refugees (*İskan-ı Aşair ve Muhacirin Müdüriyeti*, or İAMM) as well as other organs of the state. It is possible, as Stanford Shaw argues, that the limited nature of the tribunal's investigation was partly due to the fact that the court represented an attempt by the Liberty and Understanding Party (*Hürriyet ve İtilaf Fırkası*) to eliminate those who were close to the Young Turk wartime government. See Taner Akçam, *Armenien und der Völkermord: Die Istanbuler Prozesse und die türkische Nationalbewegung* (Hamburg: Hamburger Edition, 1996), 167–364. Balakian, *Burning Tigris*, 331–47; Shaw, *From Empire to Republic*, 303–44.

34. BOA.DH.ŞFR 53/75, 22 May 1915; BOA.DH.ŞFR 53/143, 27 May 1915; BOA.DH.ŞFR 54/104, 22 June 1915; BOA.DH.ŞFR 54/108, 22 June 1915; BOA.DH.ŞFR 54/172, 29 June 1915; BOA.DH.ŞFR 54/158, 26 June 1915; BOA.DH.ŞFR 54/371, 10 July 1915; BOA.DH.ŞFR 63/217, 6 May 1916; BOA.DH.ŞFR 63/264, 10 May 1916; BOA.DH.ŞFR 70/107, 27 Nov. 1916; BOA.DH.ŞFR 70/109, 27 Nov. 1916. According to these documents, deportees were settled in Muslim, Armenian, and Rum villages in Karesi and Hüdavendigar (such as Soma) as well as in Bandırma. Others later emigrated to Greece. In the autumn of 1916, despite the need to solve this 'crowd control' problem, Rum were not permitted to return or be sent to neighbouring districts.

35. BOA.DH.ŞFR 54/118, 23 June 1915; BOA.DH.ŞFR 54/157, 26 June 1915; BOA.DH.ŞFR 68/9, 15 Sept. 1916. According to one telegram, the transfer of Rum to the interior was completed in September 1916.

36. Arnold J. Toynbee, *The Western Question in Greece and Turkey: A Study in the Contacts of Civilizations* (London: Constable and Company, 1923), 143; BOA.DH.ŞFR 53/306, 9 June 1915; BOA.DH.ŞFR 54/224, 28 June 1915; BOA.DH.ŞFR 60/110, 24 Jan. 1916; BOA.DH.ŞFR 64/61, 23 May 1916.

37. BOA.DH.ŞFR 54/180, 29 June 1915; BOA.DH.ŞFR 54/276, 1 July 1915; BOA.DH.ŞFR 54/279, 1 July 1915; BOA.DH.ŞFR 54–A/185, 30 July 1915; BOA.DH.ŞFR 54–A/338, 10 Aug. 1915.
38. BOA.DH.ŞFR 54–A/19, 18 July 1915. According to the Commission for the Settlement of Tribes and Refugees, 1,060 Rum were transferred to Ertruğul.
39. Akçam, *From Empire to Republic*, 146; Çağlar Keyder, 'The Consequences of the Exchange of Populations in Turkey', in Renée Hirshon (ed.), *Crossing the Aegean: An Appraisal of the 1923 Compulsory Population Exchange between Greece and Turkey* (New York: Berghahn Books, 2003), 42; Mourelos, '1914 Persecutions', 391–2; 'Muhacirler', *Tesvir-i Efkar*, 1 Jan. 1919. According to documents found by Yannis Mourelos, more than 60,000 Greeks were forced from eastern Thrace during the first year of the war. The newspaper *Tesvir-i Efkar* offers the following statistics: Şile, Kartal, Gebze, and the Prince's Islands: 4,166; Edirne: 58,955; Çatalca: 966; Hüdavendigar: 13,558; Kale-i Sultaniye: 15,423.
40. ABCFM 16.9.3, vol. 44, doc. 204: 'Report of Miss Parsons Need of Relief in the Villages (Brousa)', n. d.; ABCFM 16.9.3, vol. 48, doc. 372: Letter to Dr Reverend James Barton from Mr Peet, 21 Aug. 1916; ABCFM 16.9.3, vol. 48, doc. 365: Letter to Dr Reverend James Barton from Mr Peet, 7 Aug. 1916. Edith Parsons, who had remained in Bursa through the autumn of 1915, estimated that some 3,100 families from various coastal villages were settled in town. Only 165 were then settled in abandoned Armenian homes.
41. ABCFM 16.9.3, vol. 48, doc. 431: Confidential letter to Dr Reverend James Barton from Mr Peet, 13 Jan. 1917. Of one group of 150 peasants deported from Marmara island communities, American missionaries reported that eighty had died on the road to Istanbul.
42. ABCFM 16.9.3, vol. 48, doc. 396: Letter to Dr Reverend James Barton from Mr Peet, 30 Oct. 1916.
43. Erik Jan Zürcher, 'Ottoman Labour Battalions in World War I', in Hans-Lukas Kieser and Dominik Schaller (eds.), *Der Völkermord an den Armeniern und die Shoah* (Zürich: Chronos Verlag, 2002), 187–94.
44. Dikranian, Interview.
45. ABCFM 16.9.3, vol. 48, doc. 268: Letter to Dr Reverend James Barton from Mr Peet, 27 Aug. 1915. Dikranian, Interview.
46. BOA.DH.ŞFR 54/238, 29 June 1915; BOA.DH.ŞFR 54/335, 7 July 1915; BOA.DH.ŞFR 54/336, 7 July 1915; BOA.DH.ŞFR 54/376, 10 July 1915.
47. Wolfgang Gust (ed.), *Der Völkermord an den Armeniern 1915/16: Dokumente aus dem Politischen Archiv des deutschen Auswärtigen Amts* (Munich: Zu Klampen Auflage, 2005), 236–7.
48. Mehmet Kanar (ed.), *Ermeni Komitelerinin Emelleri ve İhtilal Hareketleri, Meşrutiyetten Önce ve Sonra* (Istanbul: Der Yayınevi, 2001), 301–4; Talat Paşa, *Hatıralarım ve Müdafaam* (Istanbul: Kaynak Yayınları, 2006), 76–7. In fact, I would say that both Talat's 'memoir' and this piece of Ottoman propaganda are virtually the same account.
49. After the passing of the deportation law, there are reports of the storing of weapons in an Armenian school in Bursa (BOA.DH.ŞFR 54–A/29, 29 July 1915), collaboration with Allied forces on the occupied island of Midilli (BOA.DH.ŞFR 60/169, 30 Jan. 1916), Armenian 'bandit' activity in İzmit and Bursa (BOA.DH.ŞFR 55/327,

30 Aug. 1915; BOA.DH.ŞFR 55–A/104, 7 Sep. 1915; BOA.DH.ŞFR 59/169, 1 Jan. 1916), as well as the arrest and deportation of various Dashnaktsutiun sympathizers and 'defeatists' (BOA.DH.ŞFR 54–A/28, 19 July 1915; BOA.DH.ŞFR 54–A/269–270, 5 Aug. 1915; BOA.DH.ŞFR 60/173, 30 Jan. 1916; BOA.DH.ŞFR 61/173, 3 Mar. 1916; BOA.DH.ŞFR 61/192, 6 Mar. 1916; BOA.DH.ŞFR 61/290, 12 Mar. 1916). According to one newspaper report, several Armenian men were executed in Bandırma for organizing a revolt. See Özdemir, *Balıkesir Cepheleri*, 58.
50. Although there is no sign of any sort of insurrection among the Rum before the opening of the Gelibolu front, Arnold Toynbee reports that some Rum in Ayvalık did spy on Ottoman forces for the British. See Toynbee, *Western Question*, 144.
51. Dikranian, Interview.
52. Ibid.
53. Aghavni Guleserian (Kabakian), Interview, Zoryan Institute Oral History Project, conducted on 21 Nov. 1986 in Fresno, California, video recording; Manik Kouyoumjian, Zoryan Institute Oral History Project, conducted on 25 Apr. 1985 in Los Angeles, video recording. For the sake of the narrative, it is not possible to summarize the stories of these two women in full. Yet it can be said that both experienced the very worst of the genocide. Aghavni lost her entire immediate family during the march to northern Syria. After the abduction of her sister, a local sheikh bought, tattooed, and raped her. Eventually a member of her extended family from Adapazarı found Aghavni and brought her back home at the end of the war. Manik, who was age 7 at the time of the deportations, and her sister were the sole survivors of their family. With the aid of an older girl from Adapazarı (whom she believed granted sexual favours to the Ottoman gendarmes in exchange for food and protection), the two miraculously endured a forced march across the Syrian desert to Mosul. She later settled and married in Iraq.
54. Guleserian, Interview.
55. BOA.DH.ŞFR 54–A/276, 6 Aug. 1915; BOA.DH.ŞFR 54/238, 29 June 1915; BOA.DH.ŞFR 54/335, 7 July 1915; BOA.DH.ŞFR 54/336, 7 July 1915; BOA.DH.ŞFR 54/376, 10 July 1915; BOA.DH.ŞFR 60/144, 26 Jan. 1916; BOA.DH.ŞFR 60/196, 1 Feb. 1916; BOA.DH.ŞFR 60/308, 12 Feb. 1916; BOA.DH.ŞFR 61/61, 19 Feb. 1916. The lack of communiqués related to Armenians in Hüdavendigar and Kale-i Sultaniye is puzzling considering that both provinces possessed equal or greater numbers of Armenians in comparison to Karesi and were of equal strategic value.
56. ABCFM 16.9.3, vol. 44, doc. 204: 'Report of Miss Parsons Need of Relief in the Villages (Brousa)'.
57. ABCFM 16.9.3, vol. 40, doc. 269: James McNaughton, 'A Byproduct of a Great Tragedy', 25 Aug. 1919; ABCFM 16.9.3, vol. 48, doc. 372: Letter to Dr Reverend James Barton from Mr Peet, 21 Aug. 1916; ABCFM 16.9.3, vol. 48, doc. 396: Letter to Dr Reverend James Barton from Mr Peet, 30 Oct. 1916. McNaughton recounts a conversation with a former native pastor from the village of Karaağaç near Adapazarı. According to the Armenian man, Ottoman authorities had forcibly marched all 126 members of his village through the mountains without stipulating a destination. Twenty-six died along the way. As Protestants, they were eventually

allowed to return. Nevertheless, the Armenians had to rely upon the charity of local Muslims, themselves rendered destitute by the war, to supply them with food and farming equipment.

58. ABCFM 16.9.3, vol. 40, doc 269: McNaughton, 'Byproduct of a Great Tragedy'; ABCFM 16.9.3, vol. 48, doc. 268: Letter to Dr Reverend James Barton from Mr Peet, 27 Aug. 1915; ABCFM 16.9.3, vol. 48, doc. 284: Letter to Dr Reverend James Barton from Mr Peet, 17 Nov. 1915; ABCFM 16.9.3, vol. 49, doc. 133: Letter to Mr Bell from Annie Allen, 18 Mar. 1920. All of the pupils and teachers at the Bardezag High School were deported.

59. Gust (ed.), *Der Völkermord an den Armeniern 1915/16*, 222–3. Interestingly, German officials and officers in the Ottoman Empire also followed the deportation's statistical data. Vahakh Dadrian points out that both German and Austrian officers were often deeply disturbed by Ottoman policies and were compelled to contradict the official conclusions passed on to them by Ottoman officials. See Vahakn Dadrian, 'The Armenian Question and the Wartime Fate of the Armenians as Documented by the Officials of the Ottoman Empire's World War I Allies: Germany and Austria-Hungary', *International Journal of Middle East Studies*, 34 (2002): 76.

60. BOA.DH.ŞFR 59/76, 21 Dec. 1915; BOA.DH.ŞFR 54/312, 5 July 1915; BOA.DH.ŞFR 54–A/116, 28 July 1915; BOA.DH.ŞFR 54–A/211, 2 Aug. 1915; BOA.DH.ŞFR 54–A/262, 5 Aug. 1915; BOA.DH.ŞFR 55/139, 22 Aug. 1915; BOA.DH.ŞFR 64/51, 23 May, 17 May 1916; BOA.DH.ŞFR 66/63, 24 July 1916; BOA.DH.ŞFR 66/132, 4 Aug. 1916; BOA.DH.ŞFR 70/11, 16 Nov. 1916.

61. BOA.DH.ŞFR 54–A/263, 5 Aug. 1915; BOA.DH.ŞFR 55/70, 19 Aug. 1915; BOA.DH.ŞFR 58/13, 16 Nov. 1915; BOA.DH.ŞFR 60/244, 5 Feb. 1916; BOA.DH.ŞFR 61/61, 21 Feb. 1916; BOA.DH.ŞFR 61/72, 21 Feb. 1916; BOA.DH.ŞFR 61/223, 8 Mar. 1916; BOA.DH.ŞFR 62/49, 16 Mar. 1916; BOA.DH.ŞFR 71/79, 24 Dec. 1916.

62. BOA.DH.ŞFR 54–A/309, 10 Aug. 1915; BOA.DH.ŞFR 55/18, 16 Aug. 1915; BOA.DH.ŞFR 55/19, 16 Aug. 1915; BOA.DH.ŞFR 55/49, 16 Aug. 1915; BOA.DH.ŞFR 60/172, 30 Jan. 1916.

63. BOA.DH.ŞFR 54–A/276, 5 Aug. 1915; BOA.DH.ŞFR 55/56, 18 Aug. 1915; BOA.DH.ŞFR 57/115, 26 Oct. 1915; BOA.DH.ŞFR 59/230, 6 Jan. 1916; BOA.DH.ŞFR 61/71, 21 Feb. 1916; BOA.DH.ŞFR 61/285, 13 Mar. 1916.

64. BOA.DH.ŞFR 54–A/68, 23 Aug. 1915; BOA.DH.ŞFR 54–A/92, 25 July 1915; BOA.DH.ŞFR 57/358, 10 Nov. 1915; BOA.DH.ŞFR 57/366, 10 Nov. 1915.

65. BOA.DH.ŞFR 58/119, 26 Nov. 1915; BOA.DH.ŞFR 60/74, 20 Jan. 1916; BOA.DH.ŞFR 60/110, 24 Jan. 1916; BOA.DH.ŞFR 61/74, 3 Mar. 1916; BOA.DH.ŞFR 90/205, 25 Aug. 1918.

66. BOA.DH.ŞFR 54/53, 17 June 1915; BOA.DH.ŞFR 54–A/186, 30 July 1915; BOA.DH.ŞFR 54–A/212, 2 Aug. 1915. ABCFM 16.9.3, vol. 48, doc. 372: Letter to Dr Reverend James Barton from Mr Peet, 21 Aug. 1916. Americans also lent support to members of the Rum clergy in administering aid.

67. BOA.DH.ŞFR 66/224, 12 Aug. 1916; BOA.DH.ŞFR 68/24, 18 Sep. 1916.

68. A possible reason could be the absolute lack of resources in terms of professional manpower. According to Mari Tomasyan, an Armenian woman from Çatalca, local

Armenians were spared because of the state's need for ironworkers like her father. She also claims that Ottoman officials brought other Armenians to Çatalca to work during the First World War as well. See Yahya Koçoğlu, *Hatırlıyorum: Türkiye'de Gayrimuslim Hayatlar* (Istanbul: Metis Yayınları, 2003), 33.
69. BOA.DH.ŞFR 60/144, 26 Jan. 1916.
70. Dadrian, *History of the Armenian Genocide*, 222–4.
71. BOA.DH.ŞFR 54/296, 4 July 1915. In a separate telegram sent two weeks earlier, the *mutasarrıf* of Karesi received instructions on how Armenian property was to be handled. It also delegated the managing of property left on the Marmara islands to the Edremit Abandoned Property Commission (*Edremid Emval-ı Metrüke Komisyonu*). See BOA.DH.ŞFR 54/187, 27 June 1916.
72. BOA.DH.ŞFR 55/107, 20 Aug. 1915; BOA.DH.ŞFR 60/290, 9 Feb. 1916; BOA.DH.ŞFR 61/31, 15 Feb. 1916; BOA.DH.ŞFR 67/201, 7 Sep. 1916; BOA.DH.ŞFR 71/56, 21 Dec. 1916.
73. 'Muhacirler', *Tesvir-i Efkar*, 1 Jan. 1919.
74. BOA.DH.ŞFR 54–A/241, 3 Aug. 1915; BOA.DH.ŞFR 55/146, 22 Aug. 1915.
75. BOA.DH.ŞFR 57/208, 1 Nov. 1915; BOA.DH.ŞFR 59/260, 10 Jan. 1916; BOA.DH.ŞFR 89/180, 28 July 1918.
76. BOA.DH.ŞFR 59/279, 12 Jan. 1916; BOA.DH.ŞFR 69/252, 14 Nov. 1916.
77. BOA.DH.ŞFR 54/442, 14 July 1915.
78. BOA.DH.ŞFR 59/239, 6 Jan. 1916. This policy of strengthening Muslim businesses is also enunciated in a later telegram. See BOA.DH.ŞFR 64/39, 16 May 1916. This aspect of the deportations, facilitated in part by the *Teşkilat-ı Mahsusa*, is confirmed in the memoirs of Celâl Bayar, a member of the Special Organization in İzmir and a future confidant of Mustafa Kemal. See Bayar, *Ben de Yazdım*, 1573–4.
79. ABCFM 16.9.3, vol. 48, doc. 266: Letter to Dr Reverend James Barton from Mr Peet, 17 Aug. 1915; ABCFM 16.9.3, vol. 48, doc. 284: Letter to Dr Reverend James Barton from Mr Peet, 17 Nov. 1915; ABCFM 16.9.3, vol. 48, doc. 302: Dr Reverend James Barton from Mr. Peet, 29 Dec. 1915; ABCFM 16.9.3, vol. 48, doc. 311: Dr Reverend James Barton from Mr Peet, 29 Jan. 1916.
80. ABCFM 16.9.3, vol. 48, doc. 342: telegram, 20 Apr. 1916, p. 1. Evidently by 1916, the American Red Cross was allowed again to aid in helping refugees of all stripes. The telegram goes on to state the state of affairs in truly stark terms:

> Great suffering throughout country particularly at Constantinople and suburbs, along shores of Marmara, at Adrianople, Brusa and Smyrna. In these regions, five hundred thousand not comprising Armenian refugees urgently need help for bread. Hundred dying of starvation [with] no relief in sight. Sugar, petroleum, quinine, castor oil at famine prices. Typhus spreading. High mortality. For immediate relief fifty thousand dollars estimated required for Constantinople chapter administration before May first to procure food stuffs.

81. BOA.DH.ŞFR 41/22, 26 Nov. 1914; BCA 272.12.35.4.6, 5 May 1915.
82. BOA.DH.ŞFR 54/216, 28 May 1915; BOA.DH.ŞFR 54/246, 30 June 1915. Fuat Dündar, *İittihat ve Terakki'nin Müslümanları İskan Politikası (1913–1918)* (Istanbul: İlestişim Yayınları, 2001), 121.
83. Dündar, *İskan Politikası*, 119.
84. Güven, *Anzavur İsyan*, 15. Zühtü Güven notes in his memoir that Albanian gendarmes were transferred to other provinces during the middle of the war. This act was to the detriment of his unit's ability to police the environs of Lapseki.

85. BCA 272.12.35.6.18, 15 Sept. 1915.
86. BCA 272.14.74.9.15, 18 Sept. 1917; Dündar, *İskan Politikası*, 113–14.
87. Dündar, *İskan Politikası*, 120–1.
88. BOA.DH.ŞFR 54/216, 28 May 1915; BOA.DH.ŞFR 56/290, 7 Oct. 1915; H. Yıldırım Ağanoğlu, *Osmanlı'dan Cumhuriyet'e Balkanları'ın Makûs Talihi Göç* (Istanbul: Kum Saati, 2001), 113–14; Dündar, *İskan Politikası*, 118.
89. Even American missionaries caught glimpses of this policy in western Anatolia in reporting the recent arrival of both Circassians and Kurds to the region. See ABCFM 16.9.3, vol. 48, doc. 365: Letter to Dr Reverend James Barton from Mr Peet, 7 Aug. 1916.
90. See Alişan Akpınar, *Osmanlı Devletinde Aşiret Mektebi* (İstanbul: Göçebe Yayınları, 1997).
91. While it may be argued that the hostility towards Christian Albanians may in part reflect Istanbul's general wariness towards the Christian populations overall, the prohibition placed on Christian Albanians is far more reflective of their role in the Albanian nationalist movement of the turn of the century. See Blumi (ed.), *Rethinking the Late Ottoman Empire*, 23–42.
92. Ağanoğlu, *Osmanlı'dan Cumhuriyet'e*, 115; Dündar, *İskan Politikası*, 118–19.
93. BCA 272.11.11.31.3, 7 Oct. 1917. It was decided that fifty-four would go to Ertuğrul while forty would go north to Orhangazi and Gemlik.
94. BCA 272.11.11.32.25, 10 Nov. 1917.
95. BCA 272.11.11.31.3, 7 Oct. 1917.
96. BCA 272.11.11.34.5, 10 Dec. 1917.
97. BCA 272.11.11.31.3, 7 Oct. 1917.
98. BCA 272.11.11.32.25, 10 Nov. 1917.
99. BCA 272.14.74.11.33, 26 Dec. 1917. The author of this report associated these acts of Albanian insolence with the Çetmi, an Alevi sect found particularly in the counties surrounding Balıkesir. During the War of Independence, the Çetmi would be generally criminalized by the Nationalist Forces as a group of traitors for their role in aiding the Greek occupation.
100. BCA 272.11.8.13.16, 5 Nov. 1916. They are listed as being from Gostivar, Debre, and Morava. The first two were once situated in the *vilayet* of Manastır and are now located in the western portion of the Republic of Macedonia.
101. For guidelines for visa and citizenship requirements for Albanians entering the Ottoman Empire from the Balkans, see Dündar, *İskan Politikası*, 110–12.
102. BOA.DH.ŞFR 71/14, 17 Dec. 1916; BOA.DH.ŞFR 71/15, 17 Dec. 1916; BOA.DH.ŞFR 71/18, 17 Dec. 1916; Dündar, *İskan Politikası*, 130–4.
103. BOA.DH.İUM 10/2//2/31, 7 Apr. 1920.
104. ABCFM 16.9.4, vol. 6: 'Easter in Adabazar', 26 May 1919.
105. Foti Benlisoy, 'Patrikhanenin Faaliyetleri ve 1918–1920 Arasında Tehcir Edilmiş Rum Ahalinin İadesi', *Tarih ve Toplum*, 234 (June 2003): 21; Stanford Shaw, 'Resettlement of Refugees in Anatolia, 1918–1923', *Turkish Studies Association Bulletin*, 22, no. 1 (Spring 1998): 58. According to documents found by Shaw, the Ottoman government commenced with a plan to return peoples sent into exile as early as March 1918. This reversal in policy, Shaw claims, was due to the disruptions in trade, agriculture, and supplies caused by the deportations.

106. Tayyib Gökbilgin, *Millî Mücadele Başlarken* (Ankara: Türk Tarih Kurumu Basimeri, 1959), 15–16; Gotthard Jäschke, *Türk Kurtuluş Savaşı Kronolojisi: Modros'tan Mudanya'ya Kadar (30 Ekim 1918–11 Ekim 1922)* (Ankara: Türk Tarih Kurumu Basımevi, 1970), 2, 8. In addition to the Istanbul Tribunal, ten regional committees were formed to investigate the deportations and massacres of Armenians and Greeks. Among the ten, committees were formed in Bursa (responsible for the *vilayet*s of Hüdavendigar and Edirne and the *sancak* of Çatalca) and in İzmir (responsible for the *vilayet* of Aydın and the *sancak*s of Çanakkale and Karesi). Little is known about their investigations or conclusions.
107. Ayhan Aktar, 'Son Osmanlı Meclisi ve Ermeni Meselesi: Kasım-Aralık 1918', *Toplum ve Bilim*, 91 (Winter 2001–2): 142–65; Gökbilgin, *Millî Mücadele Başlarken*, 6.
108. Benlisoy, 'Patrikhanenin Faaliyetleri', 2–2.
109. PRO/FO 371/4157/62437, 5 Apr. 1919; PRO/FO 371/4158/105778, 27 June 1919.
110. PRO/FO 371/4157/62437, 5 Apr. 1919.
111. Ibid.
112. PRO/FO 371/4160/154462, 22 Nov. 1919.
113. PRO/FO 371/4158/124458, 3 Sept. 1919; PRO/FO 608/113/6476, 7 Mar. 1919; PRO/FO 608/113/10733, 22 May 1919; PRO/FO 371/4160/154462, 22 Nov. 1919. Interestingly, only 10 per cent of Greeks were deported from Gemlik. Yet most of the Rum living in villages outside town were deported.
114. ABCFM 16.9.3, vol. 51, doc. 177: McNaughton, 'Notes on Brousa Field,' 18, Sept. 1920.
115. BOA.DH.ŞFR 95/88, 9 Jan. 1919; BOA.DH.ŞFR 96/41, 2 Feb. 1919; BCA 272.74.68.37.14, 8 Feb. 1919. Ottoman officials in Orhangazi telegrammed Istanbul in February with requests for aid in order to help Armenians there in 'an extreme situation of ruin'.
116. PRO/FO 371/4157/62437, 5 Apr. 1919.
117. Ibid. One British report from early April states that in addition to the Armenian houses in Adapazarı occupied by refugees or destroyed for firewood, all of the silk factories in town were closed with the exception of a Muslim-owned establishment.
118. ABCFM 16.9.4, vol. 6: 'Easter in Adabazar'.
119. Shaw, '*Resettlement of Refugees*', 62–5, 72–3. Shaw, in looking at the Secret Telegrams collections, argues that the Ottoman government in 1918 and 1919 made every attempt to return property to Armenians, Greeks, and other deported Christians (going as far as to mandate that *all* property, including that sold or given to Muslims, be returned). What Shaw fails to take into account is the influence of CUP loyalists in resisting the will of the central government (which by the fall of 1918 was under the stewardship of the sultan and the Liberty and Understanding Party). What is also not taken into account in his argument is the degree to which the sale and transfer of Christian property was part and parcel of the state's 'national economy' project (which was again one of the core planks of the CUP).
120. PRO/FO 371/4158/124458, 3 Sept. 1919; PRO/FO 371/4160/154462, 22 Nov. 1919; PRO/FO 371/4161/161867, 12 Nov. 1919. In Bursa, British officer Lieutenant C. Hadkinson recommended the disbandment of the mixed commissions due to the rise in hostility that caused the Armenian representatives to withdraw. In

Mudanya, Armenians sent 134 complaints to the Armenian Patriarchate concerning government inaction with regard to the wartime sale of land and property, an amount that totalled £896,414 worth of assets. In Adapazarı, despite the progress made by the mixed commission, another British representative recommended at one point that no Armenians should return from their exile in Aleppo due to the lack of gendarmes. Resistution in Bandırma purportedly progressed smoothly until the occupation of İzmir. After May 1919, both Rum or Ottoman officials refused to work together.

121. BOA.DH.ŞFR 98/117, 10 Apr. 1919; BOA.DH.ŞFR 98/256, 23 Apr. 1919.
122. PRO/FO 371/4159/144275, 22 Oct. 1919. Ironically, the appointment of village guards to the role of facilitators in the case of returned property appears on the surface to have been a half-hearted measure. During this period, most Christians remained unarmed (due to the government policy of disarmament during the First World War), giving the ultimate advantage to Ottoman gendarmes and officials (not to mention disgruntled Muslim neighbours and paramilitaries).
123. BOA.DH.ŞFR 96/3, 1 Feb. 1919; BOA.DH.ŞFR 96/7, 1 Feb. 1919.
124. ABCFM 16.9.4, vol. 6: 'Easter in Adabazar'.
125. ABCFM 16.9.3, vol. 48, doc. 363: Dr Reverend James Barton from Mr Peet, 21 July 1916.

CHAPTER 3

1. This description of the town and the arrival of Selahettin comes in part from Kâzim Özalp, *Milli Mücadele, 1919–1922* (Ankara: Türk Tarih Kurumu Basimeri, 1985), 9.
2. Selçuk, *Yüzbaşı Selahattin'in Romanı, II. Kitap*, 57; Muhittin, Ünal, *Miralay Bekir Sami Günsav 'in Kurtuluş Savaşı Anılavı* (Istanbul: Cem Yaylnevi, 2002), 27.
3. Selçuk, *Yüzbaşı Selahattin'in Romanı, II. Kitap*, 58–9.
4. The most definitive study of this phenomenon is Karen Barkey, *Bandits and Bureaucrats: The Ottoman Route to State Centralization* (Ithaca, NY: Cornell University Press, 1994).
5. See Duncan Perry, *The Politics of Terror: The Macedonian Liberation Movement 1893–1903* (Durham, NC: Duke University Press, 1988), 133–40.
6. Akyut Kansu, *The Revolution of 1908 in Turkey* (Leiden: E. J. Brill, 1997), 90–1; 'The Turkish Army Officers', *The Times (London)*, 24 July 1908.
7. Hanioğlu, *Preparation for a Revolution*, 221–7, 254–8.
8. PRO/FO 608/113/12063, 7 June 1919. British officers on the scene claimed that Reşit had all the Circassians in Bandırma under his control.
9. Ferdan Ergut, 'State and Social Control: The Police in the Late Ottoman Empire and the Early Republican Turkey, 1839–1939' Ph.D. (diss., New School for Social Research, 1999), 327.
10. BOA.DH.ŞFR 47/196 27 Nov. 1914; BOA.DH.ŞFR 47/245, 30 Nov. 1914; BOA.DH.ŞFR 48/28, 17 Dec. 1914; BOA.DH.ŞFR 49/164, 30 Jan. 1915.
11. Akçam, *Armenien*, 318–19; Tarık Zafer Tunaya, *Türkiye'de Siyasal Partiler:İttihat ve Terakki, Cilt III* (Istanbul: Hürriyet Vakfı Yayınları, 1989), 283.
12. Akçam, *From Empire to Republic*, 160–3.
13. Rauf graduated from the *Deniz Harbiye* (the Ottoman Naval College). Şükrü and Eşref attended the *Harbiye*. Fuat, on the other hand, attended the *Mülkiye* (Civil

Service School). Sami meanwhile graduated from the *Harbiye*. See Berzeg, *Çerkes Göçmenleri*, 9, 21, 33; Philip Hendrick Stoddard, 'The Ottoman Government and the Arabs, 1911 to 1918: A Preliminary Study of the Teşkilat-ı Mahsusa (Ph.D. diss., Princeton University, 1963), 162.
14. Stoddard, 'Ottoman Government and the Arabs', 165–6. In the case of Rauf Orbay, it is unclear at what point and by what means he became a member of the CUP. However, it has been documented that through both his family's connections and his service in the navy, Rauf was acquainted with several seminal members of the CUP. See Cemal Kutay, *Osmanlı'dan Cumhuriyet'e Yüzyılımızda bir İnsanımız, Hüseyin Rauf Orbay, 1881–1964* (Istanbul: Kazanç Kitap Ticaret, 1995), 59.
15. Berzeg, *Çerkes Göçmenleri*, 21.
16. Ibid. 9.
17. Ibid. 18; Stoddard, 'Ottoman Government and the Arabs' 161, 171.
18. Stoddard, 'Ottoman Government and the Arabs', 166.
19. Berzeg, *Çerkes Göçmenleri*, 13–14.
20. İzzet Aydemir, *Muhacerettteki Çerkes Aydınları* (Ankara: n.p., 1991), 9; Berzeg, *Çerkes Göçmenleri*, 9, 34. Founded in 1914, the *Şimali Kafkas Cemiyeti* was an organization formed to promote the CUP's interests in the North Caucasus. It is through the actions of this committee that a rebellion was sparked in Ajaria (in southwestern Georgia) at the start of the First World War (an action that Yusuf İzzet was instrumental in fomenting). See Avagyan, *Osmanlı İmperatorluğu*, 134–9.
21. Berzeg, *Çerkes Göçmenleri*, 13, 22, 47.
22. Ibid. 15; Özcan Mert, 'Anzavur'un İlk Ayaklanmasına Ait Belgeler', *Belleteu* 56, no. 217 (1992)': 856. Mert states, however, that Anzavur spent most of the war at his horse farm in Biga.
23. Berzeg, *Çerkes Göçmenleri*, 86; Kamil Erdeha, *Yüzellilikler yahut Milli Mücadelenini Muhasebesi* (Istanbul: Tekin Yayınları, 1998), 215.
24. See Hans-Lukas Kieser, 'Dr. Mehmed Reshid (1873–1919): A Political Doctor', in Kieser and Schaller (eds.), *Der Völkermord*, 245–80; Muhittin Ünal, *Kurtuluş Savaşında Çerkeslerin Rolü* (Ankara: Takav Matbaası, 2000), 36–7.
25. Çerkes Ethem, *Hatıralarım* (Istanbul: Berfin Yayınları, 1998) 7.
26. Hüsameddin Ertürk, and Samih Nafiz Tansu, *İki Devrin Perde Arkası* (Istanbul: Ramazan Yusar, 1969), 120.
27. It is possible that two other Albanians were members or were associated with the Special Organization: (Köprülülü) Hamdi Bey and Abdülhalik (Renda). Both were members of the bureaucracy (the former was the *kaymakam* of Malkara, Keşan, and Edremit; the latter was the *vali* of Aleppo). As CUP members responsible for areas where numerous non-Muslim were murdered or deported, it is possible that both Hamdi and Abdülhalik were at the very least complicit in the actions of the *Teşkilat-ı Mahsusa*.
28. Ertürk and Tansu, *İki Devrin Perde Arkası*, 109, 120. Ertürk lists a Bosnian, *Müftü* Cemaleddin, with (Debreli) Zinnun and gendarmerie commander *Arnavud* Hayreddin as fellow conspirators against Italian activities in Albanian lands. While Ertürk offers few details as to the nature of these activities, the CUP's interest in the Balkans demonstrates that Istanbul's efforts to undermine the Allied war effort were broader than is usually understood. The *Teşkilat-ı Mahsusa*'s operations in the Balkans also suggest the possibility of continued contact between the Ottoman

government and the remaining Muslim notables in the southern Balkans. Eyüp's role in espionage in Albania is also confirmed by Atıf Bey, a witness in the Istanbul Military Tribunal hearings. See Akçam, *Armenien*, 244; PRO/FO 371/3393/4674, 16 Feb. 1917.
29. Akçam, *From Empire to Republic*, 162–3. According to Akçam, one telegram from İsmet (İnönü), who was working in the War Department, states that refugees from Thrace and Macedonia could serve as a good source for recruitment into the *Teşkilat-ı Mahsusa*.
30. This may also hold true for Kurdish members of the Special Organization. Despite the CUP's effort to resettle and 'civilize' Kurds fleeing the fighting in eastern Anatolia, Kurd notables remained an invaluable conduit of fighting men through-out the First World War and the War of Independence.
31. PRO/FO 371/4158/96965, 8 June 1919; PRO/FO 371/5054/9302, 3 Aug. 1919.
32. Erik Jan Zürcher, 'Little Mehmet in the Desert: The Ottoman Soldier's Experience', in Hugh Cecil and Peter Liddle (eds.), *Facing Armageddon: The First World War Experienced*, (London: Cooper Press, 1996), 244–5; Ahmed Emin Yalman, *Turkey in the World War* (New Haven: Yale University Press, 1930) 262. Despite the victories at Gelibolu and Kut al-Amara, the gradual retreat of the Ottoman armies from the Arab lands, as well as dire living conditions, provoked some 300,000 soldiers to desert their units by 1917. By war's end, the number was more than 500,000.
33. BOA.DH.ŞFR 71/156, 3 Jan. 1917.
34. BOA.DH.ŞFR 81/31, 5 Nov. 1917.
35. Examples of bandit activity can be seen during this period of time in Bursa (BOA.DH.ŞFR 88/19, 1 June 1918; BOA.DH.ŞFR 91/125, 12 Sept. 1918), in Bandırma (BOA.DH.ŞFR 92/286, 29 Oct. 1918; BOA.DH.ŞFR 81/15, 4 Nov. 1917), in Karacabey (BOA.DH.ŞFR 83/66, 10 Jan. 1918; BOA.DH.ŞFR 88/245, 25 June 1918), in Kirmasti (BOA.DH.ŞFR 83/66, 10 Jan. 1918; BOA.DH.ŞFR 91/73, 8 Sept. 1918), in Susurluk (BOA.DH.ŞFR 86/203, 22 Apr. 1918), in Balıkesir (BOA.DH.ŞFR 89/25, 6 July 1918), in Gemlik (BOA.DH.ŞFR 90/187, 22 Aug. 1918), in Çan (BOA.DH.ŞFR 91/72, 8 Sept. 1918), in Gönen (BOA.DH.ŞFR 92/208, 22 Oct. 1918; BOA.DH.ŞFR 93/205, 18 Nov. 1918), and in Adapazarı (BOA.DH.ŞFR 88/139, 13 June 1918; BOA.DH.ŞFR 90/123, 13 Aug. 1918).
36. BOA.DH.ŞFR 79/17, 2 Aug. 1917; BOA.DH.ŞFR 79/190, 22 Aug. 1917; BOA.DH.ŞFR 81/31, 5 Nov. 1917; BOA.DH.ŞFR 88/3, 1 June 1918; BOA.DH.ŞFR 89/25, 6 July 1918.
37. BOA.DH.ŞFR 64/232, 5 June 1916; BOA.DH.ŞFR 89/185, 28 July 1918.
38. BOA.DH.ŞFR 78/224, 25 July 1917; BOA.DH.ŞFR, 82/11, 3 Dec. 1917; BOA.DH.ŞFR 90/36, 6 Aug. 1918; BOA.DH.ŞFR 90/48, 5 Aug. 1918; BOA.DH.ŞFR 91/125, 12 Sept. 1918; BOA.DH.ŞFR 92/317, 31 Oct. 1918.
39. BOA.DH.ŞFR 89/61, 61–1, 12 July 1917; BOA.DH.ŞFR 89/105, 16 July 1917; BOA.DH.ŞFR 92/155, 14 Oct. 1918; BOA.DH.ŞFR 96/95, 8 Feb. 1919; BOA.DH.ŞFR 96/122, 9 Feb. 1919; BOA.DH.ŞFR 96/330, 27 Feb. 1919; BOA.DH.ŞFR 97/351, 31 Mar. 1919.
40. An interesting case in point is the emergence of a notorious bandit named *Kürd* Mehmet in the environs of Biga. He was a Kurdish officer who had deserted the

Ottoman army in 1916. Along with two other Kurdish deserters, Mehmet 'quickly proved' himself as a bandit since he was 'nastier and more wicked' than others. See Güven, *Anzavur İsyan*, 17.
41. Ibid. 10.
42. Ibid. 18; Uluğ İğdemir, *Biga Ayaklanması ve Anzavur Olayları* (Ankara: Türk Tarih Kurumu Basımevi, 1989), 86.
43. Güven, *Anzavur İsyan*, 20–2.
44. 'Yalova'da İki Gün', *Alemdar*, 27 Aug. 1919; BOA.DH.İUM 19/5//1/31, 14 Mar. 1919; BOA.DH.şFR 95/279, 30 Jan. 1919; Yüce, *Kocaeli Tarih ve Rehberi*, 64. According to a journalist from the anti-Nationalist newspaper *Alemdar*, the Yetimoğlus held considerable sway in the environs of Yalova.
45. BOA.DH.EUM.AYŞ 18/119, 8 Aug. 1919; BOA.DH.KMS 53–1/78, 22 June 1919.
46. Yüce, *Kocaeli Tarih ve Rehberi*, 75, 82. In the summer of 1919, over sixty notables from twenty-four villages in the İzmit and Değirmendere region sent an open complaint to the Interior Ministry, demanding that the government put an end to the Albanian band. Despite Talat's departure, the Interior Ministry appears to have been unwilling to move on the concerns of these prominent local citizens.
47. BOA.DH.EUM.AYŞ34/24, 4 Mar. 1920.
48. BOA.DH.ŞFR 90/90, 9 Aug. 1918; BOA.DH.ŞFR 90/94, 9 Aug. 1918; BOA.DH.ŞFR 90/95, 9 Aug. 1918; BOA.DH.ŞFR 90/98, 11 Aug. 1918. Zühtü Güven states that a general amnesty towards both bandits and deserters was given in November 1918 and not in August. It is unclear whether his recollections are false or whether the government elaborated on a previously announced policy at that later date. See Güven, *Anzavur İsyan*, 23.
49. In Karacabey, *Deli* Hürşid and *Çerkes* Davud, a Circassian paramilitary who had recently returned home after serving in the *Teşkilat-ı Mahsusa* in Diyarbakir, both accepted the Sultan's amnesty. They would go to war against one another, however, within a few short months. See PRO/FO 371/4158/124458, 3 Sept. 1919.
50. Güven, *Anzavur İsyan*, 24–6.
51. Ibid. 26.
52. BOA.DH.EUM.AYŞ 34/24, 4 Mar. 1920.
53. Shaw, *From Empire to Republic*, 83.
54. Şerif Güralp, *Kurtuluş Savaşı'nın İçyüzü: Bir Albayın Anıları* (İstanbul: Güncel Yayıncılık, 2002), 17–18.
55. Erik Jan Zürcher, *The Unionist Factor: The Role of the Committee of Union and Progress in the Turkish Nationalist Movement, 1905–1926* (Leiden: E.J. Brill, 1984), 84–6.
56. Ertürk and Tansu, *İki Devrin Perde Arkasv*, 180–5.
57. Gökbilgin, *Millî Mücadele Başlarken*, 24; Shaw, *From Empire to Republic*, 86, 463–4, 862, 866. Urfa and Edirne were occupied by French troops in early November 1918. The French occupation was later extended to Adana in mid-December. British forces occupied Çanakkale, Batumi, and Kars in November.
58. Shaw, *From Empire to Republic*, 2097.
59. By 2 Apr. 1919, thirty French soldiers occupied the Bandırma railway station. See PRO/FO 608/113/10733, 22 May 1919.

60. Rahmi Apak, *İstiklal Savaşında Garp Cephesi Nasıl Kuruldu* (Ankara: Türk Tarih Kurumu Basımevi, 1990), 13–14; Shaw, *From Empire to Republic*, 386–401; Sofuoğlu, *Kuva-yı Milliye Döneminde*, 31–6.
61. Sofuoğlu, *Kuva-yı Milliye Döneminde*, 37–41. Sofuoğlu makes this connection in a section he entitles 'The Activities of the Minorities (Native Rum and Armenians) in Northwestern Anatolia'.
62. Mustafa Kemal Atatürk, *A Speech Delivered by Mustafa Kemal Atatürk 1927* (Istanbul: Ministry of Education, 1963), 1.
63. Çam, *Milli Mücadele*, 9; Sabahattin Özel, *Kocaeli ve Sakarya İllerinde Milli Mücadele (1919–1922)* (Istanbul: Türkiyat Mathaacılık, 1987), 11–12; Yüce, *Kocaeli Tarih ve Rehberi*, 65.
64. PRO/FO 371/4158/90012, 13 Apr. 1919; PRO/FO 371/4158/105778, 27 June 1919. Armenian bandit activity on the south side of the Gulf of İzmit is reported to have been ongoing in April 1919.
65. Fahri Can, 'Birinci Dünya Harbından Sonra İlk Milli Kuvvet Nasıl Kuruldu?', *Yakın Tarihimiz*, 1, no. 2 (10 May 1962): 334.
66. Fahri Can, 'Kuva-yı Milliye Ruhu', *Yakın Tarihimiz*, 1, no. 8 (19 April 1962): 249–50; idem, 'Birinci Dünya Harbından Sonra İlk Milli Kuvvet Nasıl Kuruldu?', *Yakın Tarihimiz*, 2, no. 14 (31 May 1962): 28–9.
67. İbrahim Çolak, *Milli Mücadele Esnasında Kuva-yı Seyyare Kumandalığıma Ait Hatıratım* (Istanbul: Emre Yayınları, 1996), 16, 31–43; Fahri Can, 'Birinci Dünya Harbından Sonra İlk Milli Kuvvet Nasıl Kuruldu?', *Yakın Tarihimiz*, 1, no. 13 (24 May 1962): 394; idem, 'Birinci Dünya Harbından Sonra İlk Milli Kuvvet Nasıl Kuruldu?,' *Yakın Tarihimiz*, 2, no. 14: 28; PRO/FO 371/4158/96965, 8 June 1919; Yüce, 75. *Kocaeli Tarih ve Rehberi*, Interestingly, Yahya Kaptan and *Kara Arslan* were çete leaders in Macedonia during the period before the Balkan Wars. During the First World War, the two fought together in Iraq in the *Osmancık* division under the command of Süleyman Askeri (which raises the likelihood that they also were clandestine service officers). Sadık Baba, a Bulgarian (possibly a Pomak), may have served with Eşref in the early days of the *Teşkilat-ı Mahsusa*.
68. PRO/FO 371/4158/105778, 27 June 1919.
69. PRO/FO 371/4157/62437, 5 Apr. 1919.
70. BOA.DH.İUM 19/5/1/28, 13 Mar. 1919. Despite both the deportation and the violence that the Armenians of Karacabey suffered, the petitioner claimed that the refugees would continue their fealty towards the sultan.
71. BOA.DH.İUM 19/5//1/31, 14 Mar. 1919; BOA.DH.ŞFR 95/279, 30 Jan. 1919.
72. Can, 'Birinci Dünya Harbından Sonra İlk Milli Kuvvet Nasıl Kuruldu?', *Yakın Tarihimiz*, 1, no. 2: 334.
73. Sofuoğlu *Kuva-yı Milliye Döneminde*, 62. Large-scale demonstrations and public meetings were also organized in Gemlik, Bursa, Edremit, Ezine, İnegöl, and Bayramiç. In the town of İnegöl, 5,000 people attended a protest meeting.
74. Özdemir, *Balıkesir Cepheleri*, 67; idem, *Önderleri*, 71–3.
75. Apak, *İshkal Savaşında Garp*, 11–12; Özalp, *Milli Mücadele*, 3–6. On the night of 14 May 1919, Kazım (Özalp) purportedly attended a public meeting in the centre of town where Ragıp Nurettin was addressing the audience. Afterwards, he went to a coffee-house across from the governor's offices where he met with two fellow officers, Captain Hüsnü (Konyalı) and Lieutenant Osman (Manisalı). Kazım

was later joined by Haydar Rüştü (who seemingly knew Hüsnü and Osman but may have not known Kazım). According to Haydar Rüştü, Kazım (Özalp) and his compatriots spoke at length about the impending invasion and what steps needed to be taken. During the conversation, Kazım outlined in detail the state of Ottoman forces in the area and his plans to vacate the city for Ödemiş, where he would rendezvous with Celal Bayar and organize a base for the resistance. Interestingly, Kazım omits any mention of the contents of this meeting with Haydar Rüştü and the other officers in his memoirs.

76. Tarık Tunaya, *Türkiye'de Siyası Partiler, 1859–1952* (Istanbul: Doğan Kardeş Yayınları, 1952), 481–3.
77. Özalp, *Milli Mücadele*, 8–13. As in the case of many War of Independence memoirs, Kazım's account is crafted to give the impression that his actions were spontaneous and unscripted. It just so happened, he appears to explain, that he was in Izmir for a holiday when the Greeks invaded. He gives no indication that his subsequent tours of western Anatolia were directed or prearranged.
78. Ibid. 13; Selçuk, *Romanı II. Kitap*, 59–60; Ünal, *Miralay Bekir Sami*, 30.
79. Özalp, *Milli Mücadele*, 24.
80. Tülay Alim Baran, *Vasıf Çınar ve İzmir'e Doğru Gazetesi Yazıları* (Istanbul: Arma Yayınları, 2001), 11–12; Özdemir, *Önderleri*, 49. *İzmir'e Doğru* was first published 16 Nov. 1919.
81. Hacim Muhittin Çarıklı, *Balikesir ve Alaşehir Kongreleri ve Hacim Muhittin Çovikli 'nin Kuva-yı Milliye Hatiralari, 1919–1920* (Ankara: Türk lukılâp Tarihi Enstitüsü, 1967), 14–15.
82. His journal entry for 9 June 1919 reads: 'This morning I went to Muhtar Bey's house. Later we found [*Kara*] Vasıf at his home. That afternoon we met at his office. We discussed the Aydın Province question. Hopefully I will depart for Bandırma the day after tomorrow.' Hacim's encounters with *Kara* Vasıf in certain ways mirror Mustafa Kemal's own meeting with *Kara* Kemal during his final days in Istanbul, a coincidence that similarly hints at the role of the *Karakol* in launching and directing the *Kuva-yı Milliye*. See Zürcher, *Unionist Factor*, 112–14.
83. Several sources say that there was a first congress held at the Darül Nafia *medrese* in Balıkesir between 28 June and 13 July (Hacim Muhittin's memoir contains no record of this meeting). At this meeting, delegates chose Hacim Muhittin to preside over a much larger congress that would be held later. Exactly who these delegates were, and what other decisions were made, are not known. See Hasan Basri Çantay, *Kara Günler ve İbret Levhaları* (Istanbul: Ahmet Said Matbaası, 1964), 35; Mücteba İlgürel, *Milli Mücadele'de Balıkesir Kongreleri* (Istanbul: Atatürk Araştırma Merkezi, 1999), 87–100; Özalp, *Milli Mücadele*, 38.
84. Çarıklı, *Balıkesir ve Alaşehir Kongreleri*, 112–15.
85. Ibid. 114. In this regard, financial responsibility would be divided along the following provincial lines: Balıkesir 21 per cent, Edremit 17 per cent, Burhaniye 7 per cent, Balya 4 per cent, Bandırma 10 per cent, Gönen 6 per cent, Sındırgı 4 per cent, Gördes 4 per cent, Soma 5 per cent, and Bergama 2 per cent.
86. Atatürk, *Speech*, 10–11. Mustafa Kemal argued that he kept his true feelings secret for fear that they would be looked upon as 'dreams'. Still, we must be circumspect as to what his true ideological intentions were in the summer of 1919.

87. Çarıklı, *Balıkesir ve Alaşehir Kongreleri*, 33–4, 115, 126. In addition to the total expulsion of the Greek army, Hacim also advocated a population exchange between Greece and the Ottoman lands.
88. Ibid. 116.
89. For greater detail about the debate over the meaning and evolution of the term *milli/millet*, see Niyazi Berkes, *The Development of Secularism in Turkey* (Montreal: McGill University Press, 1964), 318, 331; Davison, 'Turkish Attitudes'.
90. *Harb Tarihi Vesikaları Dergisi*, 1, no. 2 (Dec. 1952): doc. 37.
91. Çarıklı, *Balıkesir ve Alaşehir Kongreleri*, 157. During the Alaşehir Congress of August 1919, Abdülgafur stated: 'The money that will be collected [for the National Movement] is not a donation. A donation is never compulsory. An amount that will be collected will be for the defence, religion and honour of the fatherland. It is a duty of every Muslim to give this.'
92. Ibid. 115–16.
93. Ibid. 118.
94. For examples see Baran, *Vasıf Çınar* 62–3, 104–6; Çantay, *Kara Günler*, 78–80.
95. For further discussion of the meaning and significance of the Nationalist debate on 'Turkishness' and Islam, see Howard Eissenstat, 'The Limits of Imagination: Debating the Nation and Constructing the State in Early Turkish Nationalism,' (Ph.D. diss., University of California at Los Angeles, 2007), 67–127.
96. Atatürk, *Speech*, 56–7.
97. Shaw, *From Empire to Republic*, 659, 708–9.
98. I have no definitive evidence suggesting that Hüseyin Rauf Orbay was the ringleader of the National Movement during these early stages. Yet his rank and noted presence at several key meetings in both Istanbul and the provinces leads me to believe that he was probably the pivital organizer of resistance efforts in the South Marmara following the events of 15 May 1919.
99. TTK Bekir Sami Dosya, ii. 188, 17 Sept. 1919. This document was later released by Mustafa Kemal during his *Nutuk*. In the despatch received by Bekir Sami, only a portion of the full document released later by Mustafa Kemal was transcribed (points 4–6). See Mustafa Kemal Atatürk, *Nutuk-Söylev* (Ankara: Türk Tarih Kurumu Basımevi, 1989), 1654.
100. Orhan Hülagü, Kemal Özer, and Zühtü Güven give cursory accounts of the construction of resistance organizations in Bursa, Gönen, and Biga respectively. While they list the names of those who joined, no details are given as to the process by which these organizations came into being or functioned. See Güven, *Anzavur İsyan*, 27–9; Hülagü, *Milli Mücadele'de Bursa*, 33–6; Özer, *Gönen*, (1964), 41–50.
101. TTK Bekir Sami Dosya, ii. 151, 23 Oct. 1919.
102. Ibid. ii. 164, 27 Oct. 1919. The committee was established by a man named İsmail (Çelikzade).
103. Ibid. ii. 165, 27 Oct. 1919.
104. Ibid. ii. 185, 31 Oct. 1919.
105. Ibid. ii. 222, 2 Nov. 1919.
106. Ibid. ii. 260, 5/6 Nov. 1919.
107. Ibid. ii. 235, 3 Nov. 1919.

108. PRO/FO 371/4161/161867, 12 Nov. 1919.
109. BOA.DH.İUM 19/13/1/56, 7 Aug. 1920; BOA.DH.KMS 53–4/48, 25 Apr. 1920. In Karamürsel, gendarmes and army officers working in the local recruiting office (*ahz-ı asker şubesi*), as well as the director of the town pier, were known to Ottoman authorities to be collecting money for the *Kuva-yı Milliye*. Further west in Bayramiç, Nationalists also subverted the recruiting office. There they demanded that farmers sell their tools and animals to them or pay an exemption tax (*bedel-i nakdi*) in lieu of not serving in the *Kuva-yı Milliye*.
110. BOA.DH.KMS 53–2/80, 17 Aug. 1919; BOA.DH.KMS 53–3/42, 1 Oct. 1919; BOA.DH.KMS 53–4/43, 11 Apr. 1920; BOA.DH.KMS 53–4/44, 15 Apr. 1920. In October 1919, two Nationalist representatives arrived in Biga with the intention of signing up men available for military service. Similar campaigns of forced recruitment and fund raising by gendarmes (who were considered to be deserters by the imperial Ottoman bureaucracy) were also reported in Balıkesir, Bilecik, Çanakkale, İzmit, and Adapazarı.
111. Thousands of Muslims from the Aegean would take up residence to the north and west of the coast in effort to escape the fighting. From the outset, refugees from Bergama, Aydın, and Izmir clung together in an effort to turn the Greeks back. Meanwhile, wealthy and politically connected men came together to act as advocates and recruiters for the National Movement. See Çarıklı, *Balıkesir ve Alaşehir Kongreleri*, 14.
112. BOA.DH.KMS 49–1/29, 10 Nov. 1918; Emrah Cilasun, *Bâki İlk Selam* (Istanbul: Belge Yayınları, 2004), 31–5. The Ottoman document suggests that Ethem may have been active in the Bandırma region soon after the armistice. In it, the Interior Ministry directs local authorities 'to give service' (*dahalet etmek*) to Ethem and his band.
113. Güven, *Anzavur İsyan*, 28–9; Recai Sanay, *Türk Casusu İngiliz Kemal: Milli Mücadele'de* (Istanbul: Geçit Kitabevi, 2005), 177, 180–5.
114. Two noted clandestine service officers from the South Marmara known to have been approached during the spring of 1919 were Şah İsmail and Çerkes Çakır. Şah İsmail, a notorious *çeteci* and deserter from Gönen, joined Ethem's Mobile Forces soon after the landing at İzmir. Çakır, who was once Enver Paşa's bodyguard and driver, also joined Ethem. Before the outbreak of hostilities, Çakır also helped to smuggle arms into the South Marmara. See BOA.DH.ŞFR 93/205, 18 Nov. 1918; Berzeg, *Çerkes Göçmenleri*, 65; Ertürk and Tansu, *İki Devri Perde Arkası* 385; Özer, *Gönen* (1964), 140.
115. Çam, *Milli Mücadele*, 30; Sofuoğlu, *kuva-yı Milliye Döneminde*, 182.
116. PRO/FO 371/5047/4272, 6 May 1920.
117. Berzeg, *Çerkes Göçmenleri*, 91. Members of the Istanbul gendarmerie later arrested Ahmet Kuşçubaşı on the road between İzmit and the capital. In a report to the *vali* of Istanbul, Eşref's brother is identified as a 'commander' of the *Kuva-yı Milliye* in Adapazarı and was purportedly travelling to Istanbul under the guise of being a merchant.
118. Ertürk, 197.
119. Çam, *Milli Mücadele*, 38; İlyas Sami Kalkavanoğlu, *Milli Mücadele Hatıralarım* (Isanbul: Ekicigil Yayınevi, 1957), 19–20; TTK Bekir Sami Dosya, ii. 153, 23 Oct.

1919. Even Bekir Sami (Günsav), from his headquarters in Bursa, stated that control over the İzmit area was 'very important'.
120. Ertürk, 197. Ertürk states that it was Enver Paşa who issued the order for Eşref to go to Adapazarı to deal with the Abkhazians and Circassians. If that is so, this revelation raises the issue of Enver's overall role within the National Movement. Zürcher has pointed out that Enver, while based in Europe and the Soviet Union, had aligned himself with the left wing of the National Movement and still attracted the loyalty of members of the CUP old guard (particularly within the *Teşkilat-ı Mahsusa*). See Zürcher, *Unionist Factor*, 123–30.
121. Çarıklı, *Balıkesir ve Alaşehir Kongreleri*, 108. According to a letter written in 1965, Hacim Muhittin stated that Eşref had maintained connections with current or former servants or slaves (*köle*) around Adapazarı (who were 'rebelling at that time'). He also mentions that the Kuşçubaşı family continued to possess some loyalty to the sultan despite joining the *Kuva-yı Milliye*.
122. Ibid. 18–20.
123. Sofuoğlu, *Kuva-yı Milliye Döneminde*, 332.
124. TTK Bekir Sami Dosya, ii. 30, 29 July 1919. According to the report, the division possessed 325 soldiers and 71 officers.
125. Ibid. ii. 351–1, 15 Nov. 1919; ii. 352, 16 Nov. 1919.
126. Ibid. ii. 164, 27 Oct. 1919; ii. 352, 16 Nov. 1919.

CHAPTER 4

1. PRO/FO 371/4160/154462, 22 Nov. 1919.
2. Ibid.
3. PRO/FO 371/4161/161867, 12 Nov. 1919.
4. Çarıklı, *Balıkesir ve Alaşehir Kongreleri*, 24. The commander of this unit, Takığ Şevket, was a native of the village of Mürvvetler, near Manyas. He was purportedly a close friend of *Çerkes* Ethem and later joined him in the defence of Salihli. He is of note only for the fact that he would later be among the first North Caucasian guerrillas to participate in the Greek-run campaign to subvert the Kemalist government in 1923. See Özdemir, *Balıkesir Cepheleri*, 143–5. For biographical data on Takığ Şevket, see Berzeg, *Çerkes Göçmenleri*, 91.
5. Çarıklı, *Balıkesir ve Alaşehir Kongreleri*, 19–20, 30; Özer, *Gönen* (1964), 67, 74.
6. TTK Bekir Sami Dosya, ii. 126, 18 Oct. 1919; ii. 135, 20 Oct. 1919; ii. 146, 23 Oct. 1919; Ünal, *Miralay Bekir Sami*, 186.
7. BOA.DH.KMS 53–4/32, 19 Jan. 1920; Çarıklı, *Balıckesir ve Alaşehir Kongreleri*, 31, 34, 37, 56; *Harb Tarihi Vesikaları Dergisi*, 3, no. 9 (Sept. 1954): doc. 220; 4, no. 12 (June 1955): doc. 305.
8. TTK Bekir Sami Dosya, ii. 163, 26 Oct. 1919.
9. Türk Cumhuriyet Genelkurmay Başkanlığı Harb Tarihi Dairesi, *Türk İstiklal Harbi: VI'ıncı Cilt, İç Ayaklanmalar (1919–1921)* (Ankara: Genelkurmay Basımevi, 1964), 134–5.
10. Ibid. 151–72.
11. Ibid. 90–110.
12. Shaw, *From Empire to Republic*, 157–9.
13. PRO/FO 371/4161/41914, 19 Mar. 1919. A British intelligence report dated March 1919 suggests that the death of his cousin, Yusuf, in 1916 weighed heavily

on Mehmet's mind when confronting the CUP. He purportedly suspected that his cousin may in fact have been murdered before taking the throne. In a comprehensive intelligence report on the state of Ottoman political life, an unnamed British official stated that the sultan's suspicions regarding his cousin's death were raised after it was revealed that it was Enver Paşa's personal physician who declared Yusuf's passing to be a suicide. The officer also stated that the CUP viewed Yusuf's accession to the throne with 'singular disfavour'. It was for this reason that Mehmet Vahdeddin came to both loathe and fear the Young Turks.

14. Tarik Tunaya, *Türkiye'de Siyasal Paritler: Mütareke Dönemi, Cilt II* (Istanbul: Hurriyet Vakfı Yayınları, 1989), 263–264.
15. Ahmad *Young Turks*, 99.
16. Tarik Mümtaz Göztepe, *Osmanoğlularının Son Padışahı: Sultan Vahideddin Mütarebe Gayyasinda* (Istanbul: Sevil Yayinevi, 1969), 116; Mahmud Kemal İnal, *Osmanlı Döneminde Son Sadnazamlar* (Istanbul: Milli Eğitim Basımevı, 1969), 2034; Küçük, 'Damad Ferid Paşa', *Türkiye Diyanet Vakfı Islam Ansiklopedesi*, 8 (1993): 436.
17. Between November 1918 and November 1922, the position of grand vizir would change hands a total of six times, with Tevfik Paşa and *Damat* Ferid serving the bulk of the time. While Ferid accumulated the most antagonistic reputation in regards to the National Movement, the shared tenure of Tevfik Paşa and Ali Rıza Paşa (the regular army general who had commanded the Ottoman armies during the Balkan Wars) was marked by a more conciliatory approach towards the *Kuva-yı Milliye*.
18. Erdeha, *Yüzellilikler*, 213; Shaw, *From Empire to Republic*, 167; Tunaya, *Siyasal Partiler, Cilt II*, 474. According to Tarık Tunaya, Sait *Molla* briefly held a position within the Ministry of Justice through 1920.
19. Fethi Tevetoğlu, *Milli Mücadele Yıllarındaki Kuruluşlar* (Istanbul: Türk Tarih Kurumu Basımevi, 1988), 55.
20. Tunaya, *Siyasal Paritler, Cilt II*, 474–5.
21. Shaw, *From Empire to Republic*, 171–3; Tunaya, *Siyasal Paritler, Cilt II*, 382–5.
22. Tunaya, *Siyasal Paritler, Cilt II*, 338.
23. Kamil Erdeha, *Milli Mücadele'de Vilayetler ve Valiler* (Istanbul: Remzi Kitapevi, 1975), 333.
24. Ibid. 335; Hülagü, *Milli Mücadele'de Bursa*, 37–8.
25. Ünal, *Miralay Bekir Sami*, 153. Among the other accusations that Bekir Sami (Günsav) levelled against İsmail Hakkı was allowing French officers to establish themselves in town, allowing an increase in banditry in the area, and appointing anti-Nationalist sympathizers. It was during this time, Bekir went on to explain, that 'Armenian and Rum clubs sprung from every side'.
26. Erdeha, *Vilayetler ve Valiler*, 337; Ünal, *Miralay Bekir Sami*, 153.
27. Çam, *Milli Mücadele*, 28–9; Erdeha, *Yüzellilikler*, 196–7; Yüce, *Kocaeli Tarih ve Rehberi*, 67. As *mutasarrıf* of İzmit, he replaced İbrahim Süreyya (Yiğit), an Abkhazian CUP officer and active organizer in the *Kuva-yı Milliye*. During the post-war period, the Liberty and Understanding Party appointed Mahmut Mahir as governor of Mersin, Afyon-Karahisar (where he organized anti-Nationalist paramilitaries), and Çanakkale (then under Greek occupation). He later fled to Albania after the war and was declared among the traitorous '150's' in 1923 and stripped of his Turkish citizenship.

28. Çam, *Milli Mücadele*, 34.
29. Ibid. 30; PRO/FO 371/3158/90012, 13 Apr. 1919; PRO/FO 371/3158/96965, 8 June 1919; PRO/FO 371/3158/105778, 27 June 1919; Yüce, *Kocaeli Tarih ve Rehberi*, 70. While Turkish observers have mentioned little of Ahmet Anzavur's actions in İzmit in the spring and summer of 1919 (Rifat Yüce mentions only that he was unsuccessful in curbing Albanian and Laz brigands in Değirmendere), British sources referred to Anzavur as 'a competent and efficient officer' (he is noted in a June report for his promise to return abandoned property to Armenian refugees and his attempt to ban the sale of alcohol). However, British officials also declared that Anzavur lacked the basic material and personnel to adequately uphold law and order in the *sancak*.
30. BOA.BEO. nu. 345, 166, lef: 1/1, cited in Mert, 'Anzavur'un İlk Ayaklanmasına', 963; BOA.DH.KMS 53–3/36, 17 Sept. 1919; BOA.DH.ŞFR 103/219, 23 Sept. 1919. *Çerkes* Bekir and his compatriots are specifically accused of patrolling Abkhazian and Circassian villages with armed men and calling for recruits to his force. At one meeting, Bekir denounced the *mutasarrıf* of Bolu, Ali Haydar, and claimed that the sultan supported this move against the *Kuva-yı Milliye*.
31. M. Naim Turfan, *Rise of the Young Turks: Politics, the Military and Ottoman Collapse* (London: I. B. Taurus, 2000), 329–30.
32. Atatürk, *Nutuk-Söylev*, 1611; Berzeg, *Çerkes Göçmenleri*, 42.
33. Among these early North Caucasian Loyalists were (Berzeg) Safer, an Ubih war veteran from Düzce (his father was a notable *şehit*, or martyr, during the Second Balkan War); (Bağ) Kamil, a village notable from the *liva* of Adapazarı; (Bağ) Taluastan, another notable from Adapazarı; and two brothers who had served in the gendarmerie, (Çule) Beslan and İhsan. See Berzeg, *Çerkes Göçmenleri*, 26, 82.
34. TTK Bekir Sami Dosya, ii. 152, 24 Oct. 1919.
35. Atatürk, *Nutuk-Söylev*, 1623; Tevetoğlu, *Milli Mücadele*, 83, 91.
36. Berzeg, *Çerkes Göçmenleri*, 83; Ertürk and Tansu,*İki Devrin Perde Arkası*, 384. Bekir is said to be from either Bandırma, Manyas, or Adapazarı. He had served under Eşref Kuşçubaşı during the retaking of Edirne during the Second Balkan War.
37. Tacettin Akkuş, *Gönen ve Köyleri Tarihçesi* (Istanbul: Ekin Yayıncılık, 2001), 273–82.
38. Çarıklı, *Balıkesir ve Alaşehir Kongreleri*, 19; Özer, *Gönen* (1964), 60.
39. Çarıklı, *Balıkesir ve Alaşehir Kongreleri*, 19–20.
40. Ibid. 20. In addition to receiving no commitment from representatives of this district, Hacim and his party were held up by bandits from the town (who discovered to their disappointment that the official and his entourage had no money to spare).
41. BOA.DH.EUM.AYŞ 9/38, 22 May 1919; BOA.DH.EUM.AYŞ 16/27, 19 July 1919. This conflict between Albanians and the Yetimoğlu family appears to have been a continuation of tensions that had emerged in the First World War. By July 1919, it was reported that the two sides had come to a truce.
42. Çarıklı, *Balıkesir ve Alaşehir Kongreleri*, 77.
43. BOA.DH.EUM.AYŞ 34/24, 4 Mar. 1920.
44. Ibid.

45. PRO/FO 371/4158/124458, 3 Sept. 1919.
46. BOA.DH.EUM.AYŞ 34/24, 4 Mar. 1920; BOA.DH.KMS 55–2/56, 16 Sept. 1919.
47. BOA.DH.EUM.AYŞ 34/24, 4 Mar. 1920; BOA.DH.KMS 55–3/20, 4 Oct. 1919.
48. BOA.DH.EUM.AYŞ 34/24, 4 Mar. 1920.
49. Ibid.; BOA.DH.KMS 55–3/4, 29 Sept. 1919.
50. BOA.DH.KMS 55–3/4, 29 Sept. 1919.
51. BOA.DH.EUM.AYŞ 34/24, 4 Mar. 1920.
52. BOA.DH.KMS 55–3/3, 23 Sept. 1919; BOA.DH.KMS 55–3/7, 29 Sept. 1919.
53. BOA.DH.EUM.AYŞ 34/24, 4 Mar. 1920.
54. Ibid.; DH.EUM.AYŞ 23/102, 8 Oct. 1919. (Gostivarlı) İbrahim was also a member of the Albanian Mutual Aid Society (*Arnavud Teavün Cemiyeti*), an expatriate group based in Istanbul and founded in March 1919. Although devoted primarily to affairs in Albania, the organization also opened up several branches in Anatolia, including in Bursa, Balıkesir, Konya, Aydın, Edirne, Eskişehir, İzmit, and Kütahya. See Tunaya, *Siyasal Paritler, Cilt II*, 452–5.
55. BOA.DH.EUM.AYŞ 34/24, 4 Mar. 1920. More than three-quarters of these losses were the result of stolen animals, totalling 67,000 lira.
56. Ibid.
57. See Erdeha, *Vilayetler ve Valiler*, 342–3; Ünal, *Miralay Bekir Sami*, 185.
58. Ünal, *Miralay Bekir Sami*, 184.
59. Özer, *Gönen* (1964), 144–5.
60. BOA.DH.KMS 55–3/29, 30 Oct. 1919.
61. Ibid.
62. Çarıklı, *Balıkesir ve Alaşehir Kongreleri*, 102; Ünal, *Miralay Bekir Sami*, 197.
63. Çarıklı *Balıkesir ve Alaşehir Kongreleri*, 102.
64. Ünal, *Miralay Bekir Sami*, 197.
65. PRO/FO 371/4158/105778, 27 June 1919. In a conversation with Circassian gendarmes ('very tough customers') from Adapazarı and İzmit, one British officer was told that the men resorted to dishonest practices during the First World War after their officers sold their rations. These men also admitted to being members of the 'CUP's murder gangs' and talked openly about their 'misdeeds'. However, the Circassians defended themselves by saying that they were driven to them.
66. BOA.DH.KMS 55–3/23, 29 Oct. 1919. The reporting official cited an incident of one *Arnavud* Abubekir, a particularly bad official who had served in Kirmasti in 1912, as the historical precedent for changing local recruitment practices.
67. BOA.DH.YUM 11/1/2/84, 7 Dec. 1919.
68. TTK/Bekir Sami Dosya 2, Belge 151, 23 Oct. 1919. Bekir Sami revealed in one memo that some of the men involved in the clashes were unemployed Albanians from Istanbul who were contracted by Karacabey notables. In a move that was reminiscent of CUP policy during the First World War, Bekir Sami stated that he would deport these men to the east as soon as possible.
69. Çantay, *Kara Günler*, 43.
70. Ibid. 42–3.
71. Çarıklı, *Balıkesir ve Alaşehir Kongreleri*, 96; Özdemir, *Milli Mücadele Önderleri*, 291–2; Özer, *Gönen* (1964), 146. *Müftü* Şevket Efendi was born in Gönen and

was educated in the local *rüştiye*. He went on to study at the Abdürrahim Efendi *medrese* in the Fatih section of Istanbul, and later became a teacher and *müftü* in the local *medrese* of Gönen. He was executed by Ahmet Anzavur's forces during April 1920.

72. Çarıklı, *Balıkesir ve Alaşehir Kongreleri*, 97–8.
73. Ibid.
74. *Harb Tarihi Vesikaları Dergisi*, 3, no. 9 (Sept. 1954): doc. 219.
75. Shaw, *From Empire to Republic*, 173–5; Mert, 'Anzavur'un İlk Ayaklanmasına', 905. Kiraz Ahmet Hamdi Paşa was purportedly a member of the Friends of England Society as well as of the *Nigehban* Society. His participation in these organizations, as well as his other anti-Nationalist activities, assured him a place among the '150's'. He died in exile in 1935.
76. Çarıklı, *Balıkesir ve Alaşehir Kongreleri*, 98.
77. Ibid. 100.
78. Bekir Sıtkı Baykal, *Heyet-i Tensiliye Kararları* (Ankara: Türk Tarih Kurumu, 1974), 38.
79. *Harb Tarihi Vesikaları Dergisi*, 3, no. 9 (Sept. 1954): doc. 219; 4, no. 11 (Mar. 1955): doc. 269; Mert, 'Anzavur'un İlk Ayaklanmasına', 896.
80. Mert, 'Anzavur'un İlk Ayaklanmasına', 873–4.
81. Ibid. 905.
82. Sofuoğlu, *Kuva-yı Milliye Döneminde*, 289; *Harb Tarihi Vesikaları Dergisi*, 5, no. 18 (Dec. 1956): doc. 452.
83. Mert, 'Anzavur'un İlk Ayaklanmasına', 904–5; Ünal, *Miralay Bekir Sami*, 211.
84. Mert, 'Anzavur'un İlk Ayaklanmasına', 906. Somewhat curiously, Hacim Muhittin's diary ends abruptly on 29 Oct. and begins again on 1 July 1920. It is not clear whether this was Hacim's own doing or was the result of the editor's decision making.
85. Ibid. 907.
86. Ünal, *Miralay Bekir Sami*, 219.
87. *Harb Tarihi Vesikaları Dergisi*, 4, no. 11 (Mar. 1955): doc. 272.
88. Çarıklı, *Balıkesir ve Alaşehir Kongreleri*, 100; Mert, 'Anzavur'un İlk Ayaklanmasına', 913.
89. Ünal, *Miralay Bekir Sami*, 184, 225, 230.
90. Ibid. 230–1.
91. Türk Cumhuriyet Genelkurmay, *Türk İshkal Harbi*, 21. The official account of the Battle of Demirkapı lists Anzavur's losses as ten dead and forty wounded. *Kuva-yı Milliye* losses are listed as eight dead and seventeen wounded (including two officers).
92. Ibid.; Özalp, *Milli Mücadele*, 70.
93. Türk Cumhuriyet Genelkurmay, *Türk İshkal Harbi*, 21–2; Mert, 'Anzavur'un İlk Ayaklanmasına', 877–83.
94. Berzeg, *Çerkes Göçmenleri*, 58–60.
95. Mert, 'Anzavur'un İlk Ayaklanmasına', 950.
96. Özalp, *Milli Mücadele*, 70–1.
97. BOA.DH.EUM.AYŞ 29/45, 31 Dec. 1919; Atatürk, *Nutuk-Söylev*, 1649–53. The letter is represented as a document in the *Nutuk*.

98. Regarding foreigners, it is my suspicion that Anzavur used the character of the Jewish merchant to highlight the alien (or at least urban, non-provincial) nature of many merchants and traders found within the region. While there were two very small Jewish communities in Bandırma and Biga (only 4 and 103 Jews respectively), the total number of Jews living in the South Marmara was around 8,500. It is likely that the figure of the Jewish merchant ranked in Anzavur's mind as a sort of stock character or villain found in popular storytelling (such as in *Karagöz*).
99. Kamil Su, *Köprülülü Hamdi Bey ve Akbaş Olayları* (Ankara: Kurtuluş Ofset Basımevi, 1984), 124–6.
100. Özdemir, *Milli Mücadele Önderleri*, 115.
101. Güven, *Anzavur İsyan*, 30.
102. Ibid. 31–2.
103. Ibid. 34–9; Su, *Köprülülü Hamdi Bey*, 173–82.
104. Güven, *Anzavur İsyan*, 41.
105. Sofuoğlu, *Kuva-yı Milliye Döneminde*, 285. According to Sofuoğlu, some 200 men armed with rifles and another 1,000 men armed with sticks, axes, and other farm equipment marched on Biga that day.
106. Güven, *Anzavur İsyan* 46–7; Özalp, *Milli Mücadele*, 98; Ünal, *Miralay Bekir Sami*, 279. Bekir Sami states that Kani Bey murdered eleven men.
107. İğdemir, *Biga Ayaklanması*, 10–11.
108. Güven, *Anzavur İsyan*, 48.
109. İğdemir, *Biga Ayaklanması*, 13. İmam Fevzi was born in Asmalı, a village in the county of Çan. His parents were purportedly refugees from the Balkan Mountains region of contemporary Bulgaria. He studied in a *medrese* in the village of Çırpılar (near Bayramiç). While working as a village teacher (*imam*) near Biga, local townspeople bestowed on him the name '*gavur*' because of his blasphemous teachings. The figure of Gavur İmam raises several intriguing issues with regard to Ahmet Anzavur and the social history of the South Marmara. First, little is known about the strength and diversity of religious orders or *tarikat*s in the region, let alone the interpretation of popular Islam in the day-to-day lives of the various native and immigrant groups there. Secondly, few religious figures appear to have played any role in the growth of the anti-Nationalist opposition in the South Marmara. While local pro-Nationalist *imam*s and *müftü*s are often highlighted in Turkish historiography, the Loyalist leadership of the South Marmara appears to be confined to social networks that have no direct religious affiliation (such as among merchant or Circassian family networks). See Özer, *Gönen* (1964), 92.
110. İğdemir, *Biga Ayaklanması*, 18.
111. Türk Cumhuriyet Genelkurmay, *Türk İstikal Harbi*, 37; İğdemir, *Biga Ayaklanması*, 44–53.
112. Türk Cumhuriyet Genelkurmay, *Türk İstikal Harbi*, 38; Ünal, *Miralay Bekir Sami*, 314. According to a secret telegram from Rahmi Bey, a total of 182 men from various Nationalist detachments deserted his column during the retreat from Biga to Gönen.
113. Ünal, *Miralay Bekir Sami*, 325–6.
114. Türk Cumhuriyet Genelkurmay, *Türk İstikal Harbi*, 37; Ünal, *Miralay Bekir Sami*, 331–2.

115. Ünal, *Miralay Bekir Sami*, 331.
116. Türk Cumhuriyet Genelkurmay, *Türk İstikal Harbi*, 39–40; Özalp, *Milli Mücadele*, 109; Özer, *Gönen* (1964), 80.
117. İğdemir, *Biga Ayaklanması*, 61. In an event that occurred a month later, Anzavur purportedly burned down the farm of one (Gönenli) Çerkes Murat Bey, who, in Uluğ's words, had 'gathered up significant forces and attacked Anzavur'.
118. Çerkes Ethem, *Hatıralarım*, 20. Özalp, *Milli Mücadele*, 112; PRO/FO 371/5167/5039, 20 May 1920; Sofuoğlu, *Kuva-yı Milliye Döneminde*, 317–18; Ünal, *Miralay Bekir Sami*, 336.
119. Ünal, *Miralay Bekir Sami*, 298.
120. Ibid. 279.
121. PRO/FO 371/5167/4510, 10 May 1920.
122. Ibid.
123. Türk Cumhuriyet Genelkurmay, *Türk İstikal Harbi*, 41; Özalp, *Milli Mücadele*, 114–15; Sofuoğlu, *Kuva-yı Milliye Döneminde*, 332.
124. Çerkes Ethem, *Hatiralarim*, 21; Türk Cumhuriyet Genelkurmay, *Türk İstikal Harbi*, 41; Sofuoğlu, *Kuva-yı Milliye Döneminde*, 333; Ünal, *Miralay Bekir Sami*, 355.
125. Çerkes Ethem, *Hatiralarim*, 21–4; PRO/FO 371/5167/5255, 25 May 1920; Sofuoğlu, *Kuva-yı Milliye Döneminde*, 333; Ünal, *Miralay Bekir Sami*, 352, 360. One British report stated that Gavur İmam and Şah İsmail both claimed to be sick after their respective defeats and retired home.
126. Sofuoğlu, *Kuva-yı Milliye Döneminde*, 333.
127. PRO/FO 371/5047/4407, 8 May 1920.
128. PRO/FO 371/5167/5353, 27 May 1920. According to one rumour, Nationalist agents offered Ahmet Anzavur a bribe of between £100,000 and £500,000 to cease his activities following his flight from Bandırma. Anzavur reportedly refused the money. See PRO/FO 371/5168/5738, 3 June 1920.
129. Çerkes Ethem, *Hatiralarim*, 24.
130. Güven, *Anzavur İsyan*, 69.
131. PRO/FO 371/5168/5738, 3 June 1920; 371/5168/5861, 4 June 1920.
132. PRO/FO 371/5049/5841, 6 June 1920; 371/5167/5466, 27 May 1920; Ünal, *Miralay Bekir Sami*, 357–8. British intelligence officials talk of continued fighting in Manyas into May and of possible massacres in Biga. In one interesting telegram reprinted in Bekir Sami's autobiographical account of the war, a detachment officer by the name of Emin asked Bekir Sami to arrest Çerkes Ethem as well as several other Nationalist and Loyalist *çete* leaders for acts of banditry. The fact that Ethem was included within this rogues' gallery further suggests that Ethem was held in low esteem by rank and file Nationalists.
133. PRO/FO 371/5169/6904, 22 June 1920.
134. BOA.DH.EUM.AYŞ 39/37, 26 Apr. 1920.
135. Ibid.; Türk Cumhuriyet Genelkurmay, *Türk İstikal Harbi*, 45–6; Sofuoğlu, *Kuva-yı Milliye Döneminde*, 337–8.
136. Berzeg, *Çerkes Göçmenleri*, 22.
137. Türk Cumhuriyet Genelkurmay, *Türk İstikal Harbi*, 48–9; Sofuoğlu, *Kuva-yı Milliye Döneminde*, 344–346; Ünal, *Miralay Bekir Sami*, 365–6. One of the most significant events to emerge was the killing of a Circassian Nationalist officer, (Hendekli) Mahmut Bey, on 22 Apr. 1920.

138. Berzeg, *Çerkes Göçmenleri*, 27.
139. Özel, *Kocaeli ve Sakarya*, 73; Sofuoğlu, *Kuva-yı Milliye Döneminde*, 348.
140. BOA.DH.EUM.AYŞ 39/37, 26 Apr. 1920. Safer Bey led the rebels in the occupation of Adapazarı.
141. Yüce, *Kocaeli Tarih ve Rehberi*, 85.
142. Özel, *Kocaeli ve Sakarya*, 61; Sofuoğlu, *Kuva-yı Milliye Döneminde*, 336.
143. Berzeg, *Çerkes Göçmenleri*, 44.
144. Özel, *Kocaeli ve Sakarya*, 61.
145. Ibid. 61–3; Yüce, *Kocaeli Tarih ve Rehberi*, 85.
146. Türk Cumhuriyet Genelkurmay, *Türk İstikal Harbi*, 44.
147. Ibid. 47.
148. Ibid. 46.
149. Ibid. 49–58; Sofuoğlu, *Kuva-yı Milliye Döneminde*, 348–9.
150. Türk Cumhuriyet Genelkurmay, *Türk İstiklal Harbi*, 60–3; Özel, *Kocaeli ve Sakarya*, 78–83. Ethem is also accused of extorting money and property from notables in his retaking of the province.
151. *Çerkes Ethem, Hatiralarim*, 32–3, 34–5; Türk Cumhuriyet Genelkurmay, *Türk İstikal Harbi*, 64. In Çerkes Ethem's memoirs, he categorically defends his decision to execute Safer and Koç, claiming that they were not true Circassians who were faithful to the fatherland and that their actions deserved the severest of punishments.
152. Türk Cumhuriyet Genelkurmay, *Türk İstikal Harbi*, 66.
153. Ibid. 66–8; Sofuoğlu, *Kuva-yı Milliye Döneminde*, 353.
154. Türk Cumhuriyet Genelkurmay, *Türk İstikal Harbi*, 69; Özel, *Kocaeli ve Sakarya*, 85; Sofuoğlu, *Kuva-yı Milliye Döneminde*, 356.
155. Türk Cumhuriyet Genelkurmay, *Türk İstikal Harbi*, 70, 72; Özel, *Kocaeli ve Sakarya*, 86.
156. BOA.DH.KMS 60–2/10, 19 Apr. 1921; Güven, *Anzavur İsyan*, 97–9.
157. Güven, *Anzavur İsyan*, 112.
158. Ibid.

CHAPTER 5

1. BOA.DH.ŞFR 53/75, 22 May 1915.
2. Ahmet Anzavur may have had some sympathizers in Ezine. According to one Interior Ministry report, three dervishes, one Pomak and two Bosnians, wrote letters of support to Ahmet Anzavur during his second uprising. See BOA.DH.EUM.AYŞ 49/63, 5 Jan. 1921.
3. Mustafa Turan *et al.* (eds.), *Türkiye'de Yunan Fecâyii* (Ankara: Berikan, 2003), 34.
4. Ibid. 228, 229.
5. BOA.DH.EUM.AYŞ 61/64, 19 June 1922. For example, *Arnavud* Aziz, a prominent pro-Nationalist guerrilla, had attacked a village in Ezine that had sought refuge under Greek protection. After Aziz's men killed the *muhtar* and two local Armenians, Greek soldiers arrived and fired upon the Nationalists. After losing Aziz's trail near an 'Arab Turkmen' village, the Greek detachment purportedly exacted retribution on the Turkmen upon the instigation of Armenian villagers who had accompanied the detachment.

Notes to Chapter 5

6. BOA.DH.EUM.AYŞ 52/18, 20 Mar. 1921; BOA.DH.EUM.AYŞ 54/30, 19 June 1921; BOA.DH.EUM.AYŞ 56/92, 16 Oct. 1921; BOA.DH.EUM.AYŞ 57/36, 6 Nov. 1921; BOA.DH.EUM.AYŞ 58/70, 2 Jan. 1922; BOA.DH.EUM.AYŞ 59/98, 14 Mar. 1922; BOA.DH.EUM.AYŞ 61/16, 23 May 1922; BOA.DH.EUM.AYŞ 61/29, 4 June 1922; BOA.DH.EUM.AYŞ 61/43, 11 June 1921; BOA.DH.EUM.AYŞ 61/64, 19 June 1922; BOA.DH.EUM.AYŞ 62/11, 2 July 1922; BOA.DH.EUM.AYŞ 62/5, 25 July 1922. Only four battles occurred in Ezine. Half of these battles between security personnel (either Ottoman, Greek or British forces) concerned unidentified men.
7. BOA.DH.EUM.AYŞ 54/30, 28 June 1921; BOA.DH.EUM.AYŞ 57/36, 6 Nov. 1921; BOA.DH.EUM.AYŞ 57/64, 20 Nov. 1921; BOA.DH.EUM.AYŞ 61/64, 19 June 1922.
8. Özalp, *Milli Mücadele*, 138; Ünal, *Miralay Bekir Sami*, 413.
9. Özalp, *Milli Mücadele*, 134–7; Shaw, *From Empire to Republic*, 1178.
10. PRO/FO 371/5052/7662, 2 July 1920.
11. PRO/FO 371/5052/7668, 3 July 1920; PRO/FO 371/5053/8192, 13 July 1920.
12. Ünal, *Miralay Bekir Sami*, 414–15.
13. PRO/FO 371/5171/12327, 5 Oct. 1920.
14. BOA.DH.EUM.AYŞ 52/1, 2 Apr. 1921.
15. Aydın Ayhan, 'İşgal Yıllarında Balıkesir Çevresi ve Gönen', in Kemal Özer (ed.), *Kurtuluş Savaşında Gönen ve Çevresi* (Ankara: Türk Diyanet Vakfı, 1998), 14–15.
16. ABCFM 16.9.4, vol. 6: Letter from Kate Lamson to Sophie Holt, 14 June 1920; PRO/FO 371/5054/9665, 10 Aug. 1920. Letters received by the British embassy in Istanbul suggest that massacres of Armenians in Adapazarı were widespread.
17. BOA.DH.EUM.AYŞ 51/54, 9 Mar. 1921; BOA.DH.EUM.AYŞ 52/18, 20 Mar. 1921.
18. ABCFM 16.9.3, vol. 49, doc. 4: Letter to Mr Bell from Charles Riggs, 14 July 1921; ABCFM 16.9.3, vol. 51, doc. 74: Letter to Ernest Riggs from Mary Kinney, 11 Oct. 1922; ABCFM 16.9.3, vol. 51, doc. 34: Letter to Enoch Bell from Sophie Holt, 25 Mar. 1920; ABCFM 16.9.4, vol. 6: Letter to Miss Lamson from Sophie Holt, 25 Oct. 1920.
19. Dikranian, Interview; Guleserian, Interview.
20. ABCFM 16.9.3, vol. 49, doc. 134: 'Remarks by Mr. W. S. Woolworth concerning Brousa', 29 Aug. 1920.
21. ABCFM 16.9.3, vol. 51, doc. 238: untitled, 14 May 1923. As the war dragged on, the American missionaries would even take in the children and orphans of Muslim refugees.
22. ABCFM 16.9.3, vol. 51, doc. 73: Letter to Dr Barton from Mary Kinney, 14 May 1921; ABCFM 16.9.3, vol. 49, doc. 133: 'Station Reports and Business Correspondence, Brousa', 18 Mar. 1920.
23. BOA.DH.EUM.AYŞ 48/1, 27 Nov. 1920; BOA.DH.EUM.AYŞ 55/3, 29 July 1921; BOA.DH.İUM 20/32/14/4, 1 Sept. 1922; BOA.DH.İUM 20/32/14/9, 7 Sept. 1922; Turan *et al.* (eds.), *Türkiye'de Yunan Fecâyii*, 56.
24. BOA.DH.EUM.AYŞ 48/1, 21 Nov. 1920.
25. Turan *et al.* (eds.), *Türkiye'de Yunan Fecâyii*, 56.
26. Görgülü, *Yunan İşgalinde Kirmasti*, 52.

27. 'Ermeniler Yunan Ordusuna Gönüllü Yazıyor', *Açık Söz*, 6 Mar. 1922; 'Yunaniler ve Ermeniler: Yunan Hükümeti İzmir Ermenilerini de Askere Alıyor', *Yeni Şark*, 25 Apr. 1922.
28. Yüce, *Kocaeli Tarih ve Rehberi*, 109.
29. BOA.DH.EUM.AYŞ 55/5, 19 July 1921.
30. Sabahattin Özel, *Milli Mücadele'de İzmit-Adapazarı ve Atatürk* (Istanbul: Derin Yayınları, 2005) 202–18; Toynbee, 241–242.
31. Toynbee, *Western Question*, 275. Toynbee traces the beginning of the atrocities to mid-April 1921.
32. BOA.DH.KMS 60–2/20, 19 May 1921; Toynbee, *Western Question*, 310–11.
33. BOA.DH.KMS 60–2/39, 12 June 1921.
34. Toynbee, *Western Question*, 295–6.
35. Ibid. 298. The massacre purportedly happened on 24 June 1921, four days before the Greek ceded the town to the Nationalist army. Rıfat Yüce states in his memoir, however, that ninety people had been killed during the Greek retreat. See Yüce, *Kocaeli Tarih ve Rehberi*, 103–6.
36. ABCFM 16.9.3, vol. 51, doc. 238: untitled, 14 May 1923.
37. BCA 272.12.39.35.5, 10 Jan. 1922.
38. Toynbee, *Western Question*, 293. Toynbee cites other examples of this phenomenon: In Ihsaniya, five people were killed, two were wounded out of a hundred; in Sultaniye one person was killed and one person was wounded out of a population of fifty-six; in Mecidiye two people were missing out of a population of 250.
39. BOA.DH.KMS 60–2/39, 28 June 1921.
40. BCA 272.12.39.34.12, 31 Dec. 1921; BCA 272.12.39.36.2, 12 Jan. 1922.
41. Toynbee, *Western Question*, 294–5. Armudlu was reportedly attacked by Rum from Katırlı, Arnavutköy, Koyru, Gemlik, and Yalova. This group was later implicated in attacks on Karacaali.
42. Ibid. 263.
43. Ibid. 266, 276, 284, 292. Despite the fact that the Greek high command had declared that villages destroyed in the Yalova–Gemlik–İzmit region were havens for Nationalist guerrillas, Toynbee asserts that the plan was organized 'from above' and that the region north of Bursa was targeted for complete destruction. He submits the anecdote that the village of Umerbey, just south of Gemlik, was spared the torch (and was in fact guarded by Greek troops), while all settlements north of Gemlik were completely destroyed.
44. Ibid. 241–2, 297. According to Toynbee, the Greek military pull-out from İzmit and northern Bursa was accompanied by the Christian population's complete desertion of this region.
45. PRO/FO 371/4160/154462, 22 Nov. 1919.
46. Toynbee, *Western Question*, 282.
47. Born in Mendik in Aegean Macedonia, İbrahim Ethem was educated in both Salonika and Istanbul. After graduating from law school in Istanbul, he was appointed to the administration of a village near Sındırgı. After leaving the bureaucracy, he practised law for a time in Balıkesir. After the war, he served as governor for the provinces of Yozgat, Siirt, Ağrı, Balıkesir, and Malatya. He

died in 1950 and was buried in Sındırgı. See Özdemir, *Milli Mücadele Önderleri*, 191–7.
48. İbrahim Ethem Akıncı, *Demirci Akıncıları* (Ankara: Türk Tarih Kurumu, 1989), 112, 114. It was also mandated that no alcohol be consumed by the troops.
49. Ibid. 113, 119.
50. Ibid. 114–15.
51. Ibid. 119, 125, 129, 133.
52. Ibid. 114, 119.
53. Ibid. 129.
54. Ibid. 119, 133, 163, 173, 177, 180.
55. Ibid. 133.
56. Ibid. 173.
57. BOA.DH.KMS 60–3/36, 31 Dec. 1921.
58. Akıncı, *Demirci Akıncıları*, 34.
59. BOA.DH.EUM.AYŞ 54/54, 27 June 1921.
60. BOA.DH.EUM.AYŞ 58/38, 18 Dec. 1921.
61. BOA.DH.İUM 20/32//14/4, 1 Sept. 1922.
62. BOA.DH.EUM.AYŞ 57/64, 20 Nov. 1921. This incident ironically preceded Parti Pehlivan's own attack on Mecidiye by three days: Akıncı, *Demirci Akıncıları*, 127.
63. BOA.DH.EUM.AYŞ 57/64, 20 Nov. 1921; Akıncı, *Demirci Akıncıları*, 127.
64. Akıncı, *Demirci Akıncıları*, 127, 144–145.
65. The *muhtar* and *imam* of Mecidiye sent a telegram to İbrahim Ethem complaining of the incident. It stated pointedly: 'We did not understand what happened. Are they infidels [*gavur*]? Are they Muslims? A number of people came and robbed our village. They went in the direction of Sarnıç village and spoke the Çetmi language. Please come!' İbrahim Ethem himself called the Çetmi an intelligent (*zeki*) but devilish or crafty (*şeytan olmak*) people. See ibid. 127, 289.
66. BOA.DH.EUM.AYŞ 56/92, 16 Oct. 1921; BOA.DH.EUM.AYŞ 57/10, 23 Oct. 1921; BOA.DH.EUM.AYŞ 58/34, 16 Dec. 1921.
67. BOA.DH.EUM.AYŞ 56/92, 16 Oct. 1921.
68. Akıncı, *Demirci Akıncıları*, 185.
69. Ibid. 372, 393.
70. Ibid. 393.
71. BOA.DH.EUM.AYŞ 52/9, 14 Mar. 1921; BOA.DH.EUM.AYŞ 54/30, 19 June 1921; BOA.DH.EUM.AYŞ 55/65, 23 July 1921; BOA.DH.EUM.AYŞ 57/36, 6 Nov. 1921; BOA.DH.EUM.AYŞ 57/64, 20 Nov. 1921; BOA.DH.EUM.AYŞ 57/80, 27 Nov. 1921; BOA.DH.EUM.AYŞ 58/38, 18 Dec. 1921; BOA.DH.EUM.AYŞ 59/11, 14 Feb. 1922.
72. BOA.DH.EUM.AYŞ 54/74, 3 July 1921; BOA.DH.EUM.AYŞ 58/53, 27 Nov. 1921.
73. BOA.DH.EUM.AYŞ 57/10, 23 Oct. 1921; BOA.DH.EUM.AYŞ 57/36, 6 Nov. 1921; BOA.DH.EUM.AYŞ 59/11, 4 Feb. 1922.
74. BOA.DH.EUM.AYŞ 55/10, 20 July 1921.
75. BOA.DH.EUM.AYŞ 50/42, 30 Jan. 1921. Kadir's gang was also accused of perpetrating several thefts around Biga, and, like their Nationalist rivals, his men were also subject to arrest. See BOA.DH.EUM.AYŞ 54/54, 27 June 1921.

Notes to Chapter 5

76. Ismail Aydın Hoşgür, *Kurtuluş Savaşında Biga* (Biga: Cahit Renda Matbaası, 1970), 121–2.
77. BOA.DH.EUM.AYŞ 54/30, 19 June 1921; BOA.DH.EUM.AYŞ 57/10, 23 Oct. 1921; BOA.DH.EUM.AYŞ 62/11, 2 July 1922.
78. BOA.DH.EUM.AYŞ 55/65, 21 Aug. 1921.
79. Ünal, *Çerkeslerin Rolü*, 286–8.
80. PRO/FO 371/5054/9302, 3 Aug. 1919.
81. Ibid.
82. BOA.DH.İUM 20/28//14/77, 13 Aug. 1921.
83. PRO/FO 371/5054/9302, 3 Aug. 1919. İbrahim Ethem reports a similar situation among Circassians in Bigadiç, where in one village rich notables compelled the townspeople to dig trenches and stand guard in the case of a Circassian or *Kuva-yı Miliye* attack. Ethem explained to the villagers that the *Kuva-yı Milliye* were neither 'Circassians or bandits'. See Akıncı, *Demirci Akıncıları*, 125.
84. Akıncı, *Demirci Akıncıları*, 217; PRO/FO 371/5054/9302, 3 Aug. 1919.
85. According to one British report prepared in May 1922, as many as 60,000 native Rum, Armenians, and Circassians served under arms in the Greek occupation. Of this number, it is estimated that anywhere between 6,000 and 10,000 were Circassians drawn from areas under Greek occupation. See PRO/WO 158/485/2489, 22 May 1922.
86. Akıncı, *Demirci Akıncıları*, 216–17.
87. Ibid. 217.
88. Ibid. 285.
89. BOA.DH.İUM 19/18/1/36, 15 Nov. 1921.
90. BOA.DH.KMS 60–2/34, 12 June 1921; BOA.DH.KMS 60–2/39, 12 June 1921.
91. Toynbee, *Western Question*, 282.
92. Özel, *İzmit-Adapazarı*, 77–85.
93. BOA.DH.KMS 60–1/22, 4 Dec. 1920; BOA.DH.KMS 60–1/23, 6 Dec. 1920.
94. BOA.DH.KMS 60–2/39, 2 July 1921.
95. Berzeg, *Çerkes Göçmenleri*, 51.
96. Özel, *İzmit-Adapazarı*, 107.
97. BOA.DH.KMS 60–2/16, 28 Apr. 1921.
98. 'Adapazarı Kaymakamın İdame Mahkumiyyet', *İkdam*, 9 Dec. 1921.
99. PRO/FO 371/6580/13914, 13 Dec. 1921.
100. Görgülü, *Yunan İşgalinde Kirmasti*, 52.
101. In the book *Greek Calamities in Hüdavendigar*, e.g., Ottoman officials implicate Davut in the murder of one *ağa* in the village of Balyaz in the county of Bursa. See Canip Bey, *Bürsa'da İşgal Gülüğü (Bursa Vilayetinde Yunan Fecayii)* (Istanbul: Düşünce Kitabevi Yayınları, 2004), 87.
102. Despite the frequent references to *Çerkes* Davut in the memoirs and secondary histories of the Greek occupation, Ottoman gendarmerie reports from Hüdavendigar make no reference to his activities during the year 1921.
103. Ethem, *Hatıralarım*, 133.
104. See Recep Albayrak, *Ethem'in Sürgün Yılları ve Simav Olayları, 1919–1948* (Ankara: Berikan Yayınları, 2004); Ergün Hiçyılmaz, *Gizli Belgelerle Çerkes Ethem* (Istanbul: Varlık Yayınları, 1993); Cemal Kutay, *Çerkez Ethem Tamamlanmış Dosya* (Istanbul:

Özgür Yayınları, 2004); Zeki Sarıhan, *Çerkez Ethem'in İhaneti* (Istanbul: Kaynak Yayınları, 1984); Cemal Sener, *Çerkes Ethem Olayı* (Istanbul: Okan Yayınları, 1984).
105. Çerkes Ethem, *Hatiralarım*, 92.
106. Akıncı, *Demerci Akıncıları*, 32–3.
107. BOA.DH.İUM 20/28/14/77, 13 Aug. 1921. In reporting on the state of (Anzavuroğlu) Kadir's activities in Manyas, the head of the local gendarmenie had this to say about Circassians in general: 'Any place that they were accepted into our kind homeland, these refugee Circassians would threaten, "Give over the cash box otherwise I will kill you," before attacking a house and stealing.' The gendarme's words open up another aspect that remains very murky: the feelings of provincial citizens about how the settlement of Circassian immigrants (or Albanians or any other group) changed their lives. Considering the radical changes that must have occurred in the social structure of such communities as Manyas, the gendarme's opinion must have been widespread.
108. BOA.DH.KMS 60–3/26, 31 Dec. 1921. This document suggests that the organization and intentions of the Near Eastern Circassian Association were known three weeks before the commencement of the meeting.
109. Tunaya, *Siyasal Partiler, Cilt II*, 589–91.
110. Ibid. 591.
111. Ibid. 590–1.
112. Edward Said talks about this contrast between the ancient and the modern in some detail in his seminal work, *Orientalism*. With regard to Arabs, colonial Egypt took on particular significance as the seat of great learning and cultural achievement. Yet with the onset of British rule, Egypt was transformed into a showplace where 'a modern power would naturally demonstrate its strength and justify history'. With that, the Arab historical claim to Egypt would be 'annexed' to Europe. See Edward Said, *Orientalism* (New York: Vintage Books, 1994), 84–5.
113. 'President Woodrow Wilson's Fourteen Points', in *The World War I Document Archive*; http://www.lib.byu.edu/~rdh/wwi/1918/14points.html.
114. Tunaya, *Siyasal Partiler, Cilt II*, 215–22.
115. PRO/FO 371/6580/12582, 15 Nov. 1921.
116. Görgülü, *Yunan İşgalinde Kirmasti*, 50.
117. Avagyan, *Osmanlı İmparatorluğu*, 211.
118. Görgülü, *Yunan İşgalinde Kirmasti*, 51; Akıncı, *Demerci Akıncıları*, 250. The Kirmasti chapter appeared to have been opened in May 1922.
119. PRO/FO 371/5171/13982, 16 Oct. 1920.
120. PRO/FO 371/6580/13914, 13 Dec. 1921.
121. Ibid.
122. 'Çerkesler'in Dünkü İctimai', *Vakit*, 29 Nov. 1921.
123. 'Çerkeslerle Türkler arasında Münasebet', *İkdam*, 29 Nov. 1921; 'Türkler ve Çerkesler Kütle ve Ahdedarlar', *Vakit*, 30 Nov. 1921.
124. 'Düzce Çerkesleri' and 'Aziziyeli Çerkesler', *Hakimiyet-i Milliye*, 12 Dec. 1921.
125. 'Düzce Çerkesleri', *Hakimiyet-i Milliye*, 12 Dec. 1921; 'Türkler ve Çerkesler Kütle ve Ahdedarlar', *Vakit*, 30 Nov. 1921.
126. Görgülü, *Yunan İşgalinde Kirmasti*, 74.
127. 'Arnavudlar'ın Nazar Dıkkatı', *İkdam*, 13 Oct. 1921.

128. Tunaya, *Siyasal Partiler, Cilt II*, 445. While it appears that some of the founding members of *Arnavud Teavün Cemiyeti* were from Macedonia and Kosova (such as (Kalkendelenli) Hasan Hüseyin and (Piriştineli) Hüseyin Fuat), the contingent from Albania proper also seemed quite large. In a memo of 1919, the society offered to send a six-man delegation to the peace conference in Versailles. Comprising Muslims, Catholics, and Orthodox Christians, the six notables were almost uniformly from Albania (although one delegate, (Dibralı) Fuad Bey, owned large tracts of land in both Albania and Macedonia). British officials in London refused to entertain the idea, stating that they would accept the views only of natives from Albania, not 'Ottomanized Stambuli Albanians'. See PRO/FO 608/97/27/1062, 31 Jan. 1919.
129. ABCFM 16.9.3, vol. 51, doc. 67: Report by Jeanie Jillson, 20 Sept. 1922.
130. 'İtalyan Mıntakası', *Açık Söz*, 24 Oct. 1922.
131. ABCFM 16.9.3, vol. 51, doc. 238: untitled, 14 May 1923.

CHAPTER 6

1. After the retaking of Izmir, Nationalist forces pressed on into the environs of Çanakkale, which British forces had occupied as a 'neutral zone' since the end of the war. After gaining Çanakkale on 23 Sept. 1922 (at the risk of restarting hostilities with Great Britain), the Nationalists asserted their control over eastern Thrace on 31 Oct. 1922. See Patrick Kinross, *Atatürk: Rebirth of a Nation* (London: Phoenix Giant, 1995), 330–9.
2. The most noted retreat in this National Pact was the ceding of the former Ottoman *vilayet* of Mosul to Iraq in 1925. Although Atatürk would later forswear any claim to the province, İsmet İnönü argued in 1923 that Mosul was truly Turkish territory and ludicrously claimed that the Kurds were a Turkic-speaking nation akin to their neighbours in Anatolia. See *Lausanne Conference on Near Eastern Affairs, 1922–1923: Records of Proceedings and Draft Terms of Peace* (London: His Majesty's Stationery Office, 1923), 342–5.
3. Mango, *Atatürk*, 357.
4. Zürcher, *Unionist Factor*, 133–4.
5. Ibid. 140.
6. Ibid. 145–54.
7. Ibid. 153–7.
8. Akıncı, *Demerci Akıncıları*, 360–2.
9. Zülfikar Ali Aydın, *İkinci Susurluk: Bir Kasaba Cinneti* (Istanbul: Metis Yayınevi, 2002), 50.
10. Mehmed Fetgerey Şoenu, *Çerkes Mes'elesi* (Istanbul: Bedir Yayınevi, 1993), 62. It appears that Mehmet Ali accompanied the group of men heading towards Manyas.
11. Ibid. 62–3.
12. Ibid. 64.
13. Güven, *Anzavur İsyan*, 111.
14. Ibid.
15. BCA 30.10.105.688.9, 12 May 1923; Güven, *Anzavur İsyan*, 112; Şoenu, *Çerkes Mes'elesi*, 64.

16. PRO/FO 371/9170/9255, 17 Sept. 1923. On 11 Aug. 1923, thirty-two Circassians reportedly landed off the coast of Söke. As an effort organized by Eşref Kuşçubaşı, Çerkes Ethem, and Çerkes Reşit, the band supposedly operated under the auspices of the Revolutionary Committee of Turkey based in Midilli. Two other attacks off the coast of Söke and Dikili occurred in December 1923, but it is unclear whether this was at all the work of exiled North Caucasians. See PRO/FO 371/9170/12134, 27 Dec. 1923; PRO/FO 371/9170/12263, 31 Dec. 1923.
17. Cilasun, *Bâki İlk Selam*, 212–13.
18. Ibid. 213.
19. Rıza Nur, *Hayat ve Hatıratım, Cilt III* (Istanbul: AtındağYayınevi, 1968), 952.
20. PRO/WO 158/485/2489, 22 May 1922. The British War Office painted an overwhelmingly bleak scenario of a Greek defeat that spring. Considering the fact the Greeks had failed that winter to crush the Kemalist formation in inner Anatolia, British planners suggested to their superiors that the Greeks would have no other choice but to pull out eventually. The exodus of civilians, in consequence of this withdrawal, was projected to be enormous. Analysts suggest that anywhere between 600,000 and 700,000, both Muslim and Christian, natives living in the Greek occupied zone would be expected to flee their homes with the retreating Greek forces. In the South Marmara, British analysts gave the following anticipated number of refugees: Hüdavendigar (Bursa): 136,000; Karesi (Balıkesir): 120,000; Kale-i Sultaniye (Çanakkale): 14,000. It is still not entirely known how many civilians fled between the Greek evacuation of September 1922 and the initiation of the population exchange in 1923.
21. PRO/FO 371/7919/14515, 12 Dec. 1922.
22. Ibid.
23. PRO/FO 371/7915/13155, 24 Nov. 1922.
24. PRO/FO 371/9120/611, 13 Jan. 1923.
25. PRO/FO 371/7919/14515, 12 Dec. 1922. It is not known what became of the option of sending İbrahim Hakkı and the other Circassians to Cyprus.
26. PRO/FO 371/7918/13942, 12 Dec. 1922.
27. PRO/FO 371/9120/34, 22 Dec. 1922.
28. PRO/FO 371/9120/2953, 19 Mar. 1923.
29. PRO/FO 371/7919/14515, 12 Dec. 1922.
30. PRO/FO 371/9120/2953, 19 Mar. 1923.
31. PRO/FO 371/9120/3391, 23 Mar. 1923.
32. PRO/FO 371/7915/13155, 24 Nov. 1922; PRO/FO 371/9120/2953, 19 Mar. 1923.
33. Cilasun, *Bâki İlk Selam*, 173–4.
34. BCA 30.10.0.0.105.688.7, 24 Apr. 1923. One statement transcribed by members of the Turkish Interior Ministry read as follows:

   A) The revolutionary commanders will hold all of those responsible if they give taxes to the Ankara government, accept soldiers, promote disorder in the name of the Ankara government or gather soldiers.

   B) Any person found working [with] or assisting [forces] against the Revolutionary Committee will be immediately executed.

C) It will be necessary for the members of the Revolutionary Committee of Anatolia to meddle and attack the people's property, life and freedom in accordance with today's situation.

35. PRO/FO 371/9101/4031, 20 Apr. 1923. The admonition of the British Foreign Office reads, 'Your proposed action is approved. If information is compromised, please make clear that it is against the letter of the Mudanya convention.'
36. Cilasun, *Bâki İlk Selam*, 173, 213.
37. The memoirs recorded by Philip Stoddard fail to mention any of Eşref's activities after the War of Independence. Stoddard falsely states that Eşref was accused of being among the '150's' after coming back from his exile in Malta (which is not possible, since there is a three-year gap between the two events). It has been assumed that Eşref was a devoted follower of Enver Paşa and left the National Movement in order to support Enver's return to Anatolia. This does seem plausible, since his brother Haci Sami was one of Enver's lieutenants in Central Asia. After Haci Sami came to Greece following Enver's death in Tajikistan, the two were instrumental in the organization of one of the assassination attempts against Mustafa Kemal. What is not clear is Eşref's connection with Çerkes Ethem, since the two seemed to have had little contact during the War of Independence (although Eşref was a long-time friend of Ethem's brother Reşit). One odd Nationalist dispatch from 1921, for example, complains that Eşref was released on bail because of a lack of evidence (along with Ethem and *Abaza* Sait, one of the founders of the Near Eastern Circassian Society!). This document suggests that there was a great deal more to the Ethem/Eşref split with the Nationalist Movement than meets the eye (possibly a much earlier connection between İbrahim Hakkı's group, Eşref Kuşçubaşı, and Çerkes Ethem). See BCA 30.18.01.01.03.29.16, 5 July 1921; Erdeha, *Yüzellikliler*, 105–9; Stoddard, 'Ottoman Government', 171–2.
38. Cilasun, *Bâki İlk Selam*, 77.
39. Ibid. 212.
40. BCA 30.10.0.0.107.699.4, 7 May 1923.
41. BCA 30.10.0.0.253.708.52, 15 June 1923. In this dispatch, local Turkish authorities were actively monitoring the encampment of Circassian militants across the sea from the island of Sisam.
42. BCA 30.10.0.0.64.427.7, 26 July 1925; PRO/FO 371/7919/14515, 12 Dec. 1922. İbrahim Hakkı reckoned that 3,000 Circassian cavalrymen were stationed in Salonika and Drama.
43. Şoenu, *Çerkes Mes'elesi*, 70.
44. Ibid. 71.
45. Ibid. 72. The villages and dates of deportation are as follows. Gönen *Kaza*: Üçpınar, 28 May 1923; Muratlar, 5 June 1923; Sızı, 9 June 1923; Keçidere, 13 June 1923; Keçeler, 16 June 1923. Manyas *Kaza*: Kızıl kilise, 7 June 1923; Yeniköy, 7 June 1923; Dömye, 7 June 1923; Ilıca, 11 June 1923; Karaçalılık, 13 June 1923; Bolcaağaç, 13 June 1923; Değirmenboğazı, 21 June 1923; Hacı Osman, 21 June 1923.
46. Ibid. 74. This figure is based on the 755 Circassian households that Şoenu reports in these villages, allotting five members per household.

47. Şoenu, *Çerkes Mes'elesi*, 76–7. Şoenu does not provide exact dates for these deportations, but they must have occurred sometime between the end of the first round of deportations (ending 21 June 1923) and publication of his pamphlet in November 1923. In addition to the names and population statistics, Şoenu also notes whether or not the village was 'mixed' or 'entirely' North Caucasian. The names of these villages and population characters are: In Manyas *Kaza*: Darıca (mixed); Aşaklar (mixed); Hacı Yakup (completely Circassian); Süleymanlı (mixed); Doruk (mixed); Çakırca (mixed); Elkese (mixed); Çavuşköyü (mixed); Kızık (mixed); Kulak (mixed); Eski Manyas (mixed); Tatar Köyü (mixed); Haydar (mixed); Eşen (mixed); Ergili (mixed); Sallur (mixed); Hamamlı (mixed); Muradiye (mixed); Geyikler (mixed). In Gönen *Kaza*: Karalar Çiftliği (completely Circassian); Tuzakça (mixed); Karaağaç Alan (mixed); Hacı Menteş (mixed); Çalıoba (mixed); Ayvalıdere (completely Circassian); Obaköy (mixed); Kumköy (completely Circassian); Ayvacık (mixed); Bayramiç (mixed); Balcı (mixed).
48. Ibid. 74.
49. Ibid. 73, 74, 76.
50. Ibid. 74, 75. The Circassians were forced to sell their property and animals, in Mehmet Şoenu's words, 'for the price of a glass of water'. Şoenu then goes on to describe the area around Manyas and Gönen as a region renowned for the growing of vegetables and tobacco, and the raising of horses.
51. BCA 272.11.18.86.9, 11 June 1923.
52. Hilmi Ziya Ülken, 'Gönen Bölgesi Monografisi', *Sosyoloji Dergisi*, 10–11 (1955–6): 142.
53. İzzet Aydemir, in a piece he wrote for the Kuzey Kafkas Derneği website, states that Rauf Orbay and others had intervened on behalf of the Circassians and had allowed them to return. Yet Rauf Orbay makes no statement as to this fact in any of the writings or memoirs attributed to him. Tacettin Akkuş does confirm that many of the Circassians from Gönen were allowed to return. See Akkuş, *Gönen, passim*; Aydemir, *Muhaceretteki*, 17; İzzet Aydemir, 'Gönen-Manyas Çerkeslerinin Sürgünü', *Nart*, no. 15 (Nov. 1999); <http://www.kafkasfederasyonu.org/v1/index.php?goster=nart&id=201>.
54. Ülken, 'Gönen Bölgesi Monografisi', 142. Ülken tells of this very situation in the village of Keçidere (now called Dereköy), which was then rebuilt by the Circassians who had returned after living in exile for two years. By 1955, the village became further repopulated by immigrants from the Balkans.
55. Aydemir, *Muhaceretteki*, 17.
56. Şoenu, *Çerkes Mes'elesi*, 60.
57. Ibid. 67.
58. Ibid. 60, 65. Şoenu seems to suggest here that Circassians were no more and no less rebellious than 'real Turks'. For this reason, the Circassians of Gönen and Manyas did not deserve to be singled out and sentenced to a life in exile. What is left unspoken is that exile (*tehcir*) was an extreme sentence, a sentence reserved for groups who had committed egregious acts of treason. In short, Circassians could not be compared to Greeks and Armenians.
59. Ibid. 69.
60. Ibid. 53, 73.
61. Ibid. 53.

62. Ibid. 73.
63. Ibid. 56.
64. Erdeha, *Yüzellilikler*, 17–21.
65. Interestingly, the sultan himself was left off the list. To this day, debate rages as to whether Sultan Vahdeddin was 'a traitor to the state'.
66. Among these former administrators was the former *kaymakam* of Adapazarı, (Mann) Mustafa Namık, who in the proceedings was called *Hain* Mustafa (Mustafa the Traitor). See İlhami Soysal, *150'liker* (Istanbul: Gür Yayınları, 1985), 48.
67. Erdeha, *Yüzellilikler*, 227. The four other men who were included among Ethem's retainers are Küçük Ethem (former Akhisar *Kaymakam*), (Düzceli) Mehmet Oğlu Sami, (Burhaniyeli) Halil İbrahim, and (Demirkapılı) Hacı Ahmet.
68. Soysal, *150'liker*, 111.
69. The individuals who were included in the list were Adapazarı representative, (Bağ) Talustan Bey; Hendek representative, (Bağ) Osman Bey; İzmit representative, (Çule) İbrahim Bey; Bandırma representative, (Brau) Sait Bey; Bandırma representative, (Berzek) Tahir Bey; Aydın representative, (Kavaca) Hüseyin Bey; Kandıra and Karasu representative, (Maan) Şiirin Bey; Düzce representative, (Hamete) Ahmet Bey; Düzce representative, (Maan) Ali Bey; Bursa representative, Harunelreşit Efendi; Eskişehir representative, (Kamil) Bey (not clear); Biga representative, (Ancuk) İsa Nuri Bey; İzmit representative, (Çiyo) Kazım Bey; Gönen representative, (Lampez) Yakup Efendi; Gönen representative, Hafız Sait Efendi; Kütahya representative, (Açofit) Sami Bey; Balıkesir representative, (Bazadoğ) Sait Bey; and Manisa representative, (Pasavv) *Çerkes* Reşit Bey (included among *Çerkes* Ethem's retinue).

The names left off the list were Bilecik representative, (Bağ) Rifat Bey; Yalova–Karamürsel representative, (Ancuk) Yakup Bey; Geyve representative, (Çule) Arslan Bey; Erdek representative, (Şahabel) Hasan Bey; and Bandırma representative, (Neçoku) Hasan Bey.
70. Erdeha, *Yüzellilikler*, 229–30. The names of the men are Gönen (Tuzakçı): Yusuf oğlu Remzi; Gönen (Bayramiç): Hacı Kasım Oğlu Zühtü; Gönen (Balcı): Kocagözün Osman oğlu Şakir; Gönen (Muratlar): Koç Mehmet oğlu Koç Ali; Gönen (Ayvacık): Mehmet oğlu Aziz; Gönen (Keçeler): Bağcılı Ahmet oğlu Osman; Gönen (Muratlar): Hüseyin oğlu Kazım; Gönen (Balcı): Bekir oğlu Arap Mahmut; Gönen (Rüstem): *Gardiyan* Yusuf; Gönen (Balcı): Ömer oğlu Eyüp; Gönen (Keçeler): Talustan oğlu İbrahim Çavuş; Gönen (Balcı): Topallı Şerif oğlu İbrahim; Gönen (Keçeler): Topal Ömer oğlu İdris; Manyas (Bolcaağaç): Kurhoğlu İsmail; Gönen (Keçeler): *Muhtar* Hacı oğlu İshak; Manyas (Kızlık): Ali Bey oğlu Sabit; Gönen (Balcı): Veli oğlu Selim; Gönen (Çerkez Mahallesi): *Makinacı* Mehmet oğlu Osman; Manyas (Değirmenboğazı): Kadir oğlu Kamil; Gönen (Keçidere): Hüseyin oğlu Galip; Manyas (Hacıyakup): Çerkez Sait oğlu Salih; Manyas (Hacıyakup): *Maktul* Şevket's brother İsmail; Gönen (Keçeler): Abdullah oğlu Deli Kasım; Gönen (Çerkez Mahallesi): Hasan Onbaşı oğlu Kemal; Manyas (Değirmenboğazı): Kadir oğlu Kamil's brother Kazım Efe; Gönen (Kızlık): Pallaç oğlu Kemal; and Gönen (Keçeler): Tuğ oğlu Mehmet.
71. Ibid. 68–9. Many of these individuals were imprisoned at the time in Balıkesir.

72. For a concise list of the present-day villages of Gönen and their ethnic make-up, see Akkuş, *Gönen*, 47–9.
73. BCA 272.12.52.126.24, 7 June 1927. According to this digest of news from Balıkesir, it was reported that Circassians from the village of Hafız Hüseyin, near the town of Gönen, had sued a group of refugees from Greece for the return of their property and had won. Hafız Hüseyin interestingly was not among the villages targeted in the 1923 deportations.
74. Soner Çagaptay, 'Crafting the Turkish Nation: Kemalism and Turkish Nationalism in the 1930s' (Ph.D. diss., Yale University, 2003), 221.
75. PRO/FO 371/9170/11493, 3 Dec. 1923. The fate of the Ottoman Revolutionary Committee is a curious one. According to British agents, the Committee remained active and expanded its influence among a wide variety of anti-Kemalist dissidents. Among these dissidents were former Loyalists from Istanbul, as well as erstwhile supporters of the National Movement (including, e.g., Rahmi (Arslan), the wartime governor of Izmir). The group claimed to have maintained contact with tens of thousands of armed anti-Kemalists in towns and villages as far away as Trabzon, Sivas, Aydın, and Kurdistan. Although the Greek government had declared that it had dispersed the Circassian camps responsible for attacks on the Turkish mainland sometime before September of 1923, Athens remained attentive in its support of the Committee and other anti-Kemalist cabals alike. See also PRO/FO 371/9170/9290, 18 Sept. 1923.
76. Berzeg, *Çerkes Göçmenleri*, 91.
77. Çagaptay, 'Crafting the Turkish Nation', 218–19. This report from 1935 stated that Ethem was aided by his younger brother, Emin.
78. Ibid. 220. According to documents Çagaptay obtained from the Interior Ministry, groups of Circassian labourers from Kütahya were placed under surveillance while working on the railroads in Afyon and Antalya.
79. Zürcher, 'Young Turks, Ottoman Muslims and Turkish Nationalists', in Karpat (ed.), *Ottoman Past*, 174.
80. Avagyan, *Osmanlı Imparatorluğu*, 256.
81. Çagaptay, 'Crafting the Turkish Nation', 190.
82. Ibid. 185.
83. Ibid. 190.
84. *Human Research Affairs Foundation* (1956), 429, 431. Soviet statistics state that 56,957 Abkhazians, 139,925 Kabardians (Adige), and 65,270 other Circassians still resided in the Caucasus in 1926. Those numbers had increased to 58,969, 164,106, and 87,973 respectively by 1939. Many thanks to John Colarusso for help on this particular point.
85. See Terry Martin, *Affirmative Action Empire: Nations and Nationalism in the Soviet Union, 1923–1939* (Ithaca, NY: Cornell University Press, 2001).
86. BCA 272.12.42.51.8, 7 July 1924. According to these statistics compiled in 1924, more than 8,000 refugees arrived from Armenia between 1921 and 1922. See Suny, *Looking toward Ararat*, 130.
87. Çagaptay, 'Crafting the Turkish Nation', 233. In 1935, Albanian Bektaşis were rumoured to have hatched a plot to kill Mustafa Kemal. Yet this possibility may have

been interpreted as a conspiracy linked to the ban placed upon Islamic brotherhoods (*tarikats*).
88. BCA 30.18.11.7.27.4, 5 Aug. 1923. It is possible that this anecdote is related to a story related by Noel Malcolm. According to Malcolm, a member of Prishtina's *ulema* led a group of 2,000 out of Kosova and found himself stranded in Sofia. The *hoca* was hired by the Yugoslav government to lead his flock of Albanians out of Prishtina and take them to Anatolia in order to be closer to the head of their dervish order (*baba*). They were purportedly assured that 'great mounds of pilaf' awaited them upon their arrival. See Malcolm, 286–7.
89. BCA 30.18.11.7.27.4, 5 Aug. 1923. There is not a record of this decision made by the Grand Turkish National Assembly at this early date.
90. Shaw, *From Empire to Republic*, 216–20.
91. BCA 272.11.16.66.1, 4 Aug. 1923. Beginning that December, Ankara was already establishing governmental commissions for the population exchange with Greece. See Önür Yıldırım, 'Diplomats and Refugees: Mapping the Turco-GreekExchange of Populations, 1922–1934' (Ph.D. diss., Princeton University, 2002), 238–9.
92. BCA 272.11.16.66.1, 4 Aug. 1923.
93. Ibid. The *vali* of Trabzon stated that he had not yet officially settled any Albanians in the province. Officials in Osmaniye stated that the families that came nine years earlier had not yet been settled and that they should be placed in villages outside town. Yet they requested that the Albanians not be given any property formerly held by Armenians or Greeks.
94. BCA 272.11.16.66.1, 4 Aug. 1923.
95. BCA 272.12.43.58.20, 29 Nov. 1924.
96. No other statistical data exist in regards to the number of Albanians living in Sinop (or Canık *sancak* during the late Ottoman period). It is known, however, that in 1925, a group of Albanians were settled in Sinop (see BCA 272.12.44.59.15, 31 Mar. 1925). Much more is known about the neighbouring district of Samsun. During the Turkish War of Independence, Ottoman security documents speak of the presence of Albanian (as well as North Caucasian) paramilitaries in the region around Bafra, between Samsun and Sinop, in 1919. Andrews states that the village of Koşuköy, located outside Bafra, continues to be inhabited by Albanians. The 1965 Turkish census also reports that 650 Albanians were living in the town of Samsun. See Andrews, *Ethnic Groups* 132, 362; BOA.DH.EUM.AYŞ 7/102, 9 May 1919.
97. BCA 272.11.16.66.1, 4 Aug. 1923. The statistics from İzmit/Adapazarı are puzzling in general. According to the table provided by the *mutasarrıf* of Kocaeli, the number of Bosnians vastly outweighed the number of Albanians (6,687 Bosnians in Adapazarı alone). While this is possible, it appears highly dubious that the number of Albanians in places such as İzmit, Adapazarı, Karamürsel, and Yalova were that low. If the Albanians of Karamürsel found themselves among the tens of thousands of refugees from the Greek occupation, where did they go afterwards?
98. BCA 272.11.16.66.1, 4 Aug. 1923. While giving the names of these individuals, who comprised a total of forty families, the *vali* gave no indication of exactly where they would be deported to.

99. PRO/WO 158/485/2489, 22 May 1922. Interestingly, British officials also took an interest in the number and ethnic nature of so-called 'non-Turkish' Muslims in the Greek occupied zone shortly before the pull-out of September 1922. In anticipation of the great refugee crisis to come, British analysts sent to their superiors several tables detailing the ethnic make-up of various counties located along the immediate interior of the Aegean Sea. A total of 2,951 Albanians, for example, were supposed to be living in the Sevres Treaty Zone (presumably in the portion allotted to the Kingdom of Greece). Precisely where they received this information is unclear. The rough breakdown of the Aegean's Albanian population, exclusive of Izmir, Buca, and other coastal centres, is as follows: Çeşme: 5; Urla: 150; Foça: 5; Karaburun: 6; Manisa: 235; Bayındır: 600; Tire: 150; Seferihisar: 395; Menemen: 215; Nefer: 27; Kasaba: 1163.
   It is interesting to note the differences between these statistics and those accounted for by these municipalities in 1923.
100. BCA 272.11.16.66.1, 4 Aug. 1923.
101. Ibid. It is not clear what happened to the Albanians in Urla, even though their population exceeded 10 per cent.
102. BCA 272.11.18.88.22, 17 July 1924; BCA 272.11.19.90.10, 6 Aug. 1924; BCA 272.11.19.93.10, 4 Sept. 1924; BCA 272.11.29.100.5, 2 Dec. 1924.
103. BCA 272.12.42.55.6, 4 Oct. 1924.
104. BCA 272.11.18.88.22, 17 July 1924; BCA 272.11.19.90.10, 6 Aug. 1924; BCA 272.11.19.93.10, 4 Sept. 1924; BCA 272.11.29.100.5, 2 Dec. 1924.
105. BCA 272.11.29.100.5, 2 Dec. 1924.
106. BCA 272.12.52.122.30, 31 Mar. 1927.
107. Seha Meray, *Lozan Barış Konferansı: Tutanaklar-Belgeler, Cilt II* (Istanbul: Yapı Kredi Yayınları, 2001), 345.
108. Nazmi Sevgen, *Celal Bayar Diyorki* (Istanbul: Tan Matbaası, 1951), 35. During a session of parliament, both Rıza Nur and Celal Bayar reasserted that no Albanians would be included in the exchanges.
109. BCA 272.11.19.92.22, 31 Aug. 1924; BCA 272.11.21.103.16, Jan. 1925.
110. BCA 30.18.1.12.65.5, 28 Dec. 1923.
111. Dimitris Michalopoulos, 'The Moslems of the Chamuria and the Exchange of Populations between Greece and Turkey', *Balkan Studies*, 26, no. 2 (1985): 303; PRO/FO 286/869, 31 Dec. 1923. Blinishti went on to say that the Çams would have to give up their property and their last harvest and give it to the Rum arriving from Anatolia. Otherwise, they would not be able to buy or sell property or vote and would have to house refugees in their homes. Caclamanos countered that since few Muslims wanted to leave Greece, that proved that there had been no abuses. The British for their part believed that the Greeks were intent on taking away the property of urban Muslim landowners.
112. PRO/FO 286/869, 31 Dec. 1923.
113. Michalopoulos, 'Moslems of the Chamuria', 309. Athens and Ankara agreed to transfer the Çams in July 1925. It is estimated that 7,500 people from the Epirus (from Jannina and Preveza) were deported to Anatolia. Before the commencement of the exchange, Ankara was prepared to settle up to 55,000 refugees from the Epirus. See Kemal Arı, *Büyük Mübadele: Türkiye'ye Zorunlu Göç(1923–1925)* (Istanbul: Tarih Vakfı Yurt Yayınları, 2003), 91; Yıldırım, 'Diplomats and Refugees', 241.

114. Kaplanoğlu, *Bursa'da Mübadele*, 86–7.
115. Ibid. 66, 67, 69. Of the refugees from Jannina settled in Gemlik, Kaplanoğlu claims that most did not speak Turkish. A good portion of the Preveza refugees who were settled alongside the Jannina refugees in Gemlik were also purportedly Albanian. As for those from Florina, who were settled between Bursa and Orhangazi, Kaplanoğlu also admits that large numbers of them were Albanian.
116. *Lausanne Conference*, 678. According to Turkish government statistics submitted at Lausanne, 25,883,091 Turkish lira in lost animals was reported in the *sancak*s of Bursa, Ertuğrul, İzmit, and Karesi.
117. BCA 272.11.19.95.22, 29 Sept. 1924.
118. Nur, *Hayat ve Hatıratım*, 1097.
119. Ibid. The refugees from Jannina that Rıza Nur encountered in Ankara in fact spoke Greek.
120. Ibid.
121. ibid. 1097–8.
122. BCA 272.11.16.66.1, 4 Aug. 1923; BCA 272.11.16.68.9, 10 Nov. 1923.
123. Nurcan Özgür-Baklacıoğlu, 'Devletlerin Dış Politikaları Açısından Göç Olgusu: Balkanlar'dan Türkiye'ye Arnavut Göçleri (1920–1990)' (Ph.D. diss., Istanbul University, 2003), 227. According to statistics cited here, 115,427 people migrated from Yugoslavia, 117,095 from Romania, and 198,688 from Bulgaria.
124. Kaplanoğlu, *Bursa'da Mübadele*, 86–7.
125. There is some disagreement on the number of immigrants that left Yugoslavia between 1923 and 1939. One source (The Historical Institute in Kosova) claims that 180,272 people fled Yugoslavia between 1923 and 1939 (255,878 between 1919 and 1940). By 1934, 5,371 individuals in Bursa had been born in Yugoslavia. See Kaplanoğlu, *Bursa'da Mübadele*, 88; Özgür-Baklacıoğlu, 'Devletlerin Dış Prlitikaları', 215.
126. Ramiz Abdyli, 'The Expropriation of the Albanian Population and Attempts at Colonisation of Albanian Territories (1918–1941)', in *The Kosova Issue: A Historical and Current Problem* (Tirana: Institute of History, 1996), 9; Millovan Obradović, 'Kolonizimi dhe Reforma Agrare në Funksion të Spastrimit Etnik të Shqiptarëvë', in Hivzi Islami (ed.), *Spastrimet Etnike: Politika Gjenocidale Serbe Ndaj Shqiptarëvë* (Pejë: Botoi Dukagjini, 2003) 175–88.
127. Malcolm, *Kosovo*, 280. While other scholars have stated that the redistribution of property solely favoured Serbs, Noel Malcolm argues that of the 14,000 families given reapportioned land, 4,000 were Albanian.
128. Hivzi Islami, *Kosova dhe Shqiptarë të: Çështje Demografike* (Prishtinë: Pena, 1990), 61.
129. Malcolm, *Kosovo*, 282.
130. Ibid. 273; Xheladin Shala, 'Ndjekja dhe Vrasja e Patriotëve Shqiptarë në Vitet 1912–1916', in *Gjenocidi dhe Aktet gjenocidiale të Pushtetit Serb Ndaj Shqiptarëve nga Kriza Lindore e Këndej (më Vështrim të Veçantë mbi Burimet Serbe të Fakteve* (Prishtinë: Akademia e Shkencave dhe e Arteve e Kosovës, 1995), 99–105.
131. 'Naši Podisi', *Stara Srbija*, 1 Apr. 1921.
132. 'Naši Podisi', *Stara Srbija*, 15 Mar. 1921.

133. 'Kačaci u Tetevu', *Stara Srbija*, 3 Apr. 1921; 'Kačaci u Tetevu', *Stara Srbija*, 8 Apr. 1921.
134. 'Naši Dopici: Kičevska Anarahja', *Stara Srbija*, 26 May 1921. In the case of this attack and robbery in Kičevo, the journalists referred to the *kaçak*s as a 'mafia' band.
135. 'Razbojniski Napad: Kačaci na Meruju', *Stara Srbija*, 23 June 1921.
136. 'Kačaci i Komite na Delu', *Stara Srbija*, 18 Aug. 1922; 'Kačaci i Komite na Delu', *Stara Srbija*, 19 Aug. 1922; 'Borba sa Odmetnitzima', *Stara Srbija*, 21 Aug. 1922.
137. 'Napad Kačaci', *Stara Srbija*, 24 Aug. 1922.
138. 'Napad Kačaka', *Stara Srbija*, 5 Jan. 1920; 'Naši Podisi: Anarhi na Kosovu', *Stara Srbija*, 6 Jan. 1920; 'Kačaci i Komite na Delu', *Stara Srbija*, 19 Aug. 1922.
139. 'Borba sa Odmetnitzima', *Stara Srbija*, 21 Aug. 1922.
140. Ibid.
141. Malcolm, *Kosovo*, 278.
142. Vasa Čubrilović, 'The Expulsion of the Albanians by the Serbs', *That was Yugoslavia: Information and Facts*, nos. 4–5 (1993): 11–12.
143. 'Socialna Pitanja: Muslimani i Agrarni Problem', *Stara Srbija*, 23 Mar. 1921.
144. Hakif Bajrami, 'Konventa Jugosllavo-Turke e Vitit 1938 për Shpërngulen e Shqiptarëve', *Gjurmime Albanolgjike*, no. 12 (1982): 243–51; idem, 'Rreth Përgatitjes së Konventës Jugosllave-Turke për Shpërnguljen e Shqiptarëve në Turqi (1938)', *Gjurmime Albanolgjike*, no. 18 (1988): 209–38.
145. Bajrami, 'Konventa Jugosllavo-Turke', 251.
146. Ibid. 253; Zamir Shtylla, 'Aspekte të Politikës së Shpërnguljes me Dhunë të Shiptarëve nga Kosova në Vitet 1936–1941', *Studime Historike*, 26, no. 3 (1990): 97.
147. Bajrami, 'Konventa Jugosllavo-Turke', 252–8.
148. Čubrilović, 'Expulsoion of the Albanians', 13.
149. Ibid. 12. Čubrilović also acknowledges that the Kingdom of Albania presented another possible destination for Yugoslavia's Albanian population (if Tirana was given the right amount of money). It is estimated that during the inter-war period, between 1930 and 1934, Albania received a minimum of 8,000 Albanians from Kosova. See Özgür-Baklacıoğlu, 'Devletlerin Dış Politikaları', 208.
150. Čubrilović, 'Expulsion of the Albanians', 14–15.
151. Ibid. 16.
152. Bajrami, 'Konventa Jugosllavo-Turke', 246. Atatürk purportedly met with Milan Stojadinović in late 1936 during his visit to Ankara. At this meeting 'the cleansing of the absolute majority of the Albanians of Kosova' was purportedly discussed.
153. Malcolm, *Kosovo*, 286.
154. Zamir Shtylla, 'The Forced Deportation of Albanians from Kosova and Other Territories between the Two World Wars (1918–1941)', in *The Kosova Issue: A Historical and Current Problem* (Tirana: Institute of History, 1996), 98.
155. Çagaptay, 'Crafting the Turkish Nation', 172; Shtylla, 'Forced Deportation of Albanians', 98.
156. Malcolm, *Kosovo*, 286. Noel Malcolm rejects Hakif Bajrami's estimated figure of 240,000 as a baseless statistic. Malcolm estimated that between 90,000 and 150,000 Albanians emigrated to Turkey during the inter-war period.

157. See Howard Eissenstat, 'Metaphors of Race and Discourse of Nation: Racial Theory and the Beginnings of Nationalism in the Turkish Republic', in Paul Spickard (ed.), *Race and Nation: Ethnic Systems in the Modern World* (New York: Routledge, 2005), 239–56.

CONCLUSION

1. See Theo Nichols *et al.*, 'Muhacir Bulgarian Workers in Turkey: The Relation to Management and Fellow Workers in the Formal Employment Sector', *Middle Eastern Studies*, 39, no. 2 (April 2003): 37–56.
2. Aydın, *İkinci Susurluk*, 50.
3. François Furet, *Interpreting the French Revolution* (Cambridge: Cambridge University Press, 2001), 15. As Furet puts it, 'By destroying, not the aristocracy, but the aristocratic principle in society, the Revolution put an end to the legitimacy of social resistance against the central State. But it was Richelieu who set the example, and so did Louis XIV.'
4. Şerif Mardin, 'Ideology and Religion in the Turkish Revolution', *International Journal of Middle East Studies*, 2, no. 3 (July 1971): 198.
5. Many descendants of Circassian and Albanian immigrants have sought to participate in Turkish national politics by joining local and national cultural associations (*dernek*). There are a wide range of Albanian and North Caucasian associations, ranging from the more Islamist (*Rumeli Türk Derneği* and *Şeyh Şamil Vakfı*) and ethno-nationalist (*Türk-Arnavut Kardeşliği* and *Kafder*) to the more community-based (such as the *Sakarya Arnavutları Kültür ve Dayanışma Derneği*). See, e.g., Alexandre Toumarkine, 'Kafkas ve Balkan Göçmen Dernekleri: Sivil Toplum ve Milliyetçilik', in Stefanos Yerasimos *et al.* (eds.), *Türkiye'de Sivil Toplum ve Milliyetçilik*, (Istanbul: İletişim Yayınları, 2001), 425–50.

Bibliography

ARCHIVES

American Board of Commissioners of Foreign Missions, Houghton Library, Harvard College Library (ABCFM)

    Missions to Asia
        ABC 16.9.3 Western Turkey Mission
        ABC 16.9.4 Western Turkey Mission, Woman's Board

Başbakanlık Cumhuriyet Arşivi (BCA)

    Bakanlar Kurulu Karaları (30.18)
    Başbakanlık Özel Kalem Müdürlüğü (30.10)
    Toprak Muhacir İskan Komisyonu (272)

Başbakanlık Osmanlı Arşivi (BOA)

    Dahiliye Nezareti
        Emniyet-i Umumiye
            Asayiş Kalemleri (BOA.DH.EUM.AYŞ)
        İdare-i Umumiye (BOA.DH.İUM)
        Kalem-i Mahsus (BOA.DH.KMS)
        Muhaberat-ı Umumiye İdaresi (BOA.DH.MUİ)
        Şifre Kalemleri (BOA.DH.ŞFR)
        Umur-ı Mahalliye-i Vilayet Müdüriyeti (BOA.DH.UMVM)
    Sadaret
        Mühimme Kalemi (BOA.A.MKT.MHM)
        Nezaret ve Devair (BOA.A.MKT.NZD)
        Umum Vilayet (BOA.A.MKT.UM)

Public Records Office (PRO)

    Foreign Office (FO)
    War Office (WO)

Türk Tarih Kurumu (TTK)

    Bekir Sami Dosya

Zoryan Institute

    Zoryan Institute Oral History Project

NEWSPAPERS, DOCUMENT COLLECTIONS, AND PERIODICALS

Açik Söz
Alemdar
The Daily News (London)
Hakimiyet-i Milliye
Harb Tarihi Vesikaları Dergisi
Human Research Affairs Foundation
İkdam
Osmanischer Lloyd
Stara Srbija
Tanin
Tehvir-i Efkar
Tesvir-i Efkar
The Times (London)
Vakit
Yakın Tarihimiz
Yeni Şark

BOOKS AND MANUSCRIPTS

Abadan, Yavuz. *Mustafa Kemal ve Çetecilik*. Istanbul: Varlik Yayınevi, 1972.

Abdyli, Ramiz. 'The Expropriation of the Albanian Population and Attempts for Colonisation of Albanian Territories (1918–1941)', in *The Kosova Issue: A Historical and Current Problem* (Tirana: Institute of History, 1996), 91–6.

Adanır, Fikret. *Die Makedonische Frage: Ihre Entstehung und Entwicklung bis 1908*. Wiesbaden: Steiner Verlag, 1979.

―― and Suraiya Faroqhi (eds.). *The Ottomans and the Balkans*. Leiden: E. J. Brill, 2002.

Adıvar, Halide Edib. *The Turkish Ordeal*. Westport, Conn.: Hyperion Press, 1981.

Ağanoğlu, H. Yıldırım. *Osmanlı'dan Cumhuriyet'e Balkanları'ın Makûs Talihi Göç*. Istanbul: Kum Saati, 2001.

Ahmad, Feroz. *The Young Turks: The Committee of Union and Progress in Turkish Politics*. Oxford: Oxford University Press, 1969.

Akan Ellis, Burcu. *Shadow Genealogies: Memories and Identity among Urban Muslims in Macedonia*. Boulder, Col.: Eastern European Monographs, on behalf of Columbia University Press, 2003.

Akçam, Taner. *A Shameful Act: The Armenian Genocide and Turkish Responsibility*. New York: Metropolitan Books, 2006.

―― 'Anatomy of a Crime: The Turkish Historcal Society's Manipulation of Archival Documents', *Journal of Genocide Research*, 7, no. 2 (June 2005): 255–77.

―― *Armenien und der Völkermord: Die Istanbuler Prozesse und die türkische Nationalbewegung*. Hamburg: Hamburger Edition, 1996.

―― *From Empire to Republic: Turkish Nationalism and the Armenian Genocide*. New York: Zed Books, 2004.

Akçam, Taner. *İnsan Hakları ve Ermeni Sorunu: İttihat ve Terakki'den Kurtuluş Savaş'ına*. Ankara: İmge Kitabevi, 1999.
Akıncı, İbrahim Ethem. *Demerci Akıncıları*. Ankara: Türk Tarih Kurumu, 1989.
Akkuş, Tacettin. *Gönen ve Köyleri Tarihçesi*. Istanbul: Ekin Yayıncılık, 2001.
Akpınar, Alişan. *Osmanlı Devletinde Aşiret Mektebi*. İstanbul: Göçebe Yayınları, 1997.
Aktar, Ayhan. 'Son Osmanlı Meclisi ve Ermeni Meselesi: Kasım-Aralık 1918', *Toplum ve Bilim*, 91 (Winter 2001–2): 142–65.
Albayrak, Recep. *Ethem'in Sürgün Yılları ve Simav Olayları, 1919–1948*. Ankara: Berikan Yayınları, 2004.
Alonso, Ana Maria. *Thread of Blood: Colonialism, Revolution and Gender on Mexico's Northern Frontier*. Tucson: University of Arizona Press, 1997.
Andonyan, Aram. *Balkan Savaşı*. Istanbul: Aras Yayıncılık, 1999.
Andrews, Peter Alford. *Ethnic Groups in the Republic of Turkey*. Wiesbaden: Dr Ludwig Reichert Verlag, 1989.
Anscombe, Fredrick (ed.). *The Ottoman Balkans 1750–1830*. Princeton: Markus Wiener Publishers, 2006.
Apak, Rahmi. *İstiklal Savaşında Garp Cephesi Nasıl Kuruldu*. Ankara: Türk Tarih Kurumu Basımevi, 1990.
Arai, Masami. *Turkish Nationalism in the Young Turk Era*. Leiden: E. J. Brill, 1992.
Arı, Kemal. *Büyük Mübadele: Türkiye'ye Zorunlu Göç (1923–1925)*. Istanbul: Tarih Vakfı Yurt Yayınları, 2003.
Arıkan, Zeki. *Mütareke ve İşgal Anıları*. Ankara: Türk Tarih Basımevi, 1991.
Asgar, Khan, M. Ali. 'Turkish Nationalists and the Indian Khaliphatists', *Journal of the Asiatic Society of Bangladesh*, 19, no. 3 (1974): 39–50.
Atatürk, Mustafa Kemal. *Nutuk-Söylev*. Ankara: Türk Tarih Kurumu Basımevi, 1989.
―― *A Speech Delivered by Mustafa Kemal Atatürk 1927*. Istanbul: Ministry of Education, 1963.
Avagyan, Arsen. *Osmanlı İmparatorluğu ve Kemalist Türkiye'nin Devlet-İktidar Sisteminde Çerkesler*. Istanbul: Belge Yayınları, 2004.
Avcıoğlu, Doğan. *Milli Kurtuluş Tarihi, 1838'den 1995'e*. Istanbul: Tekin Yayınevi, 1995.
Aydemir, İzzet. *Göç*. Ankara: Gelişim Matbaası, 1988.
―― 'Gönen-Manyas Çerkeslerinin Sürgünü', *Nart*, no. 15 (November 1999); <http://www.kafkasfederasyonu.org/v1/index.php?goster=nart&id=201>.
―― *Muhaceretteki Çerkes Aydınları*. Ankara: n. p., 1991.
Aydın, Zülfikar Ali. *İkinci Susurluk: Bir Kasaba Cinneti*. Istanbul: Metis Yayınevi, 2002.
Bajrami, Hakif. 'Konventa Jugosllavo-Turke e Vitit 1938 për Shpërngulen e Shqiptarëve', *Gjurmime Albanolgjike*, no. 12 (1982): 243–69.
―― 'Rreth Përgatitjes së Konventës Jugosllave-Turke për Shpërnguljen e Shqiptarëve në Turqi (1938)', *Gjurmime Albanolgjike*, no. 18 (1988): 209–38.
Balakian, Peter. *The Burning Tigris: A History of the Armenian Genocide*. London: William Heinemann, 2003.
Baran, Tülay Alim. *Vasıf Çınar ve İzmir'e Doğru Gazetesi Yazıları*. Istanbul: Arma Yayınları, 2001.

Barkey, Karen. *Bandits and Bureaucrats: The Ottoman Route to State Centralization*. Ithaca, NY: Cornell University Press, 1994.

―――― and Mark von Hagen (eds.). *After Empire: Multiethnic Societies and Nation-Building*. Boulder, Col.: Westview Press, 1997.

Başbakanlık Devlet Arşivleri Genel Müdürlüğü. *Osmanlı Belgelerinde Ermeniler, 1915–1920*. Ankara: Başbakanlık Devlet Arşivleri Genel Müdürlüğü, 1994.

Bayar, Celâl. *Ben de Yazdım: Millî Mücadele'ye Gidiş*. Istanbul: Baha Matbaası, 1965.

Baykal, Bekir Sıtkı. *Heyet-i Tensiliye Kararları*. Ankara: Türk Tarih Kurumu, 1974.

Benjamin, Thomas and Mark Wasserman. *Provinces of the Revolution: Essays on Regional Mexican History, 1910–1929*. Albuquerque: University of New Mexico Press, 1990.

Benlisoy, Foti. 'Patrikhanenin Faaliyetleri ve 1918–1920 Arasında Tehcir Edilmiş Rum Ahalinin İadesi', *Tarih ve Toplum*, 234 (June 2003): 21–31.

Berkes, Niyazi. *The Development of Secularism in Turkey*. Montreal: McGill University Press, 1964.

Berzeg, Sefer. *Kuzey Kafkasya Cumhuriyet, 1917–1922*. Istanbul: Birleşik Kafkasya Dernegi, 2004.

―――― *Türkiye Kurtuluş Savaş'ında Çerkes Göçmenleri, Cilt II*. Istanbul: Ekin Yayıncılık, 1990.

Blok, Anton. *The Mafia of Sicilian Village, 1860–1960: A Study of Violent Peasant Entrepreneurs*. Oxford: Blackwell, 1974.

―――― *Honour and Violence*. Cambridge: Polity, 2001.

Bloxham, Donald. *The Great Game of Imperialism, Nationalism and the Destruction of the Armenians*. New York: Oxford University Press, 2007.

Blumi, Isa. 'The Consequences of Empire in the Balkans and the Red Sea: Reading Possibilities in the Transformations of the Modern World'. Ph.D. dissertation, New York University, 2005.

―――― 'Recent Studies on Albanian Nationalism at the End of the Ottoman Empire from Turkey and the Arab World', *Balkanistica*, 14 (2001): 139–44.

―――― (ed.), *Rethinking the Late Ottoman Empire: A Comparative Social and Political History of Albania and Yemen, 1878–1918*. Istanbul: Isis Press, 2003.

Brailsford, H. N. *Macedonia: Its Races and their Future*. London: Methuen & Co., 1906.

Brower, Daniel and Edward Lazzerini (eds.). *Russia's Orient: Imperial Borderlands and Peoples, 1700–1917*. Bloomington: Indiana University Press, 1997.

Buda, Aleks *et al*. *Historia e Popullit Shqiptar: Vëllimi i Dytë, Rilindja Kombëtare*. Tirana: Toena, 2000.

Can, Fahri. 'Birinci Dünya Harbından Sonra İlk Milli Kuvvet Nasıl Kuruldu?' *Yakın Tarihimiz*, 1, no. 2 (10 May 1962): 334–5.

―――― 'Birinci Dünya Harbından Sonra İlk Milli Kuvvet Nasıl Kuruldu?' *Yakın Tarihimiz*, 1, no. 13 (24 May 1962): 394–5.

―――― 'Birinci Dünya Harbından Sonra İlk Milli Kuvvet Nasıl Kuruldu?' *Yakın Tarihimiz*, 2, no. 14 (31 May 1962): 28–9.

―――― 'Kuva-yı Milliye Ruhu', *Yakın Tarihimiz*, 1, no. 8 (19 April 1962): 249–50.

Canip, Bey. *Bürsa'da İşgal Günlüğü (Bursa Vilayetinde Yunan Fecayii)*. Istanbul: Düşünce Kitabevi Yayınları, 2004.

Cecil, Hugh and Peter Liddle (eds.). *Facing Armageddon: The First World War Experienced.* London: Cooper Press, 1996.

Cilasun, Emrah. *Bâki İlk Selam.* Istanbul: Belge Yayınları, 2004.

Cole, Juan. 'Of Crowds and Empires: Afro-Asian Riots and European Expansion, 1857–1882', *Comparative Studies in Society and History*, 31, no. 1 (January 1989): 106–33.

Cutbell, David Cameron. 'The Muhacir Komisyonu: An Agent in the Transformation of Ottoman Anatolia, 1860–1866'. Ph.D. dissertation, Columbia University, 2005.

Çagaptay, Soner. 'Crafting the Turkish Nation: Kemalism and Turkish Nationalism in the 1930s'. Ph.D. dissertation, Yale University, 2003.

Çam, Yusuf. *Milli Mücadele'de İzmit Sancağı.* İzmit: İzmit Rotary Kulubü, 1993.

Çankaya, Ali. *Mülkiye Tarihi ve Mülkiyeliler.* Ankara: Örnek Matbaası, 1954.

Çantay, Hasan Basri. *Kara Günler ve İbret Levhaları.* Istanbul: Ahmet Said Matbaası, 1964.

Çarıklı, Hacim Muhittin. *Balıkesir ve Alaşehir Kongreleri ve Hacim Muhittin Çarıklı 'nın Kuva-yı Milliye Hatıraları, 1919–1920.* Ankara: Türk Inkılâp Tarihi Enstitüsü, 1967.

Çelik, Bilgin. *İttihatçılar ve Arnavudlar: II. Meşrutiyet Dönemminde Arnavud Ulusçuluğu ve Arnavudluk Sorunu.* Istanbul: Büke Kitapları, 2004.

Çerkes Ethem. *Hatıralarım.* Istanbul: Berfin Yayınları, 1998.

'Čerkezi u Naši Zemli', *Glasnik: Skopskog Naučnog Društva*, no. 1 (1928): 143–53.

Çolak, İbrahim. *Milli Mücadele Esnasında Kuva-yı Seyyare Kumandalığıma Ait Hatıratım.* Istanbul: Emre Yayınları, 1996.

Čubrilović, Vasa. 'The Expulsion of the Albanians by the Serbs', *That was Yugoslavia: Information and Facts*, nos. 4–5 (1993): 6–28.

Dadrian, Vahakn. 'The Armenian Question and the Wartime Fate of the Armenians as Documented by the Officials of the Ottoman Empire's World War I Allies: Germany and Austria-Hungary', *International Journal of Middle East Studies*, 34 (2002): 59–85.

——— *The History of the Armenian Genocide: Ethnic Conflict from the Balkans to the Caucasus.* Providence, RI: Berghahn Books, 1995.

Dağlı, Yücel *et al. Evliya Çelebi Seyahatnamesi (5. Kitap).* Istanbul: Yapı Kredi Yayınları, 2001.

Davison, Roderic. 'Turkish Attitudes Concerning Christian–Muslim Equality in the Nineteenth Century', *American Historical Review*, 59, no. 4 (July 1954): 844–64.

Deringil, Selim. *The Well-Protected Domains: Ideology and the Legitimation of Power in the Ottoman Empire, 1876–1909.* London: I. B. Taurus, 1998.

Dündar, Fuat. *İttihat ve Terakki'nin Müslümanları İskan Politikası (1913–1918).* Istanbul: İlestişim Yayınları, 2001.

——— *Türkiye Nüfus Sayımlarında Azınlıklar.* Istanbul: Doz Yayıcılık, 1999.

Dyer, Gwynne. 'Turkish "Falsifiers" and Armenian "Deceivers": Historiography and the Armenian Massacres', *Middle Eastern Studies*, 12, no. 1 (1976): 99–107.

Edwards, David. 'Mad Mullahs and Englishmen: Discourse in the Colonial Encounter', *Comparative Studies in Society and History*, 31, no. 4 (October 1989): 647–70.

Eissenstat, Howard. 'The Limits of Imagination: Debating the Nation and Constructing the State in Early Turkish Nationalism'. Ph.D. dissertation, University of California at Los Angeles, 2007.

Erdeha, Kamil. *Milli Mücadele'de Vilayetler ve Valiler*. Istanbul: Remzi Kitapevi, 1975.

―――― *Yüzellilikler yahut Milli Mücadelenini Muhasebesi*. Istanbul: Tekin Yayınları, 1998.

Erdem, Hakan. *Slavery in the Ottoman Empire and its Demise, 1800–1909*. New York: St Martin's Press, 1996.

Ergil, Doğu. *Milli Mücadele'nin Soysal Tarihi*. Istanbul: Turhan Yayınevi, 1981.

Ergut, Ferdan. 'State and Social Control: The Police in the Late Ottoman Empire and the Early Republican Turkey, 1839–1939'. Ph.D. dissertation, New School for Social Research, 1999.

Erikson, Edward J. *Ordered to Die: A History of the Ottoman Army in the First World War*. Westport, Conn.: Greenwood Press, 2001.

Ertürk, Hüsameddin and Samih Nafiz Tansu. *İki Devrin Perde Arkası*. Istanbul: Ramazan Yasar, 1969.

Faroqhi, Suraiya. *Towns and Townsmen of Ottoman Anatolia: Trade, Crafts and Food Production in an Urban Setting*. Cambridge: Cambridge University Press, 1984.

Fischer, Bernd J. 'Albanian Highland Tribal Society and Family Structure in the Process of Twentieth Century Transformation', *East European Quarterly*, 33, no.3 (September 1999): 281–301.

Foley, Neil. *The White Scourge: Mexicans, Blacks and Poor Whites in Texas Cotton Culture*. Berkeley: University of California Press, 1997.

Fortna, Benjamin. *Imperial Classroom: Islam, the State and Education in the Late Ottoman Empire*. Oxford: Oxford University Press, 2002.

Fraenkel, Eran and Christina Kramer (eds.). *Language Contact, Language Conflict*. New York: Peter Lang, 1993.

Frashëri, Sami. *Shqipëria: Ç'ka Qenë, Ç'është e Ç'do të Bëhet?* Tirana: Perparim Xhixha, 1999.

Furet, François. *Interpreting the French Revolution*. Cambridge: Cambridge University Press, 2001.

Georgeon, François. *Abdülhamid II: Le Sultan Calife (1876–1909)*. Paris: Fayard, 2003.

Ginio, Eyal. 'Port Cities as an Imagined Battlefield: The Boycott of 1913'. Paper presented at the Eighth Mediterranean Social and Political Research Meeting, Florence, Italy, 21–5 March 2007.

Gologlu, Mahmut. *Üçüncü Meşrutiyet 1920*. Ankara: Başnur Matbaası, 1970.

Gondicas, Dimitri. *The Greeks of Asia Minor: Confession, Community, and Ethnicity in the Nineteenth Century*. Kent, Ohio: Kent State University Press, 1992.

―――― and Charles Issawi (eds.). *Ottoman Greeks in the Age of Nationalism: Politics, Economy, and Society in the Nineteenth Century*. Princeton: Darwin Press, 1999.

Göçek, Fatma Müge. *Rise of Bourgeoisie, Demise of Empire: Ottoman Westernization and Social Change*. New York: Oxford University Press, 1996.

Gökalp, Ziya. *The Principles of Turkism*. Leiden: E. J. Brill, 1968.

Gökbilgin, Tayyib. *Millî Mücadele Başlarken*. Ankara: Türk Tarih Kurumu Basımevi, 1959.

Görgülü, Fahri. *Yunan İşgalinde Kirmasti (Mustafakemalpaşa)*. Mustafakemalpaşa: Yeni Müteferrika Basımevi, 1960.

Göztepe, Tarık Mümtaz. *Osmanoğlularının Son Padişahı: Sultan Vahıdeddin Mütareke Gayyasında*. Istanbul: Sevil Yayınevi, 1969.

Graham, Richard. *The Idea of Race in Latin America: 1870–1940*. Austin: University of Texas Press, 1990.

Guha, Ranajit. *Elementary Aspects of Peasant Insurgency in Colonial India*. New York: Oxford University Press, 1991.

Güner, Zekai and Orhan Kabataş. *Milli Mücadele Dönemi Beyannameleri ve Basını*. Ankara: Atatürk Kültür Merkezi Yayını, 1990.

Güralp, Şerif. *Kurtuluş Savaşı'nın İçyüzü: Bir Albayın Anıları*. Istanbul: Güncel Yayıncılık, 2002.

Gürün, Kamuran. *Ermeni Dosyası*. Ankara: Türk Tarih Kurumu, 1983.

Gust, Wolfgang (ed.). *Der Völkermord an den Armeniern 1915/16: Dokumente aus dem Politischen Archiv des deutschen Auswärtigen Amts*. Munich: Zu Klampen Auflage, 2005.

Güven, Zühtü. *Anzavur İsyan: İstiklâl Savaşı Hatıralarından Acı Bir Safha*. Ankara: Türkiye İş Bankası, 1965.

Haddad, Mahmoud. 'The Rise of Arab Nationalism Reconsidered', *International Journal of Middle East Studies*, 26, no. 2 (1994): 201–22.

Hanioğlu, Şükrü. *Preparation for a Revolution: The Young Turks, 1902–1908*. Oxford: Oxford University Press, 2001.

———. *The Young Turks in Opposition*. Oxford: Oxford University Press, 1995.

Hart, John. *Revolutionary Mexico: The Coming and Process of the Mexican Revolution*. Berkeley: University of California Press, 1997.

Hiçyılmaz, Ergün. *Gizli Belgelerle Çerkes Ethem*. Istanbul: Varlık Yayınları, 1993.

Hirshon, Renée (ed.). *Crossing the Aegean: An Appraisal of the 1923 Compulsory Population Exchange between Greece and Turkey*. New York: Berghahn Books, 2003.

Hobsbawm, Eric. *The Age of Revolution, 1789–1848*. New York: New American Library, 1962.

———. *Bandits*. New York: New Press, 2000.

———. *Nations and Nationalism since 1780: Programme, Myth, Reality*. New York: Cambridge University Press, 1992.

Holquist, Peter. *Making War, Forging Revolution: Russia's Continuum in Crisis, 1914–1921*. Cambridge, Mass.: Harvard University Press, 2002.

Hoşgür, İsmail Aydın. *Kurtuluş Savaşında Biga*. Biga: Cahit Renda Matbaası, 1970.

Hovannisian, Richard (ed.). *The Armenian Genocide: History, Politics, Ethics*. London: Macmillan, 1992.

Hroch, Miroslav. *Social Preconditions of National Revival in Europe: A Comparative Analysis of the Social Composition of Patriotic Groups among the Smaller European Nations*. New York: Cambridge University Press, 1985.

Hunt, Lynn Avery. *Politics, Culture and Class in the French Revolution*. Berkeley: University of California Press, 1984.

Hülagü, Orhan. *Milli Mücadele'de Bursa*. Istanbul: Emre Yayınları, 2001.

Islami, Hivzi. *Kosova dhe Shqiptarët: Çështje Demografike*. Prishtinë: Pena, 1990.

——— (ed.). *Spastrimet Etnike: Politika Gjenocidale Serbe Ndaj Shqiptarëvë*. Pejë: Botoi Dukagjini, 2003.

İğdemir, Uluğ. *Biga Ayaklanması ve Anzavur Olaylar Günlük Anılar*. Ankara: Türk Tarih Kurumu Basımevi, 1989.

İlgürel, Mücteba. *Milli Mücadele'de Balıkesir Kongreleri*. Istanbul: Atatürk Araştırma Merkezi, 1999.
İnal, Mahmud Kemal. *Osmanlı Devrinde Son Sadrıazamlar*. Istanbul: Milli Eğitim Basımevi, 1969.
İnalcık, Halil. 'Arnawutluk', *Encyclopedia of Islam*, i (1960): 656.
____ and Donald Quataert (eds.). *An Economic and Social History of the Ottoman Empire, ii: 1600–1914*. Cambridge: Cambridge University Press, 1994.
İpek, Nedim. *Rumeli'den Anadolu'ya Türk Göçleri (1877–1890)*. Ankara: Türk Tarih Kurumu, 1994.
Jäschke, Gotthard. 'Der Turanismus und der Jungtürken zur Osmanischen Aussenpolitik im Weltkrieg', *Die Welt des Islams*, 23 (1941): 1–53.
____ *Türk Kurtuluş Savaşı Kronolojisi: Modros'tan Mudanya'ya Kadar (30 Ekim 1918–11 Ekim 1922)*. Ankara: Türk Tarih Kurumu Basımevi, 1970.
Johnson, Chalmers. *Revolutionary Change*. Boston: Little & Brown, 1966.
Kalkavanoğlu, İlyas Sami. *Milli Mücadele Hatıralarım*. Istanbul: Ekicigil Yayınevi, 1957.
Kanar, Mehmet (ed.). *Ermeni Komitelerinin Emelleri ve İhtilal Hareketleri, Meşrutiyetten Önce ve Sonra*. Istanbul: Der Yayınevi, 2001.
Kansu, Aykut. *Politics in Post-Revolutionary Turkey, 1908–1913*. Leiden: E. J. Brill, 2000.
____ *The Revolution of 1908 in Turkey*. Leiden: E. J. Brill, 1997.
Kaplanoğlu, Raif. *Bursa'da Mübadele*. Orhangazi: Avrasya Etnografya Vakfı, 1999.
Kappler, Andreas. *The Formation of National Elites*, iv. Dartmouth, NH: New York University Press, 1992.
Karpat, Kemal. *Ottoman Population, 1830–1914: Demographic and Social Characteristics*. Madison: University of Wisconsin Press, 1985.
____ (ed.). *Ottoman Past and Today's Turkey*. Leiden: E. J. Brill, 2000.
____ (ed.). *The Politicization of Islam: Reconstructing Identity, State, Faith and Community in the Late Ottoman State*. Oxford: Oxford University Press, 2001.
____ (ed.). *Studies on Ottoman Social and Political History*. Leiden: E. J. Brill, 2002.
____ (ed.). *The Turks of Bulgaria: The History, Culture and Political Fate of a Minority*. Istanbul: Isis Press, 1990.
____ and Robert W. Zens (eds.). *Ottoman Borderlands: Issues, Personalities and Political Changes*. Madison: University of Wisconsin Press, 2003.
Katz, Friedrich. *The Secret War in Mexico: Europe, the United States and the Mexican Revolution*. Chicago: University of Chicago Press, 1981.
Kayalı, Hasan. *Arabs and Young Turks: Ottomanism, Arabism and Islamism in the Ottoman Empire, 1908–1918*. Berkeley: University of California Press, 1997.
'Kazım Özalp Anlatiyor', *Yakın Tarihimiz*, 2, no. 20 (5 July 1962): 196–7.
Khodarkovsky, Michael. *Russia's Steppe Empire: The Making of a Colonial Empire, 1500–1800*. Bloomington: Indiana University Press, 2002.
Kieser, Hans-Lukas. *Der Verpasste Friede: Mission, Ethnie und Staat in den Ostprovinzen der Türkei*. Zürich: Chronos Verlag, 2000.
____ and Dominik Schaller (eds.). *Der Völkermord an den Armeniern und die Shoah*. Zürich: Chronos Verlag, 2002.
Kinross, Patrick. *Atatürk: Rebirth of a Nation*. London: Phoenix Giant, 1995.

Kırımlı, Hakan. *National Movements and National Identity among the Crimean Tatars, 1905–1916.* Leiden: E. J. Brill, 1996.
Klein, Janet. 'Power in the Periphery: The Hamidiye Cavalry and the Struggle over Ottoman Kurdistan, 1890–1914'. Ph.D. dissertation, Princeton University, 2002.
Knight, Alan. *The Mexican Revolution.* New York: Cambridge University Press, 1986.
Koçoğlu, Yahya. *Hatırlıyorum: Türkiye'de Gayrimuslim Hayatlar.* Istanbul: Metis Yayınları, 2003.
Köklü, H. Nusret. *Manisa: İşgalden Kurtuluşa.* Ankara: H. Nusret Köklü, 1967.
Kuşçubaşı, Eşref. *Hayber'de Türk Cengi.* Istanbul: Araba Yayınları, 1997.
Kutay, Cemal. *Çerkez Ethem Tamamlanmış Dosya.* Istanbul: Özgür Yayınları, 2004.
____ *Osmanlı'dan Cumhuriyet'e Yüzyılımızda bir İnsanımız, Hüseyin Rauf Orbay, 1881–1964.* Istanbul: Kazanç Kitap Ticaret, 1995.
Küçük, Cevdet. 'Damad Ferid Paşa', *Türkiye Diyanet Vakfı İslam Ansiklopedisi,* 8 (1993): 436.
____ 'Mehmet VI', *Türkiye Diyanet Vakfı İslam Ansiklopedisi,* 1 (1993): 422.
Kzhnachov, Vasil. *Makedonja: Etnografiya i Statistika.* Sofia: Drzhvana Pechatnitsa, 1900.
Landau, Jacob. *Pan-Turkism: From Irredentism to Cooperation.* London: Hurst Press, 1995.
Lausanne Conference on Near Eastern Affairs, 1922–1923: Records of Proceedings and Draft Terms of Peace. London: His Majesty's Stationery Office, 1923.
Lewis, Bernard. *The Emergence of Modern Turkey.* Oxford: Oxford University Press, 1968.
____ *The Political Language of Islam.* Chicago: University of Chicago Press, 1988.
Lewis, Stephen. *The Ambivalent Revolution: Forging State and Nation in Chiapas, 1910–1945.* Albuquerque: University of New Mexico Press, 2005.
Lewy, Guenter. *The Armenian Massacres in Ottoman Turkey: A Disputed Genocide.* Salt Lake City: University of Utah Press, 2005.
Lopasic, Alexander. 'Islamization of the Balkans with Special Reference to Bosnia', *Journal of Islamic Studies,* 5, no. 2 (1994): 163–86.
Luzbetak, Louis J. *Marriage and the Family in Caucasia.* Vienna: St Gabriel's Mission Press, 1951.
Magnarella, Paul. *Tradition and Change in a Small Town in Turkey.* New York: John Wiley and Sons, 1974.
Majer, Hans Georg (ed.). *Osmanische Studien zur Wirtschafts und Sozialgeschichte: In Memoriam Vančo Boškov.* Wiesbaden: O. Harrasowitz Verlag, 1986.
Makdisi, Ussama. *The Culture of Sectarianism: Community History and Violence in Nineteenth-Century Ottoman Lebanon.* Berkeley: University of California Press, 2000.
Malcolm, Noel. *Kosovo: A Short History.* London: Macmillan, 1998.
Mallon, Florencia. *Peasant and Nation: The Making of Postcolonial Mexico and Peru.* Berkeley: University of California Press, 1995.
Mango, Andrew. *Atatürk: The Biography of the Founder of Modern Turkey.* Woodstock, NY: Overlook Press, 2000.
Mardin, Şerif. 'Ideology and Religion in the Turkish Revolution', *International Journal of Middle East Studies,* 2, no. 3 (July 1971): 197–211.
Martin, Terry. *Affirmative Action Empire: Nations and Nationalism in the Soviet Union, 1923–1939.* Ithaca, NY: Cornell University Press, 2001.

McCarthy, Justin. *Death and Exile: The Ethnic Cleansing of Ottoman Muslims, 1821–1922*. Princeton: Darwin Press, 1995.
Meray, Seha. *Lozan Barış Konferansı: Tutanaklar-Belgeler, Cilt II*. Istanbul: Yapı Kredi Yayınları, 2001.
Mert, Özcan. 'Anzavur'un İlk Ayaklanmasına Ait Belgeler', *Belleten*, 56, no. 217 (1992): 847–972.
Michalopoulos, Dimitris. 'The Moslems of the Chamuria and the Exchange of Populations between Greece and Turkey', *Balkan Studies*, 26, no. 2 (1985): 303–13.
Miller, Donald E. and Lorna Touryan Miller. *Survivors: An Oral History of the Armenian Genocide*. Berkeley: University of California Press, 1993.
Mourelos, Yannis G. 'The 1914 Persecutions and the First Attempt at an Exchange of Minorities between Greece and Turkey', *Balkan Studies*, 26, no. 2 (1985): 389–413.
Nakracas, Georgios. *Anadolu ve Rum Göçmenlerin Kökeni*. Istanbul: Kitabevi Yayınları, 2005.
Nalbandian, Louise. *The Armenian Revolutionary Movement*. Berkeley: University of California Press, 1963.
Nichols, Theo *et al*. 'Muhacir Bulgarian Workers in Turkey: The Relation to Management and Fellow Workers in the Formal Employment Sector', *Middle Eastern Studies*, 39, no. 2 (April 2003): 37–56.
Niyazi, Resneli Ahmet. *Hürriyet Kahramanı Resneli Niyazi*. Istanbul: Örgün Yayınevi, 2003.
Nolte, Richard (ed.). *Modern Middle East*. New York: Atherton Press, 1963.
Nur, Rıza. *Hayat ve Hatıratım, Cilt III*. Istanbul: Atındağ Yayınevi, 1968.
The Other Balkan Wars: A 1913 Carnegie Endowment Inquiry in Retrospect with a New Introduction and Reflections on the Present Conflict by George F. Kennan. Washington: Carnegie Endowment for International Peace, 1933.
Ozdalga, Elisabeth (ed.). *Late Ottoman Society: The Intellectual Legacy*. London: Routledge Curzon Press, 2005.
Özalp, Kâzım. *Milli Mücadele, 1919–1922*. Ankara: Türk Tarih Kurumu Basımevi, 1985.
Özbek, Nadir. 'Philanthropic Activity, Ottoman Patriotism and the Hamidian Regime, 1876–1909', *International Journal of Middle East Studies*, 37, no. 1 (2005): 59–81.
Özdemir, Zekeriya. *Balıkesir Bölgesinde Milli Mücadele Önderleri*. Ankara: Zekeriya Özdemir, 2001.
———. *Milli Mücadele Yıllarında Balıkesir Cepheleri*. Ankara: Zekeriya Özdemir, 2001.
Özel, Sabahattin. *Kocaeli ve Sakarya İllerinde Milli Mücadele (1919–1922)*. Istanbul: Türkiyat Matbaacılık, 1987.
———. *Milli Mücadele'de İzmit-Adapazarı ve Atatürk*. Istanbul: Derin Yayınları, 2005.
Özer, Kemal. *Kurtuluş Savaşında Gönen*. Gönen: Türkdili Matbaası, 1964.
———. *Kurtuluş Savaşında Gönen ve Çevresi*. Ankara: Türk Diyanet Vakfı, 1998.
Özgür-Baklacıoğlu, Nurcan. 'Devletlerin Dış Politikaları Açısından Göç Olgusu: Balkanlar'dan Türkiye'ye Arnavut Göçleri (1920–1990)'. Ph.D. dissertation, Istanbul University, 2003.
Öztürkmen, Arzu. 'Remembering through Material Culture: Local Knowledge of Past Communities in a Turkish Black Sea Town', *Middle Eastern Studies*, 39, no. 2 (April 2003): 179–94.

Pandey, Gyandendra. *The Ascendancy of the Congress in Uttar Pradesh: Class, Community and Nation in Northern India, 1920–1940*. London: Anthem Press, 2002.
―― *The Construction of Communalism in Colonial North India*. New York: Oxford University Press, 1990.
Perry, Duncan. *The Politics of Terror: The Macedonian Liberation Movement 1893–1903*. Durham, NC: Duke University Press, 1988.
Pinson, Marc. 'Ottoman Colonization of the Circassians in Rumeli after the Crimean War', *Etudes Balkaniques*, 3 (1972): 71–85.
'President Woodrow Wilson's Fourteen Points', *The World War I Document Archive*; <http://www.lib.byu.edu/~rdh/wwi/1918/14points.html>.
Provence, Michael. *The Great Syrian Revolt and the Rise of Arab Nationalism*. Austin: University of Texas Press, 2005.
Raleigh, Donald J. *Experiencing Russia's Civil War: Politics, Society and Revolutionary Culture in Saratov, 1917–1922*. Princeton: Princeton University Press, 2002.
'Rauf Orbay'ın Hatıraları', *Yakın Tarihimiz*, 1, no. 6 (5 April 1962): 177–80.
Rexhepi, Zeqirja. *Zhvillimet Politiko-Shoqërore te Shqiptarët në Maqedoni, 1990–2001*. Tetova: Tringa Design, 2005.
Reynolds, Michael. 'Myths and Mysticism: A Longitudinal Perspective on Islam and Conflict in the North Caucasus', *Middle Eastern Studies*, 41, no. 1 (January 2005): 31–54.
―― 'The Ottoman–Russian Struggle for Eastern Anatolia and the Caucasus, 1908–1918: Identity, Ideology and the Geopolitics of World Order'. Ph.D. dissertation, Princeton University, 2003.
Rogan, Eugene. *Frontiers of the State in the Late Ottoman Empire: Transjordan 1850–1921*. Cambridge: Cambridge University Press, 1999.
―― (ed.). *Outside In: On the Margins of the Modern Middle East*. London: I. B. Taurus, 2002.
Said, Edward. *Orientalism*. New York: Vintage Books, 1994.
Sakallı, Bayram. *Milli Mücadele'nin Soysal Tarihi: Mudafaa-i Hukuk Cemiyetleri*. Istanbul: İz Yayıncılık, 1997.
Sakaoğlu, Saim. *Türk Gölge Oyunu Karagöz*. Ankara: Akçağ Yayınları, 2003.
Sanay, Recai. *Türk Casusu İngliz Kemal: Milli Mücadele'de*. Istanbul: Geçit Kitabevi, 2005.
Sarıhan, Zeki. *Çerkez Ethem'in İhaneti*. Istanbul: Kaynak Yayınları, 1984.
Sarıkoyuncu, Ali. *Milli Mücadelede Din Adamları, Cilt II*. Ankara: Diyanet İşeri Başkanlığı Yayınları, 1999.
Schwandner-Sievers, Stephanie and Bernd J. Fischer (eds.). *Albanian Identities: Myth and History*. London: Hurst & Company, 2002.
Scott, Peter Dale. *Deep Politics and the Death of JFK*. Berkeley: University of California Press, 1996.
Selçuk, İlhan. *Yüzbaşı Selahattin Romanı, I. Kitap*. Istanbul: Remzi Kitabevi, 1975.
―― *Yüzbaşı Selahattin Romanı, II. Kitap*. Istanbul: Remzi Kitabevi, 1975.
Selek, Sebahattin. *Anadolu İhtilali*. Istanbul: Burçak Yayınevi, 1968.
Sener, Cemal. *Çerkes Ethem Olayı*. Istanbul: Okan Yayınları, 1984.
Sever, Metin. *Kafdağı'nın Bu Yüzü: Türkiye'deki Kafkas Kökenliler*. Istanbul: Doğan Kitapçılık, 1999.

Sevgen, Nazmi. *Celal Bayar Diyorki*. Istanbul, Tan Matbaası, 1951.
Shala, Xheladin. 'Ndjekja dhe Vrasja e Patriotëve Shqiptarë në Vitet 1912–1916', in *Gjenocidi dhe Aktet Gjenocidiale të Pushtetit Serb Ndaj Shqiptarëve nga Kriza Lindore e Këndej (me Vështrim të Veçantë mbi Burimet Serbe të Fakteve* (Prishtinë: Akademia e Shkencave dhe e Arteve e Kosovës, 1995), 99–105.
Shaw, Stanford. *From Empire to Republic: The Turkish War of National Liberation, 1918–1923: A Documentary Study*. Ankara: Türk Tarih Kurumu Basımevi, 2000.
____ 'Resettlement of Refugees in Anatolia, 1918–1923', *Turkish Studies Association Bulletin*, 22, no. 1 (Spring 1998): 58–90.
Shissler, Holly. *Between Two Empires: Ahmet Ağaoğlu and the New Turkey*. London: I. B. Taurus, 2003.
Shtylla, Zamir. 'Aspekte të Politikës së Shpërnguljes me Dhunë të Shiptarëve nga Kosova në Vitet 1936–1941', *Studime Historike*, 26, no. 3 (1990): 79–97.
____ 'The Forced Deportation of Albanians from Kosova and Other Territories between the Two World Wars (1918–1941)', in *The Kosova Issue: A Historical and Current Problem* (Tirana: Institute of History, 1996), 97–101.
Skocpol, Theda. 'Reconsidering the French Revolution in World-Historical Perspective', *Social Research*, 56, no. 1 (1989): 53–70.
____ *States and Social Revolutions: A Comparative Analysis of France, Russia and China*. Cambridge: Cambridge University Press, 1979.
Slatta, Richard (ed.). *Bandidos: The Varieties of Latin American Banditry*. Westport, Conn.: Greenwood Press, 1987.
Sofuoğlu, Adnan. *Kuva-yı Milliye Döneminde Kuzeybatı Anadolu, 1919–1921*. Ankara: Genelkurmay Basım Evi, 1994.
Sohrabi, Nader. 'Constitutionalism, Revolution and the State: The Young Turk Revolution of 1908 and the Iranian Constitutional Revolution of 1906 with Comparisons to the Russian Revolution of 1905'. Ph.D. dissertation, University of Chicago, 1996.
____ 'Global Waves, Local Actors: What the Young Turks Knew about Other Revolutions and Why It Mattered', *Comparative Studies in Society and History*, 44, no. 1 (2002): 45–79.
Soysal, İlhami. *150'likler*. Istanbul: Gür Yayınları, 1985.
Soward, Steven. *Austria's Policy of Macedonian Reform*. Boulder, Col.: East European Monographs; distributed by Columbia University Press, New York, 1989.
Spagnolo J., (ed.). *Problems of the Modern Middle East in Historical Perspective: Essays in Honor of Albert Hourani*. Reading: Ithaca Press, 1992.
Spickard, Paul (ed.). *Race and Nation: Ethnic Systems in the Modern World*. New York: Routledge, 2005.
Stoddard, Philip Hendrick. 'The Ottoman Government and the Arabs, 1911 to 1918: A Preliminary Study of the Teşkilat-ı Mahsusa'. Ph.D. dissertation, Princeton University, 1963.
Su, Kamil. *Köprülülü Hamdi Bey ve Akbaş Olayları*. Ankara: Kurtulus Ofset Basımeri, 1984.
Suny, Ronald Gregor. *Looking toward Ararat: Armenia in Modern History*. Bloomington: University of Indiana Press, 1993.
____ and Terry Martin (eds.). *A State of Nations: Empire and Nation-Making in the Age of Lenin and Stalin*. Oxford: Oxford University Press, 2001.

Süreyya, Münir. *Ermeni Meselesinin Siyası Tarihçesi, 1877–1914.* Ankara: Türk Cumhuriyet Devlet Arşivleri Genel Müdürlüğü, 2001.
Şoenu, Mehmed Fetgerey. *Çerkes Mes'elesi.* Istanbul: Bedir Yayınevi, 1993.
Talat Paşa. *Hatıralarım ve Müdafaam.* Istanbul: Kaynak Yayınları, 2006.
Tambiah, Stanley. *Leveling Crowds: Ethnonationalist Conflicts and Collective Violence in South Asia.* Berkeley: University of California Press, 1997.
Tevetoğlu, Fethi. *Milli Mücadele Yıllarındaki Kuruluşlar.* Istanbul: Türk Tarih Kurumu Basımevi, 1988.
Thompson, E. P. *The Making of the English Working Class.* New York: Pantheon Books, 1964.
Thompson, Elizabeth. *Colonial Citizens: Republican Rights, Paternal Privilege and Gender in French Syria and Lebanon.* New York: Columbia University Press, 2000.
Tilly, Charles. *From Mobilization to Revolution.* Reading, Mass.: Addison-Wesley, 1978.
Toledano, Ehud R. *Slavery and Abolition in the Ottoman Middle East.* Seattle: University of Washington Press, 1998.
Toprak, Zafer. *İttihad-Terakki ve Cihan Harbi: Savaş Ekonomisi ve Türkiye'de Devletçilik.* Istanbul: Homer Kitabevi, 2003.
_____ *Türkiye'de 'Milli İktisat' (1908–1918).* Ankara: Yurt Yayınları, 1982.
Toynbee, Arnold J. *The Western Question in Greece and Turkey: A Study in the Contact of Civilizations.* London: Constable and Company, 1923.
Tunaya, Tarik Zafer. *Türkiye'de Siyasal Partiler, 1859–1952.* Istanbul: Doğan Kardeş Yayınları, 1952.
_____ *Türkiye'de Siyasal Partiler: Mütareke Dönemi, Cilt II.* Istanbul: Hürriyet Vakfı Yayınları, 1989.
_____ *Türkiye'de Siyasal Partiler: İttihat ve Terakki, Cilt III.* Istanbul: Hürriyet Vakfı Yayınları, 1989.
Tuncay, Mete and Erik Jan Zürcher (eds.). *Socialism and Nationalism in the Ottoman Empire 1876–1923.* New York: Palgrave Macmillan, 1994.
Turan, Mustafa *et al.* (eds.). *Türkiye'de Yunan Fecâyii.* Ankara: Berikan, 2003.
Turfan, M. Naim. *Rise of the Young Turks: Politics, the Military and Ottoman Collapse.* London: I. B. Taurus, 2000.
Türk Cumhuriyet Genelkurmay Başkanlığı Harb Tarihi Dairesi. *Türk İstiklal Harbi: VI'ıncı Cilt, İç Ayaklanması (1919–1921).* Ankara: Genelkurmay Basımevi, 1964.
Uzer, Tahsin. *Makedonya Eşkiyalık Tarihi ve Son Osmanlı Yönetimi.* Ankara: Türk Tarih Kurumu, 1979.
Ülken, Hilmi Ziya. 'Gönen Bölgesi Monografisi', *Sosyoloji Dergisi*, 10–11 (1955–6): 142.
Ünal, Muhittin. *Kurtuluş Savaşında Çerkeslerin Rolü.* Ankara: Takav Matbaası, 2000.
_____ *Miralay Bekir Sami Günsav'in Kurtuluş Savaşı Anıları.* Istanbul: Cem Yayınevi, 2002.
Vanderwood, Paul. *Disorder and Progress: Bandits, Police and Mexican Development* (Lincoln: University of Nebraska Press, 1981).
Vardar, Galip. *İttihat ve Terakki İcinde Dönenler.* Istanbul: İnkılap Kitapevi, 1960.
Watenpaugh, Keith. 'Bourgeois Modernity, Historical Memory and Imperialism: The Emergence of an Urban Middle Class in the Late Ottoman and Inter-war Middle East: Aleppo, 1908–1939'. Ph.D. dissertation, University of California at Los Angeles, 1999.

Webb, Gary. *Dark Alliance: The CIA, the Contras and the Crack Cocaine Explosion.* New York: Seven Stories Press, 1998.

Wells, Allen and Gilbert M. Joseph. *Summer of Discontent, Seasons of Upheaval: Elite Politics and Rural Insurgency in Yucatan, 1876–1915.* Stanford, Calif.: Stanford University Press, 1996.

White, Paul J. and Joost Jongerden (eds.). *Turkey's Alevi Enigma: A Comprehensive Overview.* Leiden: E. J. Brill, 2003.

Winnifrith, Tom (ed.). *Perspectives on Albania.* London: Macmillan, 1992.

Wolf, Eric. *Peasant Wars in the Twentieth Century.* New York: Harper & Row, 1969.

Yalman, Ahmed Emin. *Turkey in the World War.* New Haven: Yale University Press, 1930.

Yamauchi, Masayuki. 'Reflections on the Social Movements during the National War of Liberation War of Turkey: A Tentative Analysis of Partisan Activities in Western Anatolia', *Journal of Asian and African Studies* (Tokyo), no. 15 (1978): 15–50.

Yanıkdağ, Yücel. '"Ill-Fated" Sons of the Nation: Ottoman Prisoners of War in Russia and Egypt, 1914–1922'. Ph.D. dissertation, Ohio State University, 2002.

―― 'Ottoman Prisoners of War in Russia, 1914–1922', *Journal of Contemporary History*, 34, no. 1 (1999): 69–85.

Yasmaoğlu, İpek. 'The Priest's Robe and the Rebel's Rifle: Communal Conflict and the Construction of National Identity in Ottoman Macedonia, 1878–1908'. Ph.D. dissertation, Princeton University, 2005.

Yerasimos, Stefanos, *et al.* (eds.). *Türkiye'de Sivil Toplum ve Milliyetcilik.* Istanbul: İletişim Yayınları, 2001.

Yetkin, Sabri. *Ege'de Eşkıyalar.* Istanbul: Tarih Vakfı Yurt Yayınları, 2003.

Yıldırım, Önür. 'Diplomats and Refugees: Mapping the Turco-Greek Exchange of Populations, 1922–1934'. Ph.D. dissertation, Princeton University, 2002.

Yüce, Rifat. *Kocaeli Tarih ve Rehberi.* İzmit: Türkyolu Matbaası, 1945.

Zavallani, T. 'Albanian Nationalism', in Peter F. Sugar and Ivo Lederer (eds.), *Nationalism in Eastern Europe* (Seattle: University of Washington Press, 1994), 62–76.

Ze'evi, Dror. '*Kul* and Getting Cooler: The Dissolution of Elite Collective Identity and the Formation of Official Nationalism in the Ottoman Empire', *Mediterranean Historical Review*, 11, no. 2 (1996): 177–96.

Zeidner, Robert. *The Tricolor over the Taurus: The French in Cilicia and Vicinity, 1918–1922.* Ankara: Atatürk Supreme Council for Culture, Language, and History, 2005.

Zürcher, Erik Jan. 'Kosovo Revisited: Sultan Reşad's Macedonian Journey of June 1911', *Middle East Studies*, 35, no. 4 (1999): 26–39.

―― *The Unionist Factor: The Role of the Committee of Union and Progress in the Turkish Nationalist Movement, 1905–1926.* Leiden: E. J. Brill, 1984).

Index

150's (*Yüzelilikleri*) 145–6

Abdülgafur Hoca 73, 75, 171
Abdülhalik (Renda) 160–1, 171
Abdülhamid II 14–15, 19, 26–7, 48, 57, 84, 94–5, 143, 171, 173
Abdülvehab 121, 171
Adapazarı (Sakarya) 2, 8–9, 20–2, 25, 28–9, 37, 43–5, 51–4, 58, 63, 65–6, 69, 70, 79, 80, 86, 96, 104–5, 110, 121, 122, 124, 127, 133, 137, 139, 145, 154, 156, 171, 172, 173, 174, 175, 178, 179
Ahmet Anzavur 58, 62–3, 82, 83, 85–6, 94–110, 116, 118–21, 128, 130, 138, 141–2, 144, 145–6, 167, 171, 172, 173, 174, 176, 177, 178, 179, 180, 181
Ahmet Esat Tomruk (*İngiliz* Kemal) 171
Ahmet Kuşçubaşı 79, 171, 213 n.
Ahmet (Mercimekizade) 78, 171
Albanian/Albanians
  Deportations of 41, 47–51, 148–65
  Emigration to Anatolia 32–3, 35–6, 148–65
  First World War and 47–51, 64–5
  Identity and society of 12–13, 30–6
  Loyalist Movement and 103
  National Movement and 80, 133
  Paramilitarism and 33–4, 64–5, 66–8, 80, 88–94
  Yugoslavia and 133, 137, 148–9, 155, 156, 161–64
Ali Fuat (Cebesoy) 90, 92, 96, 136
Ali Suat 79, 171
Alim Efendi 172
American Board of Commissioners for Foreign Missions (ABCFM)
  Armenians and 22
  Deportations of non-Muslims and 38, 40, 45–6, 52–4, 110, 140, 166
  Prewar war activities in the South Marmara 21–3
Anadolu ve Rumeli Müdafaa-i Hukuk Cemiyeti 76, 77
Armenian Genocide *see* Armenians
Armenians
  Abandoned property of 45–6, 53–4, 159
  Deportations/massacres of 41–6, 52–4, 134
  Greek occupation and 110–13

Identity and society of 19–23, 37
Ottoman history and 19–23
Paramilitarism and 44, 69–70, 111–13
Armutlu 71, 111, 112, 223
Arab Ali Osman Efe 115–16, 172
Arnavud Arslan Ağda 115, 172
Arnavud Aziz 107, 117, 172
Arnavud Kazım 67, 172, 179
Arnavud Mahmut Mahir 85, 86, 172
Arnavud Rahman 66, 106, 117–18, 171, 172
Arnavud Teavün Cemiyeti 133
Association for the Strengthening of Near Eastern Circassian Rights (*Şark-ı Karib Çerkesleri Temin-I Hukuk Cemiyeti*) 124–133, 145, 172, 173, 174, 175, 178
Artin 66, 172
Ayvalık 100
Aziz (Captain) 80, 172

(Bağ) Kamil 127, 172
(Bağ) Taluastan 127, 128, 172
Bahçecik 8, 22, 44, 45, 46, 53, 69, 110, 167
(Bakırlı) Mehmet Efe 115, 172
Balıkesir 2, 8–9, 20–1, 25, 28, 44, 50, 52, 59, 70–5, 79, 82, 87, 95, 98, 102–3, 109, 111, 113–17, 119, 120, 124, 127, 131, 137, 138, 144, 146, 167, 171, 172, 176, 177, 178, 179, 181
Balkan Wars 35–6, 37–39
Bandırma 8, 20–2, 28, 35, 40, 50, 52–3, 55, 57, 62, 70, 72–3, 77, 89, 102–3, 109, 111, 119, 120, 124, 127, 133, 137, 160, 167, 181
Bayramiç (Karesi) 20, 89, 107
Bayramiç (Kale-i Sultaniye) 138, 142, 144, 151
Bekir Sami (Günsav) 55–6, 72, 77–80, 82, 85, 90–2, 97, 108–9, 172, 176, 178, 180, 181
Bekir Sami (Kunduhk) 62, 173
Benoit Blinishti 158, 173
(Berzeg) Safer 104–5, 173
(Big) Ahmet Fevzi 98, 132, 173
Biga 28–9, 45, 53–4, 66–8, 79, 87, 95, 100–6, 110–11, 113, 117–18, 123–4, 138, 172, 174, 175, 176, 177, 178, 181
Bilecik 21, 23, 25, 28, 53, 59, 78, 80, 82, 111, 124, 127, 160, 171

Bolu 25, 104, 124, 150
Boşnak Karabulut İbrahim Çavuş 117, 173
British, Great Britain 28, 40–1, 52–3, 58,
    68–71, 76, 78–79, 81, 85–86, 89, 96,
    102, 105, 109–10, 112, 117–22, 131–2,
    139–41, 158, 171, 173, 176, 181
  Occupation of the South Marmara
      by 52–3, 68–70, 109
Bursa 2, 8–9, 20–3, 25, 28, 3–3, 36, 38, 40,
    43, 4–5, 50, 52–4, 63, 66, 72, 78–80,
    82, 85, 89–90, 92, 95, 102–3, 109,
    110–13, 124, 127, 131–34, 137, 148,
    155–56, 159, 160–61, 164, 166–67

Caclamanos, Demetrius 158, 175
Çanakkale (Kale-i Sultaniye) 2, 9, 21, 25, 38,
    39, 40, 41, 43, 44, 65, 66, 69, 82, 90, 99,
    100, 101, 107, 109, 137, 138, 146, 151,
    152, 167
Celal Bayar 72, 173
Çallı Kadir Efe 138, 173
(Canbazlı) Safer 88, 90, 173
Cemal Paşa 68, 173
Çerkes Bekir Sıtkı 86, 145, 173
Çerkes Çakır 173, 213 n., 114
Çerkes Davut 58, 88, 90, 96, 98, 103, 122,
    133, 141, 145, 173
Çerkes Ethem 63, 79, 82, 88, 96, 98, 103,
    105, 116, 123–24, 128, 138, 141,
    144–46, 171, 172, 173, 174, 179,
    180
Çerkes Fuat 122, 123, 174
Çerkes Hikmet 87, 174
Çerkes İttihat ve Teavün Cemiyeti 27, 175
Çerkes Kazım 87, 174
Çerkes Mehmet Reşit 63, 174
Çerkes Neş'et 66, 87, 172, 174
Çerkes Reşit 55, 57, 58, 63, 78–79, 124, 133,
    174
Çerkes Tevfik 103, 123, 174
Çetmi 9, 18, 96, 99, 116–17, 130
Çingene/Kıbti Ali 117–18, 174
Circassian/Circassians
  Deportations of 50–1, 92–3, 142–4
  Emigration to Anatolia 24–6, 147
  First World War and 58–63
  Greek occupation and 110–13
  Identity and society of 23–30
  Loyalist Movement and 91–106
  National Movement and 78–80
  Paramilitarism and 29, 30, 58–63, 66–8,
      78–9, 88–94
  Separatism and 123–33, 138–45
Committee of Union and Progress (Young
    Turks)
  Balkan Wars and 38–9

Establishment of the Republic of Turkey
    and 136–7
First World War and 41–3
Identity and 13–18
National Movement and 68–71, 76–7
Origins of 13–18
(Çule) Beslan 127, 174
(Çule) İbrahim Hakkı 87, 103, 121, 127, 174,
    179

Damat Ferid Paşa 55, 71, 72, 83–6, 102–3,
    105, 145, 175
(Debreli) Ziya Bey 68, 88, 175
Değirmendere 36, 67–8, 71, 88, 103,
    112–13, 133, 172, 179, 181
Deli Fuat Paşa 27–8, 132, 175
Deli Hurşid 67, 88–9, 91, 175
(Dramalı) Ali Rıza 100–1, 175
(Dürrızade) Abdullah Efendi 145, 175
Düzce 98, 104–5, 124, 127, 133, 173, 178

Ebubekir Hazım 90, 97, 175
Edremit 36, 50, 71–2, 100, 102, 151
Enver Paşa 44, 52, 58, 68–70, 139, 173, 175,
    176
Erdek 21, 42, 69, 72, 124, 127, 158, 231
Eşref Kuşçubaşı 58, 62–3, 70, 79, 80, 104–5,
    141, 144–6, 171, 175, 176, 180
Eyüp Sabri 64, 175
Ezine 107, 116–17, 151, 172, 180

Fahri Can 71, 176
First World War 41–52, 58–68

Galip Paşa 88, 89, 90, 91, 176
Galipoli (Gelibolu) 39, 43, 47, 154
Gavur İmam (İmam Fevzi) 101–3, 176
Gemlik 21, 43, 50, 52–3, 81, 111–13
Geyve 105, 124, 127, 154
Gönen 8, 28–9, 63, 66, 72–3, 80–1, 86–7,
    89, 91, 95–8, 101–3, 111, 121, 124,
    127, 133, 138, 142–7, 173, 174, 176,
    177, 179, 181
(Gostivarlı) İbrahim 67, 89, 91, 96, 162, 176
Greece
  Circassians and 118–34, 138–45
  Irrendentism of 55, 71–5, 108–11
  Occupation of the South Marmara
      by 107–35
(Gümülcineli) İsmail Hakkı 68, 85, 176

Hacı Sami Kuşçubaşı 146, 171, 176
Hacim Muhittin (Çarıklı) 73, 80–1, 87, 92,
    95–6, 172, 176

Hadkinson, Vivian 70, 81, 139, 140, 181
Halil Pehlivan 66, 172, 176
Halit (Moralızade) 72, 176
Hasan Basri (Çantay) 72, 75, 176
Hasan Tahsin 93–4, 176, 178
Haydar Rüştü (Öktem) 72, 177
Hendek 104–5, 124, 178
Hüsamettin (Ertürk) 63, 69, 79, 177
Hüseyin Ragıp Nurretin 72, 177

İbrahim Ethem Akıncı 114–17, 120, 124, 172, 177, 179
İbrahim Süreyya (Yiğit) 177, 215 n., 27
İnegöl 124
İngiliz Ali Kemal 96, 102, 177
İsmail Efe 138, 177
Izmir 20, 25, 41, 55, 62, 69, 71–6, 79, 100, 111–12, 114, 120, 124, 128, 131–9, 147–8, 151, 155–7, 160, 164, 172, 174, 175, 176, 177, 179, 181
İzmir'e Doğru 73, 75, 181, 211
İzmit (Kocaeli) 2, 8–9, 20–1, 25, 28–9, 43–5, 47, 49, 52–4, 58, 67, 69–71, 79–80, 82, 85–7, 95–6, 102–5, 109, 110, 112–13, 118, 121–22, 124, 127, 131, 132, 137, 139, 140, 146, 150–52, 154–6, 159–60, 164, 166, 171, 172, 173, 174, 175, 177, 178, 179, 180, 181
İznik 154, 160

Kadir (Anzavuroğlu) 98, 118–19, 134, 138, 141–2, 144, 177
Kale-i Sultaniye: *see* Çanakkale
Kani Bey 101, 177
Kanlı Mustafa 138, 141–2, 144, 177
Kara Arslan 64, 70, 177
Kara Hasan 66–7, 79, 87, 98–101, 171, 174, 177, 178
Kara Kemal 70, 178
Kara Vasif 70, 73, 178
Karabiga 66, 103, 106, 109–10, 118, 171, 172, 174, 177
Karacabey 28–9, 32, 35–6, 40, 43, 50, 53, 67–8, 71, 78, 80, 88, 89–91, 93–4, 96–8, 102–3, 109, 124, 133, 172, 173, 174, 175, 176, 178
Karakol see Special Organization
Karamürsel 36, 67, 71, 113, 124, 127, 133, 153–4, 159–60, 181
(Karzeg) Sait 103, 122, 178
Kasap Hüseyin 88, 178
Kazım (Özalp) 65, 72–3, 77, 80, 96, 98, 100, 103, 108, 136, 178
(Keçeci) Hafız Mehmet Emin 73, 178
Kel Aziz 138, 141–2, 144, 178
Kel Hüseyin 92–4, 176, 178

(Kıbrıslı) Sırrı 70, 79, 178
Kirmasti (Mustafakemalpaşa) 28–9, 35–6, 43, 50–3, 64, 67, 78, 80, 88–91, 94, 96–7, 102–3, 111, 121–4, 131, 133, 145, 166, 172, 173, 174, 175, 176, 178
Kocaeli *see* İzmit
(Köprülülü) Hamdi 65, 96, 98, 100–1, 104, 175, 177, 178
Kürd Mehmet 178, 208
Kurdistan, Kurds 4, 9, 27, 34, 48–9, 83, 130, 140, 147–8, 163, 166–7, 178
Kuva-yı İnzibatiye 105, 108, 180, 183
Kuva-yı Milliye see National Forces/National Movement

Lamb, Harry 131–2, 176
Lapseki 47, 103, 109
Loyalist Movement 81–106, 141–5
  British support for 85, 102
  Collapse of 104–6
  Origins of 83–6

(Maan) Ali 58, 62, 104–5, 127–8, 178
(Maan) Koç 104–5, 178
(Maan) Mustafa Namık 122, 179
(Maan) Şirin 62, 127, 179
Macedonia
  Albanians and 31–33
  Committee of Union and Progress and 15, 57
Manyas 28–9, 73, 80–1, 87–9, 92, 95–8, 103, 119–20, 123, 138, 142–6, 173, 174, 176, 178, 179, 180
Mehmet VI Vahdeddin 83–5, 179
Mehmet Ali 138, 141, 179
Mehmet Aydemiroğlu 81, 179
Mehmet Fertgerey (Şoenu) 142–4, 179
Mehmet Fuat (Çarım) 58, 179
Mehmet Vehbi (Bolak) 179
Mudanya 20, 40, 43, 53, 109, 111, 141, 197
Müftü Şevket Efendi 95, 179
Mustafa Necati 72, 179
Mustafa Kemal (Atatürk) 3–4, 7, 12, 35, 68–9, 74, 76–7, 83, 86, 92, 96, 105, 117, 123, 125, 129, 134–7, 139, 146, 149, 159, 164, 167, 174, 175, 180
Mustafa Sabri Efendi 145, 179

National Forces (*Kuva-yı Milliye*)/National Movement
  Greek occupation and 113–18, 134
  Islam and 74–5
  Nationalism and 75–6
  Organization of 71–80
  Origins of 55–6, 68–74
Nigehban Cemiyeti 85

North Caucasians *see* Circassians
Nurettin Bey 67, 179

Orhangazi 50, 53, 111, 113, 137
Ottoman Revolutionary Committee 141, 143–4, 146, 179

Parti Mehmet Pehlivan 103, 115–16, 179
Pendik 70, 160
Pomaks 9, 66, 79, 87, 98–103, 119, 130, 146–7, 176, 177, 180

Rahmi Bey 79, 179
Rauf Orbay 58, 62–3, 72–80, 136–37, 143, 147, 172, 180
Redd-i İlhak Cemiyeti 73–4, 77, 95, 171
Rıfat Yüce 78, 85–6, 111, 180
Rıza Nur 139, 158, 159–61, 180
Rum (Anatolian Greeks)
  Abandoned Property of 45–6, 53–4, 159
  Boycott of Businesses of 38–40
  Deportations/Massacres of 40–1, 41–6, 52–4, 134, 149
  Greek occupation and 110–13
  Identity and society of 19–23
  Ottoman history and 19–23
  Paramilitarism and 69–70, 111–13
Rumbold, Horace 132, 177
Rüştü Aras 163, 180

Sabanca 28, 105, 109, 167, 174
Sadık 107, 117, 180
Sadık Baba 70, 180
Şah İsmail 88, 90–1, 96, 98, 120, 133, 180
Sait Molla 85, 87, 180
Sakarya *see* Adapazarı
Şark-ı Karib Çerkesleri Temin-I Hukuk Cemiyeti see Association for the Strengthening of Near Eastern Circassian Rights
Selahettin Bey (Captain) 12–13, 35, 55, 72, 180

Ses 72, 75
Şimali Kafkas Cemiyeti 27, 62, 63, 132
South Marmara
  Ethnic Breakdown of 9, 10–11
  Geography of 8–9
Special Organization (*Teşkilat-ı Mahsusa*)
  Circassians and 58–65
  Karakol and 70–1, 73, 79, 177, 178, 182
  Loyalist opposition and 87, 93–4
  Origins of 57–65
Süleyman Askeri 58, 70, 180
Süleyman Şefik Paşa 105, 180

Tahsin (Uzer) 35, 180
Takığ Şevket 138, 142, 144, 180
Talat Paşa 44, 50, 52, 67–8, 70, 179, 180
Teal-i İslam Cemiyeti 85, 179
Turkey and Turks
  Establishment of the Republic of Turkey 136–7
  Legacy of the Turkish War of Independence and 7, 166–67
  Nationalism and 15–18
  Revolution and Reform in 1–2, 13–18, 136–7

Vasıf (Çınar) 73, 75, 179, 181

Yahya Kaptan 64, 70, 181
Yarbay Rahmi Bey 90–1, 102, 181
Yalova 28, 33, 54, 102, 111–13, 127, 154, 160
(Yenibahçeli) Şükrü 58, 70–1, 79, 181
Yenice 39, 101
Yenişehir 78, 111, 124, 160
Yetimoğlu family 67, 71, 81, 88, 181
Young Turks *see* Committee of Union and Progress
Yusuf İzzet Paşa 62–3, 89, 181
Yüzelilikleri see 150's

(Zarbalı) Hulusi 73, 181
Zeybeks 9, 18, 66